THE GOOD OLD CAUSE

THE ENGLISH REVOLUTION OF 1640–1660

Its Causes, Course and Consequences

Extracts from contemporary sources
edited by

Christopher Hill and Edmund Dell

SECOND EDITION

Revised and with a new Introduction by

CHRISTOPHER HILL

FRANK CASS & CO. LTD
1969

Published by
FRANK CASS AND COMPANY LIMITED
67 Great Russell Street, London WC1
by arrangement with Lawrence & Wishart, Ltd.

Originally published as Volume One of the
History in the Making Series

First edition	1949
Second edition	1969

SBN 7146 1483 1

Printed in Great Britain by Clarke, Doble & Brendon Ltd.
Plymouth and London

CONTENTS

PART THREE

THE STATE MACHINE BEFORE 1640

PART FOUR

CHURCH AND STATE BEFORE 1640

PART FIVE

THE INTERNATIONAL SITUATION

PART SIX

THE STORM BREAKS

PART SEVEN

THE CIVIL WAR

PART EIGHT

THE SECTS AND DEMOCRACY

PART NINE

THE LEVELLERS

PART TEN

ARMY DEMOCRACY

PART ELEVEN

THE END OF THE OLD ORDER

PART TWELVE

THE DIGGERS

PART THIRTEEN

THE DEFEAT OF THE LEVELLERS

PART FOURTEEN

ECONOMIC PROBLEMS OF THE REVOLUTION

PART FIFTEEN

GROWING CONSERVATISM

PART SIXTEEN

THE RESTORATION AND AFTER

ABBREVIATIONS

Abbott—ed. W. C. Abbott: *Writings and Speeches of Oliver Cromwell*, 4 vols. (1937–47).
B.B. and T.—ed. A. E. Bland, P. A. Brown and R. H. Tawney: *English Economic History, Select Documents* (4th impression, 1920).
Burton—ed. J. T. Rutt: *Parliamentary Diary of Thomas Burton*, 4 vols. (1828).
C.S.P.D.—*Calendar of State Papers, Domestic Series.*
C.S.P.Ven.—*Calendar of State Papers, Venetian.*
Dugdale—Sir W. Dugdale, *A Short View of the Late Troubles in England* (1681).
Gardiner—ed. S. R. Gardiner: *Constitutional Documents of the Puritan Revolution, 1625–60* (3rd edition, 1906).
H. and D.—ed. W. Haller and G. Davies: *The Leveller Tracts, 1647–53* (1944).
Hamilton—ed. L. D. Hamilton: *Selected Writings of Gerrard Winstanley* (1944).
J. and W.—James and Weinstock: *England during the Interregnum* (1935).
J.C.D.—ed. J. R. Tanner: *Constitutional Documents of the Reign of James I* (1930).
Ludlow—ed. C. H. Firth: *Memoirs of Edmund Ludlow*, 2 vols. (1894).
May—T. May: *History of the Parliament* (1647).
Newcastle—ed. C. H. Firth: *Life of the Duke of Newcastle, by the Duchess* (2nd edition, n.d.).
Oglander—ed. F. Bamford: *A Royalist's Notebook* (1936).
Pepys—ed. H. B. Wheatley: *Diary of Samuel Pepys*, 9 vols. (1904).
Prothero—ed. G. W. Prothero: *Statutes and Constitutional Documents, 1558–1625*.(4th edition, 1913).
Rushworth—ed. J. Rushworth: *Historical Collections*, 8 vols. (1st edition, 1659–1701).
T. and P.—ed. R. H. Tawney and E. Power: *Tudor Economic Documents*, 3 vols. (1924).
T.C.D.—ed. J. R. Tanner: *Tudor Constitutional Documents* (2nd edition, 1930).
Walker—Clement Walker: *History of Independency* (1648).
Warburton—E. Warburton: *Memoirs of Prince Rupert and the Cavaliers*, 3 vols. (1849).
Williams—ed. R. F. Williams: *The Court and Times of Charles I*, 2 vols. (1848).
Wilson—ed. F. J. Fisher: *Sir Thomas Wilson's State of England* (1600), *Camden Miscellany*, Vol. XVI (1936).
Wolfe—ed. D. Wolfe: *Leveller Manifestoes of the Puritan Revolution* (1944).

SOME IMPORTANT DATES

1603–25.	Reign of James I.
1618–48.	Thirty Years' War—Spain, Austria and German catholic princes *versus* France, Sweden and German protestants.
1625.	Accession of Charles I.
June, 1628.	Petition of Right.
August, 1628.	Assassination of Duke of Buckingham.
March, 1629.	Dissolution of Charles's third Parliament. Personal government begins.
1637.	Trials of Prynne, Burton, Bastwick and Lilburne.
1637–8.	Ship Money case: trial of Hampden.
1639–40.	"Bishops' War" against Scotland. Scots occupy Northumberland and Durham.
April, 1640.	Short Parliament.
November, 1640.	Long Parliament meets.
1641.	Seizure of power by Parliament (Triennial Act, Acts against dissolution without Parliament's consent, against unparliamentary taxation, abolition of Star Chamber and High Commission, execution of Strafford, imprisonment of Laud, control of armed forces).
November, 1641.	Revolt in Ireland.
December, 1641.	The Grand Remonstrance.
January, 1642.	Attempted arrest of five Members.
August, 1642.	Charles I raises his standard at Nottingham. Civil War begins.
October, 1642.	Battle of Edgehill. Charles advances on London.
1643.	Resistance of Parliamentary forces in Hull, Gloucester and Plymouth checks advance on London.
September, 1643.	Parliament signs agreement with Scots (Solemn League and Covenant).
January, 1644.	Scottish army enters England.
July, 1644.	Battle of Marston Moor. Great Royalist defeat.
November, 1644.	Milton publishes *Areopagitica*.
April, 1645.	Self-denying Ordinance leads to establishment of New Model Army.

June, 1645.	Battle of Naseby. Organised Royalist opposition broken.
1646.	Parliamentary forces mopping up.
February, 1646.	Abolition of feudal tenures and Court of Wards.
October, 1646.	Abolition of episcopacy and sale of bishops' lands.
March–November, 1647.	Agitators in the Army.
June, 1647.	Cornet Joyce seizes the King. General Council of the Army set up.
August, 1647.	The Army occupies London, becomes the chief power in the land.
October–November, 1647.	Putney Debates on the *Agreement of the People*.
November, 1647.	Defeat of Agitators at Ware. General Council of Army suppressed.
1648.	Second civil war. Scottish army defeated by Cromwell at Preston.
December, 1648.	Pride's Purge.
January, 1649.	Trial and execution of Charles I.
March–May, 1649.	Abolition of House of Lords. Proclamation of Republic.
May, 1649.	Leveller revolt defeated at Burford.
1649–50.	Cromwell's Irish campaign.
1649–50.	Diggers cultivating St. George's Hill.
1649–51.	Sale of crown, dean and chapter and cavaliers' lands.
1650.	Charles II established in Scotland as King. Cromwell invades Scotland. Battle of Dunbar (September).
1651.	Charles invades England. Routed at Worcester (September).
October, 1651.	Navigation Act.
1652–4.	Anglo-Dutch War.
April, 1653.	Cromwell dissolves Long Parliament.
July – December, 1653.	Barebones Parliament.
December, 1653.	Oliver Cromwell established as Lord Protector (Instrument of Government).
April, 1654.	Union of England and Scotland.
September, 1654–January, 1655.	First Protectorate Parliament.

1655–60.	War with Spain. Blake's fleet sweeps the Mediterranean. Jamaica (1655) and Dunkirk (1658) conquered.
1655–6.	Rule of Major-Generals.
September, 1656–February, 1658.	Second Protectorate Parliament. Crown offered to Oliver (Petition and Advice). Second chamber established.
September, 1658–April, 1659.	On death of Oliver, Richard Cromwell becomes Lord Protector.
April, 1659–March, 1660.	Restoration of Rump of Long Parliament.
August, 1659.	Rising of Sir George Booth (Presbyterian) for Charles II defeated.
December, 1659–February, 1660.	Monck marches from Scotland to London.
March–April, 1660.	Long Parliament dissolved. Convention Parliament meets.
April, 1660.	Declaration of Breda.
May, 1660.	Restoration of Charles II.
1685.	Death of Charles II and accession of James II.
1688–9.	"Glorious" Revolution. James II expelled. William III and Mary succeed. Bill of Rights. Parliamentary sovereignty secured.

INTRODUCTION

> "*Historians desiring to write the actions of men ought to set down the simple truth, and not say anything for love or hatred; also to choose such an opportunity for writing, as it may be lawful to think what they will and write what they think, which is a rare happiness of the time. In commending or disallowing the actions of men, it is a course very requisite to consider the beginning, the proceeding, and the end: so shall we see the reasons and causes of things, and not their bare events only, which for the most part are governed by fortune*" (Sir Walter Raleigh).

I

This book originally appeared in 1949, the tercentenary year of the execution of Charles I and the proclamation of the English Republic. Its interpretation of the English Revolution then seemed highly controversial; the Introduction and Notes were written accordingly. But much water has flowed under many bridges since 1949, and a new Introduction is called for. It would be foolish to claim that the interpretation which these documents are intended to illustrate is generally accepted by historians. But the original Introduction is out of date for two reasons. First, the orthodoxies which it was primarily concerned to attack no longer prevail. Secondly, I have published half a dozen books in which I have elaborated at length the interpretation then put forward in twelve summary pages. The reader is referred especially to my *Century of Revolution*, 1603–1714 (Nelson History of England, Vol. 5, 1961).

Briefly, what I felt was fairly new in 1949 was this book's *social* interpretation of the English Revolution. The Victorian conception of "the Puritan Revolution" was still widely taught in schools; and so were expositions which stressed the narrowly constitutional aspect of the struggles. But since that date controversies in *Economic History Review* between Professors Tawney, Trevor Roper and Stone, and the writings of a score of other historians, have changed all that. Some of the notes would have been worded rather differently and less brusquely if this book were now being published for the first time (e.g. those to Nos. 104 and 161, and the title of No. 108). This consideration applies most of all to words like "feudal" and "bourgeois". They are used in a technical Marxist sense which is unfamiliar to most English readers. In this reprint I have sometimes replaced them by other phrases, and should have liked to make even more changes. The word "bourgeois", where it remains, is not used in an exclusively urban sense, since capitalism in 16th and 17th century England grew up mostly in the countryside (sheep farming, the clothing industry, mining, market-gardening). "Bourgeoisie" is sometimes used in the notes to include those landlords and farmers who were producing for the market. "Bourgeois society" is capitalist society. "Bourgeois revolution" signifies a revolution which—whatever the subjective intentions of the revolutionaries—had the effect of establishing conditions favourable to the development of capitalism. "Feudal" describes those landlords whose mode of life was more traditional, less closely linked with market production; also the hierarchical social structure which had characterized mediaeval England and of which much still remained down to the 17th century Revolution.

II

This book argues that the 17th century English Revolution marked the transition from mediaeval to modern English society. Although capitalist relations developed apace during the inflationary century between Reformation and Revolution, the possibility always existed that England might go the way of the continental absolute monarchies. Because England was an island, because there was no land frontier to defend, the Tudor and Stuart monarchy was never able to build up a standing army such as existed in most continental monarchies; so in England absolutism was tempered by respect for the landed class as Members of Parliament and Justices of the Peace rather than by respect for the wishes of that class as army officers. But with this important difference it was a monarchy of the same type as that of Louis XIII.

The difference however proved crucial. Because of the largely rural nature of capitalism in England, Parliament, the representative assembly of property, came more and more to represent groups favourable to a freer capitalist development of the economy. Yet the crown suffered financially from the inflation which benefited many gentlemen farmers and merchants; and it could not increase taxes against the will of the House of Commons. Hence the various financial devices of the first two Stuarts, and the use of outmoded feudal methods of extortion. The government was apt to interfere in the economic life of the country, either in the interests of social stability (against enclosures, for example) or to make money (monopolies, for example) or to keep the new economic developments under its control (monopolies again, the Cokayne Project). This interference was no less aggravating because it rarely achieved its object: it was harmful to the economy out of all proportion to any fiscal return. In foreign policy the government did not forward the interests of the commercial classes or of gentlemen investors as vigorously or as successfully as they wished (see Parts II and V).

III

The constitutional and religious conflicts are related to this deeper conflict from which was to emerge an England in which capitalism could develop freely. But contemporaries did think about politics in religious terms, religious groupings often formed the basis of political parties. Why?[1]

In the first place, the Bible was the main item of intellectual diet. It was read and re-read, and its phraseology passed into the secular language. Secondly, the pulpit was by far the most powerful instrument of propaganda. To control it was as important as to control press, radio and TV today. Thirdly, the established church acted as a principal support of the state: it was a monopolistic spiritual organization with power, wealth, electoral influence and educated personnel at its disposal; and it had twenty-six episcopal votes in the House of Lords, often a majority of those attending. Thus a conflict with the state was bound to involve a conflict with the church—and vice versa. Lastly, the word "religion" today means something rather less inclusive than the same word 300 years ago. In religion was included much of what today is considered politics and philosophy. The Revolution was a religious conflict only in this wider sense; it was a conflict between two ways of life, two attitudes towards the world.

The Bible is infinitely interpretable. Men found in it what they were looking for. The Puritans discovered in it justification for the bourgeois virtues of the independent producer: the simple life, industry, sobriety, frugality. And if an elect—evident by its works—was predestined to eternal bliss, it soon followed that poverty might be a sign of sin, of defeat by economic forces controllable in themselves by the leading of a Puritan life. Thus on the home front Puritanism was an ideology uniting those who opposed existing authority in church and state, though it ceased to unite them once the monarchy and state church had been overthrown. The conflict had at the same time the characteristic of a struggle for national

[1] I have elaborated on the paragraphs which follow in my *Economic Problems of the Church* (1956) and *Society and Puritanism in pre-Revolutionary England* (1964).

independence, rather like the Revolt of the Netherlands in which Calvinism had played a similar role. When James I and Charles I, through a mixture of financial necessity and ideological affinity, adopted a policy of subservience to Spain, they seemed to have subordinated the independence of England, so hardly won under Elizabeth, to the international Catholic movement of which Spain was the head (see Part V).

Puritanism was also revolutionary in that it relied for its sanction not primarily on the authority of an institutionalized church, but on individuals' experience of direct contact with God. In this way it links up with the contemporaneous development of scientific method whereby science too freed itself from the church and sought only for the authority which experiment—personal experience of natural phenomena—would give it. But the history of science shows that a great mental effort was required to break from old paths and create new ideas. In politics, as in science and religion, authority was crumbling; and crumbling before the same new corrosive—the test of experience. The authority of precedent was being overthrown—the belief that "we have good laws but they want their execution"; that somewhere in the past an ideal constitution had existed to which return was possible (see No. 124). As the crisis developed it became clear to the Parliamentary leaders that their theory did not fit the facts. The impeachment of Strafford, for instance (see No. 71), showed that what was needed was new law, not the restitution of the old. New situations were arising, for which no precedent could even be pretended; justification had to be sought not in the past but in reason.

But for the Parliamentary leaders the enthronement of reason bore with it its own dangers. Reason entirely unrestrained by precedent might give rise to democratic or even communist theories (see Parts IX, X, XII). To the Parliamentary leaders precedent acted as a cement binding them to the past, ensuring them against the radicalism of the left-wing groups. But their ability to restrain pamphleteering declined, especially with the increasing participation of radicals in the conduct of the war; and there came into existence a practical freedom of thought and publication which for a privileged few—mainly the population of London and the Army—gave something as near the Miltonic ideal of a free market in ideas as has ever been known (see No. 117). The Protectorate and Restoration put the lid back on the pot; but not before much had been said that future generations would reiterate. In this respect Levellers, Diggers and Harringtonians are of especial note. That is why considerable attention has been paid to them.

IV

The List of Contents makes clear the plan of the book. It tries first to show the social structure of England before the Revolution—the landed ruling class, merchants, yeomen, the mass of the population. But society was not static. Some merchants made vast profits out of overseas trade, including plunder and the slave trade. They tended to invest in land. Some yeomen and gentlemen were producing for the market, and doing very well out of the steep rise in prices during the 16th and early 17th century. The lower classes were correspondingly worse off. The new purchasers and lessees of land probably accelerated the introduction of commercial methods into agriculture—racking of rents, enclosure, eviction, engrossing. Peasants driven from their holdings created unprecedented problems of pauperism and vagrancy, and were only slowly absorbed by the new industries as cottage workers or a proletariat. They rioted helplessly and desperately in the endeavour to recover their lost security (Part I).

The Tudors had concentrated in a central power much of the authority which had previously been wielded by feudal lords or (before the Reformation) by the church. The organs of power which they had developed for this purpose (the Courts of Star Chamber, and High Commission, the Councils in the North and in Wales) were originally used against feudal separatism, against the unruly great magnate, or against peasant disorder. Their activites had been viewed with benevolent neutrality by gentry and merchants, whose economic activities depend on royal maintenance of law and order.

But after the defeat of the northern earls in 1569 the internal danger to the national state was over; after the defeat of the Spanish Armada in 1588 the external danger was over too; and meanwhile the commercial classes had profited by the Tudor peace, and were becoming conscious both of their economic power and of their political weakness. The monarchy was now less necessary to them, and was becoming increasingly dependent on what they paid in taxation. The House of Commons tried to use its control of the purse to control the state. Thus challenged, the Stuart monarchy began to use against the Parliamentary opposition those instruments of repression formerly directed against feudal separatism and peasant revolt. James I elaborated his theory of divine right of kings in response to opposition theories of the superiority of Parliament or the common law. Fiscal feudalism was reinforced. The whole machinery of the state was bent to serve the purposes of royal policy—a policy for which support in the political nation was diminishing. A revolutionary situation developed. Finance and control of the armed forces and the church were the immediate causes, but issues far deeper than the narrowly constitutional were at stake: the economic future of the country, its political alignment in the international struggle then being waged, freedom of thought, *power* (Part III).

The struggle to control the church was part of the political struggle. Church courts were part of the state administrative machine; bishops were civil servants; Archbishop Laud was in effect Prime Minister. The church had a monopoly in the manufacture of public opinion, and this monopoly was used to support the old order; the opposition wanted to control this machine in their interests. So both on religious and on secular grounds there was opposition to the Laudian church. Any independent thinker was likely to oppose a persecuting church whose leading officials were enforcing an unpopular government policy by supernatural sanctions. This had been the case of radical protestants against the Roman church; they had aimed at winning the right of individuals to think for themselves, to discuss more freely, to organize more democratically. It was because the state church seemed to be trying to go back behind the Reformation in this respect (as well as in doctrine) that there was sense in accusing Laud of being a papist, though we now know that he refused a cardinal's hat. In the early 17th century two worlds were at war: the whole power of catholic Europe was aligned against the new forces fighting for the right of self-expression. No wonder the Parliamentarians passionately hated those who aligned themselves with the catholic camp (Parts IV and V).

Charles I would no doubt have liked to imitate the King of France by getting rid of Parliament altogether. He nearly succeeded in this in the decade after 1629. But despite rigid economy and a variety of financial expedients, the government was only just able to pay its way, not to build up the surplus necessary to finance a standing army—though if he had once been able to create such an army all Charles's problems would have been solved: taxation could have been collected forcibly. The sixteen-thirties were one of the most ignoble decades in English history. The government had no independent foreign policy. As soon as the system was challenged, it collapsed. An attempt to extend English control over Scotland, with a threat that secularized church lands there might be resumed, produced a national movement which Charles, in his penniless state, was unable to combat. He was forced to call a Parliament. He quarrelled with the Short Parliament (April, 1640) and dissolved it after three weeks; but there was still no way out for him. In November, 1640, the Long Parliament met, which sat until 1653.

This Parliament made short work of Charles's system of personal government. The prerogative courts were abolished; Charles's recent methods of levying money were declared illegal; his ministers were impeached, the Earl of Strafford was executed, and others fled from the country; Charles agreed to call Parliaments every three years, and not to dissolve the present Parliament without its own consent. He had surrendered effective sovereignty.

But he had no intention of allowing the surrender to be permanent. For meanwhile a conservative party was forming in Parliament, strongest in the House of Lords, but also with its supporters in the Commons. These men had been at one with Pym and his followers in attacking Charles's personal rule, but drew back when they saw that they were taking part in a revolution. For the leaders of the House of Commons went on to attack the institutions of the established church; they encouraged the people of London to demonstrate. Ideas began to be expressed which were utterly subversive of the old hierarchical order. Charles was encouraged in his opposition to Parliament's demands; and in 1642 the two sides began to arm. There is plenty of evidence to show that the general division in the civil war was on social lines. There were many personal exceptions, but broadly the economically advanced south and east of England faced the backward north and west; merchants, artisans, yeomen and some gentlemen fought for Parliament against the mass of the lords and gentry and their dependants. This is brought out by the financial and administrative methods of the two sides, by Parliament's belief in publicity, propaganda and wide discussion. Contemporaries had a clear idea of the social nature of the struggle (Part VI).

Civil war produced general social unrest, riots against enclosures, criticism of established institutions, the rise of sectarian congregations free from the supervision and control either of a state church or of Parliament. Many of the wealthier classes on the Parliamentary side began to get anxious. They worked for a compromise settlement with the King rather than complete victory; and they called in a Scottish army, well-disciplined and officered by conservatives, to offset the radical forces which were gathering under Oliver Cromwell. Cromwell thought the cause was worth fighting for; wanting to beat the King, he did not mind if the vulgar helped to beat him. He advocated religious toleration, the widest unity of those who had "the root of the matter in them". He was helped by the obstinate refusal of Charles and his supporters to compromise: and in 1645 the win-the-war party at last succeeded in forcing through Parliament the Self-Denying Ordinance, by which all members of either House of Parliament surrendered their military commands. So those (peers especially) who owed their rank to social position and not ability were got rid of; and the New Model Army was founded. Cromwell, however, was reappointed to his command, although an M.P. (Part VII.)

The conservatives had been right to fear the growth of the sects. In their congregations and in the Army the middling and lower classes were now discussing politics in a way that had never before been possible for them. Parts IX, X and XII deal with the Leveller and Digger movements and rank-and-file democracy in the Army. The conservative Parliamentarians were loosely spoken of as Presbyterians. They had in fact supported a Presbyterian church establishment as the price of a Scottish alliance and in the hope of preserving some central control over the religious life and thought of the country (Nos. 103–4): but the labels "Presbyterian" and "Independent" are political as well as religious (Part VIII). In 1647 the rank and file of the Army took the lead in bringing pressure to bear on Parliament for a more democratic settlement; and in December 1648—after the second civil war—the Presbyterians were purged from Parliament. The King was tried and executed; the House of Lords abolished; a republic was proclaimed, which was in effect a dictatorship of the Army (Part XI).

This was a second revolution, but a political rather

than a social revolution. New men were in power, but the republican government broke with the extreme left—the Levellers and Diggers (Part XIII). The achievements of the Commonwealth—conquest of Scotland and Ireland, land sales, the Navigation Act, the Dutch War—benefited above all the commercial classes (No. 143, Part XIV). There was no thoroughgoing social, economic or legal reform in the interests of the lower classes (Nos. 120–2, Part XIV, No. 200). Because of the predominantly rural nature of capitalism in England, there could be no peasant revolution such as took place in the French and Russian Revolutions. This made a restoration ultimately inevitable. The republic had cut away its support from the left. The Army, purged of Levellers, became increasingly professional: its higher officers prospered. In 1653 the Rump of the Long Parliament was dissolved. The last attempt at a deal with the left occurred with the setting up of the Barebones Parliament: but that proved too radical, and was dissolved in its turn. Cromwell became Lord Protector, and made repeated attempts to come to terms with the mass of the landed and merchant class—the old Presbyterians.

In the fifties the situation became more and more paradoxical. Only the Army could defend the gains of the Revolution, yet the Army was hated by gentry and merchants, because its upkeep demanded extremely heavy taxation, and because it continually interfered with their running of local government. By repeated purgings the Army itself lost its radical character. It became a vested interest, collecting taxes to pay its own wages. It could only be a matter of time before it was disbanded and the sovereignty of the "natural rulers of the countryside" established. But in order to disband the Army the social basis of the government had to be broadened to the right. Cromwell did this in his acceptance of the Humble Petition and Advice in 1657: that constitution brought together again the social elements which the Presbyterians and Independents had represented (Part XV). But so long as the Army existed the alliance was precarious and it broke up after Cromwell's death in 1658. Faced by a new threat of social revolution, there was a further consolidation of the ranks of all the propertied Parliamentarians and the defeated Royalists. Charles II was restored.

The restoration of King, House of Lords and bishops was not a restoration of the old order. The revolutionary legislation of 1640–1, which Charles had never seriously intended to accept, was confirmed. There was a compromise land settlement; the church ceased to include all Englishmen and lost most of its persecuting powers; the organs of absolute government were not restored. Parliament's role in government was maintained. The Navigation Act and the abolition of feudal tenures were confirmed. 1660–88 was a period of political compromise and economic expansion. The landed ruling class had to adapt itself to the new order, or go under. The peasantry failed to win security of tenure; and the decline of the yeomanry, the pauperization of the mass of the peasantry, accompanied the prosperity of great landlords and farmers, and prepared for the Agricultural and Industrial Revolutions of the 18th century. The monied men increased their direct control over governments and their indirect permeation of the administration by bribery. In 1688, when James II tried to re-establish absolutism, the real nature of the compromise of 1660 was revealed. The Tory squires, the non-resistance Church of England parsons, deserted the Lord's Anointed and followed the lead of the great Whig lords and bankers in accepting William III.

The bourgeois revolution succeeded; the Puritan revolution failed. In 1660 the leaders of the radicals were executed or driven into exile. Their rank-and-file supporters survived for some time underground, plotting unsuccessfully against Charles II's government. Their last bid for power was in Monmouth's rebellion of 1685, whose defeat freed the Whigs from anxiety lest the expulsion of James II in 1688 should produce a new republican movement. Many of the radical revolutionaries emigrated in the sixteen-fifties and sixties; others were absorbed by the Quakers or other non-conformist sects, through whom their democratic ideas were handed down. It was in the 19th century, after the Industrial Revolution had created a town working class and a radical bourgeoisie on a new scale, that the 17th century republicans were rediscovered by Godwin, Cobbett, Bronterre O'Brien and many others (Part XVI).

VI

Many changes would be needed to bring the notes up-to-date. Since 1949 this period has been the subject of vigorous and controversial historical interest. Views of the class structure and economic life of England (Parts I and II) have been modified by the writings of Professors W. G. Hoskins, W. K. Jordan, I. A. Roots, L. Stone, R. H. Tawney, H. R. Trevor-Roper, C. Wilson, Mr. Alan Everitt, Mrs. V. L. Pearl, Mrs. Prestwich, Mrs. J. Thirsk. Professor R. Ashton's *The Crown and the Money Market* and Professor G. Aylmer's *The King's Servants* would call for changes in Part III. The notes on the Levellers in Parts IX and X should be read in the light of Professor C. B. Macpherson's *The Political Thought of Possessive Individualism.* Articles by Professors J. E. Farnell and A. Woolrych throw new light on the economic policies of the Rump and on the Barebones Parliament (Nos. 172, 177–8). For a mass of other writing on this period the reader is referred to Bibliographies at the end of my *Century of Revolution* (1961) and *Reformation to Industrial Revolution* (1967). The notes on Nos. 114 and 151 have been expanded in my *Puritanism and Revolution* (1958), pp. 50–152; those on Nos. 62 and 155 in my *Intellectual Origins of the English Revolution* (1965). The prohibition on quotation from Clarendon's *History of the Rebellion* mentioned in the note to No. 85 has now been withdrawn: some of the material which had to be rejected in 1949 was used in *Puritanism and Revolution*, pp. 199–214.

VII

Spelling and punctuation have been modernized in these extracts, and occasional slight alterations have been made in conformity with modern usage (thus "propriety" becomes "property", "country" "county" when the latter seemed the sense intended). Editorial explanations in the text are contained within square brackets. Years have always been given in the New Style—i.e. any date between January 1 and March 24, 1650–1, has been written as 1651. As far as possible references are to the most accessible editions of the books quoted. With the original edition Irene Corfield gave invaluable technical help, and the late Dona Torr generous assistance and encouragement at every stage. Miss Pat Lloyd very kindly helped with the proofs of the present edition.

October, 1967 CHRISTOPHER HILL.

Part One

SOCIAL CLASSES BEFORE 1640

Freeholders and tradesmen are the strength of religion and civility in the land; and gentlemen and beggars and servile tenants are the strength of iniquity.

The Reverend Richard Baxter.

1. THE LANDED CLASS

Landowners naturally come first in any description of the class structure of England in the two generations before 1640. Land was the source of political power and social prestige. Through the manor court and as J.Ps., landowners controlled local justice and administration; the central government had difficulty in enforcing its will when it ran counter to the desires of the gentry (cf. No. 40). In extract *a*) Bacon (later James I's Lord Chancellor) is defending Elizabeth's government from the charge of neglecting the interests of the higher nobility. The five following extracts are from Sir Thomas Wilson's *State of England*, written in 1600 or 1601 by a man on the fringe of government service who had access to reasonably good information. As the younger son of a gentleman, he was a member of a social group which, as appears from *e*), was an element of unrest in the life of his time. Note his evidence of the growing dependence of landowners on court favour and the plunder of the Church (*b*) and *f*); cf. No. 34). Since the Reformation these two sources of pickings had steadily increased in importance. (See L. Stone, "The Anatomy of the Elizabethan Aristocracy," *Economic History Review*, 1948.)

a) Francis Bacon, Certain Observations upon a Libel (*Letters and Life*, by J. Spedding, I, pp. 172–3); *b*) Wilson, p. 22; *c*) p. 23; *d*) pp. 23–4; *e*) p. 24; *f*) pp. 22–3, 38.

a) THE NOBILITY, 1592

THERE have been in ages past noblemen . . . both of greater possessions and of greater commandment and sway than any are at this day. One reason why the possessions are less I conceive to be because certain sumptuous veins and humours of expense—as apparel, gaming, maintaining of a kind of followers and the like—do reign more than they did in times past. Another reason is because noblemen nowadays do deal better with their younger sons than they were accustomed to do heretofore, whereby the principal house receiveth many abatements. Touching the commandment, which is not indeed so great as it hath been, I take it rather to be a commendation of the time than otherwise. For men were wont factiously to depend upon noblemen; whereof ensued many partialities and divisions, besides much interruption of justice, while the great ones did seek to bear out those that did depend upon them; so as the kings of this realm, finding long since that kind of commandment in noblemen unsafe unto their crown and inconvenient unto their people, thought meet to restrain the same by provision of laws; whereupon grew the statute of retainers; so as men now depend upon the prince and the laws and upon no other. A matter which hath also a congruity with the nature of the time; as may be seen in other countries, namely in Spain, where their grandees are nothing so potent and so absolute as they have been in times past. But otherwise it may be truly affirmed that the rights and pre-eminences of the nobility were never more duly and exactly preserved unto them than they have been in [Elizabeth's] times; the precedence of knights given to the younger sons of barons; no *subpœnas* awarded against the nobility out of the chancery, but letters; no answer upon oath, but honour; besides a number of other privileges in Parliament, court and country. So likewise for the countenance which they receive of her Majesty and the state in lieutenancies, commissions, offices and the like, there was never a more honourable and careful regard had of the nobility . . . [even though] a few of them by immoderate expense are decayed.

b) THE STATE OF THE NOBILITY

I find great alterations almost every year, so mutable are worldly things and worldly men's affairs; as namely the Earl of Oxford, who in the year 1575 was rated at £12,000 a year sterling, within two [years] following was vanished and no name of him found [in the taxation books], having in that time prodigally spent and consumed all, even to the selling of the stones, timber and lead of his castles and houses; and yet he liveth and hath the first place amongst Earls. But the Queen is his gracious mistress and gives him maintenance for his nobility's sake . . . out of the bishopric of Ely, which since his decay could never see other bishop. Another, the Earl of Arundel, about the same time was reckoned not much inferior to him in state, and before him in dignity; and in one six months all was confiscated to the Queen for treason. The other Earls, some daily decay, some increase, according to the course of the world; but that which I have noted by perusing many of the said books [of taxation] . . . is that still the total sum groweth much to one reckoning, and that is to £100,000 rent yearly, accounting them all in gross. . . . If a man would proportion this amongst nineteen Earls and a Marquis it would be no great matter, to every one £5,000 rent, but as some exceed that much, so many come short of it.

The thirty-nine Barons and two Viscounts do not much exceed that sum: their revenue is reckoned together to amount to £120,000 yearly.

c) THE STATE AND NUMBER OF KNIGHTS

There are accounted to be in England about the number of five hundred knights. . . . These for the most part are men for living betwixt £1,000 and £2,000 yearly, and many of them equal the best barons and come not much behind many earls . . . [being] thought to be able to dispend yearly betwixt £5,000 and £7,000 of good land.

d) THE NUMBER AND STATE OF GENTLEMEN

Those which we call Esquires are gentlemen whose ancestors are or have been knights, or else they are the heirs and eldest of their houses and of some competent quantity of revenue fit to be called to office and authority in their county. . . . Of these there are esteemed to be in England, as I have seen by the book of musters of every several shire, to the number of 16,000 or thereabout; . . . these are men in living betwixt £1,000 and £500 rent. Especially about London and the counties adjoining, where their lands are set to the highest [i.e. leased at rack rents], he is not counted of any great reckoning unless he be betwixt 1,000 marks [£666 13*s.* 4*d.*] or

£1,000; but northward and far off a gentleman of good reputation may be content with £300 or £400 yearly. These are the elder brothers.

e) THE STATE OF GREAT YOUNGER BRETHREN

I cannot speak of the number of younger brothers, albeit I be one of the number myself; but for their estate there is no man hath better cause to know it, nor less cause to praise it. Their state is of all stations for gentlemen most miserable, for if our fathers possess £1,000 or £2,000 yearly at his death he cannot give a foot of land to his younger children in inheritance, unless it be by lease for twenty-one years or for three lives . . . or else be purchased by himself and not descended. Then he may demise as much as he thinks good to his younger children, but such a fever hectic hath custom brought in and inured amongst fathers, and such fond desire they have to leave a great show of the stock of their house, though the branches be withered, that they will not do it, but my elder brother forsooth must be my master. He must have all. . . . This I must confess doth us good some ways, for it makes us industrious to apply ourselves to letters or to arms, whereby many times we become my master elder brother's masters, or at least their betters in honour and reputation; while he lives at home like a [dolt] and knows the sound of no other bell but his own.

f) THE STATE OF THE CLERGY

The Bishops' revenues amount to about £22,500 yearly altogether. . . . The Deans' . . . commodities in letting the church lands and bestowing the places and offices is very great, otherwise their revenue is not much; . . . their whole revenue accounted through England amounted to the sum of £4,500 yearly or thereabouts.

But this must be understood, that the state of the clergy is not altogether so bare as may perhaps be conjectured by the smallness of their revenue, for that they never raise nor rack their rents nor put out tenants as the noblemen and gentlemen do to the uttermost penny; but do let their lands as they were let 100 years since, reserving to themselves and their successors some commodities besides the bare rent, as corn, muttons, beef, poultry or such like; but to say the truth their wings are well clipped of late by courtiers and noblemen, and some quite cut away, both feather, flesh and bone. . . .

[Royal policy aimed at] the keeping low of the clergy from being over rich, for that order of men have most damnified [i.e. caused loss to] England by their profuse spending upon their pleasures, and upon idle serving men and other moth-worms which depended upon them and ate the fat of the land and were no way profitable; for it is not long since you should not ride nor go through country or town but you should meet such troops of these priests' retinue as exceeded 100 or 200 of these caterpillars, neither fit for war nor other service, attending upon this pontifical crew, furnished and appointed in the best manner that might be; but since their wings were clipped shorter they [i.e. we] hold opinion that England hath flourished more.

2. FEUDAL SOURCES OF REVENUE

These extracts are from *The Lives of the Berkeleys*, written by John Smyth, steward to the family, about 1620. (For the management of the Berkeley estates, see No. 4.) The sources of revenue of a great landed family were still mediæval; a new grant of rights in traditional feudal form could still be obtained from the Crown—for a price (*b*).

a) J. Smyth, *Lives of the Berkeleys* (1883–5), II, p. 333; *b*) *ibid.*, II, pp. 435–7.

a) FEUDAL DUES

NOT long after [1611–12] this lord [Berkeley] (. . . partly to pursue the precedents of his ancestors . . .) had a benevolence from all his tenants, whether holding by copy of court roll or by indenture; and also Aid *pur faire fitz chevalier*, according to the statutes of 3 E. I and 25 E. III, from all his freeholders, whether holding by knight's service or in socage, whereby the sum of £700 and upwards was raised. And for anything I perceived . . . [it was] willingly paid.

b) FEUDAL RIGHTS GRANTED BY THE CROWN

[In 1616], this lady [Lord Berkeley's mother] at her only charges obtained from his Majesty a large grant of liberties in the name of this lord her son in all his hundred of Berkeley [and other places] . . .; which liberties were these, viz. a view of frankpledge and whatsoever thereto belongeth; and all felons' goods of what kind soever . . .; waived [i.e. forsaken] goods, strays, treasure trove, deodands; year, day and waste; estrepments [waste by tenants]; goods of fugitives, and of convict, attainted, outlawed and of waived [i.e. fugitive] persons, before what judge soever, or in what court wheresoever such goods shall come to be forfeited; and all whale fishes, sturgeons, and all other great and royal fishes, in whatsoever free fishings within the river of Severn; and all such fairs and markets as have been accustomed, together with a court of pie-powders, with all stalls, pickages, weights, fines, amercements, tolls, liberties and free customs to such fairs and markets belonging; and also free warren in all his demesne lands within the said hundred, and in all other places where his ancestors have used to have free warren, with others the like, . . . enriching the whole with more regal liberties than were attained unto by any of his former ancestors. . . .

From which charter of liberties in Berkeley hundred she in the last year [1617] (amongst some others) reaped these fruits in the manors and lands of other men:

i) One Cullen, an inn-holder in Dursley, by stabbing of himself with his own knife, becoming thereby *felo de se*, his goods escheated, which she had.

ii) A servant to John Hollister working at his water-mill in Wike near Berkeley, coveting with a feather in his hand to oil the cogs, was by their swift motion caught and drawn in by the arm, and ground almost to pieces, whereby Hollister made composition for the deodand—cogs, wheel and upper millstone: for whatever causes death is a deodand. . . .

iii) The like deodand of wain and 6 oxen happening about the same time at Nimpesfield, a manor of Mr.

John Bridgeman's, as it was entering into his gates with wood, when the owner perished under the wheel of the wain. . . .

iv) In this present month of May, 1618, . . . one Thomas Caston, a tiler, in taking down an old farm house . . . found hidden between the tiling and ceiling over an old oven four and thirty pieces of gold of the coin of King Henry VI . . .; which he with others coveting to conceal, a bill was by her exhibited against them into the Court of Wards, making her title to that treasure trove under the said charter of King James. But they, seeking peace, found it; and upon receipt of an account of the whole she honorably gave back a part, rewarded some others, retaining the residue to herself.

3. THE LIFE OF THE GENTRY

Extract *a*) is from Peacham's *Compleat Gentleman*, a handbook of polite behaviour first published in 1622. It became a favourite in cavalier circles because of its calm assumption that gentlemen deserve their social privileges. The last sentence of *a*), however, shows that even blue blood is beginning to have a market value. Extract *b*) shows that in 1631 it was still normal for tenants to render dues in kind. This and *c*) show the court as a cause of extravagant expenditure as well as a source of pickings for the fortunate (cf. Nos. 12, *b*) and 90, *a*)). But then *c*) is from Braithwaite's *The English Gentleman* (first published in 1630), the Puritan rival of Peacham. The old ideas of the *duty* of landowners to provide hospitality and charity lost their reality as gentlemen, faced with rising prices, came to regard their estates as sources of money income rather than as a means of maintaining dependent tenants (see No. 4).

a) H. Peacham, *The Compleat Gentleman* (1634), pp. 13–14;
b) Wye Saltonstall, *Picturæ Loquentes* (1631), No. 26;
c) R. Braithwaite, *The English Gentleman* (1633), p. 332.

a) ADVANTAGES OF GENTLE BIRTH

FIRST, noble or gentlemen ought to be preferred in fees, honours, offices and other dignities of command and government, before the common people.

They are to be admitted near and about the person of

the prince, to be of his council in war, and to bear his standard.

We ought to give credit to a noble or gentleman before any of the inferior sort.

He must not be arrested, or pleaded against upon cosenage.

We must attend him, and come to his house, and not he to ours.

His punishment ought to be more favourable and honourable upon his trial, and that to be by his peers of the same noble rank. . . .

They ought to take their recreations of hunting, hawking, etc., freely, without control in all places.

Their imprisonment ought not to be in base manner, or so strict as others'.

They may eat the best and daintiest meat that the place affordeth; wear at their pleasure gold, jewels and best apparel, and of what fashion they please, etc.

Besides, nobility stirreth up emulation in great spirits . . . It many times procureth a good marriage.

b) COUNTRY LIFE

A gentleman's house in the country is the prime house of some village, and carries gentility in the front of it. The tenants round about travel thither in pilgrimage with their pig and goose offerings, and their duty increases with the near expiring of their leases. . . . Their master allows [his servingmen] to make men drink for his credit, while they sound forth his fame of hospitality. . . . They envy most their own coat, for if a gentleman bring half a dozen men with him, they'll not suffer a man to come off alive, and that expresses their master's welcome. . . . [If a chambermaid and a servingman marry] she obtains of her mistress a poor copyhold, and they both turn tenants to the family; and are called retainers. The master of the house is adored as a relic of gentility, and if his wife come by some home-match, he dares not let her see London or the court, for fear she should make his woods pay for it. He observes all times and seasons of the year, and his Christmas is the butler's jubilee. To conclude, his house is the seat of hospitality, the poor man's court of justice, the curate's Sunday ordinary, and the only exchequer of charity where the poor go away relieved and cry, "God bless the founder."

c) THE COURT

I do not approve of these who fly from their county as if they were ashamed of her, or had committed something unworthy of her. How blameworthy then are these court-comets, whose only delight is to admire themselves? These, no sooner have their bed-rid fathers betaken themselves to their last home . . . but they are ready to sell a manor for a coach. . . . Hospitality, which was once a relic of gentry and a known cognizance to all ancient houses, hath lost her title merely through discontinuance; and great houses, which were at first founded to relieve the poor and such needful passengers as travelled by them, are now of no use but only as way-marks to direct them. But whither are these Great Ones gone? To the court, there to spend in boundless and immoderate riot what their provident ancestors had so long preserved.

4. LANDOWNERS IN DEVELOPING BOURGEOIS SOCIETY

Some landowners managed to adapt their economy to the new world; others went under. The Berkeleys (*a*) nearly went under. They were involved in interminable law-suits, and Lord Henry (1534–1608?) began by living disastrously above his income. Drastic reorganisation enabled him to maintain a good deal of feudal state. His revenue henceforth was a mixture of ancient (see No. 2) and modern; e.g. he sold timber to an iron-smelter. But Smyth, the prudent steward, recommends in 1620 leasing the estates to capitalist farmers better able to wring profits from them. Extract *b*), written in 1656, shows the Holles family in similar difficulties—the grandfather contracting debts in feudal ostentation, the younger generations anxious to marry money and realising the importance of being on good terms with the local borough. Gervase Holles, author of the extract, who refused to marry the lady his father selected, was on the King's side in the Civil War; the more prosperous branch of the family was Parliamentarian (see No. 45). Extracts *c*) (dubious history, but useful evidence for the seventeenth century) and *d*) show the transition from a society in which landlords measured their wealth in terms of men who would follow them in war to a society in which they measured it in terms of money. The Royalist Sir John Oglander (*e*) passed on to his son a similar lesson, bitterly learnt, to that which Smyth wished to convey to the heir to the Berkeley estates. He again refers to the court as a source of windfalls.

a) J. Smyth, *Lives of the Berkeleys*, II, pp. 285–6, 361, 364, 370, 368–9, 378, 410, 6; *b*) Gervase Holles, *Memorials of the Holles Family* (Camden Soc., 1937), pp. 197–203; *c*) G.W., *Respublica Anglicana* (1650), p. 39; *d*) Selden, *Table-Talk* (1847), pp. 105–6; *e*) Oglander, p. 75.

a) A FEUDAL FAMILY—DECLINE AND READJUSTMENT

THUS lived this lord [Berkeley] and his wife . . . the first 13 years of Queen Elizabeth [1558–71]; in . . . their travels (if both together) they were seldom or never attended with fewer than 150 servants in their . . . coats in summer, with the badge of the white lion rampant embroidered on the left sleeve; and in coats of white frize lined with crimson taffeta in the winter . . .; amongst whom many were gentlemen and esquires of remarkable families and descent . . ., many of whom I lived to see and know and to talk of these times: and have with some of them then in nearest relation and place of his revenue expostulated why they would suffer their young lord and lady his wife to run yearly £1,500 at least into expense above their utmost income, each year (or second at least) shortening the same by sale of a manor. . . .

And in place of all these manors and lands thus sold for £41,399 13*s*. 0*d*., he purchased . . . the little poor manor of Canonbury, of the value of £5 11*s*. 8*d*. per annum. . . .

[After 1571] the check-roll of his servants was shortened 40 persons at the least, and many unuseful persons pared off. . . . [About 1584] the former check-roll of his household servants was again further shortened 20 persons at the least. . . . The number then was about three score and ten of all sorts. . . .

In his last days . . . I have observed him met by the way and accompanied with 300, 400 and 500 horse of his kindred, friends and tenants ere he came to Berkeley town, though he usually set forth . . . with seldom above 14 or 16; which confluence of train, how it daily doth and more is like to degenerate, let his posterity observe and declare to their generations. . . .

As touching this lord's alms to the poor, it was 3 days in the week, wherein the poor of 4, 5 and 6 country parishes and villages next adjoining . . . were relieved, with each of them a mess of wholesome pottage with a piece of beef or mutton therein, half a . . . loaf and a can of beer; besides the private alms that daily went out of his purse, never without 8 or 10*s.* in single money; . . . and besides his Maundy each Thursday before Easter day, wherein many poor men and women were clothed by the liberality of this lord; . . . and besides 20 marks or £20 or more, which thrice each year against the feasts of Christmas, Easter and Whitsuntide was sent by this lord to 2 or 3 of the chiefest inhabitants of those villages . . . to be distributed amongst their poor. . . .

The standing yearly wages of this lord to his household servants were ordinarily 5 marks to a gentleman, 4 marks to a yeoman [1 mark = 13*s.* 4*d.*], and 40*s.* to a groom, with a tawny coat for summer and a white frize coat for winter . . .; which I note for difference between times so lately past and these I write in, and which this family is further like to see in itself: and thereby with more caution to regulate their revenues: and yet few peers of this lord's time were served with better qualified gentlemen and yeomen than I have known this lord to be. . . .

This lord Henry . . . had much, spent much, yet left enough to continue the like honourable port, if regulated after that method which he observed in the later half of his life; whereby he knew to a penny what quarterly he was to receive, and for what the same came in, and how it was again issued out; and was able at the end of each year in the closing of his audit to say that such and such sums and expenses might have been avoided by providence [= prudence], but being past he would amend it in the year following. If like providence be not hereafter found in his heir, that portion which now descendeth will be found shortened in the next generation; which my wish is may in time be seriously thought upon. . . .

When he [the heir] shall attain to one and twenty years . . . he will have no better course than to advance his demesne lands to an improved rent payable quarterly . . . and rather to supply his provisions for wheat, oats and straw by the tithes of some appropriate parsonage not far from his abode, or by reservation upon such leases monthly or quarterly to be brought in, than to keep much tillage in his own hands (the natures of hind servants, bailiffs . . . and other incidents considered); and no more (at most) of other grounds than may supply his provisions of beef and muttons. But for the plough, none gaineth thereby but he that layeth his eye or hand daily upon it.

b) ADJUSTMENT TO NEW TIMES

My father . . . was the true heir of his grandfather's hospitable disposition, of which certainly (had his revenues been answerable) he would have given as specious an argument. He would never sit down to meals unless he had some of his friends or neighbours with him, and in case they came not he would send for them. Accordingly he was charitable to the poor and very prompt to do any civility or courtesy to a stranger. . . .

My grandfather . . . died not much above two years before my father, during whose life he had but a narrow exhibition for the maintenance of himself and his family, nor could my grandfather's estate well allow it better. So he was forced to contract some good round debts that he might the better live according to his quality and to the extensiveness of his mind and disposition. These debts hung with the more pressing weight upon him because his land being entailed and he but tenant in it for term of life he could not sell any part of it for their discharge. All his hopes was that my marriage at the least would bring him in a sum of money sufficient to free him from those incumbrances, and that with justice enough he might expect from a son that had any pity or filial affection in him. . . .

He had often been importuned by the corporation of Grimsby to become a burgess among them, which he still excused until about four years before his death. Then, willing to satisfy them from whom he had received always a great deal of love and civility, he was . . . chosen alderman, and the next election mayor. . . . I never see my grandfather so angry as when he heard he was made an alderman, because the most of them were mean and mechanic fellows. But my father besought him to be patient, telling him his neighbours loved him well and he could not but gratify them in that which divers gentlemen of very great worth had done before him.

c) ANCIENT AND MODERN ARISTOCRACY COMPARED

Those generous souls [the nobility of earlier centuries] were a terror and curb to tyrants, not their creatures and slavish instruments; as depending upon their own worth and their country's love, not Kings' mere creations. Their principles of education led them to endeavour to be lords over, not apes unto, the French; and he was counted the bravest lord who conquered most of their men, not the finest that followed most of their fashions. Scars were the ornaments of a noble face, not black patches; and hair powdered with dust and dewed with sweat, not with perfumed powders and gesmin butter, was the dress wherein England's nobles courted their mistress, *Heroic fame*. . . . Their lands were let at easy rates, with some services reserved, whereby their tenants, being able men, might not be broken-spirited, and also might be obliged to attend them when their country's service called them forth; hence came England's valiant yeomanry, and her bold barons, who, by frequent Parliaments, knew how to manage great councils, perform worthy actions, restrain and curb tyrannical monarchs. These men were rather a spur than bridle to the Commons in all good actions.

d) A SIMPLE ECONOMIC POINT

When men did let their land underfoot [i.e. at less than the economic rent] the tenants would fight for their landlords, so that way they had their retribution. But now they will do nothing for them, may be the first, if but a constable bid them, that shall lay the landlord by the heels, and therefore 'tis vanity and folly not to take the full value.

e) TRADE NECESSARY

It is impossible for a mere country gentleman ever to grow rich or to raise his house. He must have some other vocation with his own inheritance, as to be a courtier, lawyer, merchant or some other vocation. If he hath no other vocation, let him get a ship and judiciously manage her, or buy some auditor's place or be vice-admiral in his county. By only following the plough he may keep his word and be upright, but will never increase his fortune.

Sir John Oglander wrote this with his own blood, June the 25th, 1632, then aged 48 years.

5. SALES OF LAND

As the bourgeoisie prospered they aspired to land, the source of profits, power and prestige: landowners in difficulties were forced to sell. Extracts *a*) and *b*) could be matched by many others from contemporary literature. Sometimes men purchased in order to resell at a profit, as in *c*). Here the purchaser, Lionel Cranfield, was one of the biggest merchants of his day, big enough to buy himself into the government. He became Lord Treasurer and Earl of Middlesex before being disgraced in 1624. No doubt the huge profit he made on this transaction is to be explained by other favours he had rendered Lord Howard of Effingham, one of the great lords coming into the clutches of money-lenders. Extract *d*), probably written a few years before the revolution of 1640, shows a contemporary acutely conscious of the social effects of land transactions. In *e*) Wilson shows lawyers profiting by land sales, and using their skill to cut through the complexities of the still feudal law.

a) Ben Jonson, *The Devil is an Ass*, Everyman, II, p. 291; *b*) Shirley, *The Gamester* (1633), Act I, Scene 1; *c*) *Historical Manuscripts Commission, Sackville MSS.*, I (Cranfield Papers), p. 152; *d*) *Norfolk Archæology*, XV, pp. 1–2; *e*) Wilson, pp. 24–5.

a) FROM BEN JONSON

Meercraft: WE see those changes daily: the fair lands
That were the client's, are the lawyer's now;
And those rich manors there of goodman Taylor's
Had once more wood upon them than the yard
By which they were measured out for the last purchase.
Nature hath these vicissitudes. She makes
No man a state of perpetuity, sir.

b) SALE—PURCHASE—SALE

Old Barnacle: We that had
Our breeding from a trade, cits, as ye call us,
Though we hate gentlemen ourselves, yet are
Ambitious to make all our children gentlemen:
In three generations they return again.
We for our children purchase land: they brave it
I' the country; beget children, and they sell,
Grow poor and send their sons up to be prentices.
There is a whirl in fate.

c) SPECULATIVE PURCHASE OF A LEASE

March 15th, 1608. Paid my Lord of Effingham for a lease of the park and castle of Donnington—£200; the interest for £1,000 lent him gratis for 6 months—£50; other disbursements—£38 15*s.* 0*d.*; [Total—£288 15*s.* 0*d.*].

July 29th, 1608. Sold the lease to Peter van Lore and Edward Ferrers for £1,700.

So gotten clear by this bargain, for which Almighty God be praised—£1,411 5*s.* 0*d.*

d) SOCIAL CONSEQUENCES OF LAND SALES

There is a society or combination lately sprung up called the Land-buyers. These lay their purses together, and as they can light on a manor, a gentleman's seat or a good quantity of land they buy it in gross and make profit of it by retailing it in parcels, even to single acres, as a purchaser will buy; and by making other waste thereof.

[All this is] tending to the destruction of gentry, gentlemen's seats and their hospitality, manors and lordships; [to] the severing of lands and tillage from the mansion houses, contrary to the statutes in that behalf; and to depopulation; [to] the enhancing of the prices of lands and thereby of rents, farms, corn and other commodities; [to] the making of a parity between gentlemen and yeomen and them which before were labouring men; [to] the begetting of pride and stubbornness in them, and by this means to become more refractory to the government of the county.

e) THE ESTATE OF COMMON LAWYERS

This sort and order of people within these forty or fifty years, since the practice of civil law hath been as it were wholly banished and abrogated, and since the clergy hath been trodden down by the taking away of church livings, and since the long continuance of peace hath bred an inward canker and [un]rest in men's minds, the people doing nothing but jar and wrangle one with another, these lawyers by the ruins of neighbours' contentions are grown so great, so rich and so proud, that no other sort dare meddle with them. Their number is so great now that, to say the truth, they can scarcely live one by another, the practice being drawn into a few hand of those which are most renowned, and all the rest live by pettifogging, seeking means to set their neighbours at variance, whereby they may gain on both sides. This is one of the greatest inconveniences in the land, that the number of the lawyers is so great [that] they undo the country people and buy up all the lands that are to be sold, so that young gentlemen or others newly coming to their livings, some of them prying into his evidence will find the means to set him at variance with some other, or some other with him, by some pretence or quiddity; and when they have half consumed themselves in suit they are fain to sell their land to follow the process and pay their debts, and then that becomes a prey to lawyers.

6. THE NEW GENTRY

Many were the satirical references to *nouveaux riches* who purchase coats of arms and peerages to live in idleness (*a*) and *b*)); to stewards who look after their own rather than their masters' interests (*c*). In *d*) (1641) Sir John Suckling, cavalier, goes a little deeper in stressing that the kind of men who prosper by usury and commerce have new (and to him hateful) standards of values. (Cf. No. 37).

a) W. Harrison, *Description of Britain* (ed. 1877), pp. 128–9; *b*) *Witt's Recreations* (1640), No. 11; *c*) Braithwaite, *The English Gentleman*, p. 287; *d*) *Somers Tracts*, 1st edition, XV, pp. 439–40.

a) HOW TO BECOME A GENTLEMAN, 1587

WHOSOEVER studieth the laws of the realm, whoso abideth in the university . . . or professeth physic and the liberal sciences, or beside his service in the room of a captain in the wars, or good counsel given at home, whereby his commonwealth is benefited, can live without manual labour, and thereto is able and will bear the port, charge and countenance of a gentleman, he shall for money have a coat and arms bestowed upon him by heralds (who in the charter of the same do of custom pretend antiquity and service, and many gay things), and thereunto, being made so good cheap, be called master . . . and reputed for a gentleman ever after, which is so much the less to be disallowed of for that the prince doth lose nothing by it, the gentleman being so much subject to taxes and public payments as is the yeoman or husbandman.

b) CLOTH TRADE TO HOUSE OF LORDS—AND BACK

Geta from wool and weaving first began
Swelling and swelling to a gentleman;
When he was a gentleman and bravely dight
He left not swelling till he was a knight:
At last (forgetting what he was at first)
He swole to be a Lord; and then he burst.

c) UNJUST STEWARDS

Many times it falleth out that the servant is able to purchase his master, having enriched himself by feeding his humour! Yet see the unthankfulness of many of these: having made them a garment of their master's shreds, and raised themselves to a great estate by his prodigality, they can learn to put on a scornful countenance towards their landless master, entertain him with contempt, forget his bounty, and ascribe all to their own thriving providence, which proceeds mainly from his profuseness.

d) THE OLD ORDER CRITICISES THE NEW

My first complaint is of titles of honour. . . .

Observe commonly what these people are by birth, and mark the manner of their and their father's getting of wealth to compass this title, and you shall find them people most hateful, most odious to the commonwealth, by their extortion, usury and other ungodly kind of getting, as ye may instance in Roberts, Craven, Sanderson and many others.

Can there be a greater grievance to a noble mind than to see these upstart families, by their insufferable misery [i.e. miserliness], penury and extortion grown to wealth, to precede the best of you in rank, degree and calling, whose ancestors have lost their lives for king and country; and yourselves in many respects more able and capable of serving your prince and commonwealth than they, and every way better deserving?

The character of a covetous man is that he getteth his goods with care and envy of his neighbours, with sorrow to his enemies, with travail to his body, with grief to his spirit, with scruple to his conscience, with danger to his soul, with suit to his children and curse to his heirs; his desire is to live poor, to die rich; but as these vices are made virtues, even so is he honoured for them with title of nobility.

7. MERCHANTS

Extract *a*) was written by a radical poet as early as 1550. At that date capitalist morality—the idea that a man can do what he likes with his own—was new and very shocking. *b*) is from James I's advice to his son, written in 1598. It may be compared with the rather different advice of a merchant to his son in No. 11.

a) Crowley, *Selected Works* (1872), pp. 87–9; *b*) James I, *Works* (1918), p. 26.

a) THEY UPSET THE SOCIAL ORDER

So soon as they have ought to spare,
Beside their stock that must remain,
To purchase lands is all their care
And all the study of their brain.

There can be no unthrifty heir
Whom they will not smell out anon,
And handle him with words full fair
Till all his lands are from him gone.

The farms, the woods and pasture grounds
That do lie round about London
Are hedged in within their mounds [= enclosures],
Or else shall be ere they have done. . . .

If ye ask of the collier
Why he selleth his coals so dear,
And right so of the woodmonger,
They say "Merchants have all in fear."

"The wood," say they, "that we have bought
In times past for a crown of gold,
We cannot have, if it be ought,
Under ten shillings ready told. . . ."

Let it suffice thee to marry
Thy daughter to one of thy trade:
Why shouldst thou make her a lady,
Or buy for her a noble ward?

And let thy sons, every one,
  Be bound 'prentice years nine or ten,
To learn some art to live upon:
  For why should they be gentlemen? . . .

For thou canst not promote thy son,
  But thou must buy him land and rent,
Whereby some must needs be undone
  To bring to pass thy fond intent.

Some man, perchance, need doth compel
  To mortgage his land for money;
And wilt thou cause him for to sell
  The livelihood of his progeny?

b) JAMES I'S DISAPPROVAL

The merchants think the whole common-weal ordained for making them up; and accounting it their lawful gain and trade to enrich themselves upon the loss of all the rest of the people they transport from us things necessary, bringing back sometimes unnecessary things and at other times nothing at all. They buy for us the worst wares and sell them at the dearest prices; and albeit the victuals fall or rise of [i.e. in] their prices, according to the abundance or the scantness thereof, yet the prices of their wares ever rise, but never fall: being as constant in their evil custom as if it were settled law for them.

8. THE BOURGEOISIE

By now the bourgeoisie has come to stay. Wilson (*a*) coldly analyses capitalist profits: child labour (long before the industrial revolution) is seen as a source of surplus value breeding aldermen. Peacham (1622) is old-fashioned in his attitude (*b*); but Bacon (1625) realises the importance of monopolies and dishonest speculation in the all-important process of accumulating capital.

a) Wilson, pp. 20–1; *b*) Peacham, *Compleat Gentleman*, pp. 3, 11–13; *c*) Bacon, *Essay* No. XXXIV, "Of Riches."

a) THE ESTATE OF CITIZENS

THESE, by reason of the great privileges they enjoy, every city being as it were a commonwealth among themselves . . . must needs be exceeding well to pass. They are not taxed but by their own officers of their own brotherhood, every art [i.e. craft] having one or two . . . which are continually of the council of the city in all affairs to see that nothing pass contrary to their profit. Besides, they are not suffered to be idle in their cities as they be in other parts of Christendom, but every child of six or seven years old is forced to some art whereby he gaineth his own living and something besides to help to enrich his parents or master. I have known in one city (viz. Norwich) where the accounts having been made yearly what children from six to ten years have earned towards their keeping in a year, and it hath been accounted that it has risen to £12,000 sterling which they have gained, besides other keeping, and that chiefly by knitting of fine jersey stockings, every child being able at or soon after seven years to earn 4*s*. a week at that trade. . . . And in that city I have known in my time twenty-four aldermen which were esteemed to be worth £20,000 apiece, some much more, and the better sort of citizens the half; but if we should speak of London and some other maritime places we should find it much exceeding this rate. It is well known that at this time there are in London some merchants worth £100,000, and he is not accounted rich that cannot reach to £50,000 or near it.

b) TRADE IS UNGENTLEMANLY

The exercise of merchandize hath been (I confess) accounted base, and much derogating from nobility. . . . Touching mechanical arts and artists, whosoever labour for their livelihood and gain, have no share at all in nobility or gentry. . . . The reason is, because their bodies are spent with labour and travail. . . . Neither must we honour or esteem those ennobled or made gentle in blood, who by mechanic and base means have raked up a mass of wealth, or because they follow some great man, wear the cloth of a noble personage, or have purchased an ill coat [of arms] at a good rate; no more than a player upon the stage, for wearing a lord's cast suit: since nobility hangeth not upon the airy esteem of vulgar opinion, but is indeed of itself essential and absolute.

c) BUT WE CANNOT GET RICH WITHOUT NEW METHODS

The ways to enrich are many, and most of them foul: parsimony is one of the best, and yet it is not innocent; for it withholdeth men from works of liberality and charity. The improvement of the ground is the most natural obtaining of riches; . . . but it is slow; and yet, where men of great wealth do stoop to husbandry, it multiplieth riches exceedingly. I knew a nobleman in England that had the greatest audits of any man in my time, a great grazier, a great sheep-master, a great timber-man, a great collier, a great corn-master, a great lead-man, and so of iron, and a number of the like points of husbandry. . . . It was truly observed by one, "That himself came very hardly to a little riches, and very easily to great riches"; for when a man's stock is come to that, that he can expect the prime of markets and over-come those bargains which for their greatness are few men's money, and be partner in the industries of younger men, he cannot but increase mainly. . . . Monopolies and co-emption of wares for resale, where they are not restrained, are great means to enrich; especially if the party have intelligence what things are like to come into request, and so store himself beforehand.

9. THE NEW POWER OF MONEY

The mediæval Church forbade the taking of interest, though means of evading the prohibition were often found. The Protestant reformers were more sympathetic to the needs of capitalist society. In England in 1571 the House of Commons forced upon a reluctant government the legalisation of interest of 10 per cent. upon loans. Extract *a*), from R. Carew's *Survey of Cornwall* (1602), shows gentlemen falling into the clutches of tin-manufacturers who were also usurers; and suggests that the latter tended to Puritanism in religion. Extract *b*) (1628) is one of many tirades against the power of gold written in this age of accumulation. A more familiar passage is in Shakespeare's *Timon of Athens*, Act IV, Scene 3.

a) T. and P., I, pp. 289–90; *b*) Owen Feltham, *Resolves, Divine, Moral and Political* (Temple Classics), pp. 89, 101–3.

a) MONEYLENDERS

When any western gent. or person of account wanteth money to defray his expenses at London, he resorteth to one of the tin merchants of his acquaintance to borrow some; but they shall as soon wrest the club out of Hercules' fist as one penny out of their fingers, unless they give bond for every £20 so taken in loan, to deliver a thousand pound weight of tin at the next coinage, which shall be within two or three months, or at farthest within half a year after. At which time the price of every thousand will not fail to be at least £23, perhaps £25: yea, and after the promise made the party must be driven . . . to make three or four errands to his house, ere he shall get the money delivered. In this sort some one merchant will have £500 out beforehand, reaping thereby a double commodity, both of excessive gain for his loan, and of assurance to be served with tin for his money. This they say is no usury, forsooth, because the price of tin is not certainly known beforehand. . . . But if to take above fifty in the hundred be extremity, whatsoever name you list to give it, this in truth can be no other than cut-throat and abominable dealing. I will not condemn all such as use this trade, neither yet acquit those who make greatest pretence of zeal in religion.

b) GOLD

How happily they lived in Spain, till fire made some mountains vomit gold! and what miserable discords followed after. . . . If this were put down, virtue might then be queen again. . . . As for gold, surely the world would be much happier if there were no such thing in it. But since it is now the fountain whence all things flow, I will care for it, as I would for a pass, to travel the world by without begging. If I have none, I shall have so much the more misery. . . .

We magnify the wealthy man, though his parts be never so poor; the poor man we despise, be he never so well otherwise qualified. To be rich, is to be three parts of the way onward to perfection. To be poor, is to be made a pavement for the tread of the full-minded man. Gold is the only coverlet of imperfections: it is the fool's curtain, that can hide all his defects from the world. It can make knees bow, and tongues speak, against the native genius of the groaning heart. . . . Gold, that lay buried in the buttock of the world, is now made the head and ruler of the people. . . . Worth without wealth is like an able servant out of employment . . . for though indeed riches cannot make a man worthy, they can show him and the world when he is so. But when we think him wise for his wealth alone, we appear content to be misled with the multitude.

10. HYMN FOR A MERCHANT

George Wither was a Puritan poet and pamphleteer, who in James I's reign had found himself in jail for writing political satires (see No. 39, *a*)). The conclusion of the hymn expresses the insecurity which merchants still felt under a political régime which they did not control. *Hallelujah* was dedicated to Parliament. Wither, *Hallelujah* (1641), Part III, Hymn XXXV.

By the use of this hymn merchants may be kept heedful of the snares and temptations which they become liable unto by their negotiations, and what peace and profit will ensue if they be just and merciful in their dealings.

Sing this as the 4th, 5th, or 6th Psalms.

Unless, O Lord! Thy grace Thou lend
To be my hourly guide,
In every word I do offend,
In every step I slide. . . .
Yea, to great wealth men seldom rise
Through what they sell and buy,
Except to vend their merchandise
They sometimes cheat and lie.
The sins, O Lord! forgive Thou me
Which to my trading cleave;
Upright let all my dealings be,
That I may none deceive. . . .
Permit not greediness of gain
My conscience to ensnare,
Or load me with employment vain,
Or fill my heart with care:
Nor make my goods a prey to those
Who by dishonest ways,
Or by pretending all to lose,
Themselves to riches raise.
To those who poor are that way made
Which they could not prevent,
Let me no cruel burdens add
In craving what I lent;
But let me do for men distressed
As my estate may bear,
What at their hands I might request
If in their plight I were.
So though to poverty I fall,
And needy seem to be
A quiet mind possess I shall
With full content in Thee:
And if great wealth I do acquire,
It will not waste away
Like brushy fuel in the fire
But with mine offspring stay.

11. A MERCHANT'S ADVICE TO HIS SON

Mun's *England's Treasure by Foreign Trade* was written about 1630, but not printed during the author's lifetime because of its implied criticisms of royal policy (see also No. 68). It was published in 1664. So Mun's complaint of the bad treatment of merchants in England by comparison with "other countries" (i.e. especially the Netherlands; cf. Nos. 67–8) refers to the pre-revolutionary period. Trade is still despised by the landed aristocracy, and prosperous merchants abandon their profession (cf. No. 8). Nevertheless, Mun has unbounded confidence in the future of his class. T. Mun, *England's Treasure by Foreign Trade* (1928), pp. xiii, 3–4, 16.

My son, in a former discourse I have endeavoured after my manner briefly to teach thee two things. The first is piety, how to fear God aright . . .; the second is policy, how to love and serve thy country. . . . So am I now to speak of money, which doth indifferently serve to both those happy ends. . . . Many merchants here in England, finding less encouragement given to their profession than in other countries, and seeing themselves not so well esteemed as their noble vocation requireth . . . do not therefore labour to attain unto the excellency of their profession, neither is it practised by the nobility of this kingdom as it is in other states from the father to the son throughout their generations, to the great increase of their wealth and maintenance of their names and families. Whereas the memory of our richest merchants is suddenly extinguished; the son, being left rich, scorneth the profession of his father, conceiving more honour to be a gentleman (although but in name) to consume his estate in dark ignorance and excess, than to follow the steps of his father as an industrious merchant to maintain and advance his fortunes. . . . There is more honour and profit in an industrious life, than in a great inheritance which wasteth for want of virtue. . . . They that have wares cannot want money.

12. YEOMEN

"Yeoman" is a loose term. It covers generally the independent peasantry, particularly that section which is prospering and coming up into the gentry. Harrison (*a*) contrasts yeomen with gentlemen on the one hand and servants on the other; yeomen are buying lands; some are even rich enough to "live without labour" and thus become gentlemen. Wilson, a later and shrewder observer, paints a less idyllic picture (*b*). He sees the part played by the rise in prices (referred to by Harrison) in the prosperity of a section of the yeomanry, and notes that the enrichment of some means the decline of others (see Nos. 14–16). In 1630 John Taylor describes a *kulak* type, driving up prices, thriving in time of famine, making his son a gentleman and failing to keep up feudal standards of hospitality and alms-giving.

a) W. Harrison, *Description of Britain*, pp. 132–3; *b*) Wilson, pp. 18–19, 38–9; *c*) John Taylor, *A Brood of Cormorants*, *Works* (1630), p. 12.

a) A PROSPEROUS CLASS, 1587

YEOMEN are those which . . . may dispend of their own free land in yearly revenue to the sum of 40*s*. sterling, or £6 as money goeth in our times. . . . This sort of people have a certain pre-eminence, and more estimation than labourers and the common sort of artificers, and these commonly live wealthily, keep good houses, and travail to get riches. They are also for the most part farmers to gentlemen . . . or at the leastwise artificers, and with grazing, frequenting of markets, and keeping of servants (not idle servants, as the gentlemen do, but such as get both their own and part of their master's living), do come to great wealth, insomuch that many of them are able and do buy the lands of unthrifty gentlemen, and often setting their sons to the schools, to the universities, and to the Inns of the Court, or otherwise leaving them sufficient lands whereupon they may live without labour, do make them by those means to become gentlemen.

b) STRATIFICATION OF THE PEASANTRY

It cannot be denied but the common people are very rich, albeit they be much decayed from the states they were wont to have, for the gentlemen, which were wont to addict themselves to the wars, are now for the most part grown to become good husbands and know as well how to improve their lands to the uttermost as the farmer or countryman, so that they take their farms into their hands as the leases expire, and either till themselves or else let them out to those who will give most; whereby the yeomanry of England is decayed and become servants to gentlemen, which were wont to be the glory of the country and good neighbourhood and hospitality; notwithstanding there are yet some store of those yeomen left who have long leases of such lands and lordships as they hold, yea I know many yeomen in divers provinces in England which are able yearly to dispense betwixt £300 and £500 yearly by their lands and leases, and some twice and some thrice as much. But my young masters the sons of such, not contented with their states of their fathers to be counted yeomen and called John or Robert (such an one), but must skip into his velvet breeches and silken doublet, getting to be admitted into some Inn of Court or Chancery, must ever after think scorn to be called any other than gentleman; which gentlemen indeed, perceiving them unfit to do them that service that their fathers did, when their leases do expire turn them out of their lands (which was never wont to be done, the farmer accounting his estate as good as inheritance in times past) and let them to such as are not by their bad pennyworths able to gentleman it as others have done. . . .

Of these yeoman of the richest sort which are able to lend the Queen money (as they do ordinarily upon her letters called privy seals whensoever she hath any wars defensive or offensive or any other enterprise) there are accounted to be about 10,000 in country villages besides citizens.

There are, moreover, of yeomen of meaner ability which are called freeholders, for that they are owners of lands which hold by no base service of any lord or superior, such as are able to keep ten or eleven, or eight or six milch kine, five or six horses to till their ground, besides young beasts and sheep and are accounted to be worth each of them in all their substance betwixt £300 and £500 sterling more or less, of these I say there are accounted to be in England and Wales about the number of 80,000, as I have seen in sheriffs' books. . . .

The cause that hath made the yeomanry in England so great I cannot rightly call a policy, because it was no matter invented and set down by authority for the bettering of that state of people, but rather by the subtlety of them and simplicity of gentlemen; for the yeomanry and mean people being servants and vassals to the gents, who are the possessors and lords of the lands and lordships and could not occupy all their lands themselves, but placed farmers therein, at a time when by reason of the great wars money was scarce and all things else cheap, and so lands let at a small rent—the yeomen and farmers told the gentlemen (their landlords) that they could not be at so great charges to manure and inclose and improve their grounds, and repair and re-edify their houses ruined by war, unless they would let them the said land for some time; and if they would so do, and at a smaller rent, they would pay them some piece of money for a fine, and so much money yearly. The gentlemen, improvident of what should come after, and gladded to have money in hands, did let unto the said farmers all their lands and lordships (saving their dwelling) after the rate aforesaid, some for 30, some 40, and some 50, some 100 years. Soon after the King [Henry VIII], by reason of the want of money, altered the coin and caused that which was before but 6*d.* to go for 12*d.*, and after that again lessened it as much more. . . . Hereby it came to pass that he which paid before one pound weight in silver for his farm, paid now but a quarter; and the yeoman at that time having most money, carrying it to the mint, had for every £1 four. . . . Then the price of corn, cattle and all farmers' commodities increasing daily in price, and the gentleman who is generally inclined to great and vain expence had no more than would keep his house and some small rent and therefore could not spend away prodigally much of the wealth of the land because he hath no superfluity, and the baser sort, which by this means had got the wealth, had never the inclination to spend much . . . and so began England so rich. But since these long leases are grown to expire the gentlemen by this begin to be ware how to be so over-reached. Notwithstanding, some report that this was not done without the policy of the King, who by this means weakened the ability of his nobility and thereby clipped the wings of their insolencies.

c) THE SPECULATIVE YEOMAN FARMER

Then [i.e. in earlier days] was a farmer like a labouring ant
And not a land-devouring cormorant.
For if a gentleman hath land to let
He'll have it, at what price so e'er 'tis set,
And bids, and over-bids, and will give more
Than any man could make of it before:
Offers the landlord more than he would crave,
And buys it, though he never get nor save.
And whereas gentlemen their land would let
At rates that tenants might both save and get,
This cormorant will give his landlord more
Than he would ask, in hope that from the poor
He may extort it double, by the rate
Which he will sell his corn and cattle at.
At pining famine he will ne'er repine;
'Tis plenty makes this cormorant to whine,
To hoard up corn with many a bitter ban
From widows, orphans, and the labouring man.
He prays for rain in harvest, night and day,
To rot and to consume the grain and hay:
That so he mows and ricks and stacks that mould,
At his own price he may translate to gold.
But if a plenty come, this ravening thief
Torments and sometimes hangs himself with grief.

And all this raking toil and cark and care
Is for the clownish first-born son and heir,
Who must be *gentled* by his ill-got pelf,
Though he to get it got the devil himself. . . .
For alms, he never read the word relieve:
He knows to get, but never knows to give.

13. CONFLICTING STANDARDS

Bourgeois civilisation brought its own code of morality to challenge that of the preceding age: we saw something of the resultant conflict in No. 7. In *a*) Sir John Eliot, imprisoned in the Tower for opposing Charles I in Parliament, elaborates a philosophical attack on exclusive hereditary right, the foundation of the feudal property system and absolute monarchy. Eliot has grasped in 1630 the essential difference between the morality of a society based on free competition and that of a society based on monopoly landownership. And for him Reason is the sole judge (cf. Nos. 62 and 124). In *b*) we see the same conflict in practice. A precise calculation of the wealth of a yeoman, a demonstration of his ability to live without work, may cancel out his social inferiority and make his daughter an eligible match for a gentleman. Oxinden, in February, 1641, declares that one man is as good as another: the Civil War is at hand.

a) Sir J. Eliot, *The Monarchy of Man*, II, pp. 179–81; *b*) *The Oxinden Letters, 1607–42* (ed. Dorothy Gardiner, 1933) pp. 276–9.

a) PRIMOGENITURE OR MERIT?

We shall endeavour . . . [to] discover . . . what true honour is. And first to see whether it be confined within an order, limited to persons and degrees [i.e. classes], or left promiscuously to all, as their worths and qualities shall discern it, wherein let reason be the judge. Is it the reward of virtue or of fortune they would make it? Let them answer who so magnify this pretence. Do they apply that honour to their houses, or themselves? Is it the distinction of their families, or guerdon of their merits? If they will take it for distinction, 'tis but a name, and the poorest, the basest have as much, and a small cause there is to glory in that subject. If it be the distinction of their families, the character of their houses, though it implied a glory, what can it be to them more than treasures are to porters? But they will say, it's the glory of their ancestors, the acquisition of their virtues; "and from them it does descend hereditarily to us." So may the other [i.e. the porter] say that treasure is his master's, and by his will imposed upon his shoulders: but to whose use, and in whose right, has he received it? In his own, or to his own profit and advantage? Masters would take this ill if their servants should usurp it; and all men would condemn them both of falsehood and ingratitude. So is it, in the other, an injury to their ancestors if they pretend that honour to be theirs. They can but carry it to *their* use, as a monument of *their* virtues that acquired it, not in their own interest and right, to the glory of themselves; nay, not without their shame whose purchase cannot equal it, being but the sole inheritors of the fortune, not the worth. . . . All persons, all orders, all degrees extant, may be capable thereof [of honour].

b) SHOULD A GENTLEMAN MARRY A YEOMAN'S DAUGHTER?

I desire you to acquaint Sir James Oxinden with . . . the party's estate. . . . It is as it is now let . . . £109 12*s*. 0*d*. by the year; and this is fee simple and socage estate; the wood and timber upon the ground was valued to me by Cooper, this last year, at £400, and he said he had not overvalued it. . . . Now valuing £109 12*s*. 0*d*. by the year at £2,192, and the wood and timber at £400, it will amount to £2,592; out of this there is to be subtracted £1,400. So there remains to her £1,192; but the house and site in this valuation is reckoned at nothing, which I esteem at a considerable rate. . . .

There is one objection, which I doubt not but in the course of my life I shall hear often, and that is my mistress was a yeoman's daughter. True it is her father was a yeoman, but such a yeoman as lived in his house, in his company, and in his sports and pleasures like a gentleman, and followed the same with gentlemen; . . . and that he bred his daughter according to herself, his maintaining her four years at school amongst other gentlemen's daughters, at the same cost and charges they were at, will sufficiently demonstrate. . . . The wisest men have ever held virtue the best and truest nobility, and as sure as death it is so, and for my own part my former highly esteeming of political nobility I now reckon among the follies of my youth. Yet am not I ignorant that there be divers people in the world, and it is convenient there should be such, of so stupid and gross capacities, that conceive there is something extraordinarily inherent in this political nobility. . . . If I see a man of what low degree or quality soever that is virtuous, rich, wise or powerful, him will I prefer before the greatest lord in the kingdom that comes short of him in these. . . . I know the greater part of the world do ignorantly believe otherwise.

14. THE LOWER ORDERS

Extract *a*) is fundamental to an understanding of this volume. Written by a Secretary of State and published barely fifty years before the revolution, it perfectly expresses official theory. The ruling class is still the gentry: all others exist "only to be ruled." That is why anyone who could afford it sought to buy land. Later on we shall see "the fourth sort" trying to have a say in ruling themselves. Serfdom or villeinage had virtually ceased by the end of the sixteenth century, though examples could still be found (*c*), and a conservative gentleman like John Smyth looked back to it with nostalgia in the sixteen-thirties (*d*). Extract *f*) shows how the ruling class in 1639 still thought of the lower orders as their property, and relied on class solidarity between landowners. The descendants of villeins were copyholders and cottagers, subject to many disabilities (*b*) and *e*)). Most of them were excluded by a statute of 1563 from all industries, even the rural clothing industry: hence they formed a pool of cheap agricultural labour. Note in *b*) how the rich escape overseas military service: cf. No. 41, *c*). Extract *e*) is from a parliamentary survey taken after the sale of crown lands in 1649. The copyholders of these manors paid cash to the King to escape from the legal uncertainty of their unfree tenure, but had never secured the promised confirmation of their liberation. (Cash, of course, was all that the King intended to get from the transaction.) Copyholders tried during the revolution to get a general statutory liberation from the servile incidents of their tenure, but unsuccessfully (see Nos. 151, 170, 174–5).

a) Sir Thomas Smith, *The Commonwealth of England*, (ed. Alston, 1906), Book I, Chap. 24; *b*) Wilson, pp. 19–20; *c*) T. and P., I, pp. 71–2; *d*) J. Smyth, *History of the Hundred of Berkeley*, p. 43; *e*) *Journal of Derbyshire Archæological and Natural History Society*, Vol. XXXIV, pp. 22–3; *f*) *Oxinden Letters, 1607–42*, p. 152.

a) THREE-QUARTERS OF THE POPULATION, 1583

THE fourth sort or class amongst us is . . . day labourers, poor husbandmen, yea merchants or retailers which have no free land, copyholders and all artificers. . . . These have no voice nor authority in our commonwealth, and no account is made of them, but only to be ruled.

b) COPYHOLDERS AND COTTAGERS, 1601

The rest are copyholders and cottagers, as they call them, who hold some land and tenements . . . at the will of the lord, and these are some of them men of as great ability as any of the rest; and some poor, and live chiefly upon country labour, working by the day for meat and drink and some small wages. These last are they which are thrust out to service in war, the richer sort of yeomen and their sons being trained but not sent out of the land, but kept to defend against invasion at home—unless they will go voluntarily, as many do.

c) LIBERATION OF A SERF, 1576

Whereas the Queen's most excellent Majesty . . . hath named and appointed me Henry Lee, knight, her Majesty's Commissioner to enquire of all her Majesty's bondmen and bondwomen, with their children, . . . their goods, chattels, lands, tenements and hereditaments within this realm of England and Wales, whereunto her Majesty may in any wise be entitled . . . and [hath] further granted . . . to me . . . full power and authority to accept, receive and admit to be manumised and enfranchised such . . . of her bondmen and bondwomen in blood; . . . [I] the said Sir Henry Lee have accepted, received and admitted . . . Margaret Cawston as one bondwoman of the said number, with her posterity . . . to be manumitted, enfranchised and made free by the authority aforesaid.

d) ADVANTAGES OF SERFDOM, *c.* 1630

I conceive . . . that the laws concerning villeinage are still in force, of which the latest are the sharpest. But now . . . since slaves were made free which were of great use and service, there are grown up a rabble of rogues, cutpurses and the like mischievous men, slaves in nature though not in law. And if any think this kind of dominion not to be lawful, yet surely it is natural: and certainly we find not such a latitude of difference in any creature, as in the nature of man; wherein the wisest excel the most foolish of men by far greater degree than the most foolish of men doth surpass the wisest of beasts. And therefore when commiseration hath given way to reason, we shall find that nature is the ground of masterly power and of servile obedience which is thereto correspondent; and a man is *animal politicum*, apt even by nature to command or obey, every one in his proper degree.

e) COPYHOLDERS BUYING FREEDOM, 1621

In [1621] certain of the copyholders of the . . . manor of Wirksworth [and four other manors] . . . in the . . . county of Derby . . . belonging to the crown did compound with the King to make their fines certain and to have and use divers other privileges; and for the quiet settling of the same they had a decree in the Duchy [of Lancaster] court to confirm their customs; and by the decree and their own consent they were ordered to pay 35 years' chief and ancient rent for the same, the moiety whereof they were to pay within 3 months after the decree was passed (which they did accordingly pay) and the other moiety they were to pay within 3 months next after the decree should be confirmed by Act of Parliament unto them, which is not yet done [1649!]. And those only that paid their composition whose names are in schedule annexed unto the decree were to have the benefit of the decree and the other copyholders were to have none. And by this decree . . . they were ordered to pay for their whole composition £1,193 3*s.* 5¼*d.* . . . They are all still liable to the payment of the other moiety proportionably whensoever an Act of Parliament shall confirm the decree unto them, and they would pay in their money were the Act passed for them.

f) PROPERTY RIGHTS MUST BE RESPECTED, 1639

WORTHY COUSIN,—

I spoke to Sir Thomas Palmer that he would not take it ill if you followed the law against his man for stealing your conies [rabbits]. His answer to me was very choleric and rash, and said you did him a great discourtesy to take away his man now he had so earnest and important occasions for him, being harvest and he his pitcher, but you might prosecute the others now and after harvest hang his man if he deserved it. Moreover he does think no justice of peace will be so discourteous as to send a warrant for his man without writing him a letter beforehand to certify him the business; such things are used to clowns, never to gentlemen.

15. CONTRASTS OF WEALTH AND POVERTY

The poem by the Earl of Oxford (*a*) is a commentary on Nos. 13 and 14. His lordship was not a Socialist agitator: he went bankrupt through extravagant ostentation (No. 1, *b*)); these stanzas are merely part of an incidental simile and breathe no moral indignation at the familiar fact of exploitation. In the second stanza, "manchet" is the best quality wheaten bread, "cheat" the inferior bread which the poor ate.

a) In *Poems of Ralegh and others*, (ed. J. Hannah, 1910), pp. 145–6; *b*) H. Hall, *Society in the Elizabethan Age* (1902), pp. 203, 223; *c*) Thomas Adams, *God's Bounty*, a sermon (*Works*, 1630), pp. 866, 863.

a) THE LABOURER, 1576

THE labouring man that tills the fertile soil,
And reaps the harvest fruit, hath not indeed
The gain, but pain; and if for all his toil
He gets the straw, the lord will have the seed.

The manchet fine falls not unto his share;
On coarsest cheat his hungry stomach feeds;
The landlord doth possess the finest fare;
He pulls the flowers, the other plucks but weeds.

The mason poor that builds the lordly halls
Dwells not in them; they are for high degree;
His cottage is compact in paper walls,
And not with brick or stone as others be.

The idle drone that labours not at all
Sucks up the sweet of honey from the bee;
Who worketh most, to their share least doth fall:
With due desert reward will never be. . . .

For he that beats the bush the bird not gets,
But who sits still and holdeth fast the nets.

b) WAGES AND PRICES, 1589

Wages paid by William Darrell, Axford, Wilts

	s.	*d.*
Lovell going to plough, ten weeks	10	0
Sandes, 1 month keeping sheep	2	0
Earle, helping the shepherd	0	9
Biggs & Tymberland, hedging, three days	3	0
Two boys going to plough, five weeks	6	0
Biggs & Tymberland, threshing, five days	5	10
Boy to help the shepherd, four weeks	2	0
Tull & Colman, ten days threshing	11	10
seven days threshing oats	4	0
threshing oats, six days	3	6

One day's expenses of William Darrell on food: Monday dinner, June 2nd

3 chickens and bacon	2	9
For roasting a chine of beef	1	0
For a loin of veal	2	0
For baking thereof	1	8
For a capon	2	6
For 2 rabbits	1	8
For boiling the chickens & bacon, & roasting the capon and rabbits	1	2
For 1-lb. of sugar	1	5
3 quarts of white wine	1	6
Oranges and lemons	0	4
Bread and beer	1	2
	17	2

Supper, same day

A quart of strawberries	0	8
½ pint of claret	0	1
Bread and beer	1	0
	1	9
Total	18	11

c) FEUDAL ENGLAND, 1630

The lords of great lands yet live upon other men's moneys: they must riot and revel, let the poor commoners pay for it. . . . When the poor creditor comes to demand his own they rail at him and send him laden away, but with ill words, not good money. In the country they set labourers on work, but they give them no hire. Tut, they are tenants, vassals: must they therefore have no pay? Yet those very landlords will bate them nothing of their rents. . . .

It is easy for that man to be rich, that will make his conscience poor.

16. PAUPERS

The rise of capitalism in sixteenth-century England brought with it the expropriation of the peasantry and the beginnings of the formation of a proletariat (see Marx, *Capital*, I, Chaps. 27–8). Large numbers of landless and homeless peasants wandering about looking for work created a new problem. It was met by imposing savage penalties. In *b*) J.Ps.—themselves members of the employing class—are empowered to direct paupers to forced labour for long hours at fixed wages. (Money, as Clause III indicates, was the test of class.) The penalties for employers who infringed these regulations were proportionately much less severe than the penalties on workers. The title of *c*) is somewhat ironical. It tightens up the act of 1563 as regards forced labour and imposes a means test for relief. The control of the ruling class is again enforced by the fact that churchwardens are nominated (not elected) and are supervised by J.Ps. Extract *d*) completes the code. Note the wide definition of "rogues," and that actors "belonging to" peers are exempt from the Act. The last clause shows the fear that underlies all this savage legislation. A contemporary said that *d*) "being in substance the very law of God, is never to be repealed"; the code survived until the nineteenth century. Extract *e*) illustrates action complementary to this legislation, the attempt to prevent disorder by maintaining employment in bad times as well as good. Extract *f*) dates from the sixteen-seventies, but makes the point that even at that late date there was no developed proletariat in the modern sense of the word. So long as the mass of the workers grew their own food, they could not be driven to work by fear of starvation, as the amiable Sir William Petty wished. This absence of a proletariat should be remembered when considering the failures of the democratic movements in the revolution (Parts IX–XIII). For Petty see No. 197.

a) Harrison, *Description of Britain*, pp. 212–14; *b*) *T.C.D.*, pp. 502–5, Prothero, pp. 46–8, 52; *c*) *T.C.D.*, pp. 488–92; *d*) *ibid.*, pp. 485–7; *e*) B.B. and T., pp. 382–3; *f*) Sir W. Petty, *Economic Writings* (ed. C. H. Hull, 1899), I, pp. 274–5.

a) THREE SORTS OF POOR

THERE is no commonwealth at this day in Europe wherein there is not great store of poor people, and those necessarily to be relieved by the wealthier sort, which otherwise would starve and come to utter confusion. With us the poor is commonly divided into three sorts, so that some are poor by impotency, as the fatherless child, the aged, blind and lame, and the diseased person that is judged to be incurable; the second are poor by casualty, as the wounded soldier, the decayed householder, and the sick person visited with grievous and painful diseases; the third consisteth of thriftless poor, as the rioter that hath consumed all, the vagabond that will abide nowhere but runneth up and down from place to place (as it were seeking work and finding none), and finally the rogue and the strumpet, which are not possible to be divided in sunder, but run to and fro over all the realm, chiefly keeping the champaign [i.e. unenclosed] soils in summer to avoid the scorching heat, and the woodland grounds in winter to eschew the blustering winds.

For the first two sorts . . . there is order taken throughout every parish in the realm that weekly collection shall be made for their help and sustentation, to the end they should not scatter abroad, and by begging here and there annoy both town and country. . . . But if they refuse to be supported by this benefit of the law, and will rather endeavour by going to and fro to maintain their idle trades, then are they adjudged to be parcel of the third sort, and so, instead of courteous refreshing at home, are often corrected with sharp execution and whip of justice abroad.

b) STATUTE OF APPRENTICES, 1563

III. Every person being unmarried and every other person being under the age of thirty years that . . . shall marry, and having been brought up in any of the said arts [thirty-one named industrial crafts] and not having lands . . . of the clear yearly value of 40*s*., nor being worth of his own goods the clear value of £10 . . ., shall (during the time that he shall be so unmarried or under the age of thirty years) upon request made by any person using the art or mystery wherein the said person so required hath been exercised . . . be retained and shall not refuse to serve. . . .

IV. No person which shall retain any servant shall put away [i.e. dismiss] his or her said servant, and . . . no person retained according to this statute shall depart from his master, mistress or dame before the end of his or her term . . . unless it be for some reasonable and sufficient cause or matter to be allowed before two Justices of Peace, or one at the least. . . .

VII. None of the said retained persons in husbandry or in any of the arts or sciences above remembered, after the time of his retainer [has] expired, shall depart forth of one city, town or parish to another . . . unless he have a testimonial under the seal of the said city or of the constable or other head officer and of two other honest householders of the city, town or parish where he last served, declaring his lawful departure. . . .

IX. All artificers and labourers being hired for wages by the day or week shall betwixt the midst of the months of March and September be at their work at or before 5 of the clock in the morning, and continue at work until betwixt 7 and 8 of the clock at night, except it be in the time of breakfast, dinner or drinking, the which times at the most shall not exceed above 2½ hours in the day. . . .

XI. The Justices of Peace . . . shall yearly . . . have authority . . . to limit, rate and appoint the wages . . . of . . . artificers, handicraftsmen, husbandmen, or any other labourer, servant or workman. . . .

XXVIII. If any person shall be required by any householder having and using half a ploughland at the least in tillage to be an apprentice and to serve in husbandry or in any other kind of art, mystery or science before expressed, and shall refuse so to do; . . . then upon the complaint of such housekeeper made to one Justice of Peace . . . they shall have full power and authority . . . to commit him unto ward, there to remain until he be contented and will be bounden to serve as an apprentice should serve.

c) AN ACT FOR THE RELIEF OF THE POOR, 1598

The churchwardens of every parish and four substantial householders there . . . nominated . . . under the hand and seal of two or more Justices of the Peace in the same county . . . shall take order from time to time . . . with the consent of two or more such Justices of Peace for setting to work of the children of all such whose parents shall not by the said persons be thought able to keep and maintain their children, and also all such persons married and unmarried as having no means to maintain them use no ordinary and daily trade of life to get their living by; and also to raise . . . (by taxation of every inhabitant . . . in the said parish . . .) a convenient stock of flax, hemp, wool, thread, iron and other necessary ware and stuff to set the poor on work, and also competent sums of money for and towards the necessary relief of the lame, impotent, old, blind and such other among them being poor and not able to work. . . .

The parents or children of every poor, old, blind, lame and impotent person, or other poor person not able to work, being of sufficient ability, shall at their own charges relieve and maintain every such poor person in that manner and according to that rate as by the Justices of Peace of that county where such sufficient persons dwell . . . shall be assessed; upon pain that every one of them . . . forfeit 20*s*. for every month which they shall fail therein. . . .

All begging is forbidden by this present Act.

d) ROGUES, VAGABONDS AND STURDY BEGGARS, 1598

From time to time . . . the Justices of Peace of any county or city . . . [shall] cause to be erected one or more houses of correction within their several counties or cities. . . .

All persons calling themselves scholars going about begging, all seafaring men pretending losses of their ships or goods on the sea going about the country begging, all idle persons going about in any county either begging or using any subtle craft or unlawful games and plays, or feigning themselves to have knowledge in physiognomy, palmistry or other like crafty science, or pretending that they can tell destinies, fortunes, or such other like fantastical imaginations; all . . . common players of interludes and minstrels wandering abroad (other than players of interludes belonging to any baron of this realm, or any other honourable personage of greater degree . . .); all jugglers, tinkers, pedlars and petty chapmen wandering abroad, all wandering persons and common labourers being persons able in body, using loitering and refusing to work for such reasonable wages as is taxed [i.e. laid down by J.Ps.] or commonly given in such parts where such persons . . . dwell or abide, not having living otherwise to maintain themselves; all persons delivered out of gaols that beg for their fees or otherwise do travel begging; all such persons as shall wander abroad begging pretending [i.e. alleging] losses by fire or otherwise . . . [gipsies] . . . shall be taken, adjudged and deemed rogues, vagabonds and sturdy beggars. . . .

Every person which is by this present Act declared to be a rogue, vagabond or sturdy beggar which shall be . . . taken begging, vagrant, wandering or misordering themselves . . . shall upon their apprehension . . . be stripped naked from the middle upwards and shall be openly whipped until his or her body be bloody, and shall be forthwith sent from parish to parish . . . to the parish where he was born . . . there to put him or her self to labour as a true subject ought to do. . . .

If any of the said rogues shall appear to be dangerous to the inferior sort of people where they shall be taken, or otherwise be such as will not be reformed . . . in every such case it shall and may be lawful to the said Justices . . . [to order them to] be banished out of this realm . . . or . . . to the galleys. . . . And if any such rogue so banished . . . shall return again into any part of this realm . . . without lawful licence or warrant . . . in every such case . . . the party offending therein [shall] suffer death.

e) THE PRIVY COUNCIL TO J.PS. OF CLOTHING COUNTIES, 1622

We do hereby require you to call before you such clothiers as you shall think fitting, and to deal effectually with them for the employment of such weavers, spinners and other persons as are now out of work. . . . As we have employed our best endeavours in favour of the clothiers both for the vent of their cloth and for moderation in the price of wool . . . so may we not endure that the clothiers . . . should at their pleasure, and without giving knowledge thereof unto this Board, dismiss their workfolks, who, being many in number and most of them of the poorer sort, are in such cases likely by their clamours to disturb the quiet and government of those parts wherein they live . . .: this being the rule by which both the wool-grower, the clothier and merchant must be governed, that whosoever had a part of the gain in profitable times since his Majesty's happy reign, must now in the decay of trade . . . bear a part of the public losses as may best conduce to the good of the public and the maintenance of the general trade.

f) NOT YET A PROLETARIAT

It is observed by clothiers and others who employ great numbers of poor people, that when corn is extremely plentiful . . . the labour of the poor is proportionably dear, and scarce to be had at all (so licentious are they who labour only to eat, or rather to drink). . . . Surplusage of corn should be sent to public store-houses, from thence to be disposed of to the best advantage of the public [so keeping the price up] . . . rather than the same should be abused by the vile and brutish part of mankind to the prejudice of the commonwealth.

17. CLASS FEELING

Industry had hardly yet begun to bring the scattered peasantry together in factories; but sedentary crafts, even when carried on at home, gave men time to think, as a Minister notes in *a*). Weavers were notoriously heretical (i.e. thought for themselves). Extract *b*) shows the ruling class technique of fooling and dividing its opponents (cf. No. 88, *b*); a technique that could not be repeated indefinitely, as Sir John Oglander was soon to find. Nicholas Ferrar was wiser (*c*). He had abandoned a promising political career to found an "Anglican monastery" at Little Gidding, possibly because he foresaw the coming storm. He prudently advocated shortening leases.

a) T. and P., II, p. 45; *b*) Oglander, pp. 60–1; *c*) B. Blackstone, *Ferrar Papers* (1938), pp. 63–4.

a) CECIL ON BAD EFFECTS OF INDUSTRY, *c.* 1564

THE people that depend upon making of cloth are of worse condition to be quietly governed than the husbandmen.

b) DIFFICULTIES IN THE ISLE OF WIGHT, *c.* 1630–40

Corn hath been at a high price two or three times whilst I had the command of the Island [of Wight], insomuch as I was forced to forbid the exporting of it to any place in the Main. But . . . I would wish all men to be very provident in so doing. . . . You will make the meaner sort of people, who are always apt to rebel and mutiny, so insolent that they will hinder the transportation of all victuals and will not suffer bread and beer for the victualling of our own ships. I have often seen by experience how glad they will be to rise on the least occasion, and if you give them an inch they will take an ell. . . . On the other side, something must be done in a dearth to give the common people content. I have had 300 with me in a morning and have pacified them well. Good words at such a time will do more than harsh deeds. Yet afterwards proceed against the ringleaders, but avoid giving distaste to a multitude of desperate needy people: rather comply with them for the present. So shalt thou the better bring thine own designs to pass.

c) FOREBODINGS, 1637

The tenants to the lordship . . . desired to have new leases for fifteen years at the old rent. . . . [John Ferrar] was against it, saying to his brother that the rent was 100 marks [=£66 13*s*. 4*d*.] per annum under foot [i.e. below the market rent] by all other land about them, and that time was much too long to let leases at in that case. [Nicholas Ferrar said] let the men have ten years and a good penny worth [bargain], that so they may be willing to pay you honestly at your days of payment; for I tell you that before those times come out you will see other days, and think yourselves happy that you may receive and they pay you that rent in quiet.

18. THE PEASANT TRADITION

A strong tradition survived among the peasantry, looking back to the days when the land belonged to them and villages were run by the community. Edmund Spenser (*a*) was hostile to this tradition: for him Communism was the theory of those who *would not* work. But he was probably reproducing arguments he had heard used. (Note the religious argument. With the last line compare No. 9.) This peasant tradition was to emerge in a new form in the Leveller and Digger movements (Parts IX–XII). There were peasant risings in 1549, 1596, 1607, 1631 (Nos. 21–2). In 1631, with revolt in Gloucestershire and the west, the Privy Council feared economic breakdown and a general revolt of "the poorer sort." So they ordered the J.Ps. of Rutland to take elaborate precautions (*b*).

a) Spenser, *Mother Hubbard's Tale*, lines 132–53; *b*) B.B. and T., pp. 390–1.

a) COMMUNIST IDEAS, 1591

The Fox: For why should he that is at liberty
Make himself bond? Sith then we are free-born,
Let us all servile base subjection scorn;
And as we be sons of the world so wide,
Let us our fathers' heritage divide,
And challenge to ourselves our portions due
Of all the patrimony, which a few

Now hold in hugger-mugger in their hand;
And all the rest do rob of good and land.
For now a few have all, and all have nought,
Yet all be brethren, alike dearly bought.
There is no right in this partition,
Nor was it so by institution
Ordained first, nor by the law of Nature,
But that she gave like blessing to each creature,
As well of worldly livelihood as of life,
That there might be no difference nor strife,
Nor ought called mine or thine: thrice happy then
Was the condition of mortal men.
That was the golden age of Saturn old,
But this might better be the world of gold;
For without gold now nothing will be got.

b) SEDITIOUS TALK, 1631

We have been made acquainted with a letter written by John Wildbore, a minister in and about Tinwell [Rutlandshire] . . . to a friend of his here, wherein after some mention . . . of the present want and misery sustained by the poorer sort in those parts through the dearth of cloth and the want of work, he doth advertize in particular some speeches uttered by a shoemaker of Uppingham (whose name we find not) tending to the stirring up of the poor thereabout to a mutiny and insurrection. . . . "Hearest thou?" saith a shoemaker of Uppingham to a poor man of Liddington; "If thou wilt be secret I will make a motion to thee." "What is your motion?" saith the other. Then said the shoemaker, "The poor men of Oakham have sent to us poor men of Uppingham, and if you poor men of Liddington will join with us, we will rise, and the poor of Oakham say they can have all the armour of the county in their power within half an hour; and in faith," saith he, "we will rifle the churls."

Upon consideration had thereof, . . . to prevent all occasions which ill-affected persons may otherwise lay hold of under pretence and colour of the necessity of the time, we have thought good hereby to will and require you, the Deputy Lieutenants and Justices of Peace . . . forthwith to apprehend and take a more particular examination as well of the said shoemaker as of such others as you shall think fit . . .; and that you take especial care that the arms of that county in and about those parts be safely disposed of; and likewise (which is indeed most considerable and the best means to prevent all disorders in this kind) that you deal effectually in causing the market to be well supplied with corn and the poor to be served at reasonable prices and set on work by those of the richer sort, and by raising of stock to relieve and set them on work according to the laws.

Part Two

ECONOMIC LIFE BEFORE 1640

In popular states the merchant usually has more share in administration of public affairs; whereas in monarchies those that have the charge of the rudder have commonly little insight into trade, and as little regard of traders.

Henry Parker.

19. DEPOPULATION

One sign that money was now more valued than men (see No. 4) was the frequent conversion of arable land to sheep-farming. This was more profitable, but involved turning men off the land. Extract *a*) is one of the most famous contemporary attacks on the depopulator. It takes up the standpoint which the government, fearful of the social consequences of "depopulation," would have liked to have been able to enforce. But policy was administered by J.Ps., and the J.Ps. were often the depopulators. Extracts *b*) and *c*) bring out the contradictory situation in which Charles I's government was placed. On the one hand, it desired to prevent discontent which might result in outbreaks (*c*). On the other hand, both the government and its Parliamentary opponents wanted to protect property. Hence when enclosure did produce revolts they were severely put down (*b*).

a) R. Powell, *Depopulation Arraigned* (1636), pp. 6–8, 33–6, 40–2; *b*) Williams, II, pp. 60–1; *c*) B.B. and T., pp. 391–3.

a) DEPOPULATION ARRAIGNED

To describe it [depopulation] more plainly, it robs and pills the people of their due means and maintenance, and thereby disables them both in body and state from performing their service, and liege obedience, immediately to their prince, and mediately to the common-weal; . . . And it alters the quality of the people; from good husbands, it makes them houseless and thriftless, puts them in a course of idleness (the mother of mischief, and bane of all rule and order). So as they become aliens and strangers to their national government, and the kingdom by that means in a manner dispeopled and desolated.

The unlawful ways and means by which this grievous desolation is wrought, are next to be considered. It is not by any invasion, sacking or ransacking of places or people, by any foreign enemy, but by a bosom and home-bred enemy, either by an actual, violent, and voluntary razing and demolition of mansions and houses of habitation, or a careless and negligent suffering of them to decay, and to be unhabitable, or by enclosing, and hedging in common fields, and converting arable into pasture.

The persons actors in this oppression are (though they draw in by their example other inferior persons) griping and avaricious landlords, who commonly suffer ancient demiseable tenements to fall into their hands, and so retain them without granting further estates, at conscionable fines; and then wilfully or negligently decay the houses, and either keep their grounds in their own or a bailiff's manurance, or let it out by several parcels, at rack and extreme rents, to several persons; who to make the best of a bad bargain, are enforced (for want of . . . [a] farm to maintain a plough) to turn tillage into pasture, and thereby only keep a few sheep and a cow. . . . [39 Eliz., cap. 1] explained and enacted, that every house which at that time, or then after, had twenty acres . . . of arable land, meadow, and pasture, or more, thereunto belonging, and so let to farm for three years together, since the beginning of the Queen's reign (not being the castle, or dwelling house of any nobleman, or gentleman, nor the chief mansion house of any manor) shall be adjudged a house of husbandry for ever, with many provisions for repairing, and new-building houses of husbandry. In the same Parliament an Act . . . was made, that arable land converted to sheep pastures, or to the fatting or grazing of cattle since 1 Eliz. should be restored or laid to tillage, and so continue for ever, according to the nature of the soil and course of husbandry, with . . . a penalty of twenty shillings for every acre for every year not restored. I cannot omit the reasons of this law enforced in the entrance of it.

1. That the strength and flourishing estate of this kingdom has been always upheld and advanced by the maintenance of the plough and tillage.

2. Tillage is the occasion of multiplying of people, both for service in the wars, and time of peace.

3. A principal means that people are set on work, and thereby withdrawn from idleness, drunkenness, unlawful

games, and all other lewd practices and conditions of life.

4. That by tillage and husbandry, the greater part of the subjects are preserved from extreme poverty in a competent estate of maintenance and means to live.

5. That the wealth of the realm [be] kept dispersed and distributed in many hands, where it is more ready to answer all necessary charges for the service of the realm.

6. It is a cause that the realm doth more stand upon itself, without depending upon foreign countries, either for importation of corn, in time of scarcity, or for vent and utterance of our own commodities.

[Refers to the discontinuance of this Act and the repeal of "all the said other statutes against decay of houses" by an act of 21 Jac.] And so the remedy must have recourse to the common law, and the wisdom of the state. . . .

One of the mainest special occasions of this grand mischief is a growing evil of late years practised and set on foot by certain greedy and covetous persons, . . . grazing butchers, who under colour of their *mechanic trade* in butchery, respecting their own private gain and lucre above the general good of his Highness' subjects, do accumulate and gain into their hands, at excessive yearly rents, several great portions and parts of the grounds and lands of this realm, from several landlords, and persons, to the value of four hundred, five hundred, eight hundred, or a thousand pounds a year, more or less, from the occupation of poor husbandmen, to the intent to use it in pasture and not in tillage: and thereby not only to graze and feed great store of sheep and other cattle, which they usually buy in great numbers, to the intent to sell them alive . . . but also to . . . take to pasture in those several grounds the cattle of divers poor husbandmen and others at very high and unusual rates and prices; by means whereof the poor laborious husbandmen in most parts of the kingdom, whose tenements do most consist of arable land, are intercepted and forestalled from renting any competent quantities of meadow or pasture to maintain their oxen and other cattle, to keep the plough in use according to the season of the year; and those grounds which within the space of few years have been let at reasonable yearly rates to neighbouring husbandmen are now . . . enhanced to the full double value; to the great discomfort and discouragement of the husbandman, who ofttimes is enforced, for want of food and fodder for his oxen and cattle, to sell them away, and to leave his grounds untilled.

b) PROTECTION FOR ENCLOSING LANDLORDS, 1630

On Saturday last were censured in the Star Chamber fourscore persons, seven at £40 fine, and the residue at £100 or £200 apiece, for plucking down a pale which Sir James Fullerton and Mr. Kirke of the Bedchamber had erected about Gillingham Forest in Dorsetshire, after they had felled all the woods; the inhabitants thereabouts pretending [i.e. alleging] a [right of] commonage upon it, notwithstanding it was given by his Majesty under his broad seal to those two Scottishmen. The two ringleaders of the rout were censured also to stand upon the pillory at the next [i.e. nearest] market town.

c) STAR CHAMBER PUNISHING ENGROSSERS OF CORN, 1631

One Archer of Southchurch in Essex was . . . charged by Mr. Attorney-General for keeping in his corn and consequently for enhancing the price of corn the last year, which offence Mr. Attorney affirmed to be of high nature and evil consequence to the undoing of the poor. . . .

Justice Harvey . . . declared his offence to be very great, and fit to be punished in this Court; and adjudged him to pay 100 marks [£66 13*s.* 4*d.*] fine to the King and £10 to the poor, and to stand upon the pillory in Newgate Market an hour with a paper, wherein the cause of his standing there was to be written, put upon his hat, "For enhancing the price of corn." . . .

The Bishop of London [i.e. Laud] observed . . . that this Archer was guilty of a most foul offence, which the

Prophet hath in a very energetical phrase, "grinding the faces of the poor." He commended highly that speech of Justice Harvey, that this last year's famine was made by man and not by God, solicited by the hard-heartedness of men, and commended this observation as being made by his Majesty.

20. PEASANT GRIEVANCES

This petition illustrates one of the greatest of peasant grievances, the uncertainty of the terms on which they held their land. Either they might be expelled so that arable might be converted to pasture; or their rents might be increased to bring them into line with the 500 per cent. rise in prices in the 100 years before 1640. These risks were increased when, for example, crown lands were sold to city merchants in satisfaction of royal debts. The removal of the court rolls and records could deprive the peasants of their only evidence of what their terms of occupation traditionally were. (For later attempts to remove this grievance, see Nos. 126, 170, *b*) and 177.) From R. H. Tawney, *The Agrarian Problem in the Sixteenth Century* (1912), pp. 413–15.

To the King's most Excellent Majesty.

THE humble petition of your Majesty's poor and distressed tenants of your manor of North Wheatley in the county of Nottingham belonging to your Majesty's Duchy of Lancaster.

Most humbly showing that your poor subjects have time out of mind been copyholders of lands of inheritance to them and their heirs for ever of the manor aforesaid, and paid for every oxgang of land 16*s*. 8*d*. rent, and paid heretofore upon every alienation 1*s*. for every oxgang, but now of late, about 4 Jac. [1607] by an order of the Duchy Court they pay 2*s*. 6*d*. upon every alienation for every acre, which amounteth now to 45*s*. an oxgang.

And whereas some of your tenants of the said manor have heretofore held and do now hold certain oxgangs of lands belonging to the said manor by copy from 21 years to 21 years, and have paid for the same upon every copy 2*s*. and for every oxgang, 16*s*. 8*d*. per annum; they now of late by an order in the Duchy Court hold the same by lease under the Duchy seal, and pay £6. 13*s*. 4*d*. for a fine upon every lease and 16*s*. 8*d*. rent, with an increase of 6*s*. 8*d*. more towards your Majesty's provision.

And whereas in 11 Edw. IV [1472] your petitioners did by copy of court roll hold the demesnes of the said manor for term of years at £9. 6*s*. 8*d*. per annum, they afterwards in 6 Eliz. [1564] held the same demesnes by lease under the seal of the duchy for 21 years, at the like rent; and ten years before their lease was expired, they employed one Mr. Markham in trust to get their lease renewed, who procured a new lease of the demesnes in his own name for 21 years at the old rent, and afterwards contrary to the trust committed to him increased and raised the rent thereof upon the tenants to his own private benefit to £56. per annum.

And whereas the woods belonging to the said manor have within the memory of man been the only common belonging to the said town, paying yearly for the herbage and pannage thereof 6*s*. 8*d*., they now also hold the same under the Duchy Seal at £16. 16*s*. 2*d*. per annum.

And whereas the Court Rolls and Records of the said manor have always heretofore been kept under several locks and keys, whereof your Majesty's stewards have kept one key and your Majesty's tenants (in regard it concerned their particular inheritances) have kept another key; but now they are at the pleasure of the stewards and officers transported from place to place, and the now purchasers do demand the custody of them, which may be most prejudicial to your Majesty's poor tenants:

Now forasmuch as your Majesty has been pleased to sell the said manor unto the City of London, who have sold the same unto Mr. John Cartwright and Mr. Tho. Brudnell gent, and for that your petitioners and tenants there (being in number two hundred poor men, and there being 11 of your Majesty's tenants there that bear arms for the defence of your Majesty's realm, and 12 that pay your Majesty's subsidies, fifteens and loans) are all now like to be utterly undone, in case the said Mr. Cartwright and Mr. Brudnell should (as they say they will) take away from your tenants the said demesnes and woods after the expiration of their leases, and that your poor tenants should be left to the wills of the purchasers for their fines, or that the records and court rolls should not be kept as in former times in some private place, where the purchasers and tenants may both have the custody and view of them as occasion shall serve:

May it therefore please your Sacred Majesty that such order may be taken in the premises for the relief of your poor tenants of the manor aforesaid that they may not be dispossessed of the demesnes and leases, and that they may know the certainty of their fines for the copyholds, demesnes and leases and may have the court rolls and records safely kept as formerly they have been. . . . And your poor tenants as in all humble duty bound will daily pray for your Majesty.

Whitehall, this 10 of November, 1629.

21. AGRARIAN DISCONTENT, 1596

The peasantry hit back. The abortive Oxfordshire rising here described was caused by hunger attributed to enclosure. The deputy-lieutenant responsible for rounding up the conspirators was himself accused of enclosing common fields. These summaries from the *Calendar of State Papers* are bare; but behind them we can sense the grim interrogations on the rack. The proposed alliance of peasants and London apprentices became a reality in the Leveller movement (see Part IX). Steere's remark about Spain can only refer to the Communeros' Revolt of 1523. It is a remarkable instance of a long-surviving tradition—although it is not true. That revolt was defeated; and the poor in Spain were no more "living merrily" in 1596 than in 1949. *C.S.P.D.*, 1595–7, pp. 316–17, 319, 343–5.

Sir W. Spencer, deputy lieutenant of Oxfordshire, to the lords-lieutenant, 6th and 15th December, 1596:

There was a rising planned at Enslow Hill of 200 or 300 seditious people, from various towns [i.e. villages] of that shire, with the design of raising a rebellion. They were to spoil the neighbouring gentlemen's houses of arms and horses, and go towards London, where they expected to be joined by the apprentices. . . . They speak of hundreds who were to join them. We have laboured night and day, but cannot get confessions. . . . Their practices will very hardly be discovered unless it be on the rack, which it is likely they will taste of when they come before the Lords of the Council. . . .

[*Examination of John Steere.*] Was told of the rising by his brother Bartholomew, who said there would be 200 or 300 people . . . and they would go from one rich man's house to another, and take horses, arms and victuals. Tried to persuade him against such unlawful courses, but he said he would not always live like a slave. . . .

[*Examination of Bartholomew Steere, carpenter, "in answer to interrogatories."*] [James] Bradshaw, being a miller and travelling the country, undertook to persuade others to join. . . . At the time of his first determination to get up a rising [Steere] served Lord Norris and was a single man, and therefore stood in no need, but meant to have risen to help his poor friends and other poor people who lived in misery. . . . Mr. Power has enclosed much; Mr. Frere has destroyed the whole town of Water Eaton; Sir William Spencer has enclosed common fields. . . .

[*Examination of Roger Symonds, carpenter.*] Met Bartholomew Steere, who asked him how he did this hard year, and how he maintained his wife and children, having seven sons. Told him he did so by hard work, and could hardly find them bread and water. Steere replied "care not for work, for we shall have a merrier world shortly; there be lusty fellows abroad, and I will get more, and I will work one day and play the other," adding that there was once a rising at Enslow Hill, when they were entreated to go down and after were hanged like dogs, but now they would never yield, but go through with it; . . . that servants were so held and kept like dogs that they would be ready to cut their masters' throats. . . . Steere said he would cut off all the gentlemen's heads. . . .

[Symonds] made the less account of these speeches, as when he went to market he commonly heard the poor people say that they were ready to famish for want of corn, and thought they should be forced by hunger to take it out of men's houses. . . . Steere said that when they were up the London apprentices would join them . . . and that it would only be a month's work to overrun the realm; and that the poor once rose in Spain and cut down the gentry, since which they have lived merrily.

22. DIRECT ACTION, 1607

Extract *a*) is interesting, not only for its account of the revolt of 1607, but also for its veiled sympathy with the rebels. The latter were called Levellers and Diggers, names we shall meet later. The suggestion that they were "a puritan faction" throws some light on what contemporaries meant by the word "Puritan" (cf. No. 56): it was clearly not applied to men concerned exclusively with theology. Captain Pouch understood the political value of a claim to divine authority. Extracts *b*) and *c*) show Oliver Cromwell, some years before the Civil War, leading opposition to the Court-sponsored schemes for draining the Fens, which would have deprived many peasants of their livelihood.

a) J. Stow, *Annals* (continued by E. Howes) (1631), p. 890; *b*) *C.S.P.D.* (1631–3), p. 501; *c*) Dugdale, p. 460.

a) THE MIDLANDS REVOLT OF 1607

About the middle of this month of May, 1607, a great number of common persons suddenly assembled themselves in Northamptonshire, and then others of like nature assembled themselves in Warwickshire, and some in Leicestershire. They violently cut and broke down hedges, filled up ditches, and laid open all such enclosures of commons and other grounds as they found enclosed, which of ancient time had been open and employed to tillage. These tumultuous persons . . . grew very strong, being in some places of men, women and children a thousand together, and at Hill Norton in Warwickshire there were 3,000, and at Cottesbich there assembled of men, women and children to the number of full 5,000.

These riotous persons bent all their strength to level and lay open enclosures, without exercising any manner of theft or violence upon any man's person, goods or cattle, and wheresoever they came, they were generally relieved by the near inhabitants, who sent them not only many carts laden with victual, but also good store of spades and shovels for speedy performance of their present enterprise. . . . Until then some of them were fain to use bills, pikes and such-like tools instead of mattocks and spades.

The 27th of this month there were several proclamations made, straitly charging them to surcease their disorder, yet nevertheless they ceased not, but rather persisted more eagerly, and thereupon the sheriffs and justices had authority given them to suppress them by force, by virtue whereof they raised an army and scattered them. . . .

At the first those foresaid multitudes assembled themselves without any particular head or guide; then started up a base fellow called John Reynolds, whom they surnamed Captain Pouch because of a great leather pouch which he wore by his side. . . . He told them . . . that he had authority from his majesty to throw down enclosures, and that he was sent of God to satisfy all degrees [classes] whatsoever, and that in this present work he was directed by the Lord of Heaven; and thereupon they generally inclined to his direction, so as he kept them in good order. He commanded them not to swear, nor to offer violence to any person: but to ply their business and to make fair work, intending to continue this work so long as God should put them in mind.

At the beginning of these disordered assemblies until their suppression . . . it was generally bruited throughout the land that the special cause of their assemblies and discontent was concerning religion. Some said it was the Puritan faction, because they were the strongest, and thereby sought to enforce their pretended reformation; others said it was the practice of the Papists thereby to obtain restoration or toleration; all which reports proved false as appeared plainly by the examination of all such as were examined, whose general pretence of grievances and cause of stirring in this riotous and traitorous manner was only for the laying open of enclosures, the prevention of further depopulation, the increase and continuance of tillage to relieve their wives and children; and chiefly because it had been credibly reported unto them by many that of very late years there were 340 towns [i.e. villages] decayed and depopulated, and that they supposed by this insurrection and casting down of enclosures to cause reformation.

Some of them were indicted of high treason and executed for levying wars against the king. . . . Captain Pouch was made exemplary.

b) CROMWELL AND DIRECT ACTION

A crowd of women and men, armed with scythes and pitchforks, uttered threatening words against anyone that should drive [their cattle off] their fens. It was commonly reported by the commoners in Ely Fens and the fens adjoining that Mr. Cromwell of Ely had undertaken (they paying him a groat [4*d.*] for every cow they had on the common) to hold the drainers in suit of law for five years, and that in the mean time they should enjoy every foot of their common.

c) THE LORD OF THE FENS

[Oliver Cromwell] was especially made choice of by those who ever endeavoured the undermining of regal authority to be their orator [i.e. spokesman] at Huntingdon unto the . . . King's Commissioners of Sewers there, in opposition to His Majesty's most commendable design [of supporting the Adventurers for draining the fens].

23. PETITION AGAINST ENCLOSURE

This extract shows how enclosure affected tenants, and how landlords used their position as members of the ruling class to swindle them. Resistance was possible only when important men were involved ("the Mayor and free tenants") and even then was risky (cf. postscript). It is significant that the appeal is addressed to Parliament, not to Charles I. B.B. and T., pp. 255–8.

To the right honourable House of Parliament now assembled, the humble petition of the Mayor and free tenants of the borough of Wootton Basset in the County of Wilts.

Humbly showeth to this honourable House, That whereas the Mayor and free tenants of the said borough . . . had and did hold unto them free common of pasture for the feeding of all sorts of other beasts, as cows, etc., without stint [i.e. limitation of numbers] be they never so many, in and through Eastern Great Park, which said Park contained by estimation 2,000 acres of ground or upwards; and in [1555] . . . the manor of Wootton Basset . . . came . . . into the hands and possession of one Sir Francis Englefield, knight, who in short time after he was thereof possessed did enclose the said Park; and in consideration of the common of pasture that the free tenants of the borough had in the said park did . . . lease out unto the said free tenants of the said borough to use as common amongst them that parcel of the said Great Park . . . called by the name of Wootton Lawnd, which was but a small portion to that privilege which they had before; it doth not contain by estimation above 100 acres. But the free tenants [were] therewith contented. . . .

[Since then, however,] Sir Francis Englefield, heir of the aforesaid Sir Francis Englefield, did by some means gain the charter of our town into his hands, and, as lately we have heard, his successor now keepeth it. . . . And he thereby knowing that the town had nothing to show for their right of common but by prescription, did begin suits in law with the said free tenants for their common. . . . And this did continue so long, he being too powerful for them, that the said free tenants were not able to wage law any longer; for one John Rous, one of the free tenants, was thereby enforced to sell all his land (to the value of £500) with following the suits in law, and many others were thereby impoverished and were thereby forced to yield up their right and take a lease of their said common of the said Sir Francis Englefield for term of his life. And the said mayor and free tenants hath now lost their right of common in the said Lawnd near about twenty years. . . .

We do verily believe that no corporation in England so much is wronged as we are. For we are put out of all the common that ever we had and have not so much as one foot of common left unto us, nor never shall have any. We are thereby grown so in poverty, unless it please God to move the hearts of this honourable House to commiserate our cause and to enact something for us, that we may enjoy our right again. . . .

[23 signatures.] Divers hands more we might have had, but that many of them doth rent bargains of the lord of the manor, and they are fearful that they shall be put forth of their bargains; and then they shall not tell how to live. Otherwise they would have set to their hands.

24. LONDON'S MERCHANT COMPANIES

This extract comes from a report made by the Venetian Ambassador in 1607. James I's government accepted the exclusion of English traders from the West Indies. It was only after the revolution that a war was fought to open up trade with Spanish America. (4 crowns = £1.) *C.S.P.Ven.*, 1603–7, pp. 503–4.

It is a common opinion that the wealth of [London's] citizens is very great and entirely the fruit of trade and commerce, which is carried on by means of companies. At present there are two such companies, the Muscovy Company, trading to Muscovy, Poland, Russia; and the

Levant Company, which includes Italy. . . . Many English ships sail . . . under the name of merchants with a small amount of cargo, but their real intention is piracy. They are content to remain abroad in exile for a while, for they are quite sure that after a little, by the help of bribes, the only way in this country to overcome all difficulty, they will be able to return home and enjoy their gains. . . .

There was a proposal . . . to introduce East and West Indian goods; but as by the terms of the treaty between England and Spain the English are forbidden to trade to the West Indies—though this clause is differently read by the English—the whole proposal remains imperfect and inconclusive, though many private individuals do send their ships on that voyage. . . .

The Levant Company, and the others as well, is a close gild of men trading in the Levant, and no one who is not enrolled in the company is allowed to trade in any territory belonging to the Turk. The Company has its Directors, elected by itself, and it is bound, without any support from the Crown, to maintain at its own charges the Ambassador in Constantinople and the Consuls throughout that Empire. . . . By royal patent the Company used to enjoy the customs on currants and sweet wines on a payment of 24,000 crowns a year, but now this privilege has been taken from it and has been given by the King to the Lord Chamberlain. His Majesty gives the Company no more than the protection of his letters; for the rest, this company and the others also, govern themselves. In this way many have acquired fortunes of 100, 150 and 200,000 crowns, some even passing 400,000 and 500,000.

25. FOR FREE TRADE

Those excluded from the trading companies protested against others' privileges. Parliamentary committees were used to express this opposition. But although the attack might take place under a cry of free trade, often it was just the "outs" trying to get "in"; and some of the most vigorous Parliamentarians changed sides when through Parliamentary influence they had got themselves "in." This extract is from the House of Commons debates on free trade of 1604. Note the reference to commerce as an employment for younger sons of gentlemen (cf. No. 1, *e*)). B.B. and T., pp. 443–6.

THE Committees from the House of the Commons sat five whole afternoons upon these Bills; there was a great concourse of clothiers and merchants, of all parts of the realm, and especially of London; who were so divided, as that all the clothiers, and in effect all the merchants of England, complained grievously of the engrossing and restraint of trade by the rich merchants of London, as being to the undoing, or great hindrance, of all the rest; and of London merchants, three parts joined in the same complaint against a fourth part; and of that fourth part, some standing stiffly for their own company, yet repined at other companies. . . .

The most weighty reasons for the enlargement of trade were these:

Natural right—All free subjects are born inheritable, as to their land, so also to the free exercise of their industry in those trades, whereto they apply themselves and whereby they are to live. Merchandize being the chief and richest of all other, and of greater extent and importance than all the rest, it is against the natural right and liberty of the subjects of England to restrain it into the hands of some few, as now it is . . . .The governors of these companies, by their monopolising orders, have so handled the matter as that the mass of the whole trade of all the realm is in the hands of some 200 persons at the most, the rest serving for a show only and reaping small benefit. . . .

Wealth—The increase of the wealth generally of all the

land by the ready vent of all the commodities to the merchants at higher rate; for where many buyers are, ware grows dearer; and they that buy dear at home, must sell dear abroad; this also will make our people more industrious.

Equal Distribution—The more equal distribution of the wealth of the land, which is a great stability and strength to the realm; . . . the contrary whereof is inconvenient in all estates, and oftentimes breaks out into mischief, when too much fulness doth puff up some by presumption, and too much emptiness leaves the rest in perpetual discontent, the mother of desire of innovations and troubles: and this is the proper fruit of monopolies. Example may be in London, and the rest of the realm. The custom and import of London come to £110,000 a year, and of the rest of the realm but to £17,000.

Strength—The increase of shipping and especially of mariners, in all parts of England. How greatly the mariners of the realm have decayed in all places of latter times, and with how great danger of the state in those late wars, is known to them who have been employed in that kind of service; who do also attribute the cause thereof to this restraint of trade; free traffic being the breeder and maintainer of ships and mariners, as by memorable example in the Low Countries may be seen.

Profit of the Crown—The increase of custom and subsidy to the King, which doth necessarily follow the increase of foreign traffic and wealth. And they which say otherwise, will dare to say anything. . . .

Necessity at Home—And as there will be greater opportunity abroad, so also much greater necessity at home; for what else shall become of gentlemen's younger sons, who cannot live by arms when there is no wars, and learning preferments are common to all and mean? So that nothing remains fit for them, save only merchandize . . . unless they turn servingmen, which is a poor inheritance.

26. THE CLOTHING INDUSTRY

Wool and cloth had for centuries been England's staple products. This extract is from a State Paper dated 1615. Note in how many cases the breeder of wool and the clothier were compelled to accept credit from the merchants, who thus tended to secure control over the production of the commodities they sold, by reducing both breeders and clothiers to dependence on themselves. B.B. and T., pp. 354–5.

THE breeders of wool in all counties are of three sorts:

1. First those that are men of great estate, having both grounds and stock [i.e. capital] of their own, and are beforehand in wealth. These can afford to delay the selling of their wools and to stay the clothiers' leisure for the payment to increase the price. The number of these is small.

2. Those that do rent the king's, noblemen's and gents' grounds and deal as largely as either their stock or credit will afford. These are many and breed great store of wool; most of them do usually either sell their wools beforehand, or promise the refusal of them for money which they borrowed at the spring of the year to buy them sheep to breed the wool, they then having need of money to pay their lady-day rent . . ., and at that time the clothiers disburse their stock in yarns to lay up in stock against hay-time and harvest when their spinning fails. So that then farmers and clothiers have greatest want of money at one time.

3. The general number of husbandmen in all the wool counties that have small livings, whereof every one usually hath some wool, though not much. They are many in numbers in all counties and have great store of wool, though in small parcels. Many of these also do borrow money of the wool merchant to buy sheep to stock their commons. Their parcels being so small, the times of selling so divers, the distance of place so great between the clothier and them, it would be their undoing to stay the clothiers' leisure for the time of their sale, or to be subject to him for the price. . . .

These wools are usually converted by four sorts of people:

1. The rich clothier that buyeth his wool of the grower in the wool counties, and makes his whole year's provision beforehand and lays it up in store, and in the winter time hath it spun by his own spinsters and woven by his own weavers and fulled by his own tuckers, and all at the lowest rate for wages. . . .

2. The second is the meaner clothier that seldom or never travels into the wool country to buy his wool, but borrows the most part of it at the market, and sets many poor on work, clothes it [i.e. converts it into cloth] presently and sells his cloth in some counties upon the bare thread, as in Devonshire and Yorkshire, and others dress it and sell it in London for ready money, and then comes to the wool market and pays the old debt and borrows more. Of this sort there are great store, that live well and grow rich and set thousands on work. . . .

3. The third sort are such clothiers that have not stock enough to bestow, some in wool and some in yarn, and to forbear some in cloth as the rich clothiers do; and they buy little or no wool, but do weekly buy their yarn in the markets, and presently make it into cloth and sell it for ready money, and so buy yarn again; which yarn is weekly brought into the markets by a great number of poor people that will not spin to the clothier for small wages. . . . These yarn-makers are so many in number that it is supposed by men of judgment that more than half the cloths that are made in Wilts, Gloucester and Somersetshire is made by the means of these yarn-makers and poor clothiers. . . .

4. The fourth sort is of them of the new drapery, which are thousands of poor people inhabiting near the ports and coasts from Yarmouth to Plymouth and in many great cities and towns. . . . These people by their great industry and skill do spend a great part of the coarse wools growing in the kingdom, and that at as high a price or higher than the clothiers do the finest wools of this country.

27. ROYAL INTERFERENCE WITH THE CLOTHING INDUSTRY

The Merchant Adventurers had a monopoly of the export of cloth—exported at this time either partly finished or undyed, so that the finer cloths were dressed or dyed abroad. Some merchants, led by Alderman Cockayne of the City of London, desired to break the Merchant Adventurers' monopoly. They propounded a scheme whereby they were to be granted a patent to finish all cloth in England before export, in return for an annual grant of £300,000 to the King. James I jumped at the prospect, and in 1614 the privileges of the Merchant Adventurers were suspended and the export of unfinished and undyed cloth prohibited. The results were disastrous. The Dutch, whose dyeing industry had been threatened, prohibited the import of dyed cloth and began to manufacture cloth themselves. The project collapsed. The privileges of the Merchant Adventurers were regranted. The only people to benefit were those courtiers who had been bribed by Cockayne to influence the King. Even a scheme which on paper was decidedly advantageous to England's economic development was ruined by the incompetence of the royal government (*b*) and *c*)).

a) B.B. and T., pp. 454–6; *b*) A. Friis, *Alderman Cockayne's Project and the cloth trade* (1927), pp. 318, 365; *c*) Notestein, Relf and Simpson, *Commons Debates, 1621*, V, p. 457, IV, p. 50.

a) COCKAYNE'S PROJECT

JAMES by the Grace of God, etc.

We have often and in divers manners expressed ourselves . . . what an earnest desire and constant resolution we have that, as the reducing of wools into clothing was the act of our noble Progenitor King Edward the Third, so the reducing of the trade of white cloths, which is but an imperfect thing towards the wealth and good of this our Kingdom, unto the trade of cloths dyed and dressed, might be the work of our time.

To which purpose we did first invite the ancient Company of Merchant Adventurers to undertake the same, who upon allegation or pretence of impossibility refused.

Whereupon nevertheless not discouraged but determined to maintain our princely resolution against impediments and difficulties in a work so excellent, We did find means to draw and procure divers persons of good quality within our City of London and elsewhere with great alacrity and commendable zeal to give a beginning to this our purpose.

In respect whereof for that above all things we were to take a princely care that between the cessation of the old trade and the inception and settling of the new there should not be any stand [i.e. glut] of cloth nor failing or deadness in the vent thereof, . . . we were inforced to grant several licences under our Great Seal unto the said persons for a trade of whites to be temporary and in the interim until this work . . . might be happily accomplished. . . .

But notwithstanding, having evermore in contemplation our first end, We have still provoked and urged on the said persons unto whom the trade is now transferred to some certainty of offer and undertaking concerning a proportion of cloths dressed and dyed to be annually exported, and the same proportion to increase and multiply in such sort as may be a fruitful beginning of so good a work and also an assured pledge of the continuation thereof in due time.

Whereupon the said persons or new Company have before the Lords of our Privy Council absolutely condescended and agreed at a Court holden the seventeenth day of June one thousand six hundred and fifteen, that thirty-six thousand cloths shall be dressed and dyed out of such cloths white as were formerly used to be shipped out by the old Company undressed and undyed. . . .

And did further promise . . . to proceed . . . to the settling of the whole trade of cloths dressed and dyed. . . .

Wherefore We, in our princely judgment foreseeing that as long as the said new Company shall remain not incorporated it doth much weaken both the endeavour and expectation which belongeth to this work . . . have thought it now a fit time to extend our princely grace unto them for their incorporation and to indue and invest them with such liberties and privileges as the old Company formerly had, with such additions and augmentations as the merit of concurrence to so good an end may require, with this, nevertheless, that because the nature of the present liberties and privileges must of necessity differ from those which shall be fit and requisite when the whole trade shall be overcome and settled, there be therefore a power in Us to revoke or alter the same. . . . [Appoints William Cockayne, Alderman of our City of London, to be the first and present Governor.]

b) THE FAILURE OF THE SCHEME

September 11th, 1616. [James I ordered Sir William Cockayne] to call the rest of the Society [of the King's Merchant Adventurers] together as soon as he might, and to tell them as from his Majesty that his honour is now so far engaged in this work as, rather than it shall fail, if all the merchants of England can do it he will have a Company [which] shall perform it; but if the new Company shall fail of their contract he will be sure first to punish them. . . .

August 12th, 1617. [Royal Proclamation.] We intend not to insist and stay longer upon specious and fair shows, which produce not the fruit Our actions do ever aim at, which is the general good of this Our state and kingdom: wherefore perceiving that the former grounds proposed to Us by the undertakers of that work [the King's Merchant Adventurers] consisted more in hopes than in effects; and finding the work itself to be too great to be brought to pass in any short time, by reason of the many difficulties accompanying the same, and that as the state of trade now stands there will be greater loss in the cloth-making of the kingdom than gain in the dyeing and dressing thereof . . . [the King has restored its charter to the old company of Merchant Adventurers].

c) A PARLIAMENTARY POST-MORTEM

February 14th, 1621. [Debate in the House of Commons on a Bill "for free liberty to buy and sell wools."]

Sir Thomas Wentworth: The third [reason for the fall in the price of wool] was, the pretermitted customs, with imposing a third part more than formerly had been upon every cloth, was the cause that the merchant could not sell so cheap as other countries, and so our cloth, through dearness growing out of request amongst other nations, stuck upon the merchants' hands abroad to their great loss and damage of the trade. . . . The fourth was the patent procured by Cockayne for dyeing and dressing, which had so displaced and put the trade out of favour, that it was not yet thoroughly settled. . . .

Sir Edward Coke: [It was] Cockayne's project of dyeing which first set the Dutch into a course of making cloth. . . . If you divide that which is exported out of the kingdom into ten parts, that which comes off the sheep amounts to nine.

28. MONOPOLIES

Besides obtaining money by grants of privileges to merchant companies, the King could obtain some by grants of monopoly in industrial processes, e.g. soap and salt-making. However, the King's financial benefit was counterbalanced by the hostility engendered among all classes of the community by the rise in prices of the commodities concerned, a rise entirely out of proportion to the King's gain (*c*). There were many attempts in Parliament to secure the abolition of the monopolies. In 1601 Elizabeth promised, under strong Parliamentary pressure, to abolish some of her grants and to submit the others to test by the common law. But the evil continued. In 1624 Parliament passed the Statute of Monopolies (*a*), described by a contemporary as a "bill against monarchy." But in order to protect the City of London, corporations were exempted from its provisions, and this enabled the King to defeat the intentions of Parliament by granting industrial monopolies to corporations. Hence monopolies were still a grievance in 1640 (see No. 73, *a*)). Monopolists were often catholics: many were the complaints of "Popish soap" (*b*).

a) B. B. and T., pp. 446–7; *b*) Williams, II, pp. 229–31; *c*) Sir A. Weldon, *The Court and Character of King James and the Court of King Charles* (1651), pp. 197–8.

a) THE STATUTE OF MONOPOLIES, 1624

May it please your Majesty, . . . that all monopolies and all commissions, grants, licences, charters, and letters patents heretofore made or granted to any person or persons, bodies politic or corporate whatsoever, of or for the sole buying, selling, making, working, or using of anything within this realm or the dominion of Wales . . . are altogether contrary to the laws of this realm, and so are and shall be utterly void and of none effect, and in no wise to be put in use or execution. . . . All such commissions [etc.] . . . shall be forever hereafter examined, heard, tried and determined by and according to the common law of this realm and not otherwise. . . .

IX. Provided . . . that this act or anything therein contained shall not in any wise extend or be prejudicial unto the city of London, or to any city, borough, or town corporate within this realm, for or concerning any grants, charters, or letters patents to them or any of them made or granted, . . . or unto any corporation, companies, or fellowships of any art, trade, occupation, or mystery, or to any companies or societies of merchants within this realm.

b) A MONOPOLY AT WORK, 1633

The soap business is almost at an end. The certificate is made, but not yet published: it justifies the new soap and damns the old. Upon Monday the 23rd the Lord Mayor was sent for to the Court, where his Majesty and the lords rebuked him for his partial proceeding in favour of the old soap and disparaging the new. Their lordships sent a warrant . . . to bring a poor woman out of Southwark before them for speaking invectively against the new soap. I think she was well chidden, and so dismissed. The new company of gentlemen soapboilers have procured Mrs. Sanderson, the Queen's laundress, to subscribe to the goodness of the new soap: but she tells her Majesty she dares not wash her linen with any other but Castile soap: and the truth is that most of those ladies that have subscribed have all of them their linen washed with Castile soap, and not with the new soap. . . . .

Upon Sunday last [December 29th] the King and the Council sat again upon the soap business; and now it is determined that the patentees for this new soap shall have power given them to seize upon all such soap as hath been made since the middle of November last, or thereabout; to seize upon the pans and all their other utensils belonging to the trade of soap-boiling; and lastly to commit the soap-boilers themselves to prison. It seems the King and the lords are well satisfied in the goodness of this new soap. . . . It is granted that this new soap hath blistered the washers' hands, and done other mischiefs. But then again, it is believed that the soap was sophisticated with some obnoxious matter to work that mischief.

c) COST TO CONSUMERS IN THE SIXTEEN-THIRTIES

There was not anything (almost) that any man did eat, drink or wear, or had in his house from foreign parts, or scarce any domestic commodities exempted, but he paid, as it were, an excise for it; yea, at last even cards and dice escaped not, but they were monopolized by a great Councillor, the Lord Cottington: yea (to keep their hands in ure [in practice]) they got patents for the very rags, marrow-bones, guts and such like excrements, as were thought of no use but to be cast on the dunghills; and he was held the bravest commonwealth's-man that could bring in the most money (yet the King's private purse or public treasury little or nothing bettered, but to impoverish and vex the subject, and to no other end): for which he was ordinarily rewarded with honour.

29. FAILURE TO PROTECT INTERESTS OF MERCHANTS

For financial reasons (cf. Nos. 47–8), because of their pro-Spanish foreign policy (Nos. 63–6) and because of their fear of capitalist expansion, the governments of James I and Charles I failed to give English traders and industrialists the support they expected (*a*) and *f*)). The last sentence of *a*) makes a shrewd analysis of the position of the privileged trading companies at this time; extract *c*), from a newsletter, shows them exposed to direct political pressure. The parliamentary leader, Sir John Eliot, who had connections in the City, criticises royal policy for discouraging cloth exports and handicapping the English merchants in competition with the Dutch (*b*) and *e*)). Pym, Eliot's successor as leader of the House of Commons, was treasurer of a company trading to the West Indies—a part of the world where English merchants only got adequate support from the state after the revolution (No. 69). Bulstrode Whitelock (*d*) was later one of the republican leaders. Extract *f*) should be contrasted with the oft-quoted eulogy by Clarendon of the prosperity of the sixteen-thirties—written long after the event by a Royalist looking back through rose-coloured spectacles.

a) *C.S.P.Ven.*, 1621–3, pp. 434–5; *b*) J. Forster, *Sir John Eliot* (1865), I, pp. 168–70; *c*) Williams, I, p. 381; *d*) B. Whitelock, *Memorials of the English affairs* (1853) I, pp. 32, 37–8; *e*) Forster, *op. cit.*, II, pp. 451–2; *f*) *C.S.P.Ven.*, 1636–9, pp. 61, 210, 387–8.

a) ECONOMIC RESULTS OF STUART RULE, 1622

THIS [James I's pro-Spanish foreign policy] has also depressed all the trades, including that of cloth, to the immense disgust of countless artisans, who revolted recently for lack of food. The wars of Poland and Germany have also damaged them and severely affected the King also in the customs, which though raised do not augment his Majesty's revenue, as they [English merchants] do not sell so much merchandise as they used and therefore import less; as foreigners have to pay four times as much, many decide not to trade, and so business declines. Moreover, the burdens upon the townsmen, the difference in value with the neighbouring countries, which absorb as much gold as the Indies . . .; the rise of the Dutch, who now eclipse the fame of all other nations and seem to draw all wealth to themselves, and finally the management of all business by companies, which limits trade to a few tyrannical hands, who, by arrangement among themselves, only place such goods as they think they can sell at very high prices, while taking out a larger quantity than they can sell, proves detrimental, in addition to the things already noted. Although favoured by various privileges the companies are declining owing to the charges laid upon them by sovereigns, their expenses being very heavy, especially the Turkey Company, in keeping the ambassador at Constantinople and the consuls, and because to maintain themselves they are compelled to disburse great sums to the favourites, the lords of the council and other ministers, many being members of their society. Thus burdened and protected they are enabled and compelled to tyrannize over the sellers without and the buyers within the kingdom.

b) SIR JOHN ELIOT, HOUSE OF COMMONS, MAY, 1624

Take any large trade, and consider how it stood for its commodities before they became severally charged with impositions. Then compare it with the present condition and state it now stands in, and you will find the small increase to revenue that such additions make. The trade of cloth shall speak for the rest. . . . Was the king's benefit ever so much in that, now so heavily burdened, as when it paid but the noble [6*s.* 8*d.*] of the pack? Surely no! . . . For that easiness made the merchant's benefit more, while yet he sold the cheaper. That it was which so enlarged the vent beyond sea, where now, for the price, others undercreep us, and so forestall our markets. From 80,000 they have brought us down to 40,000 cloths a year; and as it is in this, so it is in all. The greatness of the charges lessening the merchant's benefit discourages him from trade. . . . Projectors fatten upon individual loss, but the king and the state are weakened. His majesty derives profit not from heavy duties on some, but cheapness in all. The number it is that will supply his majesty's profit, if there be vent, and not only with advantage outgo all projects in that particular, but with an infinite enriching to the whole kingdom, not only in the commodities, but in the labours of our men, to make them more industrious who now stand idle and do devour us. The town of Amsterdam can give us good testimony in this. There, as I am credibly informed, their customs come to more than in all England, and yet the proportion and rate not a third part of ours. What is the cause of this? The easiness of the charge. It is that which does not only quicken their own but draws other merchants thither. For, wherever the merchants' benefit is most, there they resort; and especially that nation [the Dutch], whose inclination hither we may easily discern. And would it not then be so with us upon the like reason? Yes, and much more. Much more; as we exceed in many opportunities and advantages which they affect and study but possess not. Our harbours are more, our harbours are better, our harbours are nearer in the course and way of trade. And that which they fear there, the danger of an enemy, in whose view they pass into their own country, our coast is free from. So that, abate the customs and they will soon be drawn hither. . . . Their example, too, . . . will likewise stir our merchants.

c) EAST INDIA CO. IN DIFFICULTIES, JULY, 1628

The East India Company have been much daunted, and are likely to dissolve, by reason his Majesty, without their privity, hath released those three Holland East India ships which he had arrested to give them satisfaction for the wrongs which had been done them [in a massacre of English traders by the Dutch] at Amboyna. Whereupon, on Wednesday, the principal of them [i.e. of the Company] went to court, and spoke their minds to the King freely. His Majesty's answer was, he could not detain those ships any longer without entering into a war with that people; which how improper it would be now, when he hath both France and Spain on his back, he left them to judge. . . . The same afternoon the Duke [of Buckingham], accompanied with seven other lords, went to animate them in their trade, from his Majesty. . . . For the company's better encouragement the Duke and some others of the lords offered to come in adventurers in their new stock. All which notwithstanding they rested disanimated, as it is thought. They will hardly be hindered from dissolution.

d) TONNAGE AND POUNDAGE, 1628–9

Some merchants were committed [to prison] for not paying tonnage and poundage according to the King's declaration. Chambers, one of them, brought his *habeas corpus*, and it was returned that he was committed for insolent words spoken by him at the Council table, that the merchants were screwed up in England more than in Turkey; . . . he was discharged by bail. The Council were offended at it and rebuked the judges. . . .

The King's attorney, Heath, a fit instrument for those times, preferred an information . . . against Chambers in the Star Chamber. . . . Chambers confessed the words [quoted above], but said he spake them of the under officers of the customs, who had much wronged him, and not reflecting upon the King or Council, or the government, yet the court fined him £2,000 and [ordered him] to make a submission, which he refused, underwriting that he did abhor and detest it as unjust and false. . . . He pleaded Magna Carta and other statutes against the fine by the King and his Council in the Star Chamber. . . . Afterwards he brought his *habeas corpus*, but the judges remanded him; and after 12 years' imprisonment, and long waiting for satisfaction for his losses from the Long Parliament, he at last died in want.

e) ELIOT ATTACKS GOVERNMENT ECONOMIC POLICY, 1629

It [tonnage and poundage] is used by him [Lord Treasurer Weston] as an engine for the removing of our trade, and if it be allowed it cannot but subvert the government and the kingdom. It was a counsel long since given against us by Hospitalis [L'Hopital], chancellor to Charles IX of France, that the way to debilitate this state, the way to weaken and infirm it and so to make it fit for conquest and invasion, was not by open attempt, not by outward strength to force it, but first to impeach our trade, to hinder or divert it, to stop it in our hands or to turn it into others', and so lay waste our walls—those wooden walls, our ships, that both fortify and enrich us. That counsel is now in practice. . . . In this work is meant our ruin and destruction. To that end already strangers are invited to drive our trade; or at least, which will be equally as dangerous, our merchants are to be driven to trade in strangers' bottoms.

f) ECONOMIC CONDITIONS

September 5th, 1636. The country is ruined everywhere by an excessive drought, causing the greatest suffering to everything and making the miserable weakness of the country people general, while even the purses of the greatest find it insupportable. . . .

May 15th, 1637. Trade has suffered great deterioration. . . .

March 19th, 1638. To every foreigner willing to pay 25 crowns they grant permission to practice any trade in London. To the old duty of 20 crowns the butt of wine they have recently added 10 crowns more. . . . Silk cloth pays 20% [import duty], currants 15 crowns the thousand, and all the rest in proportion. This causes an incredible scarcity of everything and a universal outcry among the inhabitants, who are not accustomed to pay anything but the ordinary subsidies voted by Parliament. Whenever that body comes into force again it will revoke all these impositions.

Part Three

THE STATE MACHINE BEFORE 1640

The gentry of England . . . are the garrisons of good order throughout the realm.

Sir Walter Ralegh.

30. THE CROWN

With *a*) cf. No. 90, *a*)—by Harrington, who admired the Venetian Republic. The author of *c*), Professor of Civil Law at Cambridge, was attacked in Parliament for the book quoted, *The Interpreter*. Extract *f*) is from the *Table Talk* of John Selden, first published in 1689, though Selden died in 1654. It contains an illuminating comment on the type of political judge whose views are represented by *e*). The occasion was the Ship Money case (No. 49).

a) *C.S.P.Ven.*, 1603–7, p. 509; *b*) Wilson, p. 37; *c*) Prothero, pp. 409–10; *d*) *ibid.*, pp. 293–4, *J.C.D.*, p. 15; *e*) Gardiner, pp. 121–2; *f*) Selden, *Table Talk*, pp. 97–104, 180.

a) THE VENETIAN AMBASSADOR, 1607

THE government is in the hands of the Council, who rule as the King desires, but occasion may arise where the public weal or ill is concerned, such as the introduction or the amendment of laws, supply, etc.; in such cases the King, out of modesty, is accustomed to continue the old practice and to summon Parliament in its three Estates of the Realm, the Clergy, Nobility, and Commons. It cannot be denied that originally and for many years later the authority of members was great, for each one was permitted, without fear of punishment, to speak his mind freely on all that concerned the state, even to the touching of the King's person, who, to speak the truth, was rather the head of a Republic than a Sovereign. But now that the Sovereign is absolute, matters move in a very different fashion. This absolute authority dates from the reign of Edward III in 1327. The authority and power of Parliament was greatly curtailed, and while now possessing its ancient shape, it has lost its original independence and authority; for no act is valid unless it has received the royal assent.... The crown, too, by various means, secures the exclusion of those whom it does not like and the inclusion of those upon whose support it thinks it may count. The Sovereign has now reached such a pitch of formidable power that he can do what he likes, and there is no one who could dare either in

Parliament or out of it, except at the grave risk of ruin, I do not say to oppose him, but even to make the smallest sign of running counter to his will.

b) A CIVIL SERVANT, 1601

The Prince has no authority to make laws nor to dispose of the Crown, that must be done by general consent of all in Parliament; yea, the King's eldest son, though the Kingdoms be hereditary, shall not be crowned without the consent of the parliament after the death of his father. His privileges be to make war or peace, to create and choose the principal magistrates and officers throughout the whole kingdom unless in cities and towns, and to determine [i.e. put an end to] their offices when he pleases.

c) A PROFESSOR, 1607

[The King] is above the law by his absolute power . . .; and though for the better and equal course in making laws he do admit the three estates, that is, Lords Spiritual, Lords Temporal and the Commons unto counsel, yet this, in divers learned men's opinions, is not of constraint but of his own benignity or by reason of his promise made upon oath at the time of his coronation. For otherwise were he a subject after a sort and subordinate, which may not be thought without breach of duty and loyalty. For then must we deny him to be above the law, and to have no power of dispensing with any positive law, or of granting especial privileges and charters unto any, which is his only and clear right.

d) JAMES I, 1610

The state of monarchy is the supremest thing upon earth; for kings are not only God's lieutenants upon earth and sit upon God's throne, but even by God himself they are called gods. . . . Kings are justly called gods for that they exercise a manner or resemblance of Divine power upon earth; for if you will consider the attributes to God you shall see how they agree in the person of a king. God hath power to create or destroy, make or unmake, at his pleasure; to give life or send death; to judge all, and to be judged nor accountable to none; to raise low things and to make high things low at his pleasure; and to God are both soul and body due. And the like power have kings: they make and unmake their subjects; they have power of raising and casting down; of life and of death; judges over all their subjects and in all causes, and yet accountable to none but God only. They have power to exalt low things and abase high things, and make of their subjects like men at the chess, a pawn to take a bishop or a knight, and to cry up or down any of their subjects as they do their money. And to the King is due both the affection of the soul and the service of the body of his subjects.

As to dispute what God may do is blasphemy . . . so it is sedition in subjects to dispute what a king may do in the height of his power; but just kings will ever be willing to declare what they will do, if they will not incur the curse of God. I will not be content that my power be disputed upon, but I shall ever be willing to make the reason appear of all my doings and rule my actions according to my laws. . . .

I would not have you meddle with such ancient rights of mine as I have received from my predecessors. . . . All novelties are dangerous, as well in a politic as in a natural body; and therefore I would be loath to be quarrelled in my ancient rights and possessions: for that were to judge me unworthy of that which my predecessors had and left me.

e) A JUDGE, 1638

Sir Robert Berkeley: Where Mr. Holborne [counsel for John Hampden] supposed a fundamental policy in the creation of the frame of this kingdom, that in case the monarch of England should be inclined to exact from his subjects at his pleasure, he should be restrained, for that he could have nothing from them but upon a common consent in Parliament: he is utterly mistaken herein.

I agree the Parliament to be a most ancient and supreme court, where the King and Peers, as judges, are in person, and the whole body of the Commons representatively. There Peers and Commons may, in a fitting way, *parler lour ment* [speak their mind], and show the estate of every part of the kingdom; and, amongst other things, make known their grievances (if there be any) to their sovereign, and humbly petition him for redress.

But the former fancied policy I utterly deny. The law knows no such king-yoking policy. The law is of itself an old and trusty servant of the King's; it is his instrument or means which he useth to govern his people by.

f) A PARLIAMENTARIAN LAWYER

A king is a thing men have made for their own sakes, for quietness' sake. Just as in a family one man is appointed to buy the meat. . . . A king that claims privileges in his own country because they have them in another, is just as a cook that claims fees in one lord's house because they are allowed in another. If the master of the house will yield them, well and good. . . .

The king's oath is not security enough for our property, for he swears to govern according to law; now the judges they interpret the law, and what judges can be made to do we know. . . .

The king's prerogative is not his will, or what divines make it—a power to do what he lists. The king's prerogative, that is the king's law. For example, if you ask whether a patron may present to a living after six months by law? I answer No. If you ask whether the king may, I answer he may by his prerogative; that is by the law that concerns him in that case.

31. FEUDAL MONARCHY

English society was still in many ways very feudal. The Tudors had monopolised much of the power previously wielded by great feudal lords, notably by the establishment of the Court of Wards in 1540. In feudal theory the heir of a tenant-in-chief, if a minor, needed protecting; it was the duty of his overlord to protect him, obtaining payment for his trouble out of the ward's estate. That was fair enough in days when bold bad barons roamed the land; but in the relative peace and order of the seventeenth century the system had become merely a means of exploitation, equivalent to heavy but irregularly recurring death duties. It made long-term estate management a risky business. The royal treasury rarely got the full benefit; wards were farmed out by the needy Stuarts to greedy and powerful courtiers, or pensionable civil servants (see No. 47, *a*)). But as *c*) and *d*) indicate, the Crown benefited in many other ways from the system. With *a*) compare No. 39: the price of an office in the Court of Wards was going up because suitors were being squeezed. The Court brought in about £20,000 a year at the beginning of Elizabeth's reign and £84,000 in 1640. Attempts were made in Parliament to abolish wardship and feudal tenures: in 1610 an offer of £200,000 a year compensation was refused. For all the hardships of tenants-in-chief, it could still be assumed that they, as great landowners, would support the Crown (*b*). For the subsequent history of the question see No. 163. Goodman (*a*) was one of those bishops of whom the Royalist Lord Falkland said they were "so absolutely, directly and cordially Papists, that it is all £1,500 a year can do to keep them from confessing it." After the £1,500 a year ceased, Goodman did confess it: he died a Catholic.

a) Bishop Goodman, *The Court of King James I* (1839), I, p. 271; *b*) *ibid.*, pp. 322–3; *c*) Burnet, *A History of My Own Time*, ed. Airy (1897), I, pp. 20–1; *d*) *C.S.P. Ven.*, 1603–7, p. 507.

a) A BISHOP ON THE COURT OF WARDS

ALL the lands in the kingdom either mediately or immediately were held from the crown. . . . Lord Chancellor Egerton . . . [said] that if men's estates were looked into, he did not know that man in all England whose land was not liable to wardship. And here the Court of Wards was such a tie upon the subject as no king in the world ever had the like; and how much this Court of Wards hath been improved may appear by this, that the registrar's office there was of 6 times greater value than it was. At my knowledge, a feodary's place, which in my remembrance was but the place of a servant, and for which was usually given not above 30 or 40 pieces, came to be sold for £300 or £400; and, as I have been credibly informed, the last Master of Wards took £700.

b) TENANTS-IN-CHIEF AND THE CROWN

How often hath he [the Earl of Middlesex] told the King that in selling land he did not only sell his rent, as other men did, but sold his sovereignty, for it was a greater tie of obedience to be a tenant to the King than to be his subject; for as a subject he did only obey him according to his laws, but as a tenant he was ready upon all occasions to serve him, and drew others on by his example. Thus, some counties of England did never oppose the King in anything, but were ever conformable to his will; and this was in regard of his tenants. But other counties did resist him in all things, still opposing the freedom and liberty of the subject against all his designs; and this did partly rise from the King's own tenants, who could never endure to hear that kings had ever received any power from the people, but all was derived immediately from God: so then the people did look upon them as having a distinct power from themselves, and so the greater their power was, the more was the slavery and bondage of the people; whereas if they had taken upon them to be feoffees in trust for the government, and so representing them, then the people would have looked upon them as the authors of their liberty and freedom, and would never have stood in opposition.

c) FEUDAL DEPENDENCE

The crown had a great estate over all England, which was all let out upon leases for years, and a small rent was reserved. So most of the great families of the nation were the tenants of the crown, and a great many boroughs were depending on the estates so held. The renewal of these leases brought in fines both to the crown and to the great officers; besides that the fear of being denied a renewal kept all in a dependence on the court. King James obtained of his parliament a power of granting, that is selling, those estates for ever, with the reserve of the old quit-rent: and all the money raised by this was profusely squandered away.

Another main part of the regal authority was the wards, which anciently the crown took into their own management. Our kings were, according to the first institution, the guardians of these wards: they bred them up in their court, and disposed of them in marriage as they thought fit. . . . All were under a great dependence by this means: much money was not raised this way, but families were often at mercy, and were used according to their behaviour. King James granted these generally to his servants and favourites, and they made the most of them. So that what was before a dependence on the crown, and was moderately compounded for, became then a most exacting oppression, by which several families were ruined. This went on in King Charles's time in the same method. Our kings thought they gave little when they disposed of a ward, because they made little of these.

All this raised such an outcry, that Mr. Pierpoint at the Restoration gathered so many instances of these, and represented them so effectually to that house of commons that called home King Charles II, that he persuaded them to redeem themselves by an offer of excise, which produces indeed a much greater revenue, but took away the depencence in which all families were held by the dread of leaving their heirs exposed to so great a danger.

d) DISADVANTAGES FOR LANDOWNERS

Wardship . . . has always been farmed out. . . . Grave abuses have crept in, and the subjects cry aloud to heaven and do all they can to avoid such an inheritance, which brings a plague and ruin upon their estates. Those who farm this impost are always the great lords, and in order to enrich themselves the more easily they have gradually introduced this usage—that if a man possesses 2 acres in ward and 100 free, the 2 acres bring the 100 under the operation of the wardship, and so there is hardly an estate that is not subject to this burden. Moreover, if a father dies leaving his children minors and debts on the estate, the whole income of the estate goes to the crown and to the farmer, and not to the payment of the debts; when the children come of age they are confronted with their father's debts, which might have been paid off during their minority. There is another evil, that on the death of the father many persons apply to be appointed guardian, and if, as often happens, they are not relations, they ruin the estate of the unhappy wards. If the wards are of good estate and rich their guardians marry them to a daughter or niece, assigning them any dower they please; should the ward refuse to marry, the estate is obliged to pay the amount of the dower of the lady he has refused.

32. A ROYAL FAVOURITE

One of the worst features of absolute monarchy was the opening it gave to worthless favourites. The Earl of Somerset, one of James I's Scottish minions, was found guilty of poisoning a friend who knew too much of Somerset's schemes to marry another man's wife. He was succeeded in the King's affections by George Villiers, carefully selected for his looks: for ten years Villiers was the most powerful man in the country, controlling home and foreign policy, and becoming Duke of Buckingham. He retained his position as favourite under Charles I until he was assassinated in 1628, amid general rejoicing. D'Ewes was subsequently a supporter of Parliament.

Sir Simonds D'Ewes, *Autobiography and Correspondence* (1845), I, pp. 80-2, 380.

THE Earl of Somerset . . . fell not so fast as the new favourite rose; for, being knighted, he was made, in or about the end of December this year [January 1616, actually], Master of the Horse, a place of great honour and authority, and ordinarily bestowed on a great peer;

and the year following he was made Knight of the Garter . . . and afterwards created Baron Whaddon, Viscount Villiers and Earl of Buckingham, all within the space of six months . . . I have heard Sir Robert Cotton affirm that some hundreds of monoplies and projects by which the commonwealth was oppressed were refused by my lord of Somerset, and for the present dashed, which afterwards all passed by Buckingham's means. . . . My lord of Buckingham, without regard of person or condition, prostituted all honours under the degree of a marquis to such as would buy them. . . . [He] invested so many of his name, kindred and alliance with high titles as many of them were enforced to be burdens to the crown or commonwealth, or to themselves. . . . The Duke of Buckingham was too often bid by his own lust and passion, or by the rash dictates of young heads. . . . [He] was generally conceived to be the main cause . . . of the aversion of hearts between the King [Charles I] and his subjects, and of all the other mischiefs in church and commonwealth.

33. SALE OF OFFICES AND HONOURS

Office was regarded as a property right, to be bought and sold as doctors used to sell their practices. The system was not likely to lead to efficiency. James I and Charles I extended the system to the sale of honours. There was a standard rate for peerages, and the new honour of baronet was created for purely fiscal reasons. Sir John Oglander in *a*) objects, not to the principle of sale, but to sale at too low a price. It is significant that even a convinced Royalist like himself looks to Parliament to put this right.

a) Oglander, p. 45; *b*) Sir J. Bramston, *Autobiography* (Camden Soc., 1845), p. 118; *c*) *C.S.P.D.*, 1638–9, pp. 622–3.

a) BARONETCIES GOING CHEAP

The Duke of Buckingham, not having money both to encourage the commanders and to furnish them with necessaries for that expedition to relieve Rochelle [1627] gave to the inferior sort the making of 40 baronets, which they—out of their want—sold for £150 and £200 apiece. This is the reason so many of inferior rank, both in our county and elsewhere, had precedency in honour. But a time may come, either by Parliament or his Majesty, that, since they do not perform the grounds of the first institution, as not paying £1,000 for it nor having £1,000 land yearly to maintain it, their honour may be buried in the dust as the Duke, the patron of these upstart baronets, was very shortly afterwards.

b) IT LESSENS FEUDAL DEPENDENCE

I did and do think the honour of baronets a great injury to the crown, it taking off the dependence of so many considerable families in every county which, having as much honour as their estates are capable of, are not at all solicitous to serve and apply to the crown.

c) COMPETITIVE BIDDING, MARCH, 1639

The Master of the Rolls is dead. A man unthought of and a very ass is [now] Master of the Rolls—Sir Charles Cæsar, a doctor of the civil law. . . . Sir Ed. Leech was to give £13,000 for the place—£7,000 presently [i.e. at once] and £6,000 in May. It passed the king's hand for him, and was left with the Lord Treasurer until he paid in the money, which stop raised new competitors. Sir Thomas Hatton, from my Lady Hatton, offered her house presently to the king, and money to boot, so he might be Master of the Rolls. Lord Finch would have had it, and would have brought in a sergeant, one Reeves, who should have given £14,000 for his [Finch's] place in the Common Pleas. . . . Sir Ralph Freeman also offered fair, but this woodcock [fool] Sir Charles Cæsar has outbid them all—£15,000!

34. THE ARISTOCRACY DEPEND ON COURT PICKINGS

As landlords ran more and more into economic difficulties, so they became increasingly dependent on the Court for the grant of a monopoly, a profitable office, or hard cash (cf. Nos. 1, 2, *b*), 4, *e*)). This extract (written about 1627) brings out how very personal and arbitrary such favours were. R. Cary, Earl of Monmouth, *Memoirs* (King's Classics), pp. 25, 53, 80, 84, 94, 97.

I SPENT two winters and a summer in court after this, in which time the Queen gave me out of the Exchequer £1,000 to pay my debts, which gave me great relief. Presently after this, my old Lord Scroop died at Carlisle, and the Queen gave the West Wardenry to his son that had married my sister. He . . . desired me to be his deputy . . .; and his fee being 1,000 marks [£666 13*s*. 4*d*.] yearly, he would part it with me and I should have the half. . . . The Queen . . . continued her favour to me the time I stayed, which was not long; for she took order I should have £500 out of the Exchequer for the time I had served, and I had a patent given me under the great seal to be her Warden of the East March. . . .

[After James I succeeded Elizabeth] Now was I to begin a new world; for by the King's coming to the crown I was to lose the best part of my living. For my office of Wardenry ceased, and I lost the pay of 40 horse, which were not so little (both) as £1000 per annum. . . . I only relied on God and the King. The one never left me, the other shortly after his coming to London deceived my expectation, and adhered to those that sought my ruin. . . .

By [my wife's] procurement when I was from court she got me a suit of the King that was worth to me afterwards £4 or £5,000. I had the charge given me of the Duke's [of York: later Charles I] household, and none allowed to his service but such as I gave way to, by which means I preferred to him a number of my own servants. . . .

So (for the time it lasted) we lived at no great charge, and most of the little means we had we employed as it came in to the bettering of our estate. But it continued not long thus, for within four years after, or thereabouts, the Queen died; her house dissolved, and my wife was forced to keep house and family, which was out of our way £1,000 a year that we saved before.

[When Charles I succeeded] Myself, being his Chamberlain, and the rest (as the Master of the Horse, Treasurer, Controller and Secretary) were all discharged of our places. . . . But the King dealt very graciously with us, and for the loss of our places gave the most of us good rewards. To myself in particular he gave (to me and my heirs for ever) £500 per annum in fee farm, which was a very bountiful gift, and a good satisfaction for the loss of my office; and especially because I continued my place of gentleman of the bedchamber.

35. THE STAR CHAMBER

The main instrument of royal despotism was the Star Chamber, a political court whose judges were mostly members of the government. Prynne, Burton and Bastwick (*a*) were sentenced for publishing attacks on the bishops, Prynne having previously been punished savagely for an alleged criticism of the Queen. The Star Chamber judges put men on oath and then tried to force them to incriminate themselves: hence Lilburne's refusal to take the oath (*b*) and his insistence on the illegality of any but common law procedure, whereby a man is deemed innocent until proved guilty. The Star Chamber was abolished by the Long Parliament (No. 72). We meet Lilburne again as a leader of the Levellers (Parts IX and X).

a) Rushworth, *Historical Collections* (abridged ed., 1706), II, pp. 293–4; *b*) *ibid.*, pp. 344–5.

a) SENTENCE ON PRYNNE, BURTON AND BASTWICK

[30th June, 1637.] The said three prisoners were brought to the New Palace yard at Westminster, to suffer according to their sentence. Dr. Bastwick spake first, and (among other things) said, had he a thousand lives he would give them all up for this cause. Mr. Prynne . . .

showed the disparity between the times of Queen Mary and Queen Elizabeth, and the times then (of King Charles), and how far more dangerous it was now to write against a bishop or two than against a King or Queen. . . . He said, if the people but knew into what times they were cast, and what changes of laws, religion and ceremonies had been made of late by one man [Archbishop Laud], they would look about them. . . . The Archbishop of Canterbury, being informed by his spies what Mr. Prynne said, moved the Lords then sitting in the Star Chamber that he might be gagged and have some further censure to be presently executed on him; but that motion did not succeed. Mr. Burton . . . spake much while in the pillory to the people. The executioner cut off his ears deep and close, in a cruel manner, with much effusion of blood, an artery being cut, as there was likewise of Dr. Bastwick. Then Mr. Prynne's cheeks were seared with an iron made exceeding hot; which done, the executioner cut off one of his ears and a piece of his cheek with it; then hacking the other ear almost off he left it hanging and went down; but being called up again he cut it quite off.

b) LILBURNE

An information being preferred in the Star Chamber against John Lilburne and John Wharton for printing and publishing *The News from Ipswich* and other seditious books, contrary to the . . . late decree of that court, they were brought to the office to be examined upon interrogatories, but refused to take the oath, terming it an oath *ex officio*, and insisting that no free-born Englishman ought to take it, none being bound by law to accuse himself; whence Lilburne was ever after called Free-born John. . . . The court declared them guilty of a high contempt, and an offence of a dangerous consequence and evil example in refusing to take a legal oath, without which many exorbitant offences might go away undiscovered and unpunished; and therefore decreed that the said Lilburne and Wharton should be remanded to the

Fleet, there to continue until they conformed; that they should pay £500 apiece to the King, and before enlargement be bound to their good behaviour; that Lilburne should be whipped through the streets from the Fleet to the pillory. Which sentence was on the following 18th April [1638] rigorously executed on Lilburne, who when he was whipped at the cart and stood in the pillory uttered many bold speeches against the bishops, and when in the pillory took copies of several pamphlets (said to be seditious) out of his pocket and tossed them among the people; whereof the court of Star Chamber, then sitting, having notice, ordered him to be gagged during the residue of the time he was to stand in the pillory, which was done; and when he could not speak he stamped with his feet.

36. THE HIGH COMMISSION

The High Commission was the executive organ of the Church. Like the Star Chamber, it was used for the political persecution of enemies of the government until its abolition in 1641. The unpopularity of the bishops (which led to the abolition of the episcopacy in 1646) was largely due to their association with this court, which was also obnoxious as a rival of the common law courts. Leighton was a Presbyterian Scot, whose case is described by himself in *a*). His petition was favourably received, and he became governor of a jail. Extract *b*) shows parliamentarian fear of clerical independence and of a threat to property. Many men opposed bishops for reasons which were not merely religious. For Laud see Nos. 52, *b*), 54.

a) S. Chandler, *History of Persecution* (1736), pp. 367–71;
b) Laud, *History of Troubles and Trial* (1695), pp. 161–87.

a) LEIGHTON'S PETITION TO PARLIAMENT, 1640

YOUR much and long-distressed petitioner, on the 17th of February gone ten years [1630] was apprehended in Blackfriars, coming from the sermon, by a High Commission warrant. . . . Nothing would serve Dr. Laud but the highest censure that ever was passed in that court to be put upon him; and so it was to be inflicted with knife, fire and whip at and upon the pillory, with £10,000 fine; which some of the lords conceived should never be inflicted; only it was imposed (as on a dying man) to terrify others. . . .

Your petitioner's hands being tied to a stake (besides all other torments) he received 36 stripes with a treble cord; after which he stood almost two hours on the pillory in cold frost and snow, and suffered the rest, as cutting off the ear, firing the face and slitting of the nose, so that he was made a theatre of misery to men and angels. [Here the compassion of the House of Commons was so great that they were generally in tears, and ordered the clerk to stop reading twice, till they had recovered themselves.] . . .

Now the cause of all this harsh, cruel and continued ill-usage . . . was nothing but a book written by your petitioner, called "Sion's plea against the Prelacy"; and that by the call of divers and many good Christians in the Parliament-time, after divers refusals given by your petitioner, who would not publish it being done till it had the view and approbation of the best in the City, country and university, and some of the Parliament itself: in witness whereof he had about 500 hands; for revealing of whose names he was promised more favours by Sir Robert Heath [Attorney-General] than he will speak of. But denying to turn accuser of his brethren he was threatened with a storm, which he felt to the full. . . .

Your petitioner . . . humbly and heartily entreateth that you would be graciously pleased to take this his petition into your serious thoughts and to command deliverance, that he may plead his own cause; . . . having been prisoner . . . in the most nasty prisons 11 years, not suffered to breathe in the open air.

b) LAUD ON TRIAL, 1645

The next charge . . . was that "I went about to exempt the clergy from the civil magistrate." . . . The last instance of this day was the bringing Sir Rich. Samuel into the High Commission for doing his office as justice of the peace upon some clergymen . . . After this came a charge . . . that since my coming to be Archbishop I had renewed the High Commission, and put in many illegal and exorbitant clauses, which were not in the former. . . . The fourth exception was "that by this commission I took greater power than ever any court had, because both temporal and ecclesiastical". First, whatsoever power the High Commission had was . . . given by his Majesty. . . . Secondly, they have not power of life or limb . . . as other courts have. Thirdly, they may have more various power in some respects, but that cannot make it greater. . . . This I am sure of, the Commission hath power to deprive. For the statute gives it power "to use all ecclesiastical and spiritual censures," of which deprivation is known to be one. And that power is expressly given to deprive some offenders of all their spiritual promotions. . . . Therefore I think it follows necessarily, either that we have power over freehold [i.e. property] in that case, or else, that a benefice is not a freehold.

37. CLASS PRIVILEGES SPREAD TOO WIDE.

Wisdom after the event, from Charles I's Secretary of War and Charles II's Clerk of the Council. Cf. Nos. 1, 3, 106. Sir Edward Walker, *Historical Discourses* (1705), pp. 292, 302-3.

[PEERS] are not for any offence to be judged but by their peers; their bodies are not subject to arrests; nor are they obliged (being examined) to answer by their oaths, but upon their honours; and out of them the great officers of the kingdom, especially in military affairs, have in all times been elected [i.e. chosen], and some of those are and have been hereditary to particular families. . . . In the time of Parliament they are in a capacity of advancing or opposing the good of the king and kingdom. . . .

The late frequent and numerous creations [of peers] . . . have conduced to the disservice of the king and alteration of our happy condition under the royal government. . . . [This policy] took off from the respect due to nobility, and introduced a parity in conversation; which . . . proved of ill consequences, familiarity . . . begetting contempt. . . . Again, it abated the king's revenues by fees out of the Exchequer; but most of all by pensions and gifts to enable many of them to support their dignities; whereas had they been left in private condition they would have had less confidence to demand, and smaller gratification would have satisfied them. But that which essentially was destructive was that the king was not in capacity to gratify them all; which had this ill effect, that some of them grew envious, others factious because they were not employed; others ungrateful because denied something they aimed at, how highly soever obliged. Whereas had their number been less they might every one in his time and station have had opportunity to have tasted of the royal favours; for . . . in Queen Elizabeth's time there was hardly a peer in England but in some kind or other was employed by her according to their capacities.

38. THE LAW COURTS

The Crown still retained a right of arbitrary arrest, and of imprisoning men with no cause shown. Like wardship (see No. 31), this may have been justifiable in the turbulent days of military feudalism, but was intolerable in a settled commercial society. In fact Charles I used the right for exclusively political purposes. In *a*) the Lord Chief Justice obviously sympathised with the five knights imprisoned by the King's order for refusing to pay taxes not voted by Parliament; but he was bound by the precedents. A change in the law was clearly needed. It came after the revolution, in the Habeas Corpus Act of 1679. A way round the rigours of the law could often be found by bribery (*b*). Lord Chancellor Bacon was exposed as a taker of bribes in 1621. Under Charles I a determined attempt was made to subordinate the law and the judges to the needs of royal policy (No. 30, *e*) and *f*)). The denunciation in *c*) is the more impressive since it comes from a man who was later to die fighting for the King in the civil war. The mention of "deer" refers to the attempt to recover formerly royal forests from private hands. In January, 1641, Charles I was forced to agree that judges should hold office "during good behaviour" and not "at the King's pleasure"—but this was not finally confirmed until the Act of Settlement, 1701.

a) Gardiner, pp. 63-4; *b*) *C.S.P.Ven.*, 1636–9, pp. 165–6; *c*) Rushworth, IV, p. 140; *d*) ed. Cunnington, *Wiltshire Quarter Sessions Records of the Seventeenth Century* (1932), p. 136.

a) ARBITRARY ARREST, 1627

Lord Chief Justice Hyde: He [the Warden of the Fleet Prison] doth certify that they are detained in prison by the special command of the King; and whether this be good in law or no, that is the question. . . .

The precedents are all against you, every one of them, and what shall guide our judgments, since there is nothing alleged in this case but precedents? . . . If no cause of the commitment be expressed, it is to be presumed to be for matter of state, which we cannot take notice of. You see, we find none—no, not one—that hath been delivered by bail in the like cases, but by the hand of the king or his direction. . . . The question now is, whether we may deliver these gentlemen or not. . . . What can we do but walk in the steps of our forefathers? . . . If in justice we ought to deliver you, we would do it; but upon these grounds and these records, and the precedents and resolutions, we cannot deliver you, but you must be remanded.

b) BRIBING JUDGES, 1637

The crime was only bribing the judges, . . . one to which they [the English] are not accustomed to attach much importance. The corruption of the highest judges and magistrates has made it familiar, so much so that one may any day see the judges in the public tribunals, in the very act of pronouncing sentence, oppose the arguements of the lawyers, openly interesting themselves for one of the parties. Although this is a very great scandal, yet it is tolerated, and connivance at it has become a custom, so that the practice passes without exciting comment.

c) LORD FALKLAND'S SPEECH IMPEACHING LORD KEEPER FINCH, JANUARY, 1641

He gave our goods to the king, our lands to the deer, our liberties to his sheriffs, so that there was no way by which we had not been oppressed and destroyed if the power of this person had been equal with his will. . . . He not only by this means made us liable to all the effects of an invasion from without, but by destruction of our liberties (which included the destruction of our property, which included the destruction of our industry) to the terriblest of all invasions, that of want and poverty, so that if what he plotted had taken root (and he made it as sure as his declaration could make it) . . . in this wealthy and happy kingdom there could have been left no abundance but of grievances and discontentment, no satisfaction but amongst the guilty.

d) DUE PROCESS OF LAW, 1641

[At the Wiltshire Quarter Sessions] Katherine Peters [was] indicted for stealing a . . . table cloth value 10*s*. and one holland sheet value 10*s*., the goods of Francis Goddard Esq. . . . Refusing to plead to the indictment . . . [she was] adjudged to be committed to the place from whence she came and from thence to be brought to a close room and there to be laid upon her back naked from the middle upward, her legs and arms stretched and fastened towards the four corners of the room, and upon her body to have so much weight and somewhat over than she is able to bear. The first day—she requiring food—to have three morsels of coarse bread and no drink, the second day drink of the next [i.e. nearest] puddle of water, not running, next the place she lieth, and no bread: so every day in like manner until she be dead.

39. IN PRISON

George Wither (see No. 10) was imprisoned for satirising the court and government. He was later an officer in the Parliamentary Army (*a*). Extract *b*), from a contemporary letter, gives a realistic picture of the horrors of prison life for the poor. Prison was the first place in which one would look for an insolvent debtor (see Nos. 120 and 175).

a) G. Wither, *The Shepherd's Hunting* (*Poems*, 1891), pp. 180–1; *b*) Williams, II, p. 244.

a) GEORGE WITHER, 1618

Philarete: Here thou seest me pent,
Within the jaws of strict imprisonment,
A forlorn shepherd, void of all the means
Whereon men's common hope in danger leans;
Weak in myself, exposed to the hate
Of those whose envies are insatiate;
Shut from my friends, banished from all delights;
Nay worse, excluded from the sacred rites.
Here I do live, 'mongst outlaws marked for death,
As one unfit to draw the common breath. . . .
I suffer 'cause I wished my country well;
And what I more must bear I cannot tell. . . .
But, spite of hate and all that spite can do,
I can be patient yet, and merry too. . . .
Yea, midst these bonds can slight the great'st that be
As much as their disdain mis'steems of me; . . .
And hope to turn, if any justice be,
Both shame and care on those that wished it me.
For while the world rank villanies affords,
I will not spare to paint them out in words.

b) CONDITIONS IN PRISON, APRIL, 1636

Sunday last, the City complained to the King that the prison of Newgate was so full of poor prisoners, as they feared it might breed the infection [i.e. the plague] there: that there were 47 condemned persons, which his Majesty had reprieved, that were kept there, which did starve the rest of the poor prisoners. . . . To put them out of the gaol were to send so many ravening wolves amongst lambs; and none durst venture to carry them oversea. That they of the court and the City knew not how to dispose of them; and it were hard to hang them now in cold blood. That gaol-damp of Hereford hath already killed a great many that were at the last assizes, and many more are sick even unto death. The stench of one poor prisoner suffocated them all.

40. JUSTICES OF THE PEACE

Before 1640 the J.Ps. controlled local government. Sir Thomas Smith in 1583 makes it clear that they were drawn exclusively from the ruling class (*a*). The central government had no bureaucracy to enforce its will locally: it had to rely on the J.Ps.' co-operation. So their will was decisive, as James I admitted (*b*). In matters like the maintenance of order and keeping wages down (*a*); cf. No. 16), the J.Ps. co-operated willingly. But the King had reason to complain by 1616 that some J.Ps. inclined to the views of the Parliamentary opposition. This made it increasingly difficult for the royal government to carry on.

a) *T.C.D.*, pp. 455–6; *b*) *J.C.D.*, pp. 19–21; *c*) T. and P., II, pp. 234–5.

a) SOCIAL ORIGIN AND FUNCTIONS

THE Justices of Peace be men elected out of the nobility, higher and lower, that is the dukes, marquises, barons, knights, esquires and gentlemen, and of such as be learned in the laws, such and in such number as the Prince shall think meet, and in whom for wisdom and discretion he putteth his trust, inhabitants within the county; (saving that some of the high nobility and chief magistrates for honour's sake are put in all or in the most of the commissions of all the shires of England). . . . At the first they were but four, after eight; now they come commonly to thirty or forty in every shire, either by increase of riches, learning, or activity in policy and government. . . .

The Justices of the Peace be those in whom at this time for the repressing of robbers, thieves and vagabonds, of privy complots and conspiracies, of riots and violences and all other misdemeanours in the commonwealth the Prince putteth his special trust. . . .

The Justices of the Peace do meet also at other times by commandment of the Prince upon suspicion of war, to take order for the safety of the shire, sometimes to take musters of harness [military equipment] and able men, and sometimes to take order for the excessive wages of servants and labourers, for excess of apparel, for unlawful games, for conventicles and evil orders in alehouses and taverns, for punishment of idle and vagabond persons, and generally . . . for the good government of the shire. . . . There was never in any commonwealth devised a more wise, a more dulce and gentle, nor a more certain way to rule the people, whereby they are kept always as it were in a bridle of good order, and sooner looked unto that they should not offend than punished when they have offended.

b) JAMES I'S SPEECH TO THE JUDGES, 1616

Even as a King (let him be never so godly, wise, righteous and just), yet if the subaltern magistrates do not their parts under him the kingdom must needs suffer; so let the judges be never so careful and industrious, if the justices of peace under them put not to their helping hands in vain is all your labour, for they are the King's eyes and ears in the country. . . . Be careful to give a good account to me and my Chancellor of the duties performed by all justices of peace in your circuits. . . . Let not gentlemen be ashamed of this place, for it is a place of high honour and great reputation to be made a minister of the King's justice in service of the commonwealth.

Of these there are two sorts, as there is of all companies, especially where there is a great number: that is, good and bad justices. . . . Another sort are gentlemen of great worth in their own conceit, and cannot be content with the present form of government, but must have a kind of liberty in the people, and must be gracious lords and redeemers of their liberty; and in every cause that concerns prerogative give a snatch against a monarchy, through their Puritanical itching after popularity. Some of them have showed themselves too bold of late in the lower House of Parliament; and when all is done, if there were not a King they would be less cared for than other men.

c) ANOTHER VIEW OF J.PS., 1601

Mr. Glascock: We use so much lenity in our law, as we had as good make no law. For we give a penalty, and to be taken upon conviction before a Justice of Peace. Here's wise stuff! First, mark what a Justice of Peace is, and we shall easily find a gap in our law. A Justice of Peace is a living creature, that for half a dozen of chickens will dispense with a whole dozen of penal statutes. . . . These be the basket-justices [by] whom the tale may be justified of a Justice whom I know, to whom one of his poor neighbours coming, said: "Sir, I am very highly rated [for taxation] in the subsidy-book. I do beseech you to help me." To whom he answered, "I know thee not." "Not me?" quoth the countryman; "why, your worship had my team and mine oxen such a day; and I have been ever at your worship's service." "Have you so?" quoth the Justice; "I never remember I had any such matter; not so much as a sheep's tail." So unless you offer sacrifice unto these idol-justices of sheep and oxen, they know you not. If a warrant come from the Lords of the Council to levy 100 men [for military service], he will levy 200: and what with chopping in and crossing out [i.e. letting men buy themselves off] he will gain £100 by the bargain. Nay, if he be to send forth a warrant upon a man's request, to have any fetched in [i.e. arrested] upon suspicion of felony or the like, he will write you the warrant himself, and you must put 2*s.* in his pocket as his clerk's fee. . . .

Why, we have had here [in Parliament] five bills: one against swearing, another for going to church, good ale, drunkenness, and [?]. This is as good to them as a subsidy and two fifteenths [i.e. a grant of taxation].

41. CLASS RULE

Extract *a*) is from Sir Thomas More's *Utopia*, the first sketch of a Communist society made in the modern world. More subsequently became Lord Chancellor and was executed by Henry VIII. *Utopia* was written in 1516, but not published in English until 1551. There is, however, no need to suppose that More would have changed his view of the state if he had lived till 1640 (cf. Nos 16, 146, 153). Extract *b*) tells us what the Lords and Commons thought the state and its law existed for. The right to carry a sword was the distinguishing mark of a gentleman; and the armed forces of the country were also under the control of the landed class (*c*).

a) More, *Utopia* (Everyman), p. 112; *b*) *Lords' Journals*, V, p. 258; *c*) *Letters of Charles I* (ed. Petrie, 1935,) p. 84.

a) THE STATE, 1516

WHEN I consider and weigh in my mind all these commonwealths which nowadays anywhere do flourish, so God help me I can perceive nothing but a certain conspiracy of rich men procuring their own commodities under the name and title of the commonwealth. They invent . . . all means and crafts, first how to keep safely, without fear of losing, that [which] they have unjustly gathered together, and next how to hire and abuse the work and labour of the poor for as little money as may be. These devices, when the rich men have decreed to be kept and observed under colour of the communalty, that is to say, also of the poor people, then they be made laws.

b) RESOLUTION OF PARLIAMENT, AUGUST 2ND, 1642

[It is] most improbable that the nobility and chief gentry of this kingdom should conspire to take away the law, by which they enjoy their estates, are protected from any act of violence and power, and differenced from the meaner sort of people, with whom otherwise they would be but fellow servants.

c) THE MILITIA: CHARLES I TO THE EARL OF SUFFOLK, SEPTEMBER 21ST, 1629

Those that are to be enrolled in the trained lists are to be of gentry, freeholders, good farmers and their sons, that are like to be resident in the county and ready to serve with the arms they bear and are trained in at the musters, and that the meaner sort of people, and servants whose residence cannot be expected to be constant, be avoided.

42. WHOM DID THE HOUSE OF COMMONS REPRESENT?

The parliamentary electorate was confined (in the counties) to freeholders possessing land worth 40*s*. a year. This excluded copyholders and cottagers, the mass of the rural population (see No. 14, *a*)), and left the county franchise in the hands of the gentry and rich freeholders (rural bourgeoisie): for voting was not secret, and it would have been a brave poor peasant who would openly oppose the wishes of his landlord or the local *kulak* and moneylender (see No. 12, *c*)). The electorate in boroughs varied, but in most it was controlled by the ruling oligarchy of the corporation, often in agreement with the local landowner. Borough representatives enjoyed less prestige in the Commons than the county members. Harrington was a Parliamentarian, but both parties in his dialogue (*a*) admit that "the lords" controlled elections, and believed that even after the revolution "the people" will still vote for "the better sort." In the century before 1640, the economic importance of those classes whom the House of Commons represented changed out of all recognition (*b*). The superiority of the Commons over the Lords was manifest in the Civil War, leading ultimately to the establishment of their sole power (No. 142). Even after the Restoration the supremacy of the Commons was maintained. In the years before the revolution the government tried to control elections, but generally by 1640 the power of the new classes was too great to be upset by such interference (*c*). On the whole, the wider the franchise the more likely the borough was to return an opponent of the court (see, e.g., evidence on disputed elections in *Commons Journals*, March–May, 1628).

a) Harrington, *Works* (1737), p. 479; *b*) Williams, I, p. 331; *c*) [Anon.] *The Plain Case of the Commonwealth* (1659), pp. 5–6.

a) HARRINGTON, 1659

Publicola: For England there is no way [for the institution of a popular assembly] but by [a] representative, to be made to rise equally and methodically by stated elections of the people throughout the whole nation. . . . How else will you avoid improvement in the interest of the better sort, to the detriment of those of meaner rank, or in the interest of the few to the detriment of that of the many?

Valerius: But even this way there is danger of that foul beast the Oligarchy.

Publicola: Look about you. The Parliament declares all power to be in the people; is that in the better sort only?

Valerius: Stay. The King was to observe "*Leges et constitutiones quas vulgus elegerit.*" That *vulgus* is to be understood of the Parliament; and the Parliament consisted wholly of the better sort. . . . It was, you will say, no democracy.

Publicola: And will you say it was?

Valerius: No, truly: yet this derived in part from the free election of the people.

Publicola: How free? Seeing the people, then under lords, dared not to elect otherwise than as pleased those lords.

Valerius: Something of that is true; but I am persuaded that the people, not under lords, will yet be most addicted to the better sort.

Publicola: That is certain.

b) ECONOMIC ADVANCE OF COMMONS, 1628

They say it [the House of Commons] is the most noble, magnanimous assembly that ever those walls contained; and I heard a lord estimate they were able to buy the upper house (His Majesty only excepted) thrice over, notwithstanding there be of lords temporal to the number of 118. And what lord in England would be followed by so many freeholders as some of those are?

c) LOOKING BACK IN 1659

It is true, in this last election was abundance of abuse and arbitrariness in the very sheriffs (in some places) on purpose to obstruct the fairest and freest choice (to the great grief of the people). . . . But remember then the days of old, and the elections made to the Long Parliament (much like this) . . . which yet had a happy success for the commonweal.

43. DANGER OF MILITARY ABSOLUTISM

The French States-General met in 1614 for the last time before the Revolution of 1789. The Cortes in Spain and representative assemblies in all countries (except the bourgeois Netherlands) were being suppressed by absolute monarchs. Charles I, in *e*) and *f*), is already threatening to rule without Parliament, as he actually did for eleven years from 1629. Both government and opposition were very conscious of the issues at stake (see also Nos. 59 and 65). Sir Dudley Carleton got into trouble with the House of Commons for the threat implied in *e*), and he was made to withdraw: within a month he had been awarded a peerage by Charles I.

a) J. A. Manning, *Memoirs of Sir Benjamin Rudyerd* (1841), p. 80; *b*) quoted in Forster, *Sir John Eliot*, I, p. 409; *c*) *ibid.*, p. 439; *d*) *Parliamentary History*, II, p. 60; *e*) Rushworth, I, p. 363; *f*) *Lords' Journals*, III, p. 687.

a) SPEECH OF SIR B. RUDYERD, MARCH 11TH, 1624

LET us seriously consider his [Prince Charles's] interests, and not distaste him also with Parliaments, for then are we lost from generation to generation. I am the more vehement in this business because I am afraid, if this Parliament fail, it will be the last of Parliaments.

b) SPEECH OF SIR R. PHELIPS, AUGUST 9TH, 1625

England is the last monarchy that yet retains her liberties. Let them not perish now. Let not posterity complain that we have done for them worse than our fathers did for us.

c) SPEECH OF MR. E. LITTLETON, AUGUST 11TH, 1625

By the easiness of the subjects to supply, princes become more careless of their revenues and their outlay; and . . . there is ever a doubt, in the frequent grant of subsidies, that they may turn in time and grow into revenue. What once were voluntary contributions in Naples and Spain have now become due and certain. Tonnage and poundage here with us is now reckoned in the ordinary [revenue], which at first was meant but for the guarding of the sea.

d) CHARLES I TO PARLIAMENT, MARCH 28TH, 1626

Remember that parliaments are altogether in my power for their calling, sitting and dissolution; therefore, as I find the fruits of them to be good or evil, they are to continue, or not to be.

e) SPEECH OF SIR D. CARLETON, MAY 12TH, 1626

I beseech you, gentlemen, move not his majesty with trenching upon his prerogatives, lest you bring him out of love with parliaments. . . . In [his] messages he told you, that if there were not correspondency between him and you, he should be enforced to use new counsels. Now I pray you consider what these new counsels are and may be. I fear to declare those that I conceive. In all christian kingdoms you know that parliaments were in use anciently, . . . until the monarchs began to know their own strength; and seeing the turbulent spirit of their Parliaments at length they by little and little began to stand upon their prerogatives and at last overthrew the parliaments throughout christendom, except here only with us. And indeed you would count it a great misery if you knew the subject in foreign countries as well as myself; to see them look not like our nation, with store of flesh on their backs, but like so many ghosts and not men, being nothing but skin and bones with some thin cover to their nakedness, and wearing only wooden shoes on their feet, so that they cannot eat meat or wear good clothes but they must pay and be taxed unto the king for it. This is a misery beyond expression, and that which *yet* we are free from.

f) CHARLES I TO PARLIAMENT, MARCH 17TH, 1628

Every man now must do according to his conscience, wherefore if you [the House of Commons] (which God forbid) should not do your duties in contributing what this state at this time needs, I must, in discharge of my conscience, use those other means which God hath put into my hands, to save that that the follies of particular men may otherwise hazard to lose.

Take not this as a threatening, for I scorn to threaten any but my equals.

44. PARLIAMENT AND CROWN

The liberties of the House of Commons had to be fought for step by step—against the King's attempt to influence elections or bring pressure to bear on members (*a*); for the right to discuss any matter of political importance (*b*) and *c*)); to prevent the King selling out to international reaction (*d*) and *e*); cf. Nos. 63–6); against the King's dishonesty (*g*) and his attempts to set up arbitrary government (*h*). The Commons' main weapon was their control of finance and the King's poverty (*d*), *e*), *h*); cf. Nos. 47–9); the King tried to split the opposition by appealing to the class feelings of the biggest landlords, the peers (*j*) and *k*)). Both these speeches were made on the occasion of a dissolution, the blame for which the King put on the Commons. The Petition of Right (*g*) and *h*)) was described by the eighteenth-century Tory historian Hume as "a revolution." So it would have been if revolutions could be made by "scraps of paper." In fact the Civil War had to be fought to establish the point that the classes represented in Parliament were strong enough to enforce their demands.

a) *J.C.D.*, pp. 223–4; *b*) Prothero, p. 310; *c*) *ibid.*, pp. 313–14; *d*) *ibid.*, p. 318; *e*) *ibid.*, pp. 319–20; *f*) Rushworth, I, pp. 423–4; *g*) *ibid.*, p. 564; *h*) Gardiner, p. 69; *j*) *Lords' Journals*, IV, p. 43; *k*) *ibid.*, p. 81.

a) COMMONS' CLAIMS, 1604

THE rights of the liberties of the Commons of England consisteth chiefly in these three things:

First, that the shires, cities and boroughs of England, by representation to be present, have free choice of such persons as they shall put in trust to represent them.

Secondly, that the persons chosen, during the time of the Parliament as also of their access and recess, be free from restraint, arrest and imprisonment.

Thirdly, that in Parliament they may speak freely their consciences without check and controlment, doing the same with due reverence to the sovereign court of Parliament, that is to your Majesty and both the Houses, who all in this case make but one politic body whereof your Highness is the head.

b) THE KING TO THE HOUSE OF COMMONS, DECEMBER 3RD, 1621

Mr. Speaker, We have heard by divers reports, to our great grief, that our distance from the Houses of Parliament, caused by our indisposition of health, hath emboldened some fiery and popular spirits of some of the House of Commons to argue and debate publicly of matters far above their reach and capacity, tending to our high dishonour and breach of prerogative royal. These are therefore to command you to make known in our name unto the House, that none therein shall presume henceforth to meddle with anything concerning our government or deep matters of state. . . . We think ourself very free and able to punish any man's misdemeanours in Parliament as well during their sitting as after; which we mean not to spare hereafter, upon any occasion of any man's insolent behaviour.

c) PROTESTATION OF THE COMMONS, DECEMBER 16TH, 1621

The Commons now assembled in Parliament . . . do make this protestation following: That the liberties, franchises, privileges and jurisdictions of parliament are the ancient and undoubted birthright and inheritance of the subjects of England; and that the arduous and urgent affairs concerning the king, state and defence of the realm and of the church of England, and the maintenance and making of laws and redress of mischiefs and grievances which daily happen within this realm, are proper subjects and matter of counsel and debate in Parliament: and that in the handling and proceeding of those businesses every member of the House of Parliament hath and of right ought to have freedom of speech to propound, treat, reason and bring to conclusion the same: and that the Commons in Parliament have like liberty and freedom to treat of these matters in such order as in their judgments shall seem fittest: and that every member of the said House hath like freedom from all impeachment, imprisonment and molestation (other than by censure of the House itself) for or concerning any speaking, reasoning or declaring of any matter or matters touching the Parliament or parliament business; and that, if any of the said members be complained of and questioned for anything done or said in Parliament, the same is to be showed to the King by the advice and assent of all the Commons assembled in Parliament, before the King give credence to any private information.

d) ADDRESS OF BOTH HOUSES TO THE KING, MARCH 22ND, 1624

We your Majesty's most humble and loyal subjects, the Lords and Commons in this present parliament assembled . . . have . . . resolved: That, upon your Majesty's public declaration of the utter dissolution and discharge of the two treaties of the marriage and Palatinate, in pursuit of our advice therein, and towards the support of that war which is likely to ensue . . . we will grant for the present the greatest aid which was ever granted in parliament to be levied in so short time . . .; the money to be paid into the hands and expended by the direction of such committees or commissioners, as hereafter shall be agreed upon in this present session of parliament.

e) ADDRESS OF BOTH HOUSES TO THE KING, APRIL 10TH, 1624

It having pleased your Majesty, upon our humble suit and advice, to dissolve both the treaties, . . . we . . . do in all humbleness offer unto your sacred Majesty these two petitions following: . . .

Seeing we are thus happily delivered from that danger to which those treaties (now dissolved) and that use which your ill-affected subjects made thereof would certainly have drawn upon us, . . . we are most humble suitors to your gracious Majesty to secure the hearts of your good subjects by the engagement of your royal word unto them, that upon no occasion of marriage or treaty or other request in that behalf from any foreign prince or state whatsoever, you will take away or slacken the execution of your laws against Jesuits, priests and popish recusants.

f) THREAT OF MILITARY RULE, 1627

The companies [of soldiers] were scattered here and there in the bowels of the kingdom and governed by martial law. . . . The soldiers brake out into great disorders. They mastered the people; disturbed the peace of families and the civil government of the land; there were frequent robberies, burglaries, rapes, rapines, murders and barbarous cruelties. Unto some places they were sent for a punishment; and wherever they came, there was a general outcry. The highways were dangerous and the markets unfrequented. They were a terror to all and an undoing to many.

g) NASTY SUSPICIONS, MAY, 1628

Sir Edward Coke: The King's answer is very gracious, but what is the law of the realm? That is the question. . . . All succeeding Kings will say, "You must trust me as well as you did my predecessors, and trust my messages." But messages of love never came into a Parliament. Let us put up a Petition of Right.

h) THE PETITION OF RIGHT, JUNE 7TH, 1628

They do therefore humbly pray your Most Excellent Majesty, that no man hereafter be compelled to make or yield any gift, loan, benevolence, tax, or such-like charge, without common consent by act of Parliament; and that none be called to make answer, or take such oath, or to give attendance, or be confined, or otherwise molested or disquieted concerning the same, or for refusal thereof; and that no freeman, in any such manner as is before mentioned, be imprisoned or detained; and that your Majesty will be pleased to remove the said soldiers and mariners, and that your people may not be so burdened in time to come; and that the foresaid commissions for proceeding by martial law may be revoked and annulled; and that hereafter no commissions of like nature may issue forth to any person or persons whatsoever to be executed as aforesaid, lest by colour of them any of your Majesty's subjects be destroyed or put to death, contrary to the laws and franchises of the land.

j) CHARLES I TO HOUSE OF LORDS, MARCH 10TH, 1629

Considering that justice as well consists in reward and praise of virtue as punishing of vice, I thought it necessary to come here to-day to declare to you and all the world that it was merely the undutiful and seditious carriage in the lower house that has made the dissolution of this Parliament, and you, my Lords, are so far from being any causers of it, that I take as much comfort in your dutiful demeanours as I am justly distasted with their proceedings. . . . As those vipers must look for their reward of punishment, so you, my Lords, must justly expect from me that favour and protection that a good king owes to his loving and faithful nobility.

k) CHARLES I TO HOUSE OF LORDS, MAY 5TH, 1640

I must needs confess and acknowledge that ye, my Lords of the higher house, did give me so willing an ear . . . that certainly I may say, if there had been any means to have given a happy end to this Parliament it was not your Lordships' fault that it was not so. . . . It hath been some few cunning and some ill-affectioned men that have been the cause of this misunderstanding.

45. A REVOLUTIONARY SCENE

Traditionally, the Speaker was nominated by the King and then "elected" by the Commons. He controlled the debates for the government. But as M.Ps. grew conscious of their power, they fought to make the Speaker their servant in reality These extracts show a stage in this fight. The resolutions in *b*) were recited by Holles as the King was approaching to break down the door of the House. The resolutions speak of enemies "to the kingdom and commonwealth," no longer to the person of the King. The emancipation of men's minds from the feudal idea that government was the personal concern of the king, and loyalty due to him personally, and the emergence of the idea of loyalty to the commonwealth, was one of the great advances in political thought made in the seventeenth century. It culminated in the conviction of Charles I of treason to the commonwealth (see No. 140). For Arminianism, see No. 59, *c*).

a) Williams, II, pp. 11–12; *b*) Gardiner, pp. 82–3.

a) A NEWSLETTER, MARCH 5TH, 1629

On Monday last Mr. Speaker [Sir John Finch] was appointed by the King to signify to the lower House that the Parliament was adjourned until the 10th day of this month. But as the Speaker began to deliver his message the gentlemen, foreseeing what he was to say, commanded him to be silent. Whereupon, as he was about to go out of the House, they plucked him back by force and held him in his chair. So locking the door to themselves, they laid the key upon the table; which done, after divers speeches by sundry men spoken, with a general voice they proclaimed [the three resolutions below]. . . . In the meantime, the King sending two or three messengers one after another unto them, they were kept out, the doors not suffered to be opened.

b) RESOLUTIONS OF THE COMMONS, MARCH 2ND, 1629

1. Whosoever shall bring in innovation of religion, or by favour or countenance seek to extend or introduce Popery or Arminianism, or other opinion disagreeing from the true and orthodox church, shall be reputed a capital enemy to this kingdom and commonwealth.

2. Whosoever shall counsel or advise the taking and levying of the subsidies of Tonnage and Poundage, not being granted by Parliament, or shall be an actor or instrument therein, shall be likewise reputed an innovator in the government and a capital enemy to the kingdom and commonwealth.

3. If any merchant or person whatsoever shall voluntarily yield or pay the said subsidies of Tonnage and Poundage, not being granted by Parliament, he shall likewise be reputed a betrayer of the liberties of England, and an enemy to the same.

46. FOREBODINGS OF CONFLICT, *c.* 1615

This dialogue was written by Sir Walter Ralegh whilst under sentence of death in the Tower. He was executed in 1618 at the demand of the Spanish Ambassador. He became one of the heroes of the revolutionaries, not only for his fight against Spain, but also for his contribution to the ideology of the revolution in his *History of the World* and in political works like that from which this extract is taken. (See Nos. 67 and 198; in the latter, Ralegh's name was used as a symbol by a Parliamentarian sixty years after his execution.) Sir W. Ralegh, "The Prerogative of Parliament in England," *Works* (1829), VIII, pp. 213–20.

Justice of the Peace: Is it a loss to the King to be beloved of the Commons? . . . Certainly it is far more happy for a sovereign prince that a subject open his purse willingly, than that the same be opened by violence. Besides that when impositions are laid by Parliament, they are gathered by the authority of the law, which . . . rejecteth all complaints and stoppeth every mutinous mouth. . . . But there are of your lordships . . . that imprison the King's subjects, and deny them the benefit of the law, to the King's disprofit. And what do you otherwise thereby (if the impositions be in any sort grievous) but . . . dig out of the dust the long-buried memory of the subjects' former contentions with their kings?

Councillor of State: What mean you by that?

Justice of the Peace: I will tell your lordship when I dare.

. . . If the House press the King to grant to them all that is theirs by law, they cannot in justice refuse the King all that is his by the law. And where will be the issue of such a contention? I dare not divine, but sure I am that it will tend to the prejudice both of the King and subject. . . .

Councillor of State: Well, Sir, would you, notwithstanding all these arguments, advise his Majesty to call a Parliament? . . .

Justice of the Peace: Belike your lordships have conceived some other way, how money be gotten otherwise. If any trouble should happen, your lordship knows that then there were nothing so dangerous for a King as to be without money. A Parliament cannot assemble in haste, but present dangers require hasty remedies. It will be no time then to discontent the subjects by using any unordinary ways. . . .

Councillor of State: In all that you have said against our greatest, those men in the end shall be your judges in their own cause. You that trouble yourself with reformation are like to be well rewarded. . . .

Justice of the Peace: To say that his Majesty knows and cares not, that, my lord, were but to despair all his faithful subjects. . . . For singular authority begets but general oppression.

47. THE FINANCIAL SITUATION

The financial difficulties of the Crown were those of all feudal landowners. Prices were rising; rents were relatively fixed. Those who produced for the market prospered; those who had fixed incomes and expanding expenditures went downhill. The King was supposed in time of peace to "live of his own" (i.e. from the rents of crown lands and *fixed* feudal dues); parliamentary taxation was to meet emergencies like wars. That was the theory; but as prices rocketed the Crown faced one emergency after another, and so became more and more dependent on parliamentary grants, less and less able to resist parliamentary control as the Commons demanded "redress of grievances before supply." For wardship (*a*), cf. No. 31. Extract *b*) is from a report drawn up by Sir Robert Johnson for Secretary Cecil. With Johnson's complaint that men were looking after their own interests rather than those of the government, cf. No. 167.

a) *C.S.P.Ven.*, 1603–7, pp. 506–8; *b*) *C.S.P.D.*, 1601–3, pp. 176–7.

a) THE KING HAS NOT A SOU

PASSING now to the question of the revenue; and first, of the Treasury, it is the common opinion that the King has not a sou, for the late Queen [Elizabeth] sank a great deal of money in her wars with Ireland and Spain, and it is a wonder that she did not leave debts rather than cash. Then the present King was obliged to spend a large amount on his succession and to make many presents, especially to those who had served him so long in Scotland, where the poverty of the kingdom had forbidden him to do so. When he came to the rich and opulent throne of England he showed the liberality of his nature. It is commonly calculated that between money, jewels and real estate he must have given away two millions, mostly to the Scottish, though some English, too, were participators. The consequence is the Crown is in debt, but not deeply. It owns jewels, plate, hangings of most beautiful quality, valued, they say, at three millions of gold.

The ordinary revenue is of two kinds; the income from Crown lands bringing one hundred and twenty-five thousand pounds sterling. . . . I must say that if the Crown would let out its land on new leases it would draw beyond a doubt three times as much, for the rents have not been raised for the last three hundred years, yet everything has gone up four or five fold. All the same the King may be said to make all he can out of it, for when he wants to reward anyone he lets out part of the Crown lands at the old rent, and the tenant then raises the rent three or four times over. In this way the King rewards his servants without putting his hand in his pocket.

The other source of revenue is the customs dues. All exports and imports pay duty, but once inside the country they circulate freely. This brings about 700,000 crowns [about £175,000]. Then there is the revenue of the Kingdom of Scotland, which may amount to 100,000 crowns. Ireland not only yields no revenue, but even causes a loss. Among the taxes is one called Wardship. . . . Various efforts have been made to shake off this burden, but in vain; Parliament offered the King one hundred and twenty in place of the eighty thousand crowns he draws and also a donative of four hundred thousand crowns, but as the Mastership of the Wards is in the hands of the Earl of Salisbury, who is supreme, and as he draws a large revenue from it, the bill was rejected. In fact the ordinary revenue of the Crown does not exceed 1,300,000 crowns.

To pass to the extraordinary; it consists of subsidies which may vary in amount, but taking the practice of the late Queen they amount to about 600,000 crowns a year. This sum can only be obtained with the consent of Parliament. I must mention an expedient adopted by the late Queen and employed last year by the present King, and that is the issue of obligations under the sign manual and privy seal. On these money is raised. These loans were never paid off by the late Queen, though the King declares his intention to do so.

The ordinary expenses of the Crown amount to about a million. The King's private expenses are 500,000 crowns, a very considerable sum, in spite of the fact that the Court has the ancient privilege of purveyance and carriage, both being paid at a very low rate; what was worth ten not fetching more than two; an intolerable burden on the subjects. . . . Parliament thought to remedy this abuse by offering certain concessions to the Crown, if only they could be rid of the tyranny of the Court officials; but the interested parties have had such weight with his Majesty that he has refused any kind of compromise to the great damage of his subjects. . . .

The total [expenditure] is about a million; so that without the subsidy there would be a balance of three hundred thousand crowns, but this and the subsidy as well is consumed by the malversation of his Ministers. The King himself gives to his favourites with a lavish hand.

b) LOSS OF REVENUE FROM CROWN LANDS, 1602

Whenever I have heard of the sale of her Majesty's lands I have observed that the value was seldom known, and the pig was sold in the panier, as the proverb is. . . . The chief foundation of mischiefs has been the want of authentic surveys and the preservation of court rolls, by which there has been the loss of many rents, the confounding of tenancies, the change of tenures, perverting of customs, concealing of fines, . . . [etc.]

[Suggested remedies] Some learned persons should be appointed to peruse and report upon such customs as to which are reasonable and which prejudicial, etc., comparing the modern with the ancient. . . .

The reason why her Majesty should more strictly examine these things than her predecessors is that . . . within these 60 or 80 years, and chiefly 40 or 50, the witcraft of man is more and more extended to obscure ancient customs and pervert them to private profit.

Tenants in these days, when inquisitions of survey or inquest of office are taken, do not study so much to answer what is true, as to set forth such customs as are profitable for themselves. If any say "the succeeding age may shift for itself, as this does," it is folly; for the controversies that have grown through want of preservation of records needs no argument.

48. GROWING FINANCIAL DIFFICULTIES

Contemporaries had great difficulty in understanding that the government's financial embarrassment was due not merely to extravagance and mismanagement, but to deep economic causes. Both sides in the dispute looked back to the "good old days" when the Crown asked for little and Parliament granted that little willingly (*a*). What was especially annoying for the King was that, though the government had to live on capital by selling crown lands (*d*) and No. 47), the country as a whole, merchants and gentry in particular, were richer than ever before. A wholesale reorganisation of taxation was needed (*b*) and *c*); cf. notes to Nos. 31, 167); but the taxpayers would never agree to that until they controlled state power. They were unlikely to accept measures like the forced loan of 1625, when the Deputy Lieutenants of Cheshire were "careful to inform themselves of moneyed men, who employ the same in usury" so that they might be heavily taxed. Sir Robert Naunton (*a*) was the Secretary of State who was dismissed by James I at the demand of Spain (No. 63, *b*)). He subsequently had great difficulty in getting his pension paid.

a) Sir Robert Naunton, *Fragmenta Regalia*, Somers Tracts, V, pp. 354–6; *b*) *T.C.D.*, p. 605; *c*) Sir J. Bramston, *Autobiography*, p. 40; *d*) Williams, I, p. 307.

a) SIR ROBERT NAUNTON, *c.* 1630

It is manifest she [Queen Elizabeth] left more debts unpaid, taken upon credit of her privy seals, than her progenitors did or could have taken up that were a hundred years before her. . . . And for such [parliamentary] aids it is likewise apparent that she received more, and that with the love of her people, than any two of her predecessors that took most. . . . And truly, though much may be written in praise of her providence and good husbandry, in that she could upon all good occasions abate her magnanimity and therewith comply with the Parliament, and so always come off both with honour and profit; yet must we ascribe some part of the commendation to the wisdom of the times and the choice of Parliament-men; . . . such as came not to the House with a malevolent spirit of contention, but with a preparation to consult on the public good, and rather to comply than to contest with majesty. . . . Neither do I remember that the House did ever capitulate or prefer their private interest to the public and the Queen's necessities, but waited their times, and in the first place gave their supply, and according to the exigence of her affairs; yet failed not at the last to attain what they desired, so that the Queen and her Parliaments had ever the good fortunes to depart in love and on reciprocal terms, which are considerations that have not been so exactly observed in our last assemblies. . . . Considering the great debts left on the King, and into what encumbrances the House itself had then drawn him, his majesty was not well used, though I lay not the blame on the whole suffrage of the House, where he had many good friends; for I dare avouch it, had the House been freed of half a dozen popular and discontented persons . . . the King had obtained that which in reason, and at his first occasion, he ought to have received freely and without condition.

b) UNEQUAL ASSESSMENT, 1601

Sir Walter Ralegh [in the debate in the House of Commons on the Subsidy Bill]: Our estates that be £30 or £40 in the Queen's books are not the hundredth part of our wealth.

c) NEED FOR REORGANISATION OF TAXATION

Now the subsidy was fallen extremely, partly by fault in the commissioners, but chiefly for that the estates of the lords and other great men, and of the church, were divided and come into the hands of the gentry and other inferior men, who were all to be allowed maintenance for themselves and families to their qualities, . . . the number of their children, and the ways they lived in. For in raising subsidies the same course by law ought to be taken as in letting lands, where the tenant computes his charge of ploughing, expense of his house, the town charges of all sorts, which being deducted he sets the rent.

d) CHARLES I AT THE CITY'S MERCY, 1627

Concerning the bargain with the Londoners, it was in a manner broken off on Friday last, upon some difference touching the assurances that were proffered them, they being departed with great discomfort from the King's presence, and he as ill satisfied of them. But they the next day repaired to the Duke [of Buckingham] and made all up again, so as on Monday the contract was absolutely concluded in the council between his Majesty and them, whereby they are to lend presently £120,000 to his Majesty, and he on his part doth pass over an assurance unto them of so much of his lands in Cornwall as shall satisfy them by the yearly revenue thereof not only for the interest of the said sum but also of a former debt of £160,000 which they had lent heretofore, till they be paid the principal of the same.

49. SHIP MONEY

When Charles I tried to rule without Parliament (1629–40), he had to find non-parliamentary sources of finance. Various expedients were adopted, by which the harm done to the subject was vastly greater than the advantage to the Treasury. Ship Money, the most serious of these expedients, seemed likely to be established as an annual tax. In February, 1637, the judges, in an extra-judicial decision, pronounced Ship Money legal. When this decision was confirmed in the Hampden case a year later, the choice lay between submission and a revolutionary change in the law. In 1641 Parliament declared Ship Money illegal. All these extracts testify to the extreme hostility which Ship Money aroused, although the Venetian Ambassador had little sympathy with the Parliamentary cause. For Finch ;*b*), see No. 38, *c*). Baxter (*c*) was a Puritan divine whose views we shall frequently quote. The Earl of Warwick (*d*) was a commercially-minded *nouveau riche*, iterested in colonisation and piracy. He was Lord High Admiral of the Parliamentary fleet in the Civil War. See No. 94, *f*).

a) D'Ewes, *Autobiography and Correspondence*, II, pp. 129-32; *b*) Ludlow, I. pp. 12-13; *c*) Richard Baxter, *Autobiography* (Everyman), p. 20; *d*) *C.S.P. Ven.*, 1632-6, p. 315; 1636-9, pp. 110, 124, 153-4, 376-7.

a) D'EWES

[In 1635] the liberty of the subjects of England received the most deadly and fatal blow it had been sensible of in five hundred years past; for writs were issued . . . to all the sheriffs of England, to levy great sums of money in all the counties of the same kingdom and Wales, under pretext and colour to provide ships for the defence of the kingdom. . . . The sum now to be levied came to some £320,000, and if this could be done lawfully, then by the same right the King upon the like pretence might gather the same sum ten, twelve, or a hundred times redoubled, and so to infinite proportions to any one shire, when and as often as he pleased; and so no man was, in conclusion, worth anything. . . .

This taxation was absolutely against law, and an utter oppression of the subjects' liberty, who had such a property in their goods as could not be taken from them by any taxes or levies, but such only as were enacted and set down by Act of Parliament. . . . All our liberties were now at one dash utterly ruined if the King might at his pleasure lay what unlimited taxes he pleased on his subjects, and then imprison them when they refused to pay. . . . What shall freemen differ from the ancient bondsmen and villeins of England if their estates be subject to arbitrary taxes, tallages and impositions? . . . It is the honour of a king to have his subjects rich. . . . In all my life I never saw so many sad faces in England as this new taxation, called Ship Money, occasioned.

b) LUDLOW

Many . . . illegal methods were revived and put in execution, to rob the people in order to support the profusion of the court. And that our liberties might be extirpated at once, and we become tenants-at-will to the King, that rare invention of Ship Money was found out by [Lord Chief Justice] Finch, whose solicitation and importunities prevailed with the major part of the judges of Westminster Hall to declare for law, "That for the supply of shipping to defend the nation, the King might impose a tax upon the people: that he was to be judge of the necessity of such supply, and of the quantity to be imposed for it; and that he might imprison as well as distrain in case of refusal." Some there were who, out of a hearty affection to the service of their country and a true English spirit, opposed these illegal proceedings: amongst whom Mr. John Hampden of Buckinghamshire, Judge Croke and Judge Hutton were of the most eminent.

c) BAXTER

Ship Money . . . made a wonderful murmuring all over the land, especially among the country nobility and gentry; for they took it as the overthrow of the fundamental laws or constitution of the kingdom, and of Parliaments, and of all property. . . .

The poor ploughmen understood but little of these matters; but a little would stir up their discontent when money was demanded. But it was the more intelligent part of the nation that were the great complainers.

d) THE VENETIAN AMBASSADOR

January 5th, 1635. The King . . . proposes to push on [with the collection of Ship Money] . . . with the object of preventing all need for summoning Parliament, and by these steps to approach more nearly to that advantageous position over his subjects, and to that independent dominion over affairs . . . which it has obviously been his aim to attain by every means. . . .

December 12th, 1636. The unwillingness of the people to contribute becomes more strongly felt. Not only the lower classes but the greatest lords are beginning to make themselves heard seriously, in expressing with great resolution their intention to maintain, with the common laws, . . . their own jurisdiction and privileges. . . .

January 16th, 1637. The Earl of Warwick . . . made no bones of telling the King frankly that his tenants . . . were all old and accustomed to the mild rule of Queen Elizabeth and King James, and could not bring themselves to consent to such notable prejudices. They would consider their fault too grave if they died under the stigma of having, at the end of their lives, signed away the liberties of the realm, and of their free will deprived their posterity of those benefits which had been left to them uncontaminated as a sacred treasure by their ancestors. For his own part he was as ready as anyone to sacrifice his blood as well as his goods for his Majesty, but he did not know how he could use force against his people. . . .

February 27th, 1637. Your Excellencies can easily understand the great consequences involved in this decision [that of the judges in favour of Ship Money], as at one stroke it roots out for ever the meeting of Parliament and renders the King absolute and sovereign. . . . It . . . has created such consternation and disorder that one cannot judge what the outcome will be. If the people submit to this present prejudice, they are submitting to an eternal yoke. . . . Thus finally the goal will be reached for which the King has been labouring so long. . . .

February 26th, 1638. The libels and pasquinades circulated through the City and country, and what persons of every condition say with the utmost freedom, is not easy to describe; but what counts for more is the reluctance to pay. No person of quality will pay voluntarily, and the exaction proceeds so slowly that the King decided to summon the sheriffs of the counties before the Council and reprimand them sharply for their negligence. They told him frankly that it was impossible to induce any person of account to pay amicably by persuasion or threats.

Part Four

CHURCH AND STATE BEFORE 1640

The doctrines which to this day are controverted about religion do for the most part belong to the right of dominion.

Thomas Hobbes.

50. THE DOCTRINES OF THE CHURCH OF ENGLAND

The English Reformation was a political, not a religious movement. It made the Church wholly subordinate to the state. The Thirty-nine Articles (1562) reflect this (*a*). So do the homilies (1562 and later)—officially approved sermons designed to be read out by the many parsons who were too ignorant to compose their own. (In general, preaching was encouraged by the Puritans: the government thought homilies safer.) The homilies reflect the social policy of the government, the modes of thought it wished to impose on the largely illiterate population through the authoritative pronouncements of the ministers of God (*b*) and *c*)). The canons of 1604 (*d*) were designed to stem the rising tide of Puritanism, to insist that every Englishman is a member of the state Church, punishable if he fails to conform. The canons of 1640 (*e*), passed before the Long Parliament met, were a party political document drawn up by the King's most fanatical adherents. They were condemned by Parliament in December, 1640, as "contrary to . . . the laws of the realm, the rights of Parliament, the property and liberty of the subject"; and were recognized to be illegal at the Restoration (see No. 54, *b*)). These extracts show that one need not be a religious Puritan to dislike the Laudian Church.

a) *The Book of Common Prayer*; *b*) *Sermons or Homilies appointed to be read in Churches* (1802), pp. 87–8; *c*) *ibid*., pp. 471–3; *d*) *J.C.D.*, pp. 232–3; *e*) Nalson, *An Impartial Collection of the Great Affairs of State* (1682–3), I, pp. 546–7.

a) ARTICLES OF RELIGION

XXXVII. The King's Majesty hath the chief power in this realm of England . . ., unto whom the chief government of all estates of this realm, whether they be ecclesiastical or civil, in all causes doth appertain. . . . It is lawful for Christian men, at the commandment of the magistrate, to wear weapons and serve in the wars.

XXXVIII. The riches and goods of Christians are not common, as touching the right, title and possession of the same, as certain Anabaptists do falsely boast.

b) AN EXHORTATION TO OBEDIENCE

Almighty God hath created and appointed all things in heaven, earth and waters in a most excellent and perfect order. . . . Some [people] are in high degree, some in low, some kings and princes, some inferiors and subjects, priests and laymen, masters and servants, fathers and children, husbands and wives, rich and poor. . . . Take away kings, princes, rulers, magistrates, judges and such estates of God's order, no man shall ride or go by the way unrobbed, no man shall sleep in his own house or bed unkilled, no man shall keep his wife, children and possessions in quietness, all things shall be common. . . . Wherefore let us subjects do our bounden duties, giving hearty thanks to God, and praying for the preservation of this godly order.

c) AGAINST DISOBEDIENCE AND WILFUL REBELLION

If servants ought to obey their masters, not only being gentle but such as be froward; as well, and much more, ought subjects to be obedient, not only to their good and courteous but also to their sharp and vigorous princes. . . .

What shall subjects do then? Shall they obey valiant, stout, wise and good princes, and contemn, disobey and rebel against children being their princes, or against undiscreet and evil governors? God forbid: for first, what a perilous thing were it to commit unto the subjects the judgment, which prince is wise and godly, and his government good, and which is otherwise . . .; an enterprise very heinous, and must needs breed rebellion. For who else be they that are most inclined to rebellion but such haughty spirits? . . . Is not rebellion the greatest of mischiefs? And who are most ready to the greatest mischiefs but the worst men? . . . What an unworthy matter were it then to make the naughtiest subjects and most inclined to rebellion and all evil judges over their princes, over their government and over their councillors. . . . Indeed a rebel is worse than the worst prince, and rebellion worse than the worst government of the worst prince.

d) CANONS OF 1604

IV. Whosoever shall hereafter affirm that the form of God's worship in the Church of England established by law and contained in the Book of Common Prayer . . . is a corrupt, superstitious or unlawful worship of God, or containeth anything in it that is repugnant to the Scriptures: let him be excommunicated *ipso facto*, and not restored but by the bishop of the place or archbishop, after his repentance and public revocation of such his wicked errors. . . .

VII. Whosoever shall hereafter affirm that the government of the Church of England under his Majesty by archbishops, bishops, deans, archdeacons and the rest that bear office in the same, is anti-christian or repugnant to the Word of God: let him be excommunicated . . . [etc.]

IX. Whosoever shall hereafter separate themselves from . . . the Church of England, and combine themselves together in a new brotherhood, accounting the christians who are conformable to the doctrine, government, rites and ceremonies of the Church of England to be profane and unmeet for them to join with in christian profession; let them be excommunicated . . . [etc.]

e) CANONS OF 1640

Every parson, vicar, curate or preacher, upon some one Sunday in every quarter of the year . . . shall in the place where he serves . . . audibly read these explanations of the regal power. . . .

The most high and sacred order of kings is of divine right, being the ordinance of God himself, founded in the prime laws of nature. . . . A supreme power is given to this most excellent order by God himself. . . .

For any persons to set up, maintain or avow . . . under any pretence whatsoever, any independent co-active power, either papal or popular, whether directly or indirectly, is to undermine their royal office, and cunningly to overthrow the most sacred ordinance which God himself hath established; and so is treasonable against God as well as the King. For subjects to bear arms against their

King, offensive or defensive, upon any pretence whatsoever, is at the least to resist the powers that are ordained of God; and though they do not invade but only resist, St. Paul tells them plainly "They shall receive to themselves damnation."

And although tribute and custom, and aid and subsidy, and all manner of necessary support and supply be respectively due to kings from their subjects by the Law of God, nature and nations, for the public defence, care and protection of them; yet nevertheless subjects have . . . a true and just right, title and property to and in all their goods and estates, and so ought to have: . . . as it is the duty of the subjects to supply their king, so it is part of the kingly office to support his subjects in the property and freedom of their estates. . . .

We do also hereby require all . . . priests and ministers that they . . . presume not to speak of his Majesty's power in any other way than in this Canon is expressed.

51. CHURCH AND STATE ARE ONE

In *a*) and *b*) judges tell us that Puritans in attacking the Church were also attacking the state: and therefore must be stopped. It was deliberately offensive to address Mr. White (a substantial London citizen) and the Rev. Mr. Udall as "thou," a term kept for social inferiors. (Later the Quakers insisted on calling everyone "thou" for egalitarian reasons.) The importance of the surplice (*a*) was that it marked out the priest from the rest of the congregation, established his unique position as the man who made the magic which turned the bread and wine into body and blood. The Puritans, emphasising the individual's direct relation to God and denying the need for a mediator, wished the minister to be indistinguishable from the congregation he served. The issue of human equality was at stake.

a) Neal, *History of the Puritans* (revised ed., 1837), I, pp. 209–10; *b*) Prothero, pp. 442–3; *c*) Hooker, *Of the Lawes of Ecclesiastical Politie* (1676), p. 438.

a) EXAMINATION OF MR. WHITE, JANUARY, 1573

Lord Chief Justice: Who is this?

White: White, an't please your honour.

L.C.J.: White! As black as the devil.

White: Not so, my lord; one of God's children.

L.C.J.: Why will you not come to your parish church? . . .

White: I would avoid those things that are an offence to me and others, and disturb the peace of the church; however, I crave the liberty of a subject. . . .

Master of the Requests: These things are commanded by act of parliament, and in disobeying the law of your country you disobey God.

White: I do it not of contempt but of conscience; in all other things I am an obedient subject.

L.C.J.: Thou art a contemptuous fellow and wilt obey no laws.

White: Not so, my lord; I do and will obey laws. And therefore refusing but a ceremony out of conscience, and not refusing the penalty for the same, I rest still a true subject.

L.C.J.: The Queen's majesty was overseen not to make you of her council, to make laws and orders for religion.

White: Not so, my lord; I am to obey laws warranted by God's word.

L.C.J.: Do the Queen's laws command anything against God's word?

White: I do not say so, my lord.

L.C.J.: Yes, marry, do you, and there I will hold you.

White: Only God and his laws are absolutely perfect; all men and their laws may err.

L.C.J.: . . . Thou are the wickedest and most contemptuous person that has come before me since I sat in this commission.

White: Not so, my lord; my conscience witnesseth otherwise.

Master of the Requests: What if the Queen should command to wear a gray frize gown, would you come to church then?

White: That were more tolerable than that God's ministers should wear the habit of his enemies.

L.C.J.: How if she should command to wear a fool's coat and a cock's comb?

White: That were very unseemly, my lord, for God's ministers.

Dean of Westminster: You will not then be obedient to the Queen's commands?

White: I would only avoid those things that have no warrant in the word of God, that are neither decent nor edifying but flatly the contrary, and are condemned by the foreign reformed churches.

L.C.J.: You would have no laws.

White: If there were no laws, I would live a Christian and do no wrong; if I received any, so it were.

L.C.J.: Thou art a rebel.

White: Not so, my lord: a true subject.

L.C.J.: Yea, I swear by God thou art a very rebel; for thou wouldst draw thy sword and lift up thy hand against thy prince, if time served.

b) AT CROYDON ASSIZES, JULY 24TH, 1590

Mr. Udall was called. . . . Then was his indictment read . . . that he, not having the fear of God before his eyes, but being stirred up by the instigation and motion of the Devil, did maliciously publish a slanderous and infamous libel against the Queen's Majesty, her crown and dignity. . . .

Judge Clarke: We have heard you speak for yourself to this point at large, which is nothing to excuse you; for you cannot excuse yourself to have done it with a malicious intent against the bishops, and that exercising their government which the Queen hath appointed them; and so it is by consequence against the Queen. . . .

Udall: My Lords . . . the author of this book toucheth only the corruptions of the bishops, and therefore not the person of her Majesty.

Judge Clarke: But I will prove this book to be against her Majesty's person, for her Majesty, being the supreme governor of all persons and causes in these her dominions, hath established this kind of government in the hands of the bishops, which thou and thy fellows so strive against; and they being set in authority for the exercising of this government by her Majesty, thou dost not strive against them but her Majesty's person, seeing they cannot alter the government which the Queen hath laid upon them.

c) HOOKER

There is not any man of the church of England but the same man is also a member of the commonwealth, nor any member of the commonwealth which is not also of the church of England.

52. RELIGION AS AN INSTRUMENT OF GOVERNMENT

James I's epigram, "No bishop, no king" (No. 55, *b*) and *c*)), is here confirmed by Charles I and his ministers (*b*), *d*) and *f*)), by Sir John Eliot (*a*), by Cromwell's scientist brother-in-law (*e*), and more cynically by a journalist who wrote impartially for either side (*f*); also by an academic observer (*c*). Note Burton's cautious words about censorship.

a) Sir John Eliot, *Negotium Posterorum* (1881), I, pp. 70–1; *b*) P. Heylin, *Cyprianus Anglicus* (1719), p. 103; *c*) R. Burton, *Anatomy of Melancholy* (Everyman), III, pp. 328–9, 338–9, 424; *d*) Charles I, *Letters*, pp. 200–6; *e*) Burnet, *History of My Own Time*, I, p. 114; *f*) quoted in Margaret James, *Social Problems and Policy during the Puritan Revolution* (1930), p. 32.

a) SIR JOHN ELIOT, 1625

Religion only it is that fortifies all policy, that crowns all wisdom, that is the grace of excellence; the glory of all power, the strength of all government is religion. For though policy might secure a kingdom against foreigners . . . and wisdom provide all necessaries for the rule and government at home, yet if religion season not the affections of the people, the danger is as much in our own Achitophels as from Moab and all the armies of Philistines. Religion it is that keeps the subject in obedience, as being taught by God to honour his vicegerents.

b) LAUD'S INSTRUCTIONS TO CLERGYMEN, 1626

We have observed that the church and the state are so nearly united and knit together that . . . they may be accounted but as one. . . . This nearness makes the church call in the help of the state to succour and support her whensoever she is pressed beyond her strength. And the same nearness makes the state call in for the service of the church, both to teach that duty which her members know not, and to exhort them to and to encourage them in that duty which they know.

c) BURTON: *ANATOMY OF MELANCHOLY* (1638)

It hath ever been a principal maxim with [politicans] to maintain religion or superstition, which they determine of, alter and vary upon all occasions, as to them seems best; they make religion mere policy, a cloak, a human invention. . . . No way better to curb than superstition, to terrify men's consciences and to keep them in awe: they make new laws, statutes, invent new religious ceremonies, as so many stalking horses to their ends. . . . In all these religions and superstitions amongst our idolaters, . . . the parties first affected are silly, rude, ignorant people, old folks, . . . weak women. . . . The best means they have . . . is to keep them still in ignorance, for "ignorance is the mother of devotion," as all the world knows, and these times can amply witness. . . .

I might have said more of this subject [predestination]; but forasmuch as it is a forbidden question, and in the Preface or Declaration to the Articles of the Church, printed 1633, to avoid factions and altercations, we that are university divines especially are prohibited "all curious search, to print or preach, or draw the article aside by our own sense and comments, upon pain of ecclesiastical censure," I will . . . conclude with Erasmus: . . . "It is neither safe nor pious to harbour and spread suspicions of the public authority. It is better to endure tyranny, so long as it does not drive us to impiety, than seditiously to resist."

d) CHARLES I, 1646

It is not the change of church government which is chiefly aimed at [by parliament] (though that were too much); but it is by that pretext to take away the dependency of the church from the crown, which . . . I hold to be of equal consequence to that of the militia; for people are governed by the pulpit more than the sword in time of peace. . . .

Believe it, religion is the only firm foundation of all power; that cast loose, or depraved, no government can be stable. For where was there ever obedience where religion did not teach it? . . . I am most confident that religion will much sooner regain the militia than the militia will religion. . . .

Take it as an infallible maxim from me that, as the church can never flourish without the protection of the crown, so the dependency of the church upon the crown is the chiefest support of regal authority. This is that which is so well understood by the English and Scots rebels, that no concessions will content them without the change of church government, by which that necessary and ancient relation which the church hath had to the crown is taken away.

e) CROMWELL

Dr. Wilkins told me he often said to him [Oliver Cromwell], no temporal government could have a sure support without a national church that adhered to it.

f) MARCHAMONT NEEDHAM, 1651

No state can permit ministers to pretend scruples.

53. WHAT PARLIAMENTARIANS OBJECTED TO IN THE CHURCH

These extracts show that more than theology was involved in control of the Church. Sibthorp and Manwaring (*a*) and *b*)) were protected and promoted by Charles I when attacked in the House of Commons. With *c*) compare Selden's remark in a speech in Parliament on April 26th, 1628: "Who doubts of our property? I never heard it denied but in the pulpit." The Root and Branch Petition (*e*) was "presented to the House of Commons from many of his

Majesty's subjects in and about the City of London and several counties of the kingdom." It demanded the total abolition of episcopacy. For Edwards (*d*), see note to No. 115.

a) Prothero, p. 437; *b*) *ibid.*, p. 438; *c*) Sir A. Weldon, *The Court and Character of King James I and the Court of King Charles*, pp. 207–8; *d*) Edwards, *Gangræna*, 2nd ed., 1646, Part II, p. 187; *e*) Gardiner, p. 137; *f*) Sir Philip Warwick, *Memoirs* (1813), pp. 193–4.

a) SIBTHORP, ASSIZE SERMON, 1626

IF a prince impose an immoderate, yea an unjust tax, yet the subject may not thereupon withdraw his obedience and duty: nay he is bound in conscience to submit.

b) MANWARING, SERMON ON ALLEGIANCE, 1627

All the significations of a royal pleasure are and ought to be to all loyal subjects in the nature and force of a command. . . . No subject may, without hazard of his own damnation in rebelling against God, question or disobey the will and pleasure of his sovereign.

c) PROPERTY INSECURE

To such a strange pass were disorders come unto, that every lackey of those great lords [of Charles I's Council] might give a check-mate to any gentleman, yea, to any country nobleman that was not in Court favour.

And to fill full the measure of the time's abounding iniquity, the Court chaplains (and others elsewhere), with the reverend Bishops themselves, did preach away our liberties and properties; yet kept they divinity enough for their own interests. For, they concluded, all was either God's or the King's. Their part belonged to God, in which the King had no property. Our part belonged wholly to the King, in which we had property no longer when the King were disposed to call for them: so that, betwixt the Law and the Gospel, we were ejected out of lands, liberties and lives at pleasure.

d) A PRESBYTERIAN LOOKS BACK, 1646

What was it that ruined the bishops and that party but their grasping and meddling with all at once, church and commonwealth together, England and Scotland both, provoking also all sorts of persons against them, nobility, gentry, city, ministers, common people. . . ?

e) THE ROOT AND BRANCH PETITION, 1640

The government of archbishops and lord bishops, deans and archdeacons, etc., with their courts and ministrations in them, have proved prejudicial and very dangerous both to the church and commonwealth. . . . They have claimed their calling immediately from the Lord Jesus Christ, which is against the laws of this kingdom.

f) A ROYALIST TALKS TO CROMWELL

Indeed they [the Parliamentarians] overthrow all ecclesiastical and civil establishments before they are concerted how to frame any new; or as Mr. Cromwell (who from a very mean figure of a man in the beginning of this parliament rose to that prodigious greatness before the end) said to Sir Thomas Chichele and myself once in the House in the matters concerning religion, "I can tell you, sirs, what I would not have, though I cannot what I would."

54. ARCHBISHOP LAUD

Laud (see Nos. 36, *b*) and 52, *b*)) was in effect Prime Minister during the personal government of Charles I. His diary, which was seized by the Parliamentarians on his arrest in March, 1641, reveals him as a superstitious and rather silly old man; but also, as in *a*), shows him conducting a campaign to obtain control of the government for churchmen and near-Papists (Windebanke). There were grounds for the accusation in *b*) that he tried to use the institutions of the Church as part of a system of extra-parliamentary government. Laud was executed in 1645. Since the revolution, no churchman has held such high political office.

a) Laud, Diary, in *History of Troubles and Trial* (1695), pp. 47–53; *b*) *ibid.*, pp. 151–4.

a) EXTRACTS FROM LAUD'S DIARY

June 15th, 1632. Mr. Francis Windebanke my old friend was sworn secretary of state, which place I obtained for him of my gracious master King Charles. . . .

July 10th, 1632. Dr. Juxon, then Dean of Worcester, at my suit sworn clerk of his Majesty's closet. That I might have one that I might trust near his Majesty, if I grow weak or infirm. . . .

February 5th, 1635. I was put into the great Committee of Trade and the King's Revenue, etc. . . .

March 14th, 1635. I was named one of the Commissioners for the Exchequer. . . .

March 16th, 1635. I was called against the next day into the Foreign Committee. . . .

March 6th, 1636. William Juxon, Lord Bishop of London, made Lord High Treasurer of England. No church-man had it since Henry VII's time. . . . And now if the church will not hold up themselves under God, I can do no more.

b) ARTICLES OF IMPEACHMENT AGAINST LAUD, 1641

He hath for the better accomplishment of his traitorous design advised and procured divers sermons and other discourses to be preached, printed and published, in which the authority of Parliaments and the force of the laws of this kingdom are denied, and an absolute and unlimited power over the persons and estates of his Majesty's subjects is maintained and defended, not only in the King, but also in himself and other bishops, above and against the law. . . .

He hath traitorously caused a Book of Canons to be composed and published . . . without any lawful warrant and authority . . . in which pretended Canons many matters are contained contrary to the King's prerogative, to the fundamental laws and statutes of this realm, to the right of Parliament, to the property and liberty of the subjects, and matters tending to sedition. . . .

55. WHAT CAVALIERS OBJECTED TO IN THE PURITANS

Andrew Melville (*a*) was a Scots Presbyterian minister and James's tutor as a boy. He is otherwise famous for addressing the King as "God's silly vassal." James's reaction when he became King of England was natural but disastrous. The Hampton Court Conference (*b*) and *c*)) was intended to reconcile Puritans with the Church, but it ended with renewed persecution. Hobbes's analysis (*g*) goes deeper. Since the fifteenth century, if not earlier, ordinary people had struggled and suffered to be able to read the word of God in their own language. This right had been won at the Reformation, with the democratic effects which Hobbes notes. The 1611 version of the Bible was "Authorised" by the government in opposition to other more socially radical versions which were circulating. With all these extracts compare Nos. 52, 57 and 75. With *b*), cf. No. 136, *a*).

a) T. McCrie, *Life of Andrew Melville* (1819), II, pp. 66–7; *b*) W. Barlow, *Sum and Substance of the Conference* (1604), pp. 79–83; *c*) Goodman, *Court of King James I*, I, p. 421; *d*) Wildman, "Putney Projects" (1647) (Woodhouse, *Puritanism and Liberty* (1938), pp. 426–7); *e*) Burnet, *History of My Own Time*, I, p. 195; *f*) *Petty Papers* (ed. Landsdowne), II, p. 227; *g*) Hobbes, *English Works*, VI, pp. 190–1.

a) MELVILLE TO JAMES VI OF SCOTLAND, 1596

THERE are two kings and two kingdoms in Scotland. There is Christ Jesus the King of the Church, whose subject King James VI is, and of whose kingdom he is not a King, nor a lord, nor a head, but a member. Those whom Christ hath called and commanded to watch over his Church and govern his spiritual kingdom have sufficient power and authority from him to do this, both jointly and severally.

b) JAMES AGAINST DEMOCRACY, 1604

[A Scottish presbytery] as well agreeth with a monarchy as God and the devil. Then Jack and Tom and Will and Dick shall meet, and at their pleasures censure me and my council and all our proceedings. Then Will shall stand up and say "It must be thus"; then Dick shall reply and say "Nay, marry, but we will have it thus." . . . My lords the Bishops, . . . if once you were out, and they [the Presbyterians] in place, I know what would become of my supremacy. No bishop, no king. . . . If this be all . . . that they have to say, I shall make them conform themselves, or I will harry them out of the land, or else do worse.

c) A BISHOP'S GLOSS, AFTER 1642

King James upon the conference at Hampton Court did absolutely conclude, "No bishops, no king, no nobility"; which, as you see, hath lately fallen out according to his prediction. It is the church which supports the state, it is religion which strengthens the government; shake the one, and you overthrow the other. Nothing is so deeply rooted in the hearts of men as religion, nothing so powerful to direct their actions: and if once the hearts of the people be doubtful in religion, all other relations fail, and you shall find nothing but mutinies and sedition. Thus the church and the state do mutually support and give assistance to each other; and if one of them change, the other can have no sure foundation.

d) A LEVELLER

If there should be none to preach up the King's interest, and by flattering, seducing words to beguile the people and foster high imaginations and superstitious conceits of the King in their hearts under the rude and general notion of authority, his lordliness and tyranny would be soon distasted.

e) CHARLES II

Presbyterianism is not a religion for gentlemen.

f) ECONOMICS OF RELIGIOUS DIFFERENCES

The lands belonging to bishops, deans and chapters, as also to universities and colleges, together with the value of appropriated tithes, are not worth £1 million *per annum*, but are [the] motive that makes differences in religion.

g) REVOLUTIONARY EFFECTS OF READING THE BIBLE

After the Bible was translated into English every man, nay every boy and wench that could read English, thought they spoke with God Almighty, and understood what he said, when by a certain number of chapters a day they had read the Scriptures once or twice over. The reverence and obedience due to the reformed church here, and to the bishops and pastors therein, was cast off, and every man became a judge of religion and an interpreter of the Scriptures to himself. . . . This licence of interpreting the Scripture was the cause of so many several sects as have lain hid till the beginning of the late King's [Charles I's] reign, and did then appear to the disturbance of the commonwealth.

56. WHAT WAS A PURITAN?

The word "Puritan" was loosely applied to political opponents in the seventeenth century, like the word "Red" to-day. It was not necessarily restricted to critics of the government's *religious* policy. The Royalist Hostmen of Newcastle used to dub "Puritans" those London merchants who opposed their monopoly of the export of coal. Mrs. Hutchinson (*a*) was the wife of one of the leading republicans; she wrote after the Restoration, when her husband was imprisoned.

a) Lucy Hutchinson, *Memoirs of the Life of Colonel Hutchinson*, ed. Firth (1885), I, pp. 113–15; *b*) May, I, p. 74; *c*) Selden, *Table Talk*, p. 74; *d*) *The Interpreter*, 1622, quoted in J. W. Allen, *English Political Thought, 1603–44* (1938), p. 261; *e*) Burton, IV, p. 77 (March 8th, 1659).

a) MRS. HUTCHINSON

The payment of civil obedience to the king and the laws of the land satisfied not: . . . if any were grieved at the dishonour of the kingdom, or the griping of the poor, or the unjust oppressions of the subject by a thousand ways invented to maintain the riots of the courtiers and the swarms of needy Scots the king had brought in to devour like locusts the plenty of this land, he was a puritan; if any, out of mere morality and civil honesty, discountenanced the abominations of those days, he was a puritan, however he conformed to their superstitious worship; if any showed favour to any godly, honest person, kept them company, relieved them in want, or protected them against violent and unjust oppression, he was a puritan; if any gentleman in his county maintained the good laws of the land, or stood up for any public interest, for good order or government, he was a puritan. In short, all that crossed the views of the needy courtiers, the proud encroaching priests, the thievish projectors, the lewd nobility and gentry . . . all these were puritans; and if puritans, then enemies to the king and his government, seditious, factious hypocrites, ambitious disturbers of the public peace, and finally the pest of the kingdom.

b) SIR B. RUDYERD, SPEECH IN PARLIAMENT, 1640

Whosoever squares his actions by any rule, either divine or human, he is a puritan. Whosoever would be governed by the king's laws, he is a puritan. He that will not do whatsoever other men would have him do, he is a puritan. Their great work, their masterpiece now is to make all those of the religion to be the suspected party of the kingdom.

c) SELDEN

The Puritans, who will allow no free will at all, but God does all, yet will allow the subject his liberty to do or not to do, notwithstanding the King, the God upon earth. The Arminians, who hold we have free will, yet say when we come to the King, there must be all obedience, and no liberty to be stood for.

d) His character abridged if you would have,
He's one that would a subject be, no slave.

e) NO LEVELLER

Sir Arthur Haselrig: I was bred a Puritan, and am for public liberty. . . . I am no leveller. If troubles should come, I should lose as much as another man. . . . I am against anarchy and tyranny, anyway propounded.

57. WHAT THE CAVALIERS FEARED

As the Church had become an organ of government, the Royalists could plausibly argue that democratic control of the one would lead to democratic control of the other. Archbishop Laud, in a sermon preached before Parliament (*a*), and the poet Edmund Waller, speaking in the House of Commons (*b*), continue James I's arguments in 55, *b*). The Royalist ideal is expressed in *c*) and *d*)—a docile, spoon-fed population, church services a spectacle (as in the Latin service of the Mass) rather than a stimulus to thought, as the Protestant reformers had tried to make them. John Earle (*c*) was chaplain to the Lord Chamberlain (the Earl of Pembroke) and resided at Court; later he became chaplain to the future Charles II. For *Eikon Basilike* (extract *e*)), fraudulently attributed to Charles I, see note to No. 111. Extract *f*) was written in 1682 by Sir William Petty (see No. 197), but it helps to illuminate the fears behind the attitude expressed in *c*) and *d*): how were ideas to be standardised unless the Church was a single mass-production propaganda agency tightly controlled by the government? Before 1640 the monopoly of the Laudians was broken through only in towns where the corporation subsidised a Puritan lecturer to preach *their* type of theology (*g*) and *h*); cf. Nos. 58, *b*) and *c*), and 81) or in those country parishes where the patron supported the Parliamentary opposition. Thus in 1625 the Parliamentary leader Sir John Eliot wrote to his bishop asking for the appointment of a named parson to a parish on his estate, promising that the man's stipend would be augmented by contributions from himself and other inhabitants if they got "a man of their affection and choice" (Forster, *Sir John Eliot*, I, p. 463).

a) Prothero, p. 435; *b*) *Old Parliamentary History* (1763), IX, pp. 388–9; *c*) Earle, *Microcosmography* (1628), Character No. XXII; *d*) Newcastle, p. 124; *e*) *Eikon Basilike* (1876), pp. 122–5; *f*) Sir W. Petty, "Essay of the growth of the City of London," *Economic Writings*, II, pp. 472–3; *g*) Dugdale, p. 36; *h*) *Supplement to Burnet, History of My Own Time*, ed. Foxcroft, pp. 69–71.

a) LAUD AGAINST EQUALITY, 1626

A PARITY they would have, no bishop, no governor, but a parochial consistory, and that should be lay enough too. . . . They, whoever they be, that would overthrow . . . the seats of ecclesiastical government, will not spare (if ever they get power) to have a pluck at the throne of David. And there is not a man that is for parity, all fellows in the church, but he is not for monarchy in the state.

b) ONE THING LEADS TO ANOTHER, 1641

I see some are moved with a number of hands [to the petition] against the Bishops, which, I confess, rather inclines me to their defence, for I look upon Episcopacy, as a counter-scarp, or outwork, which if it be taken by this assault of the people, and withal this mystery once revealed, that we must deny them nothing when they ask it thus in troops, we may in the next place have as hard a task to defend our property, as we have lately had to recover it from the prerogative. If by multiplying hands, and petitions, they prevail for an equality in things ecclesiastical, their next demand perhaps may be . . . the like equality in things temporal.

c) RELIGION TAKEN FROM THE LANDLORD

A plain country fellow's . . . religion is a part of his copyhold, which he takes from his landlord, and refers it wholly to his discretion; yet if he give him leave he is a good Christian to his power, that is comes to church in his best clothes and sits there with his neighbours, where he is capable only of two prayers, for rain and fair weather.

d) THE DUKE OF NEWCASTLE

There should be more praying and less preaching; for much preaching breeds faction, but much praying causes devotion.

e) VIEWS ATTRIBUTED TO CHARLES I

I must now in charity be thought desirous to preserve that government [of the Church] . . . as a matter of religion. . . . It hath . . . the constant practice of all Christian churches; till of late years, the tumultuariness of the people, or the factiousness and pride of presbyters, or the covetousness of some states and princes, gave occasion to some men's wits to invent new models. . . .

And not only in religion . . . but also in right reason, and the true nature of government . . . where parity breeds confusion and faction.

f) DANGERS OF THINKING FOR ONESELF

As to uniformity in religion, I conceive that if St. Martin's parish may (as it doth) consist of about 40,000 souls, that this great city also may as well be made but as one parish, with seven times 130 chapels, in which might not only be an uniformity of common prayer, but in preaching also; for that a thousand copies of one judiciously and authentically composed sermon might be every week read in each of the said chapels without any subsequent repetition of the same, as in the case of homilies. Whereas in England (wherein are near 10,000 parishes, in each of which upon Sundays, holy days and other extraordinary occasions there should be about 100 sermons per annum, making about a million of sermons per annum in the whole) it were a miracle, if a million of sermons composed by so many men, and of so many minds and methods, should produce uniformity upon the discomposed understandings of about 8,000,000 of hearers.

g) LECTURERS PREPARING FOR REVOLUTION?

Under a seeming devout and holy pretence, to advance and promote the preaching of the gospel, they got in a number of lecturers into most of the corporate towns and populous places of this realm (according to the pattern of Geneva), especially into the City of London, whom they maintained by voluntary contributions, to the end that they might be engaged to preach such doctrine as should (upon occasion) prepare the people for any disloyal attempt, and dispose them to rebellion when opportunity served.

h) A BISHOP'S REFLECTIONS AFTER THE RESTORATION

[Bishop Sheldon thought] that nothing had ruined the church in the late times so much as the lecturers and other churchmen that were only so far conformable that the law could not reach them, and were by little indirect ways still alienating the people from the church and making divisions everywhere. . . . Nothing had spoiled the late king's affairs so much as the credit that the factious lecturers had in all corporations, for this had so great an influence on their elections that he ascribed all the war to that half-conformity, and therefore he said it was necessary in order to the having a good parliament that all the clergy should be hearty conformists; and no wonder if this satisfied the king [Charles II], for it was very plausible.

58. PROTESTANTISM AND THE BOURGEOISIE

That Protestantism was the ideology of the rising bourgeoisie has become almost a truism since it was popularised by Professor Tawney in his *Religion and the Rise of Capitalism.* Contemporaries were aware of the connection. Ambrose Barnes (1627–1710) (*a*) was a Nonconformist merchant of Newcastle; Sir Philip Warwick (*b*) was a Royalist gentleman. For Puritan lecturers (*b*) and *c*)), see note to No. 57.

a) *Memoirs of Ambrose Barnes* (Surtees Soc., 1867), p. 47; *b*) Warwick, *Memoirs*, pp. 1–2, 60; *c*) Laud, *History of Troubles and Trial*, pp. 527–8, 538.

a) PROTESTANTISM, COMMERCE AND INDUSTRY

Popish religion creates an unaptness for trade. Whereas among the reformed, who purposely discourage idleness, the greater their zeal is, the greater is their disposition to industry and business. . . . No city in Spain or Italy can boast of any great trade driven by the natives, the greatest part of their commerce being carried on by protestant strangers, Amsterdam alone having more trade than all the sea-towns of Italy and Spain put together. But in Germany even in those cities, as at Cologne, where they are papists, without toleration to any other, the reformed may be said to carry all the trade. (In other towns where they are Lutherans, with a public toleration to papists which is denied to Calvinists, there the reformed carry the trade clearly, both from Lutherans and papists. . . .) This made the reformed flourish in France, both in number and wealth, where by reason of the industry of their traders there were no beggars found among them, though they were computed to exceed three or four millions of souls; whereas the multitude of popish beggars was such that in the compass of 2½ English miles from Rouen to the English church it would cost a louis d'or, or 17*s.* English to give every beggar no more than a double, which is scarce the sixth part of a penny.

b) PURITANS AND CORPORATIONS

Wherever the prince is not jealous of underminers, and active to maintain the established government, there will never want spirits given to change who will attempt it, and make religion their shelter for rebellion. And thus even vigilant Queen Elizabeth was troubled with her gospellers, upon pretence of a more refined purity. These men soon drew over to themselves, or party, many of the wealthy and trading citizens, generally in the corporations, and from thence crept into the neighbouring counties, and infected many of the yeomanry and gentry: and not long after broached principles which served to lessen sovereign and civil authority, and a pulse was raised towards an aristocratical government under a kingly title . . . or unto the sharing of the sovereignty between the king and the two houses of parliament (which, as this constitution of government is, is impossible).

c) LAUD'S ANNUAL ACCOUNTS

1633—Lincoln. The Company of Mercers in London . . . set up a lecturer in Huntingdon, with the allowance of £40 per annum, to preach every Saturday morning (being market day) and Sunday in the afternoon; with a proviso in his grant from them that, upon any dislike they may have of him, he shall at a month's or a fortnight's warning give over the place, without any relation to Bishop or Archbishop. My most humble suit to your Majesty is that no layman whatsoever, and least of all companies or corporations, may . . . have power to put in or out any lecturer . . . [King Charles's comment]: Certainly I cannot hold fit that any lay person or corporation whatsoever should have the power these men would take to themselves. For I will have no priest have any necessity of a lay dependency.

1635—Gloucester. My Lord the Bishop informs that the county is very full of impropriations, which makes the ministers poor; and their poverty makes them fall upon popular and factious courses. I doubt this is too true, but it is a mischief hard to cure in this kingdom.

59. THE ROMAN CATHOLIC THREAT

The Spanish Ambassador (*a*) was as interested as James I in the abolition of Parliament: a month earlier he had demanded that it be punished for its "insolence". His equation of the interest of Roman Catholicism and Spain is another pointer to show that more than religion was at stake in these quarrels. For the unity and leadership which Gondomar thought "this wretched people" of England lacked, see No. 105. The analysis of the position of Laud in *b*) is interesting; the Venetian Ambassador was right in saying that he was anti-Puritan rather than pro-Catholic, though the distinction became at times slight (see No. 64). The Laudian or Arminian party was thought, not without reason, to be opening the door to the Papists (*c*). The latter were regarded as a potential Fifth Column: in fact they all supported Charles I in the Civil War. So the non-enforcement of the statutes against them was a political as well as a religious grievance (*d*).

a) Gardiner, *History of England, 1603–42*, IV, p. 266; *b*) *C.S.P.Ven.*, 1636–9, pp. 69, 150–1, 393; *c*) Rushworth, I, pp. 657–8; *d*) *Fairfax Correspondence* (1848–9), II, pp. 282–7.

a) GONDOMAR'S REFLECTIONS ON THE DISSOLUTION OF 1621

It is certain that the King will never summon another Parliament as long as he lives, or at least not another composed as this one was. It is the best thing that has happened in the interests of Spain and the Catholic religion since Luther. . . . The King will no longer be able to succour his son-in-law [the Elector Palatine] or to hinder the advance of the Catholics. It is true that this wretched people are desperately offended against him, but they are without union among themselves, and have neither leaders nor strong places to lean upon. Besides, they are rich and live comfortably in their houses; so that it is not likely that there will be any disturbance.

b) THE ROMAN CATHOLIC DANGER—AND LAUD

September 18th, 1636. [The Pope] entertains the idea of rendering his name glorious to posterity by a work at once great, charitable and pious, in fine to bring the King [Charles I] himself over to the Roman faith. The foundations of this machinery have been laid very wide, and signs of progress become constantly more apparent. No nation is made more of at Rome just now than the English. . . . Here [in England] . . . the priests have never had so much liberty. . . . This is all due to the connivance of the ruler, and indicates, if not a leaning to the rites of the Roman church, at least an absence of aversion. . . .

February 20th, 1637. The Court of Rome . . . [builds], above all, on the King's connivance . . .; and on the other hand they believe in the success of their designs owing to what they understand of the friendly disposition towards the catholic faith of the Archbishop of Canterbury [Laud], who now governs everything. But although they may possibly rely confidently on the royal connivance, yet they ought not to be so sure of the archbishop, because his aim is to destroy the party of the Puritans, and not to increase the number of Catholics, so it is clear that if he succeeds in humbling the one he will subsequently be the most bitter enemy of the other, in his own interests. . . .

April 2nd, 1638. The archbishop [is] generally odious, to such an extent that one hears people regretting that while there was someone [Felton] venturesome enough to take the life of the Duke of Buckingham, with less cause, there is no one now to do it against this even worse minister, who is leading towards the total subversion of these realms.

c) MR. ROUS, SPEECH IN THE COMMONS, JANUARY 24TH, 1629

An Arminian is the spawn of a Papist . . . and if you mark it well you shall see an Arminian reaching out his hand to a Papist, a Papist to a Jesuit, a Jesuit gives one hand to the Pope and another to the King of Spain; and these men having kindled a fire in our neighbour country [France], now they have brought over some of it hither, to set on flame this kingdom also. Yea, let us further search and consider whether these be not the men that break in upon the goods and liberties of this Commonwealth, for by this means they make way for the taking away of our religion; it was an old trick of the Devil, when he meant to take away Job's religion he began at his goods. . . . Either they think thereby to set a distaste between prince and people, or else to find some other [than parliamentary] way of supply, to avoid or break parliaments. . . . But let us do as Job did, who being constant against temptation held fast his religion, and his goods were restored to him with advantage.

d) STOCKDALE TO LORD FAIRFAX, NOVEMBER 11TH, 1641

The conditions which by the statutes are given to the recusant party have neither wrought that good effect upon them in point of reformation as was expected, nor (as they are used) do they in any way conduce to the securing of the kingdom against their machinations and attempts to introduce alteration in the church and political government; and therefore I think it worthy of consideration how the parliament may settle some new course to be held by that party. . . .

It appears that giving the two-third parts of each recusant's estate to the King doth not much enrich the crown, and yet it unites the recusant party in too strict bonds of dependency upon the sovereignty, and so co-operates with it to advance the regal power beyond the right bounds in proportion with the subjects' legal liberties. . . .

Where any person of that profession is conceived to be of dangerous intelligence, or able to contrive or act a mischief, his person should be restrained; for although I think they of themselves are not able to do much hurt, yet I fear there are other humours in the body politic of this state that are made fluid and will move with them when there shall be opportunity.

60. THREAT TO THE REFORMATION IN SCOTLAND

In Scotland as in England, the Reformation brought the lands of the monasteries into the hands of lay owners, gentlemen and noblemen. Henceforth this class had a vested interest in Protestantism: Sir Richard Grenville expressed it neatly when he hoped that his heirs might in religious matters be of the same mind as himself for their profit. Queen Mary (1553–8) could restore the supremacy of the Pope in England, but not the monastic lands; when James II announced toleration for Catholics in 1687, he was careful to say that this would not affect monastic property; nevertheless, he was driven off the throne a year later. The situation looked black for Protestant landowners in the sixteen-twenties. Not only were parliamentary institutions falling all over Europe (see No. 43), but the Counter-Reformation was making a great onslaught on Protestantism. In 1628, Richelieu, Minister of the French absolute monarchy, subdued the Protestant stronghold of La Rochelle; in 1629 the Emperor Ferdinand II, would-be absolute monarch of Germany, ordered the restitution of all Church lands secularised in the two preceding generations. So when Charles I began to try to resume Church lands in Scotland it looked like part of an international plot, with the King on the Catholic-absolutist side; this did much to harden opposition both in Scotland and in England.

Burnet, *History of My Own Time*, I, pp. 29–40.

[In] Scotland . . . the king [Charles I] resolved to carry on the two designs that his father had set on foot, but had let the prosecution of them fall in the last years of his reign. The first of these was about the recovery of the tithes and church lands. He resolved to prosecute his father's revocation and to void all the grants made in his minority. . . . And that the two great families of Hamilton and Lennox might be good examples to the rest of the nation he, by a secret purchase and with English money, bought the abbey of Aberbroth of the former and the lordship of Glasgow of the latter, and gave them to the two archbishoprics. These lords made a show of zeal after a good bargain, and surrendered them to the king. . . . All men who pretended to favour at court offered their church lands to sale at low rates.

In the third year of his reign [1626, actually] the earl of Nithisdale, then believed a papist, which he afterwards professed . . . was sent down with a power to take the surrenders of all church lands, and to assure all who did readily surrender that the king would take it kindly and use them all very well, but that he would proceed with all rigour against those who would not submit their rights to his disposal. . . . So much heat was raised upon it that the earl of Nithisdale . . . came back to court, looking on the service as desperate. So a stop was put to it for some time.

In the year 1633 . . . the king . . . resolved to prosecute the design of recovering the church lands; and Sir Thomas Hope, a subtle lawyer, who was believed to understand that matter beyond all the men of his profession, though in all respects he was a zealous puritan, was made king's advocate, upon his undertaking to bring all the church lands back to the crown: yet he proceeded in that matter so slowly that it was believed he acted in concert with the party that opposed it. Enough was already done to alarm all that were possessed of the church lands: and they, to engage the whole country in their quarrel, took care to infuse it into all people, but chiefly into the preachers, that all was done to make way for popery. . . .

The most unaccountable part of the king's proceedings was that all this while, when he was endeavouring to recover so great a part of the property of Scotland as the church lands and tithes were, from men that were not like to part with them willingly, and was going to change the whole constitution of that church and kingdom, he raised no force to maintain what he was about to do, but trusted the whole management to the civil execution. By this means all people saw the weakness of the government at the same time that they complained of its rigour.

61. THREAT TO THE REFORMATION IN IRELAND

Wentworth became Lord Deputy of Ireland in 1632, and there applied Charles I's policy of resuming secularised church lands (see No. 60). The fact that men like the Earl of Cork had committed grave abuses, and that the Anglican Church in Ireland (the Church imposed by a minority of alien conquerors) was exceedingly corrupt, did not affect the alarm felt by Protestants and owners of Church lands in England. Wentworth's policy in Ireland led straight to his execution in 1641 (see No. 71). Richard Boyle, first Earl of Cork (1566–1643), was the younger son of a country gentleman who arrived in Ireland in 1588 with £27 3*s*. 0*d*. in his pocket, and made his fortune there by iron and copper mining and by moneylending. He was naturally a staunch Puritan: "Had there been an Earl of Cork in every province of Ireland there would have been no rebellion" against English rule, Oliver Cromwell thought. But the Earl did well enough socially for his children to be Royalists in the Civil War. Quoted in Lady Burghclere's *Strafford* (1931), I, pp. 305–6, 249, II, p. 87.

Wentworth to Laud: I did the other day make the Earl of Cork disgorge himself of two vicarages that his tenant and he had held from the poor incumbent these thirty years. . . . And was not this Thorough? I am most confident this day will gain 100 livings to the church, thus sacrilegiously taken from it by fine, force and rapine. For now the poor men, hearing of this, will do that which they durst not before, complain. . . . His lordship may say I am a damnable papist indeed thus to restore the possessions of the church. . . . Thus have I fixed the first link of that chain which, I assure myself, will draw back after it 100 livings with cure of souls into the bosom of the church; besides some thousands of acres for their glebes. I have some thirty in view already. . . .

[I did] never see or could possibly have believed to have

found men with so much alacrity divesting themselves of all property in their estates, and with great quietness and singleness of mind waiting what his Majesty may, in his gracious good pleasure and time, determine and measure out for them. . . . I . . . find myself extremely taken with the manner of their proceeding.

62. THE NEW PHILOSOPHY

Not all enemies of the old order were Puritans. The philosophy introduced to England by Bacon, with its emphasis on experiment and reason rather than authority, its optimistic belief in the possibilities of the human intellect, also reflects bourgeois modes of thought, the science which was to revolutionise production in the next three centuries. Donne, Dean of St. Paul's, is at once intellectually attracted by the new science and horrified by its dissolvent effect on the values he was paid to preach (*a*). Eliot, a prisoner in the Tower, has more confidence in humanity (*b*); cf. Nos. 117, 124 and 155).

a) J. Donne, *Complete Poetry and Selected Prose* (Nonesuch Edition), p. 202; *b*) Sir John Eliot, *The Monarchy of Man*, II, pp. 224–7.

a) AN ANATOMY OF THE WORLD (1611)

[The] new philosophy calls all in doubt;
The element of fire is quite put out;
The sun is lost, and th' earth, and no man's wit
Can well direct him where to look for it.
And freely men confess that this world's spent
When in the planets and the firmament
They seek so many new; then see that this
Is crumbled out again to his atomies.
'Tis all in pieces, all coherence gone;
All just supply, and all relation:
Prince, subject, father, son, are things forgot,
For every man alone thinks he hath got
To be a Phœnix, and that then can be
None of that kind of which he is, but he.

b) REFLECTIONS IN PRISON

All things are subject to the Mind, which . . . is the commander of them all. No resistance is against it. It breaks through the orbs and immense circles of the heavens, and penetrates even to the centre of the earth. It opens the fountains of antiquity, and runs down the stream of time, below the period of all seasons. It dives into the dark counsels of eternity, and the abstruse secrets of nature it unlocks. All places, all occasions are alike obvious to this. This does observe those subtle passages in the air, and the unknown paths and traces in the deeps. . . . It measures in one thought the whole circumference of heaven, and by the same line it takes the geography of the earth. The seas, the air, the fire, all things of either, are within the comprehension of the mind. It has an influence on them all, whence it takes all that may be useful, all that may be helpful in its government. No limitation is prescribed it, no restriction is upon it, but in a free scope it has liberty upon all. And in this liberty is the excellence of the mind; in this power and composition of the mind is the perfection of a man; in that perfection is the happiness we look for—when in all sovereignty it reigns, commanding not commanded. . . .

Man . . . is an absolute master of himself; his own safety and tranquillity by God . . . are made dependent on himself. And in that self-dependence, in the neglect of others, in the entire rule and dominion of himself, the affections being composed, the actions so divided, is the perfection of our government, that *summum bonum* in philosophy, the *bonum publicum* in our policy, the true end and object of this Monarchy of Man.

Part Five

THE INTERNATIONAL SITUATION

So you are of the opinion that subjects can dispossess their Kings? You are come in good time to England, to spread these principles among the people, that my subjects may drive me away, and place another in my room.

James I to the Ambassador from the Elector Palatine.

63. AN AMBASSADOR'S OBSERVATIONS

When James I became King (1603) he immediately ended the war with Spain which had continued since the time of the Armada. He disliked giving encouragement to the Dutch rebels who had thrown off Spanish rule (No. 67, *a*)). He desired an alliance with the Catholic King of Spain which might be a support in his conflict with Parliament. However, the position was complicated both for those who supported James in his Spanish policy and for those who desired to continue the Elizabethan policy of alliance with the Dutch. The results of appeasing Spain are shown in *b*). But the pro-Dutch party could not overlook the fact that the Dutch were already important trade rivals—a fact which the Spanish Ambassador tried to turn to his advantage (see also No. 68). No. 65 shows why the German Protestant princes sought the support of James I. Extracts are from the reports of the Venetian Ambassadors in London. For the Palatinate (*b*), see note to No. 64.

a) *C.S.P.Ven.*, 1603–7, pp. 518–22; *b*) *ibid.*, 1621–3, pp. 442–3.

a) IN 1607

THE common opinion is that this peace cannot last long; this view is founded on the fact that the English, moved by hatred of Spain and their own interests, desire war, for the peace has stopped them from privateering by which they grew rich, and under the pretext of attacking enemies they plundered friends, as is only too well known to your Serenity. Moreover the terms of the peace are frequently violated; for example, by the permission to take service with the Dutch, by the assistance rendered to them, which is in direct defiance of the clauses, and by the navigation of the Indies, another manifest infraction. On the other hand the Spanish adopt a certain harshness towards the English who trade to their ports, all of which, however, is greatly exaggerated and amplified in the reports by the English officials, partly because the English are by nature proud and vainglorious and expect that everyone should not only court but, as it were, worship them, partly from the desire which, as I have explained, they feel that the two crowns should go to war once more, as it is so profitable. Anyway my opinion is that during the life of the present King, who is so desirous and anxious for peace, things will remain quiet, unless indeed the rupture come on the Spanish side, which is unlikely as long as the Dutch war lasts, for the Spanish know by experience what the union of the Dutch and the English crown means for them. . . .

With the heretic princes of Germany relations are not cordial. More than one of them has proposed to his Majesty to declare himself head of the reformed religion as they call it, and to pledge himself to an alliance offensive and defensive. But the King, who dislikes change and loves peace, has let the matter drop. . . .

The King is very well disposed towards the Dutch, but not so well disposed as they would like, and as public opinion, perhaps, desires. They would have liked the King to undertake their protection openly, as did the late Queen, from whom they received support in money and all else. But since the King has made peace with the Spanish and the Archdukes he seems to have grown cold towards the Dutch; and I am well assured that there is nothing else that moves the King to a certain regard for them but religion. If that reason were removed he would certainly abandon them, for he has frequently expressed the opinion that it is impossible to wish well to rebels, and that all princes ought to hold this view in order to prevent their subjects from revolting. On this topic he expatiates when speaking of the Dutch. All the same, be it on account of religion, be it on the score of interest, his Majesty desires their preservation. . . . While the Dutch have in their service as many English and Scottish as they wish, the Spaniards find great difficulty in raising any; for though the King consents in appearance he privately causes it to be known that his subjects should abstain and that he will never hold for good and faithful friends those who take service with princes of another creed. . . . All this is well known to the Spanish, who, seeing that they cannot succeed on these lines, have taken to another course of action, namely to persuade his Majesty to interpose and to induce the Dutch to make peace with Spain. . . . The King has been at great pains in this business. . . . The Spanish urge the King to press the matter home in his own interests, for if peace is not made the Dutch will become masters of these seas, as they keep, as a rule, upwards of a hundred armed ships in commission, and although these are scattered about in various places, yet one may say with truth that they are masters of those very seas for supremacy in which the ancient Kings of England undertook long and costly wars with the most powerful Sovereigns of Europe. The King knows this, but he thinks that upon a sign from him the Dutch would surrender all they have acquired. This is true as long as they are at war with Spain, for it is not to be supposed that they could carry on war simultaneously against two of the most mighty Princes in Christendom; but if, in the course of time, which ripens all things, they were to make peace with the Crown of Spain, I am not sure that they would be so ready to yield, as the King of England promises himself; for the profession of the sea declines steadily in England, while it steadily acquires force and vigour among the Dutch. . . .

The Spanish have tried another device, which certainly would be very prejudicial to the Dutch if it succeeded; they have told the King that it is not to the interest of himself or of his subjects to allow the herring fishery in the northern waters about Scotland to be open to the Dutch. That fishery yields upwards of two millions of gold annually, though many say more, as the herrings are taken all over Europe.

b) LOSS OF NATIONAL INDEPENDENCE, 1622

The [Spanish] ambassador has reduced his Majesty [James I], out of simple suspicion, by making him consider as Puritans those who do not depend upon him, or even without this merely to do him pleasure, to deprive various persons of their charges and of his favour, although he really loved them, and to leave his presence, a severe punishment for innocence and honour. This happened to the Secretary Naunton, a minister of singular integrity ... the ambassador going so far against him as to threaten the king openly that otherwise there would be no marriage or restitution of the Palatinate. Upon this ruin he built his own designs, and in place of the fallen raised persons not so rigorous against the Catholics, indifferent though about the church, but very jealous for his party. Thus the principal charges of the government, council, army, treasury, admiralty, ports, in fact everything have fallen into the hands of his dependants, who have rendered him great services even against the royal intentions. . . .

It would be better . . . if matters were not guided by those who think more of their passions, private interests, and pleasing the Spaniards than of his Majesty. . . . His people have been smitten to the heart about their religion, being troubled . . . by the peril of their nation. . . . Yet though they were touched on the raw in so many ways, apparently they have not dared to do anything worse than speak, and the futility of it all even bridled that. But it is clear that if one hears of no disturbances, this is not because they lack the will, as they would flare up like straw the moment the slightest fire was applied.

64. APPEASING INTERNATIONAL REACTION

In 1618 the Thirty Years' War began with a Bohemian revolt against the Emperor. The Bohemian crown was given by the revolutionaries to James I's son-in-law, Frederick, the Protestant Elector Palatine. But at the Battle of White Mountain (1620) Frederick lost both his electorate and his new kingdom. Extract *a*) shows James I's hostility to anyone who took part in a revolution, even against a Catholic. James was ready to try to regain for Frederick his electorate, but only by obtaining the support of the Habsburg King of Spain, who might then influence the Habsburg Emperor to return the electorate. But the King of Spain would not use his influence. This helped to upset the projected marriage between Prince Charles and the Infanta of Spain. Extract *b*) is from a letter by Charles and Buckingham to James I during their visit to Madrid in 1623 to negotiate the marriage. It illustrates both the concessions they were prepared to make to English Catholics in order to win Spanish support and the peculiar relationship of Buckingham to Charles and the King. Not mentioned here is that under the agreement children of the marriage were to be brought up as Catholics. Extract *d*) illustrates the general opinion among Englishmen that Spain could be beaten in war by cutting her off from the Indies—the source of her treasure.

a) Howell, *Familiar Letters* (Temple Classics), I, p. 105; *b*) *Letters of Charles I*, pp. 20–1; *c*) Howell, *op. cit.*, p. 168; *d*) F. Bacon, *Considerations touching a War with Spain* (1624), *Works* (ed. Spedding), XIV, pp. 499–500.

a) THE TRADE UNION OF KINGS, 1619

WHEREAS Doctor Hall gave the Prince Palsgrave the title of King of Bohemia in his pulpit prayer, he had a check for his pains, for I heard His Majesty should say that there is an implicit tie amongst kings which obligeth them, though there be no other interest or particular engagement, to stick unto and right one another upon insurrection of subjects. Therefore he had more reason to be against the Bohemians than to adhere to them in the deposition of their sovereign prince. The King of Denmark sings the same note. . . .

b) THE SPANISH MARRIAGE

DEAR DAD AND GOSSIP, . . . We make no doubt but . . . Your Majesty will be pleased to begin to put in execution the favour towards your Roman Catholic subjects that you will be bound to do by your oath as soon as the Infanta comes over. . . . We send you here the articles, . . . the oaths private and public that you and your baby are to take with the Councils; wherein if you scare at the last clause of your private oath (where you promise that the Parliament shall revoke all the penal laws against the Papists within three years) we thought good to tell Your Majesty our opinions, which is that if you think you may do it in that time (which we think you may) if you do your best, although it take not effect, you have not broken your word, for this promise is only as a security that you will do your best. . . . We both humbly beg of

Your Majesty that you will confirm these articles soon, and press earnestly for our speedy return. So, craving your blessings, we rest,

Your Majesty's humble and obedient son and servant,

CHARLES.

Your Majesty's humble slave and dog,

STEENIE.

c) CLASS ATTITUDES TO THE SPANISH MARRIAGE

The English nation is better looked on now in Spain than ordinary, because of the hopes there are of a match, which the merchants and commonalty much desire, though the nobility and gentry be not so forward for it. So that in this point the pulse of Spain beats quite contrary to that of England, where the people are averse to this match, and the nobility with most part of the gentry inclinable.

d) SEA POWER *VERSUS* SPAIN

For money, no doubt it is the principal part of the greatness of Spain, for by that they maintain their veteran army, and Spain is the only state of Europe that is a money grower; but in this part of all others is most to be considered, the ticklish and brittle state of the greatness of Spain. Their greatness consists in their treasure, their treasure in their Indies, and their Indies (if it be well weighed) are indeed but an accession to such as are masters by sea. So as this axletree whereupon their greatness turneth is soon cut in two, by any that shall be stronger than they by sea. Herein therefore I refer myself to the opinions of all men (enemies or whomsoever) whether that the maritime forces of Great Britain and the United Provinces be not able to beat the Spaniard at sea. For if that be so, the links of that chain whereby they hold their greatness are dissolved.

65. THE PARLIAMENTARY ATTITUDE, 1621

Parliament held that the way to regain the Palatinate was to fight, not to conciliate Spain. Such a war, in their view, might be maintained from the loot of naval enterprises like Drake's in the last reign. This extract is from a debate on foreign affairs in the House of Commons. James I would not allow interference in foreign affairs (see No. 44, *b*)), and Parliament was dismissed. However, on the breakdown of the negotiations for the marriage alliance, war with Spain was declared (see No. 44 *d*), *e*)), but the antagonism of King and Parliament resulted in inefficiency, shortage of money and failure; though among those who made use of the opportunities for piracy thus created was the Earl of Warwick, later Admiral of the Parliamentary Fleet (see Nos. 49, *d*), and 94). Notestein, Relf and Simpson, *Commons' Debates, 1621*, II, pp. 447–51.

Sir Robert Phelips: The duty I owe to my King and country calls me up. The propositions are two: 1, for the present supply; 2, for future war. First the states that hinder our projects are the Catholic states of Germany, and the great wheel of Spain. Those that may help us are the princes of our profession in Germany, the protestants in France and the United Provinces in the Low Countries. And how unlike those are to help us. And the German confederates are fallen away, seeing we look aside, and the Low Countries are more naturally pendent upon us. They cannot consist [i.e. subsist] without us, no more than our well being without them. Thirdly, for France, the King doth cut the throats of his own [Protestant] subjects. . . .

First for the honour of our country. If we had kept the crown on the King of Bohemia's head we had made equal the state of our religion with theirs. Secondly our abilities, the want of trade and moneys wherein the care of the Lords of the Council has not produced so good effect. We have many enemies even within our own bowels which call us the protestant faction. . . . How bold they are in their disputations, openly hoping great matters. Therefore some course is to be taken with them, lest that we repent too late. Therefore I like of the war and would have it openly proclaimed thereby to unite the princes unto it, but yet I would not presently give too much until our next meeting, because our own kingdom may have some content in lieu of their subsidies already given. For we must take care that we give not such advantages for the future, that our country may find fault with us. . . .

Mr. Crew: . . . Love and fear draw us to give. It is good to know our enemies as well as our friends. If we had had trade to the West Indies, as we have had to the East Indies, that we might march with the protestant princes and not with Spain. It were excellent that we might crop the House of Austria and stop the Indies from him. Everyone would give with a swift and open hand. We would give more than enough. That all the Jesuits might be banished and the Papists depressed. . . . Not to fight with a concealed enemy but with the King of Spain. . . .

Sir Dudley Digges addeth that if we shall lose the Palatinate it will be a detriment in religion and that all Germany will be papists. That the Hanse towns will be lost and our traffic there, and that they will revolt from our religion. That the King of Spain will have a way to bring in armies and have the sole power of Germany. That if the King of Spain's navy were intercepted from the West Indies, if he were kept from it two years, he would be bankrupt as he was in the Queen's time.

66. RELATION OF HOME AND FOREIGN POLICY

The Venetian Ambassador in London, though sympathetic to Charles I's aspirations to autocracy (see No. 69, *c*)), shared Parliament's fear of Spain. The last item is from the Venetian Ambassador in Paris. *C.S.P.Ven.*, 1632–6, pp. 110, 301, 395, 397–8, 420, 433–4, 500–1, 523, 565, 571; 1636–9, pp. 20, 146, 421–2; 1640–2, pp. 77–8.

June 3rd, 1633. The government . . . devotes but scant attention to foreign affairs. . . . England at present has no minister of her own at any court of Europe . . . except the one at Constantinople, who . . . is maintained for the interests of trade at the instance of the merchants and . . . paid by them. . . .

December 1st, 1634. His Majesty [Charles I] does not appear to give a thought to the affairs of Germany. . . .

June 6th, 1635. The decision . . . to raise 10,000 men has been postponed. . . . The ministers . . . go about saying that as all their neighbours are arming, good government requires . . . that they should make every provision . . . for the safety of the realm. . . . But sensible men are not so easily impressed by such fears. . . . It is because the King wishes to use this opportunity to get together a considerable body of troops, with the intention of not disbanding them again but to use this means to enable him in the future to compel the people with more ease to submit to every demand of the crown, without the need of convoking Parliament again. . . .

June 13th, 1635. The ideas already reported of the urgent need that the King feels to arm swiftly . . . for the preservation of the realm . . . are maintained with increasing vigour, and this inducement easily wins the consent of the more simple. . . . All the above acts and operations . . . should finally result in an open declaration in favour of the Austrian party. Certainly if one looks at all the preparations that are being made there is no doubt but that they give constant reason for suspicion, since they exceed the need; and it is impossible to believe that the King would put himself to an expense which he cannot keep up alone . . .; but if on the other hand one considers the aversion he has always had for the meeting of Parliament, and that without having recourse to that body he cannot for long engage in costly affairs, and that, even if it is assembled, a very long time will be required before money can be obtained . . . it is only possible to guess at what more recondite ideas and more secret aims his Majesty may have. . . .

July 18th, 1635. If they [the Council] decided to raise these troops and oblige the country to maintain them . . . they considered that such a step would be exceedingly perilous . . . because the whole people ardently desired to see Parliament summoned, and if . . . it was called upon to bear arms, that might easily give the impulse to some troublesome rising, with manifest danger of seeing it greatly extended in a short time, with scant hope of being able to extinguish it very easily. . . .

August 9th, 1635. For the coming year estimates have been already made for the armament of fifty ships, and the whole country called upon for an annual contribution to support them. . . . The people seem to consent to it readily in the hope that this will avail to establish the sovereignty of the sea, for which they are eagerly jealous. . . .

January 11th, 1636. All experience has shown the King immovable and determined about not taking this step [summoning Parliament]; indeed those who know his inclinations are aware that he is moving in quite the opposite direction. From this it seems to me that they have no intention at present of undertaking any great things outside the kingdom. . . .

February 29th, 1636 [summary of discussion in the council]. It is not seemly that a slothful repose should triumph over this nation, once so formidable and warlike, or that the Spaniards, by keeping it immersed in its present vile lethargy, should constantly render themselves more formidable. The real state of affairs will appear if ever this war [the Thirty Years' War] is terminated without their [i.e. the Spaniards'] losing anything of their own, and if what they possess of other people is not taken from them. They will then undoubtedly put forward more far-reaching designs. These may possibly involve a disturbance of the peace these realms now enjoy, the felicity of which the Spaniards leave in tranquillity at present rather because of their own embarrassments than from any good will. . . . Thus on one side and the other the matter is debated at great length, but in the end it all concludes with the invariable decision to wait and see. . . . Accordingly I fancy that one may very reasonably conclude that this affair [an agreement with France against Spain], which has been discussed at this court for so long, will finally perish in irresolution, as they cling more particularly to the present policy that the more pacific this state remains the happier it will be; that for its security all that is required is to maintain predominance at sea, and for the rest to shut their eyes will never do them any harm. . . .

May 23rd, 1636. It is not difficult for them [the Spaniards] to find out all about the most secret principles of the government here. . . .

May 30th, 1636. [Secretary Windebanke] is a strong partisan of Spain. . . .

July 11th, 1636. [The Prince Palatine's secretary] went on to disclose . . . the reasons why he mistrusts the operations of the Court here . . . and the interested leaning of the greatest men of the government towards the House of Austria. . . .

February 20th, 1637. His Majesty [Charles I] . . . will on no account declare himself the enemy of the House of Austria. . . .

June 11th, 1638. The French and Dutch ambassadors . . . know that the interest and share of the Spaniards in the government here obscure reason. . . .

September 15th, 1640. It is certain that the King of Spain . . . will not conclude any agreement with him [Charles I], or if he does so it will be without profit. England to-day has become a nation useless to all the rest of the world, and consequently of no consideration.

67. INFLUENCE OF THE NETHERLANDS

The Dutch bourgeoisie was the first to revolt on a national scale against an absolute monarchy and a persecuting state Church, in their case the King of Spain and the Roman Catholic Church. Their example thrilled Europe and especially England, where Spain was also the national enemy and where the bourgeoisie was also becoming conscious of a new strength. Defence of the Netherlands against Spanish efforts at reconquest was very dear to all Protestant and patriotic Englishmen (*b*); and the example of Dutch prosperity convinced more worldly spirits that there was much in their system of government worthy of imitation (*c*). Holland was a refuge for English political and religious exiles. Many Englishmen fought in the Dutch service during the revolt and the Thirty Years' War; a Dutch contingent fought for Parliament during the Civil War. Extract *a*) was quoted by Milton in his defence of the execution of Charles I. Sir Walter Ralegh in *b*), though expressing himself cautiously, shows himself aware of the class issues involved in the Netherlands revolt (and in England). *The Cabinet Council*, from which this is extracted, was written after Ralegh had been imprisoned by James I, and first published in 1658 by Milton. Extract *c*) is from Hobbes' *Behemoth, a History of the Causes of the Civil War*, published in 1679.

a) Somers Tracts, XIV, p. 417; *b*) Ralegh, *Works*, VIII, pp. 295, 311–12, 332; *c*) T. Hobbes, *English Works*, VI, p. 168.

a) DECLARATION OF NETHERLANDS INDEPENDENCE, 1581

God did not create the people slaves to their prince, to obey his commands whether right or wrong, but rather the prince for the sake of the subjects (without which he could be no prince), to govern them according to equity, to love and support them as a father his children or a shepherd his flock, and even at the hazard of life to defend and preserve them. And when he does not behave thus, but on the contrary oppresses them, seeking opportunities to infringe their ancient customs and privileges, exacting from them slavish compliance, then he is no longer a prince but a tyrant, and the subjects are to consider him in no other view. And particularly when this is done deliberately and authorised by the States [i.e. the representative assembly], they may not only disallow his authority but legally proceed to the choice of another prince for their defence.

b) SIR WALTER RALEGH ON THE NETHERLANDS

The common people of England have suffered the same fate as other nations; they have been drawn with heat and fury to shed one another's blood for such a liberty as their leaders never intended they should have, and have fought many battles to redress grievances which victory, when it happened, always increased. . . .

The States [of the Netherlands] have . . . banished and put from them all their nobility but very few poor ones, and have shared all their inheritance among them; therefore they know if they render themselves to the Spaniard, those great persons will be restored and revenged. . . . Both Count Maurice and such of the nobility and gentry that remain are most addicted that way [to dependence on the French monarchy]. . . .

After my duty to mine own sovereign, and the love of my country, I honour them [the Netherlanders] most.

c) DUTCH INFLUENCE ON THE ENGLISH BOURGEOISIE

The City of London and other great towns of trade, having in admiration the prosperity of the Low Countries after they had revolted from their monarch, the King of Spain, were inclined to think that the like change of government here would to them produce the like prosperity.

68. THE DUTCH REPUBLIC—A MODEL AND A RIVAL

The sympathy which many English merchants felt for the Dutch in their struggle against Spain turned into mixed feelings when the whole power of the victorious Netherlands state began to be put behind a foreign policy aiming at commercial domination. The Dutch threatened to monopolise the trade of northern Europe just when English merchants were most conscious of lack of support from the governments of James I and Charles I (see Nos. 64–6). For Mun, see No. 11. As an East India merchant he was bitterly conscious of the advantages of the Dutch, of their debt to past English support, and of the fact that if only merchants controlled policy in England they could fight and trade the Dutch off the seas. This they began after the revolution, in a series of wars from 1650 to 1673; by the end of the seventeenth century the Netherlands had been reduced to the position of English satellite. The links of Protestantism had proved weaker than the rivalries of commerce.

T. Mun, *England's Treasure by Foreign Trade*, pp. 73–82.

SINCE they have cast off the yoke of Spanish slavery, how wonderfully are they improved in all humane policy!

What great means have they obtained to defend their liberty against the power of so great an enemy! And is not all this performed by their continual industry in the trade of merchandise? . . . If we compare the times of their subjection to their present estate they seem not the same people; for who knows not that the condition of those provinces was mean and turbulent under the Spaniards' government, which brought rather a greater charge than a further strength to their ambition? . . . It seems a wonder to the world that such a small country, not fully so big as two of our best shires, having little natural wealth, victuals, timber or other necessary ammunitions, either for war or peace, should notwithstanding possess them all in such extraordinary plenty that besides their own wants (which are very great) they can and do likewise serve and sell to other princes ships, ordnance, cordage, corn, powder, shot and what not, which by their industrious trading they gather from all the quarters of the world. In which courses they are not less injurious to supplant others . . . than they are careful to strengthen themselves. . . .

These and other circumstances make me often wonder, when I hear the Dutch vain-gloriously to brag, and many English simply to believe, that the United Provinces are our forts, bulwarks, walls, outworks, and I know not what, without which we cannot long subsist against the Spanish forces: when in truth *we are the main fountain of their happiness, both for war and peace, for trade and treasure, for munition and men, spending our blood in their defence; whilst their people are preserved to conquer in the Indies and to reap the fruits of a rich traffic out of our own bosoms*: which being assumed to ourselves (as we have right and power to do) would mightily increase the breed of our people by this good means of their maintenance [fishing]. . . .

The sum of all is this, that the United Provinces, which now are so great a trouble if not a terror to the Spaniard, were heretofore little better than a charge to them in their possession, and would be so again in the like occasion; the reasons whereof . . . are not pertinent to this discourse more than . . . to show the different effects between natural and artificial wealth. The first of which, as it is most noble and advantageous, being always ready and certain, so doth it make the people careless, proud and given to all excesses; whereas the second enforceth vigilance, literature, arts and policy. My wishes therefore are that as England doth plentifully enjoy the one, and is fully capable of the other, our endeavours might as worthily conjoin them both together, to the reformation of our vicious idleness and greater glory of these famous kingdoms.

Part Six

THE STORM BREAKS

No man that is wise will show himself angry with the people of England.

The Bishop of Lincoln to the Duke of Buckingham.

69. THE OPPOSITION ORGANISES

Since no parliament was summoned between 1629 and 1640, the revolutionaries had to proceed conspiratorially. The main group acted through the Providence Island Company (*b*), a company trading with the West Indies. Its Treasurer and leading spirit was John Pym (who, like Hampden, lived in Gray's Inn Lane (*b*)); with its activities were connected directly or indirectly most of those who were to lead the revolutionary struggle—John Hampden, the Earls of Warwick and Manchester, Lord Brooke, Lord Saye and Sele, Oliver St. John (Hampden's counsel in the Ship Money case). Opposition to Ship Money, the campaign which led to the calling of Parliament in 1640 and victory in the elections of that year were probably all organised by this group. For the Providence Island Company, see A. P. Newton, *Colonising Activities of the English Puritans* (1914).

a) *C.S.P.Ven.*, 1632–6, p. 547; 1636–9, p. 125; *b*) A. Wood, *Athenæ Oxonienses* (ed. Bliss, 1813–21), III, p. 547; *c*) *C.S.P. Ven.*, 1636–9, pp. 297–300, 308.

a) THE VENETIAN AMBASSADOR

April, 1636. The generality are certainly exceedingly irate, as it seems to them that the steps taken in every direction are leading to a complete change of system. . . . His Majesty's court is seen to become constantly poorer, and the few who frequent it are mostly Scots; all the great nobles of this realm, in despair of ever seeing Parliament called, keep away as much as possible. . . .

January, 1637. It now seems that many of the leading men of the realm are determined to make a final effort to bring the forms of government back to their former state. They hold secret meetings for the purpose of achieving this result.

b) THE PROVIDENCE ISLAND COMPANY

[At Lord Saye's house in the country at Broughton, near Banbury, the malcontents used to meet], and what embryos were conceived in the country were shaped in Gray's Inn Lane, near London, where the undertakers for the Isle of Providence did meet.

c) FORECAST OF THE REVOLUTION, OCTOBER, 1637

He [Charles I] inherits two things from his father, namely [love of] hunting and the aversion, not to say hostility, of the people. This is well known to be the final guide of his movements, the sole reason which makes him pacific. . . . He has given up governing by Parliament as his predecessors did. . . . Having shaken off his fears, he has had the laws interpreted in his favour by the lawyers of the realm, . . . there being no parliament to say him nay; and as private persons cannot refuse what is demanded according to the law, he has succeeded in raising large sums of money. . . .

The prince and the subject cannot both be rich at the same time. . . . When affairs of state are made the business of everyone, men have an inducement to devote their blood, life and goods freely to it. . . . From this I conclude that a prince who attempts, even with just cause, to reduce his subjects to servitude, who have been born under the laws of liberty, has a truly royal spirit and dares to the limits of daring, but he ought to realise that in doing so he is putting his state in a constant fever, rendering it turbulent, rebellious and greedy of change.

70. POPULAR PRESSURE ON THE GOVERNMENT

Bate's *Elenchus Motuum* (*c*) was originally published in Latin in 1649. He was a Royalist.

a) *C.S.P.Ven.*, 1640–2, pp. 48–9; *b*) Laud, *History of Troubles and Trial*, p. 178; *c*) [Bate] *A Short Narrative of the Late Troubles in England* (ed. 1902), pp. 24, 27.

a) THE PEOPLE OF LONDON FORCE CHARLES I'S HAND

May 25th, *1640*. Amid all these troubles the King adheres steadily to his resolution to obtain from the people by force the money necessary to maintain the war against Scotland. He has demanded a loan of £200,000 from this City [London]. As this has been openly refused, he now proposes in great wrath to compel the most substantial merchants to pay it down. For this he sent for the aldermen, so that they may divide it out among the richest; but as they declined he has had them imprisoned, amid universal murmurs. . . .

June 1st, 1640. [Riots by the London populace took place in the week since the Ambassador's last despatch.] The King, seized with serious fears that the discontent of his people may induce him to the straits which overtook some of his predecessors in the past, has wonderfully changed in a moment his decision to compel them to pay by force, and now all his thoughts are turned to conciliating the goodwill of his subjects once more. To this end he has promptly released the aldermen who were imprisoned, and it is reported that he will soon, by a public declaration, relieve the kingdom of the payment of many duties recently imposed.

b) ARCHBISHOP LAUD ON THE RABBLE

Whensoever there was anything proposed in the House of Commons, which it was thought the Lords would stick at, or the King not grant, by and by the rabble came about the Houses, and called for this and that justice, as they were prompted.

c) ABSURD PRETENSIONS OF THE COMMON PEOPLE

From that time [1641] all the authority of parliament seemed to be out of date, since . . . the common people challenged to themselves the right of voting. It was now manifest that these things did tend to sedition. Nor was it less clear that the multitude was stirred up not only by the assent and connivance or nod, as we say, but also by the machination and craft of many that sat in both houses, . . . these innovators, grown swellingly insolent by the power of the common people.

71. THE IMPEACHMENT OF STRAFFORD

The Scottish invasion (see Introduction) delivered Charles into the hands of the Parliament which he was compelled to call on November 3rd, 1640. One of its first objects was to bring to justice the prime mover in the oppressions of the eleven years' personal government, "Black Tom Tyrant," the Earl of Strafford. Extract *a*), from one of Strafford's letters to his friend, Sir Christopher Wandesford, relates his defence of his Irish policy before the Privy Council in 1636, and Charles's approval of his conduct. The charge against Strafford (*b*) was that he had subverted the fundamental law of England. Extract *c*) gives some idea of what Pym thought that fundamental law was. But as the trial went on it became increasingly clear how difficult it was to prove that Strafford was guilty of high treason, and eventually impeachment was abandoned in favour of an Act of Attainder which merely asserted Strafford's guilt. This incident made it clear to some on the Parliamentary side that what was necessary was not so much the enforcement of the existing law as the creation of a new one. Strafford was executed on May 12th, 1641.

a) Strafford, *Letters* (1739), II, pp. 20–1; *b*) Rushworth, IV, pp. 42–3; *c*) Rushworth, *Trial of Strafford*, pp. 662, 669–70.

a) STRAFFORD IN IRELAND

WHERE I found a crown, a church and a people spoiled, I could not imagine to redeem them from under the pressure with gracious smiles and gentle looks; it would cost warmer water than so. True it was, that where a dominion was once gotten and settled, it might be stayed and kept where it was by soft and moderate counsels; but where a sovereignty (be it spoken with reverence) was going down the hill, the nature of a man did so easily slide into the paths of an uncontrolled liberty, as it would not be brought back without strength, nor be forced up the hill again but by vigour and force. And true it was indeed, I knew no other rule to govern by, but by reward and punishment; and I must profess, that where I found a person well and entirely set for the service of my master, I should lay my hand under his foot, and add to his respect and power all I might; and that where I found the contrary I should not dandle him in my arms, or soothe him in his untoward humour, but if he came in my reach, so far as honour and justice would warrant me, I must knock him soundly over the knuckles; but no sooner he become a new man, apply himself as he ought to the government, but I also change my temper and express myself to him, as unto that other, by all the good offices I could do him. If this be sharpness, if this be severity, I desired to be better instructed by his majesty and their lordships, for, in truth, it did not seem so to me; however, if I were once told that his majesty liked not to be thus served, I would readily conform myself, follow the bent and current of my own disposition, which is to be quiet, not to have debates and disputes with any.

Here his majesty interrupted me, and said that was no severity; wished me to go on in that way, for if I served him otherwise I should not serve him as he expected from me.... His majesty was pleased to express his approbation of all I have done.

b) PYM ACCUSES STRAFFORD, NOVEMBER 11TH, 1640

A sudden motion was made by Mr. Pym, declaring that he had something of importance to acquaint the House with, and desired that the outward room be kept from strangers, and the outward doors upon the stairs locked; which being done, Mr. Pym informed the House that there were several persons who had given information which does give a good ground for the accusing of Thomas, Earl of Strafford, of High Treason. Whereupon the House named seven persons presently to withdraw, viz. Mr. Pym, Mr. Strode, Mr. St. John, the Lord Digby, Sir John Clotworthy, Sir Walter Earle and Mr. Hampden, to consider of the information against the Earl of Strafford. ... The Select Committee ... made their report, that they did find just cause to accuse the Earl of Strafford of High Treason; and further, that the House would desire the Lords that he may be sequestered from Parliament, and committed.

c) PYM'S SPEECH AT STRAFFORD'S TRIAL, APRIL 13TH, 1641

The Law is that which puts a difference betwixt good and evil, betwixt just and unjust; if you take away the law, all things will fall into a confusion, every man will become a law to himself, which in the depraved condition of human nature must needs produce many great enormities, lust will become a law and envy will become a law, covetousness and ambition will become laws; and what dictates, what decisions such laws will produce may easily be discerned in the late government of Ireland. . . .

It is the law that doth entitle the King to the allegiance and service of his people; it entitles the people to the protection and justice of the King. It is God alone who subsists by himself, all other things subsist in a mutual dependence and relation. He was a wise man that said that the King subsisted by the field that is tilled: it is the labour of the people that supports the Crown. If you take away the protection of the King, the vigour and cheerfulness of allegiance will be taken away, though the obligation remain.

The law is the boundary, the measure betwixt the King's prerogative and the people's liberty; whilst these move in their own orbs, they are a support and a security to one another. . . . If the prerogative of the King overwhelm the liberty of the people, it will be turned into tyranny; if liberty undermine the prerogative, it will grow into anarchy.

The law is the safeguard, the custody of all private interest, your honours, your lives, your liberties and estates, are all in the keeping of the law . . .; nothing can be more equal, than that he should perish by the justice of that law, which he would have subverted; neither will this be a new way of blood. There are marks enough to trace this law to the very original of this Kingdom; and if it has not been put in execution, as he allegeth, this 240 years, it was not for want of law, but that all that time has not bred a man, bold enough to commit such crimes as these.

72. ABOLITION OF THE STAR CHAMBER

The end of prerogative jurisdiction in secular matters: both that exercised by the Star Chamber and that exercised by the Privy Council. Its place was taken by the common law of the land, as interpreted by common lawyers such as those now sitting in Parliament and playing an important role in the changes coming over the nation. The Act became law on July 5th, 1641. Gardiner, pp. 181–83.

FORASMUCH as all matters examinable or determinable before the said Judges, or in the Court commonly called the Star Chamber, may have their proper remedy and redress, and their due punishment and correction, by the common law of the land, and in the ordinary course of justice elsewhere, and forasmuch as the reasons and motives inducing the erection and continuance of that Court do now cease, and the proceedings, censures and decrees of that Court have by experience been found to be an intolerable burden to the subjects, and the means to introduce an arbitrary power and government: and forasmuch as the Council Table hath of late times assumed unto itself a power to intermeddle in civil causes and matters only of private interest between party and party, and have adventured to determine of the estates and liberties of the subject contrary to the law of the land and the rights and privileges of the subject, by which great and manifold mischiefs and inconveniences have arisen and happened, and much uncertainty by means of such proceedings hath been conceived concerning men's rights and estates: for settling whereof and preventing the like in time to come, be it ordained and enacted by the authority of this present Parliament, that the said Court . . . [of] Star Chamber . . . be . . . clearly and absolutely dissolved, taken away and determined. . . .

III. Be it likewise declared and enacted . . . that neither His Majesty nor his Privy Council have or ought to have any jurisdiction, power or authority . . . to examine or draw into question, determine or dispose of the lands, tenements, hereditaments, goods or chattels of any the subjects of this kingdom, but that the same ought to be tried and determined in the ordinary Courts of Justice and by the ordinary course of the law.

73. FINANCIAL CONTROL

As soon as Parliament met, monopolists (see No. 28) were attacked by the future Royalist, Sir John Culpeper (*a*). All M.Ps. associated with monopolies were expelled from the House of Commons. Tonnage and poundage was the name of the Customs duties (levied on the tun of wine and the pound of merchandise) normally voted by Parliament to each King for life. But Charles I's first Parliament had voted them only for one year. Despite protests (see No. 45, *b*)) Charles nevertheless continued to collect after the grant had expired. The claim in *b*) was not disputed by any king again.

a) Rushworth, IV, pp. 33–4; *b*) Gardiner, p. 160.

a) THE FROGS OF EGYPT

[THERE] is a nest of wasps or swarm of vermin, . . . I mean the monopolizers and pollers of the people; these, like the frogs of Egypt, have gotten the possession of our dwellings and we have scarce a room free from them . . .; they sup in our cup, they dip in our dish, they sit by our fire; we find them in the dye-vat, wash-bowl and powdering-tub: they share with the butler in his box. . . . Mr. Speaker, they will not bate us a pin. . . . These are the leeches that have sucked the Commonwealth so hard that it is almost become hectical; . . . they shelter themselves under the name of a corporation, they make by-laws which serve their turns to squeeze us and fill their purses.

b) TONNAGE AND POUNDAGE ACT, 1641

It is hereby declared and enacted, That it is and has been the ancient right of the subjects of this realm, that no subsidy, custom, impost or other charge whatsoever ought or may be laid or imposed upon any merchandise exported or imported by subjects, denizens, or aliens without common consent in Parliament.

74. CHARLES I TRIES A *COUP D'ÉTAT*

The army gathered to oppose the Scots was still under arms in the North of England. Officered by the King's servants and behind-hand in its pay, it was a fruitful ground for intrigues against the Parliament. Of some of these plots at least Charles I was aware. On May 5th, 1641, Pym revealed the first Army Plot to the Commons and precautions, such as the closing of the ports to avoid the escape of conspirators, were ordered. Rushworth, IV, p. 240.

MR. PYM makes known to the House that there are divers informations given of desperate designs . . . against the Parliament and the peace of the nation. . . . That there is an endeavour to disaffect the army, not only against the Parliament's proceedings, but to bring them up against the Parliament to overawe them; that there is also a design upon the Tower; and endeavours used for the Earl of Strafford to escape. That these combinations at home have a correspondency with practices abroad; and that the French are drawing their forces amain to the sea-side, and that there is cause to fear their intent is upon Portsmouth. That divers persons of eminency about the Queen . . . are deeply engaged in these plots; that it is necessary that the ports be stopped, and that his majesty be desired to command that no person attending upon the King, Queen or Prince, do depart without leave of his Majesty, with the humble advice of the Parliament.

75. CONTROL OF THE CHURCH

The Church was also brought under Parliament's control. But divisions arose between those who wished to abolish episcopacy and those who desired merely to reform it. Extract *a*) expresses the first point of view, strongly held in London. But in the debate on the petition (*b*) Sir John Strangeways, a Royalist, warned of the social implications of such a revolutionary step—implications which Cromwell refused to admit. Extract *c*) shows that even Pym preferred reform to abolition. Extract *d*) is from the last Act of this Parliament to which the royal assent was given. Episcopacy was not hereby abolished, but bishops were expelled from the House of Lords and deprived of all temporal authority. The High Commission was abolished on the same day as the Star Chamber (see Nos. 36 and 72).

a) Gardiner, pp. 137–44; *b*) *Journal of Sir Simonds D'Ewes* (ed. Notestein, 1923), pp. 339–40; *c*) *A Just Vindication of the Questioned Part of the Reading of Edward Bagshaw, Esq.* (1660), pp. 3–4; *d*) Gardiner, p. 242.

a) THE ROOT AND BRANCH PETITION, DECEMBER 11TH, 1640

The humble Petition of many of His Majesty's subjects in and about the City of London, and several Counties of the Kingdom, sheweth,

That whereas the government of archbishops and lord bishops, deans and archdeacons, etc., with their courts and ministrations in them, have proved prejudicial and very dangerous both to the Church and Commonwealth . . . And whereas the said government is found by woeful experience to be a main cause and occasion of many foul evils, pressures and grievances of a very high nature unto His Majesty's subjects in their own consciences, liberties and estates, as in a schedule of particulars hereunto annexed may in part appear:

We therefore most humbly pray . . . that the said government, with all its dependencies, roots and branches, may be abolished. . . .

A Particular of the manifold evils, pressures, and grievances caused, practised and occasioned by the Prelates and their dependents.

1. The subjecting and enthralling of all ministers under them and their authority, and so by degrees exempting them from the temporal power; . . .

3. The encouragement of ministers to despise the temporal magistracy, the nobles and gentry of the land. . . .

4. The restraint of many godly and able men from the ministry, and thrusting out of many congregations their faithful, diligent, and powerful ministers. . . .

8. The swarming of lascivious, idle and unprofitable books and pamphlets, play-books and ballads. . . .

10. The publishing and venting of Popish, Arminian,

and other dangerous books and tenets; as namely, "That the Church of Rome is a true Church, and in the worst times never erred in fundamentals;" "that the subjects have no property in their estates, but that the King may take from them what he pleaseth;" . . .

11. The growth of Popery. . . .

12. The multitude of monopolies and patents, drawing with them innumerable perjuries; the large increase of customs and impositions upon commodities, the ship-money, and many other great burthens upon the Commonwealth, under which all groan.

13. Moreover, the offices and jurisdictions of arch-bishops, lord bishops, deans, archdeacons, being the same way of Church government which is in the Romish Church. . . .

28. . . . and from hence followed amongst others these dangerous consequences.

(1) The general hope and expectation of the Romish party, that their superstitious religion will ere long be fully planted in this kingdom again. . . .

(2) The discouragement and destruction of all good subjects, of whom are multitudes, both clothiers, merchants, and others, who being deprived of their ministers, and overburthened with these pressures, have departed the kingdom to Holland and other parts, and have drawn with them a great manufacture of cloth and trading out of the land into other places where they reside, whereby wool, the great staple of the kingdom, is become of small value and vends not; trading is decayed, many poor people want work, seamen lose employment, and the whole land is much impoverished. . . .

(3) The present wars and commotions happened between His Majesty and his subjects of Scotland. . . .

b) AN INFERENCE OF PARITY, FEBRUARY 9TH, 1641

Sir John Strangeways rose up . . . saying, if we made a parity in the church we must at last come to a parity in the Commonwealth. And that the Bishops were one of the three estates of the Kingdom and had a voice in

Parliament. . . . Mr. Cromwell went on: and said he did not understand why the gentleman that last spoke should make an inference of parity from the church to the Commonwealth; nor that there was any necessity of the great revenues of Bishops. He was more convinced touching the irregularity of Bishops than ever before, because like the Roman hierarchy, they would not endure to have their condition come to a trial.

c) PYM'S VIEWS

Mr. John Pym (a gentleman with whom I had familiar acquaintance, and knew his mind in that point) spake to this purpose, That he thought it was not the intention of the House to abolish either Episcopacy or the Book of Common Prayer, but to reform both, wherein offence was given to the people. And if that could be effected and assented to by them, with the concurrence of the King and Lords, they should do a very acceptable work to the people, and such as had not been since the Reformation.

d) CLERICAL DISABILITIES ACT, FEBRUARY 13TH, 1642

Be it enacted that no Archbishop or Bishop or other person that now is or hereafter shall be in Holy Orders, shall at any time after the 15 day of February in the year of Our Lord, one thousand six hundred forty-one [i.e. 1642], have any seat or place, suffrage or voice, or use or execute any power or authority in the Parliaments of this realm, nor shall be of the Privy Council . . . or Justice of the Peace . . . or execute any temporal authority by virtue of any commission.

76. THE END OF GOVERNMENT WITHOUT PARLIAMENT

Extract *a*) was intended to secure the regular summons of Parliaments; *b*) to guarantee this particular Parliament time to complete its programme.

a) Gardiner, p. 144; *b*) *ibid.*, p. 159.

a) TRIENNIAL ACT, FEBRUARY 15TH, 1641

WHEREAS by the laws and statutes of this realm the Parliament ought to be holden at least once every year for the redress of grievances, but the appointment of the time and place for the holding thereof hath always belonged, as it ought, to his Majesty and his royal progenitors: and whereas it is by experience found that the not holding of Parliaments accordingly hath produced sundry and great mischiefs and inconveniences to the King's Majesty, the church and commonwealth: for the prevention of the like mischiefs and inconveniences in time to come, be it enacted . . . [that Parliament shall meet automatically once every three years if not summoned by the King].

b) ACT AGAINST DISSOLVING PARLIAMENT WITHOUT ITS OWN CONSENT, MAY 10TH, 1641

Be it declared and enacted by the King, our Sovereign Lord, with the assent of the Lords and Commons in this present Parliament assembled, and by the authority of the same, that this present Parliament now assembled shall not be dissolved unless it be by Act of Parliament to be passed for that purpose.

77. APPEAL TO THE PEOPLE

In face of a second Army plot and rebellion in Ireland, in both of which the King's connivance was suspected, and of the delaying tactics in the House of Lords where bishops still sat, the Parliamentary leaders determined on an appeal to the people for support. The appeal was made in the Grand Remonstrance. It gives a history of the accumulated grievances of Charles I's reign; what Parliament had so far done to remove them; and what it yet intended to do. Its substance is summarised in *a*). The essential demand is that the King should employ as ministers only men such "as your Parliament may have cause to confide in." Swords were drawn in the Commons before it was agreed that the Remonstrance should be printed. Extract *c*) registers the horror of a man who stood between the parties at the idea of appealing against the King to the people. It must be remembered, however, that when Pym spoke of the "people" he meant the "better sort of people." Already in *b*) we find him apparently ready for a law against sectaries, those members of the lower classes who, not content to take their ideas from their betters, worked them out for themselves.

a) Gardiner, pp. 204–5; *b*) Verney, *Notes of the Long Parliament* (Camden Soc., 1845), p. 122–3; *c*) Rushworth, IV, p. 425.

a) PETITION ACCOMPANYING THE GRAND REMONSTRANCE, DECEMBER 1ST, 1641

WE, your most humble and obedient subjects, do with all faithfulness and humility beseech your Majesty:

1. That you will be graciously pleased to concur with the humble desires of your people in a parliamentary way, for the preserving the peace and safety of the kingdom from the malicious designs of the Popish party:—

For depriving the Bishops of their votes in Parliament, and abridging their immoderate power usurped over the clergy and other your good subjects, which they have perniciously abused to the hazard of religion, and great prejudice and oppression to the laws of the kingdom, and just liberty of your people:—

For the taking away such oppressions in religion, Church government and discipline, as have been brought in and fomented by them:—

For uniting all such your loyal subjects together as join in the same fundamental truths against the Papists, by removing some oppressive and unnecessary ceremonies by which divers weak consciences have been scrupled, and seem to be divided from the rest, and for the due execution of those good laws which have been made for securing the liberty of your subjects.

2. That your Majesty will likewise be pleased to remove

from your council all such as persist to favour and promote any of those pressures and corruptions wherewith your people have been grieved; and that for the future your Majesty will vouchsafe to employ such persons in your great and public affairs, and to take such to be near you in places of trust, as your Parliament may have cause to confide in. . . .

3. [Requests King not to alienate lands forfeited by the rebels in Ireland but to employ their revenues to support the Crown.]

Which humble desires of ours being graciously fulfilled by your Majesty, we will . . . most cheerfully undergo the hazard and expense of this war, and apply ourselves to such other courses and counsels as may support your royal estate with honour and plenty at home. . . .

b) PYM'S SPEECH ON THE REMONSTRANCE, NOVEMBER 22ND, 1641

The honour of the King lies in the safety of the people, and we must tell the truth; the plots have been very near the king, all driven home to the court and the popish party.

Let a law be made against sectaries. Ministers driven out of England for not reading the book of sports, and they are now separatists beyond sea.

The popish lords and bishops do obstruct us. No breach of privilege to name these, for we have often complained of lords being away, and lords' miscarriages. . . . We have suffered so much by counsellors of the King's choosing, that we desire him to advise with us about it, and many of his servants move him about them, and why may not the parliament? . . .

The matter of the declaration is not fit for the Lords, for the matters were only agitated in this house, and again many of them are accused by it.

Remonstrances are not directed either to the king or the people, but show the acts of this house.

This declaration will bind the peoples' hearts to us, when they see how we have been used.

c) AGAINST AN APPEAL TO THE PEOPLE

Sir Edward Dering . . . spoke . . . as follows: . . . My conscience bids me not to dare to be affirmative. . . . The Remonstrance whensoever it passeth will make such an impression and leave such a character behind both of his Majesty, the people, the Parliament, and of this present church and state, as no time shall ever eat it out. . . . To what end do we decline thus to them that look not for it? Wherefore is this descension from a Parliament to a people? They look not up for this so extraordinary courtesy. The better sort think best of us. . . . When I first heard of a Remonstrance, . . . I thought to represent unto the King the wicked counsels of pernicious Counsellors, . . . the treachery of false judges. . . . I did not dream that we should remonstrate downward, tell stories to the people, and talk of the King as of a third person.

78. CHARLES TRIES ANOTHER *COUP*

In retreat before the Parliamentary onslaught, Charles I decided on a grand *coup* to remove the leaders of the Commons and the peer he feared most, Kimbolton, afterwards Earl of Manchester (*a*). Parliament refused to give them up, and Charles I went down to the Commons on January 4th, 1642, to arrest the five himself (*b*). The members escaped to the City, where they were protected. Four thousand freeholders and gentlemen of Buckinghamshire marched to London to their defence. On January 10th the M.Ps. returned to Parliament in triumph; the same day Charles slunk out of London, to return only as a prisoner. Of the six people here charged, at the Restoration three were dead (Pym, Hampden and Strode); one became a peer (Holles); one became a member of the Privy Council (Kimbolton); and one died in the Tower (Haselrig). The Speaker's reply to the King (*b*) is a landmark in the struggle for the sovereignty of Parliament; hitherto he had been in effect appointed by the government as their agent to control the deliberations of the Commons. (cf. No. 45).

a) Gardiner, pp. 236–7; *b*) Rushworth, IV, pp. 477–8.

a) IMPEACHMENT OF ONE LORD AND FIVE M.PS.

ARTICLES of high treason and other high misdemeanours against the Lord Kimbolton, Mr. Denzil Holles, Sir Arthur Haselrig, Mr. John Pym, Mr. John Hampden and Mr. William Strode.

1. That they have traitorously endeavoured to subvert the fundamental laws and government of the kingdom of England, to deprive the King of his regal power, and to place in subjects an arbitrary and tyrannical power over the lives, liberties and estates of His Majesty's liege people.

2. That they have traitorously endeavoured, by many foul aspersions upon His Majesty and his government, to alienate the affections of his people, and to make His Majesty odious unto them.

3. That they have endeavoured to draw His Majesty's late army to disobedience. . . .

4. That they have traitorously invited and encouraged a foreign power [Scotland] to invade His Majesty's kingdom of England.

5. That they have traitorously endeavoured to subvert the rights and very being of Parliaments.

6. That for the completing of their traitorous designs they have endeavoured (as far as in them lay) by force and terror to compel the Parliament to join with them in their traitorous designs, and to that end have actually raised and countenanced tumults against the King and Parliament.

7. And that they have traitorously conspired to levy, and actually have levied, war against the King.

b) THE ATTEMPTED ARREST, JANUARY 4TH, 1642

The five members . . . were no sooner sate in their places, but the House was informed . . . that his Majesty was coming with a guard of military men. . . . Whereupon a certain member of the House having also had private intimation . . . that endeavours would be used this day to apprehend the five members, the House required the five members to depart the House forthwith, to the end to avoid combustion in the House if the said soldiers should use violence to pull any of them out. . . . As . . . his Majesty entered the House . . . he cast his eye . . . where Mr. Pym used to sit, but his Majesty not seeing him there (knowing him well), went up to the chair and said, "By your leave, Mr. Speaker, I must borrow your chair a little." . . . After he had stood in the chair awhile, casting his eye upon the members as they stood up uncovered, but could not discern any of the five members to be there . . . [the King] made this speech:

"Gentlemen, I am sorry for this occasion of coming unto you. Yesterday I sent a sergeant at arms . . . to apprehend some that by my command were accused of high treason, whereunto I did expect obedience, and not a message. . . . Albeit no King that ever was in England shall be more careful of your privileges . . . yet you must know that in cases of treason no person hath a privilege; and therefore I am come to know if any of these persons that were accused are here. For I must tell you, gentlemen, that so long as their persons that I have accused (for no slight cause, but for treason) are here, I cannot expect that this House will be in the right way that I do heartily wish it. . . . Since I see all the birds are flown, I do expect from you that you shall send them unto me as soon as they return hither. But I assure you, in the word of a King, I never did intend any force, but shall proceed in a legal and fair way. . . ."

His Majesty asked [the Speaker] whether he saw any of them, and where they were; to which the Speaker, falling on his knee, thus answered, "May it please your Majesty, I have neither eyes to see, nor tongue to speak in this place, but as the House is pleased to direct me, whose servant I am here; and humbly beg your Majesty's pardon that I cannot give any other answer than this to what your Majesty is pleased to demand of me." The King . . . went out of the House again, which was in great disorder, and many members cried out aloud so as he might hear them, "Privilege! Privilege!" and forthwith adjourned till the next day at one of the clock.

79. A REVOLUTIONARY SITUATION

On January 25th, 1642, Pym, in a speech at a conference with the Lords, analysed the situation. He desired their assistance. But if they should not give it he threatened that the Commons would act without them. (Already in 1628 Sir John Eliot had declared, "I cannot make so slight an estimation of the Commons as to think them mere cyphers to the nobility! . . . I am confident that, should the Lords desert us, we should yet continue flourishing and green." —Forster, *Sir John Eliot*, II, p. 224.) The departure of Charles from London began the reign of "King Pym." This speech illustrates his power and fitness to wield the sceptre. He died in December, 1643. John Pym, *A Speech delivered at a Conference with the Lords, January 25th, 1642.*

I SHALL take occasion from several branches of those petitions which your Lordships have heard, to observe,

1. The variety of dangers to which this Kingdom is now subject.

2. The manifold distempers which is the cause of those dangers.

3. The multiplicity of those evil influences which are the causes of that distemper.

The first danger is from enemies abroad. . . . All the states of Christendom are now armed, and we have no reason to believe but that those of greatest power [Spain and France], have an evil eye upon us in respect of our religion: And if their private differences should be composed, how dangerously, how speedily might those great armies and other preparations now ready be applied to some enterprise and attempt against us. . . . Some of the ministers of our neighbour princes may be justly suspected to have had a more immediate hand and operation in the insurrection and rebellion of Ireland, many of the commanders and most of the soldiers levied for the service of Spain are now joined with the rebels there. . . .

Another danger is from the Papists and ill-affected party at home. . . . They have still store of arms and munition at their disposing, notwithstanding all our endeavours to disarm them, they have a free resort to the City and to the Court. . . .

A third danger is of tumults and insurrections of the meaner sort of people: by reason of their ill vent of cloth and other manufactures, whereby great multitudes are set on work, who live for the most upon their daily gettings, and will in a very short time be brought to great extremity, if not employed. Nothing is more sharp and pressing than necessity and want; what they cannot buy they will take. . . .

A fourth danger is from the rebels in Ireland; . . . they have great hopes of supplies from abroad, of encouragement here . . . so that they begin to speak already of the transporting themselves hither, and making this kingdom the seat of the war. . . .

The obstructions which have brought us into this distemper are very many. . . .

1. The obstruction of reformation in matters of religion. . . . And of this obstruction (my Lords) I must clear the Commons, we are in no part guilty of it: some good bills have passed us, and others are in preparation, which might have been passed before this, if we had not found such ill success in the other [House]. . . .

2. An obstruction in trade. . . . I must protest the House of Commons has given no cause to this obstruction; we have eased trade of many burdens and heavy taxes which are taken off; we have freed it from many hard restraints by patents and monopolies; we have been willing to part with our own privileges to give it encouragement; we have sought to put the merchants into security and confidence in respect of the Tower of London, that so they might be invited to bring in their bullion to the Mint as heretofore they have done; and we are no way guilty of the troubles, the fears, and public dangers which make men withdraw their stocks, and to keep their money by them. . . .

3. The obstruction in the relief of Ireland. . . . I must declare that we are altogether innocent of any neglect herein. . . . We undertook the whole charge of it, and we suffered not 24 hours to pass, before we agreed to a great levy of money and men. . . . Many of the chief

commanders . . . of the rebels, after we had with your Lordships' concurrence stopped the ports against all Irish Papists, have been suffered to pass by his Majesty's immediate warrant. . . .

4. The obstruction in prosecution of delinquents. . . . His Majesty's own hand has been obtained, his Majesty's ships employed for the transporting of divers of those who have fled from the justice of the Parliament.

5. A general obstruction and interruption of the proceedings of Parliament, by those manifold designs of violence . . . by the great and frequent breaches of privilege; by the subtle endeavours to raise parties in our House, and jealousies betwixt the two Houses.

6. The obstruction in providing for the defence of the kingdom . . . What a pressing necessity there is of this, the exceeding great decays in the Navy, in the forts, in the power of ordering the militia of the kingdom, and means of furnishing them with munitions, are sufficient evidences. . . .

Lastly I come to the evil influences which have caused this distemper. . . .

1. In the first place, I shall remember the evil counsels about the King. . . .

2. The discouragement of good counsel: divers honest and approved Counsellors have been put from their places; others . . . discountenanced. . . .

3. The great power that an interested and factious party has in the Parliament by the continuance of the votes of the Bishops and Popish Lords in your Lordships' House. . . .

4. The fomenting and cherishing of a malignant party throughout the whole kingdom.

5. The manifold jealousies betwixt the King, his Parliament, and good Subjects. . . .

I am now come to a conclusion, and I have nothing to propound to your Lordships by way of request or desire from the House of Commons; I doubt not but your judgments will tell you, what is to be done; your consciences, your honour, your interests will call upon you for the doing of it. The Commons will be glad to have your help and concurrence in saving of the kingdom; but if they should fail of it, it should not discourage them in doing their duty. And whether the kingdom be lost or saved (as through God's blessing I hope it will be) they shall be sorry that the story of this present Parliament should tell posterity, that in so great a danger and extremity, the House of Commons should be enforced to save the kingdom alone, and that the House of Peers should have no part in the honour of the preservation of it, you having so great an interest in the good success of those endeavours, in respect of your great estates, and high degrees of nobility.

80. PREPARATIONS FOR WAR

Although armies were being mustered, still a thin line of communication connected the King in the North with Parliament at Westminster. Few men could bring themselves to believe that Civil War was inevitable; and negotiations continued long after the keener-sighted had abandoned hope of their success. Extract *a*) is the bewildered speech of a lawyer on the Parliamentary side, made, according to his own account, in July, 1642. Parliament maintained the fiction that they were fighting for the King even though so evidently they were fighting against him. This involved certain practical difficulties (*b*). With *d*), cf. No. 96.

a) Whitelock, *Memorials*, I, pp. 176–7; *b*) Gardiner, p. 257; *c*) *ibid.*, p. 261; *d*) ed. E. Hockliffe, *Diary of the Rev. Ralph Josselin* (Camden Soc., 1908), p. 13.

a) WHITELOCK, JULY, 1642

It is strange to note how we have insensibly slid into this beginning of a civil war by one unexpected accident after another, as waves of the sea, which have brought us thus far; and we scarce know how, but from paper combats, by declarations, remonstrances, protestations, votes, messages, answers, and replies, we are now come to the question of raising forces, and naming a general and officers of an army. . . .

It was truly observed by a noble gentleman, that if our enemies find us provided to resist their attempts upon us, it will be the likeliest way to bring them to an accord with us. . . .

We have tried by proposals of peace to his majesty, and they have been rejected: let us try yet again, and appoint a committee who may review our former propositions.

b) DECLARATION OF THE HOUSES, JUNE 6TH, 1642

The King's supreme and royal pleasure is exercised and declared in this High Court of law and council, after a more eminent and obligatory manner than it can be by personal act or resolution of his own.

c) PARLIAMENT PREPARED TO FIGHT, JULY 12TH, 1642

Resolved upon the question, that an army shall be forthwith raised for the safety of the King's person, defence of both Houses of Parliament and of those who have obeyed their orders and commands, and preserving of the true religion, the laws, liberty and peace of the kingdom.

Resolved . . . that the Earl of Essex shall be general.

Resolved . . . that this House doth declare that in this cause, for the safety of the King's person, defence of both Houses of Parliament and of those who have obeyed their orders and commands, and preserving of the true religion, the laws, liberty and peace of the kingdom, they will live and die with the Earl of Essex whom they have nominated general in this cause.

Resolved . . . that a petition shall be framed to move his Majesty to a good accord with his Parliament to prevent a civil war.

d) CLERICAL ZEAL AND POPULAR RESPONSE.

About midsummer [1642] we began to raise private arms. I found [i.e. paid for] a musket for my part, and the King was beginning to raise an army. The Parliament did the like. August 1st we met at Colchester to underwrite [loans to Parliament], where for my part, for my affection to God and His gospel, having endeavoured public promoting it beyond my estate, I underwrit and paid in to Mr. Crane £10. . . . Being at London I provided for myself sword, halberd, powder and match. The drums now also began to beat up: for my part I endeavoured to encourage others to go forth. Our poor people in tumults arose and plundered divers houses, papists' and others, and threatened to go farther, which I endeavoured to suppress by public and private means.

81. BOURGEOISIE AND PARLIAMENT

The author of *a*) later became Bishop of Oxford and allowed himself to be forcibly installed as President of Magdalen College, Oxford, as part of James II's scheme for the reintroduction of Roman Catholicism and absolute government into England. This pamphlet of his was answered by the poet Andrew Marvell, among others. The authors of *c*)–*f*) were Royalists. There is a nice irony in the fact that the Crown (for fiscal purposes) encouraged the growth of corporations (see No. 28, note), for the bourgeoisie, thus organised, became conscious of its strength.

a) S. Parker, *Discourse of Ecclesiastical Politie* (1671), p. xxxix; *b*) T. Hobbes, *English Works*, VI, pp. 191–2; *c*) Newcastle, p. 21; *d*) Dugdale, pp. 116–7; *e*) J. H[owell] *Some Sober Inspections made into the Carriage . . . of the late Long Parliament* (1655), pp. 36–7; *f*) [Anon.] *Lex Talionis* (1649), p. 9.

a) TRADE AND SEDITION, 1670

To erect and encourage trading combinations is only to build so many nests of faction and sedition, and to enable these giddy and humoursome people to create public disturbances. For 'tis notorious that there is not any sort of people so inclinable to seditious practices as the trading part of a nation. . . . And, if we reflect upon our late miserable distractions, 'tis easy to observe how the quarrel was chiefly hatched in the shops of tradesmen, and cherished by the zeal of prentice-boys and city gossips.

b) PRESBYTERIANS AND TOWNS

In the beginning of the late war, the power of the presbyterians was so very great that not only the citizens of

London were, almost all of them, at their devotion, but also the greatest part of all other cities and market towns of England.

c) RICH AND THEREFORE REBELLIOUS MARKET TOWNS

In two market towns south-west from Wakefield, viz. Rotherham and Sheffield, the enemy was very busy to raise forces against his Majesty and had fortified them both . . . hoping thereby to give protection and encouragement to those parts of the kingdom which were populous, rich and rebellious.

d) TOWNS FOR PARLIAMENT

As to the places of strength, throughout England (besides the Royal Navy . . .) they had the City and Tower of London; all the eastern counties, with the ports and castles thereto belonging; the strong town of Hull in Yorkshire, and in it all his Majesty's magazine of arms, artillery and ammunition . . . Manchester in Lancashire . . . Ludlow, Bridgnorth and Wem in Shropshire; Stafford in Staffordshire; the cities of Bristol and Gloucester; the towns of Leicester and Northampton; the city of Coventry, with the castles of Warwick and Kenilworth, all in Warwickshire; the city of Lincoln; the towns of Nottingham and Derby [etc.].

e) GOOD ADVICE NOT TAKEN

Polyander: The burgesses of towns are for the most part all tradesmen, and, being bred in corporations, they are more inclining to popular government and democracy. Now, these exceeding the knights in number [in the House of Commons] carry all before them by plurality of voices, and so puzzle the proceedings of matters. . . . This monstrous City [London] . . . is composed of nothing else but corporations, which smell rank of little republics . . . and it was a great error in the last two Kings to suffer this town to spread her wings so wide. . . . [Gondomar, the Spanish Ambassador, said to James I]: "Sir, I fear that these men will do you a mischief one day."

f) A SIMPLE SUMMARY

Three things have been the bane of monarchy:
(1) First, weekly lectures;
(2) Corporations;
(3) Trained bands.

82. THE TWO SIDES LINE UP

Extracts *a*)–*f*) are by supporters of Parliament, the last three by Cavaliers. All stress the fact that the division in the Civil War was *social*; and *b*) emphasises the revolutionary nature of the Parliamentary cause. Extract *c*) is confirmed by Mr. Wood in his *History of Nottinghamshire in the Civil War*, who shows that in that county all the peers, all but two of the knights, all but four of the larger gentry, were against Parliament (pp. 33, 123–4, 217–24). A Royalist alleges that Pym and Hampden shared the views expressed in *d*), and "thought the King so ill beloved by his subjects that he would never be able to raise an army to oppose them" (Heath's *Chronicles*, 1676, p. 36). Edmund Ludlow (*d*) was a general in the Parliamentary Army and a leading republican. His *Memoirs* were written in exile after the Restoration. With *e*) cf. No. 43. Compare the remark made after the Battle of Marston Moor (1644), that of those slain on the King's side two-thirds showed by the whiteness of their bodies that they were of "gentle birth." Butler (*j*) is satirical, but shows on which side the people of London stood. The "hero" of his poem, *Hudibras* (1663), is a Presbyterian knight: his squire is an Independent. That marks the class distinction between these two parties (cf. Nos. 108–9).

a) Baxter, *The Holy Commonwealth* (1659), p. 457; *b*) Baxter, *Autobiography*, pp. 34–5; *c*) Mrs. Hutchinson, *Life of Colonel Hutchinson*, I, pp. 141, 163, 187; *d*) Ludlow, I, pp. 38, 96; *e*) May, I, pp. 18-19; *f*) G. Fox the younger, *A noble salutation . . . [unto Charles Stuart]* in *A Collection of the several books* (1662), p. 109; *g*) Dugdale, pp. 87-8; *h*) *Life of Sir John Digby* (Camden Misc. XII), pp. 111-12; *j*) S. Butler, *Hudibras*, Part I, Canto II, lines 537–54.

a) ISSUES OF LONG STANDING

THE war was begun in our streets before the King or Parliament had any armies.

b) GENTRY AND RABBLE *VERSUS* THE MIDDLE SORT

A great part of the Lords forsook the Parliament. . . . A very great part of the knights and gentlemen of England in the several counties . . . adhered to the King. . . . And most of the tenants of these gentlemen, and also most of the poorest of the people, whom the other call the rabble, did follow the gentry and were for the king. On the Parliament's side were . . . the smaller part (as some thought) of the gentry in most of the counties, and the greatest part of the tradesmen and freeholders and the middle sort of men, especially in those corporations and counties which depend on clothing and such manufactures. . . . All the sober men that I was acquainted with, who were against the Parliament, were wont to say, "The King hath the better cause, but the Parliament hath the better men."

c) GENTRY AND HANGERS-ON *VERSUS* THE MIDDLE SORT

Most of the gentry of the county [Nottinghamshire] were disaffected to the Parliament; most of the middle sort, the able substantial freeholders and the other commons, who had not their dependence upon the malignant nobility and gentry, adhered to the Parliament. . . . Every county had the civil war, more or less, within itself. . . . All the devout people of the town [Nottingham] were very vigorous and ready to offer their lives and families, but there was not [a quarter] of the town that consisted of these; the ordinary civil sort of people coldly adhered to the better, but all the debauched, and such as had lived upon the bishops' persecuting courts, and had been the lackeys of projectors and monopolizers and the like, they were all bitterly malignant.

d) UNEXPECTED SUPPORT FOR THE KING

When I first took arms under the Parliament in defence of the rights and liberties of my country, I did not think that a work so good and so necessary would have been attended with so great difficulties. . . . I supposed that many of the clergy, who had been the principal authors of our miseries, together with some of the courtiers and such as absolutely depended on the King for their subsistence, as also some foreigners, would adhere to him. . . . But finding by experience the strong combination of interests at home and abroad against them [the Parliament], the close conjunction of the popish and prelatical parties in opposition to them; what vast numbers depended upon the King for preferments or subsistence; how many of the nobility and gentry were contented to serve his arbitrary designs, if they might have leave to insult over such as were of a lower order . . . I became convinced of my former error.

e) LORDS AND GENTRY PRAISE ABSOLUTISM

Another sort of men, and especially lords and gentlemen, by whom the pressures of the government were not much felt, who enjoyed their own plentiful fortunes . . . did nothing but applaud the happiness of England, and called those ungrateful and factious spirits who complained of the breach of laws and liberties . . . [They argued] that the French King had made himself an absolute lord, and quite depressed the power of Parliaments, which had been there as great as in any kingdom, and yet that France flourished and the gentry lived well. . . . But these gentlemen, who seemed so forward in taking up their own yoke, were but a small part of the nation (though a number considerable enough to make a reformation hard) compared with those gentlemen who were sensible of their birthrights and the true interest of the kingdom; on which side the common people in the generality, and country freeholders stood, who would rationally argue of their own rights and those oppressions that were laid upon them.

f) A QUAKER EXPLAINS TO CHARLES II

Those that took part with thy father were generally (according to outward appearance) accounted the wisest, richest, noblest and stoutest men, and . . . vaunted themselves over those that were made of the same blood. [God] did then appear in contemptible instruments (as to outward appearance), as in tradesmen, ploughmen, servants and the like.

g) ORGANISATION AND PROPAGANDA

Having laid such a foundation by ensnaring the people with their own petitions, they made an order . . . to regulate the Militia of the City, voting new Lords Lieutenants throughout the several counties of England and Wales. And to blow up the people into a perfect rebellion, they appointed weekly lectures to be generally set up; which was accordingly performed by the most seditious and turbulent spirits that could be found: procuring more petitions, by multitudes of people from sundry parts, setting forth great grievances: and desiring that the factious party (for so they called the most loyal of the nobility) might be expelled the House of Peers. Also, that the Divine Worship of God might be no longer proclaimed; and that they might be better furnished with arms to oppose foreign power.

h) DOCTORS FOR PARLIAMENT

Among their great advantages the Parliament hath had of his Majesty, I conceive the least hath not been that they have had so great choice both of sea and land-chirurgions [surgeons], whereby it hath happened that many of their men, though grievously and dangerously wounded, have been strangely and beyond expectation cured . . .; and on the contrary his Majesty's men have miscarried and died of slight-seeming hurts for want of good, experienced and skilful chirurgions.

j) POPULAR SUPPORT FOR PARLIAMENT

No sow-gelder did blow his horn
To geld a cat, but cried "Reform!"
The oyster-women locked their fish up,
And trudged away to cry "No Bishop!"
The mouse-trap men laid save-alls by,
And 'gainst "Ev'l Counsellors" did cry;
Botchers left "Old Clothes" in the lurch,
And fell to turn and patch the church.

Some cried "The Covenant," instead
Of pudding pies and gingerbread;
And some for brooms, old boots and shoes,
Bawled out to purge the Commons' House;
Instead of kitchen stuff, some cry,
"A gospel-preaching ministry."
And some for old suits, coats or cloak,
"No surplices nor service-book."
A strange harmonious inclination
Of all degrees to Reformation.

83. GENTRY *VERSUS* FREEHOLDERS

This Protestation was drawn up by the Yorkshire freeholders after Charles I had called the gentry of the county together in the hope of enlisting at least their support against Parliament. The freeholders—who must have had some political organisation—refused to allow the gentry to speak for the county. The class division is clear; one of the few gentlemen to side with the freeholders in their protest was Sir Thomas Fairfax, later Commander-in-chief of the New Model Army. Quoted in M. Campbell, The *English Yeoman* (1942), pp. 356–7.

PROTESTATION OF THE FREEHOLDERS OF YORKSHIRE.

WHEREAS his Majesty hath been pleased to give summons to the gentry of this county to attend him at his court at York the 12th of May instant [1642], to advise with him in some particulars concerning the honour and safety of his Majesty's person and the well-being and peace of this our county, and in the same summons was pleased to omit the freeholders of this county, out of a tender respect of putting them to any extraordinary charge, yet we, conscious of our sincere loyalty to his Majesty our gracious sovereign, and conceiving ourselves according to the proportions of our estates equally interested in the common good of the county, did take boldness to come in person to York, and were ready to attend his Majesty's pleasure there. And whereas his Majesty was pleased there to propound several things to the purpose aforesaid, at the meeting of the county to consider a fit answer to return to his Majesty thereupon the doors of the meeting house were shut, we utterly excluded, and in our absence a referee [committee] of knights and gentlemen chosen without our knowledge or consent to draw up the said answer: we the freeholders who petitioned his Majesty the day abovesaid, conceiving ourselves abundantly injured in the election (not knowing any warrant by writ or otherwise for the same) of the said referee, and that we ought not however to be concluded by any resolution of theirs without our assent in their election, do absolutely protest and declare against the said election; and as far as concerns us disavow whatsoever shall be the result of their consultation thereupon, and do desire a new and fair election of a referee be made, we admitted to our free votes in the same, and some one or more, to be nominated by us, allowed to deliver our sense for us at another meeting; and that we shall not make good in the least respect anything whatsoever which shall otherwise be concluded upon.

84. CAVALIERS AND ROUNDHEADS

Accounts of the origin of the names of the two parties differ; but all agree that they convey a social distinction. The version in *a*), by Lilly the astrologer, was first published in 1651. Extract *b*), from an address said to have been circulated among the royalist troops, shows the foreign and absolutist associations of the word "Cavalier."

a) W. Lilly, *The True History of King James I and Charles I* (1715), pp. 55-6; *b*) *Col. Weston's letter* (1642), in Warburton, II, p. 20.

a) HOW THE NAMES BEGAN

Those people or citizens who used thus [in 1641-2] to flock unto Westminster were, most of them, men of mean or a middle quality themselves, having no aldermen, merchants or Common-Council men, but set on by some of better quality. And yet most of them were either such as had public spirits, or lived a more religious life than the vulgar, and were usually called *Puritans*, and had suffered under the tyranny of the Bishops. . . . They were modest in their apparel, but not in language. They had the hair of their heads very few of them longer than their ears; whereupon it came to pass that those who usually with their cries attended at Westminster were by a nickname called *Roundheads*. The courtiers, again, wearing long hair and locks and always sworded, at last were called by these men *Cavaliers*; and so, after that this broken language had been used awhile, all that adhered unto the Parliament were termed *Roundheads*, and all that took part or appeared for his Majesty, *Cavaliers*, few of the vulgar knowing the sense of the word *Cavalier*. However the present hatred of the citizens was such unto gentlemen, especially courtiers, that few durst come into the City; or if they did they were sure to receive affronts and be abused.

b) A FRENCH APPELLATION

Friends and soldiers! You are called "Cavaliers" and "Royalists" in a disgraceful sense. . . . The valour of cavaliers hath honoured that name both in France and other countries, and now let it be known in England, as well as "horseman" or "trooper". The name of Cavalier, which our enemies have striven to make odious, signifies no more than a gentleman serving his King on horseback.

85. THE CLASS DIVISION

Unfortunately it is not possible, for reasons of copyright, to use the most valuable Royalist analysis of the class division in the counties—Clarendon's *History of the Rebellion.* We can only refer the reader to the following passages in W. D. Macray's edition (Clarendon Press, Oxford, 1888), which we should have liked to quote:— Vol. II. pp. 23, 226, 274, 296, 318, 329-30, 375, 446, 461-4, 470-2; Vol. III, pp. 21, 80, 129-30, 174-7, 222, 437, 494-6; Vol. IV, pp. 44-5, 287, 315. In extract *a*) note the cautious terms in which even a staunch royalist claims popular support for the king even in one outlying area. The authors of *b*) (who despised both parties and wished to arrange a compromise settlement) and of *d*) (a conservative Parliamentarian) tell much the same story as Clarendon and Warwick, (*a*). The nobility and most of the gentry for the King: the yeomen and common people, led by an occasional gentleman like Cromwell, for Parliament. The first person killed in the Civil War is said to have been a pro-Parliamentarian weaver, slain in Lancashire on July 15th, 1642. The Sir John Gell mentioned in (*d*) is a significant figure. Under Charles I, as sheriff of the county, he distrained the property of his neighbours who refused to pay Ship Money; during the revolution he seized his neighbours' estates for their refusal to recognise the sovereignty of Parliament. Not all the opponents of the King were Puritan heroes!

a) Warwick, *Memoirs*, pp. 238-40; *b*) [Anon.], *The Leaves of the Tree of Life for the healing of the Nation* (1648), p. 9; *c*) W. Chillingworth, Sermon I, in *Works* (1838), III, p. 14; *d*) May, II, p. 108; III, pp. 78-9, 69, 84.

a) A ROYALIST'S ANALYSIS

THE east, being an angle of this kingdom and no thoroughfare into any other parts, and all as it were impaled and shut up by London, their good affections were stifled; but, like a smothering fire, it was now and anon blazing out, but soon extinguished. So as Middlesex, Kent, Surrey, Sussex, Norfolk, Cambridge and Suffolk were full of good affections, but were kept as fresh pastures for the parliament, for they were properly and singly in their quarters. And though the king could no way receive the benefit of their good affections, yet he had divers of the chief gentry with him; and of their inclinations their masters (the two Houses) so doubted that, though they should have eased them in their taxes, as most properly belonging to themselves (more than any other parts) yet, knowing how little they were voluntarily obliged to them, they laid that load upon them, that unto this day they feel the inequality of, and hereof they never eased them, even when the whole kingdom came to be their quarters. Which could arise from no other reason but because in the generality they affected not their cause. . . .

For the sea-coasts of the west, the great trading towns of Bristol, Lyme, Falmouth, Plymouth and Exeter (the king's navy being now under the command of the two houses), their interest as well as their inclinations made them parliamentarians. Only the Cornishmen (as old bold Britons) were eminently loyal and royalists, though they had strong temptations to the contrary. The inland towns and cities in the west were most for the king. The most eminent noblemen and gentry throughout the country were firmly loyal to their prince; and the interest of those eminent members of the parliament such as Grenville . . . etc. . . . found such a disposition in the generality of the commons that when they appeared as heads for them to resort unto, those counties (though not the great towns) seemed much more the king's than the two Houses' or rebels' part.

The south bordered so much upon London that, like the east, they were not much at their own liberty. . . .

The two Houses were, with their Admiral, Warwick, the Neptunes of the sea and of the trade of it.

b) A NEUTRAL'S ANALYSIS

To the King goes men of honour, as the nobility and gentry much: whose honour is predominant over their reason and religion. The Episcopal party being monarchical, growing out of the root of the King, and paternal much the Fathers of the Church; men of implicit faith, whose conscience is much regulated by their superiors; men that are high and great admirers of kingliness; taken much with that ordinance of a King. And a vast number of loose men of no religion but the King.

To the Parliament, men who [are] of a lower state, and exercising their own reasons in religion: zealous and well-affected people; men of industry and labour, that love freedom and to be something themselves. Men whose consciences are their own and so strict in them; cities, corporations, bodies and men that highly honour the Parliament; men zealous for general and common good.

c) A ROYALIST SERMON AGAINST BOTH SIDES

Seeing publicans and sinners on the one side, against scribes and Pharisees on the other; on the one side hypocrisy, on the other profaneness; no honesty nor justice on the one side, and very little piety on the other; on the one side horrible oaths, curses and blasphemies, on the other pestilent lies, calumnies and perjury: when I see among them [i.e. the Parliamentarians] the pretence of reformation, if not the desire, pursued by anti-Christian, Mahometan, devilish means; and amongst us [Royalists] little or no zeal for reformation of what is indeed amiss, little or no care to remove the cause of God's anger towards us by just, lawful and Christian means:— I profess plainly I cannot without trembling consider what is likely to be the event of these distractions.

d) A PARLIAMENTARIAN'S ANALYSIS

East Anglia. The eastern counties—Suffolk, Norfolk and Cambridgeshire—were happily kept from the beginning without any great combustion; though it were certain that many of the chief gentry in those counties bended in their affections to the King's Commission of Array; but they were not . . . strong enough to engage their counties in a war. For the freeholders and yeomen in general adhered to the Parliament. . . .

Suffolk, *Norfolk*, *Cambridgeshire*, *Essex*, *Herts*, *Hunts*. There was as much unanimity of opinion and affection in those counties among the people in general as was to be found in any part of England; but it was especially among the common people. For a great and considerable number of the gentry, and those of highest rank among them, were disaffected to the Parliament, and were not sparing in their utmost endeavours to promote the King's cause and assist his force . . . which might have thrown those counties (if not wholly carried them to the other side) into as much distraction and sad calamity as any other part of the land had felt, . . . if those gentlemen had not been curbed and suppressed by that timely care which the Parliament took, and more particularly by the successful services of one gentleman, Master Oliver Cromwell of Huntingdon. . . .

The South-western Counties. [The Marquis of Hertford

and Sir Ralph Hopton, commanding for the King] were both opposed in their beginnings not so much by any noblemen or great commanders employed by the Parliament's commission, as by private gentlemen of those counties . . ., besides plain freeholders of the county, who seemed to understand their own liberties and interest which they had in the commonwealth. . . .

Derbyshire. The county of Derby, full of nobility and gentry, was much swayed, even from the beginning of these distractions, against the Parliament; for scarce did any gentleman in all that county, but Sir John Gell, appear for it at the first. He, with his brother and some of his kindred, by the help of those freeholders and yeomen that inclined that way, made a party to resist those great ones, at such a time as must needs renown his courage and constancy.

86. IMPORTANCE OF THE CITY

This pamphlet was written in 1646 by a Presbyterian. The account of London's share in the Civil War is not unduly exaggerated. [G. Walker] *A Model of the Government of the Church under the Gospel, by Presbyters*, Dedication.

To the honourable City of London, and all the inhabitants thereof . . .:—

Give me leave, most famous and renowned City, and ye the right honourable Lord Mayor, the right worshipful Aldermen, and religious Common Council and commoners, to congratulate and rejoice with you for that honour which the Lord hath laid on you in these days of great confusion. You, under God, have been the guard of this present Parliament, by which so great things have been done for the safety and defence of three kingdoms. Your free contributions of your wealth and substance have been the sinews of this war undertaken for the defence of our religion, laws and liberties. Few counties in this kingdom have been able to defend themselves, much less to help others, except those whom you have encouraged and set on work by your example, and to whom you have been a bulwark against the enemies who by you have been terrified from invading them. All the Associated Counties have cause to bless God for the vicinity and neighbourhood of London. And all the rest of the kingdom say, "If the Lord had not helped us by the forces, arms and supplies of men and money from London, we had been utterly destroyed and laid waste."

87. FEARS OF THE GENTRY

Royalists and Parliamentarians agree in depicting the social anxiety which accompanied the beginning of civil war.

a) *Memoirs of the Verney Family during the Civil War* (1892), II, p. 69; *b*) *Farrington Papers* (Chetham Soc., 1856), p. 88; *c*) May, I, pp. 113–14; *d*) Warburton, I, p. 414; *e*) Dudley Digges, *The Unlawfulness of Subjects taking up Arms* (1643), pp. 143–5.

a) SIR T. GARDINER TO RALPH VERNEY, AUTUMN, 1642

I AM persuaded that conscience hath much to do on both sides, which though it may . . . be erroneous yet ought to be respected. But these considerations enter not into vulgar hearts. "The gentry" (say they) "have been our masters a long time, and now we may chance to master them"; and now they know their strength it shall go hard but they will use it.

b) THE HIGH SHERIFF OF LANCASHIRE, NOVEMBER 3RD, 1642

[The gentlemen of Leyland Hundred are to appear with sons, tenants and servants] that a present course may be taken as well for the satisfaction of our royal master who we know now suffers under the pride and insolency of a discontented people, also for the securing of our own lives and estates, which are now ready to be surprised by a heady multitude.

c) T. MAY

A great party whose livelihood and fortunes depended on [the Bishops], and far more whose hopes of preferment looked that way—most of the clergy, and both the Universities—began to be daily more disaffected to the Parliament; complaining that all rewards of learning would be taken away, which wrought deeply in the hearts of the young and most ambitious of that coat.

Another thing which seemed to trouble some who were not bad men was that extreme licence which the common people, almost from the very beginning of the Parliament, took to themselves of reforming without authority, order or decency. . . . To this were added those daily reports of ridiculous conventicles, and preachings made by tradesmen and illiterate people of the lowest rank, to the scandal and offence of many: which some in a merry way would put off, considering the precedent times, that these tradesmen did but take up that which prelates and the great doctors had let fall—preaching the gospel: that it was but a reciprocal invasion of each other's callings, that chandlers, salters, weavers and such-like preached, when the Archbishop himself, instead of preaching, was daily busied in projects about leather, salt, soap and such commodities as belonged to those tradesmen.

d) A SERMON PREACHED BEFORE THE ROYAL ARMY, 1642

A complete cavalier is a child of honour. He is the only reserve of English gentility and ancient valour, and hath rather chosen to bury himself in the tomb of honour than to see the nobility of his nation vassalaged, the dignity of his country captivated or obscured by any base domestic enemy or by any foreign fore-conquered foe.

e) DANGERS FROM THE POORER SORT, 1643

The interests of the major part in the House of Commons may be opposite to the good of the kingdom in general. . . . It is very easy to conceive that the major part of the lower house may be very mean men, chosen to make more profitable laws for the poorer sort and to keep the gentry under by laying subsidies and all burdens of the commonwealth upon them. . . . The reason why such an election was never yet made is this: such a power was never heretofore challenged as could enable them to go through with any such design. . . . [If the house of Lords lost its veto] the disposal of all would be put into their hands whose interests are most disjointed from the public tranquillity, as enjoying least by the present establishment in this state.

88. HOW TO DEAL WITH DEMOCRATS

Extract *a*) is from a Parliamentarian report, and may exaggerate the violence of Lord Paulet's sentiments. His oppressions, however, were such that the people of Wells tried to lynch him, and it took a regiment of Cavaliers to rescue him. This extract helps us to understand why the inhabitants of Lord Paulet's manor of Lyme Regis so heroically withstood prolonged siege by the Cavaliers later in the Civil War. The Earl of Derby's advice to his son (*b*) shows a duplicity worthy of a follower of Charles I: cf. No. 17, *b*). The last sentence of *b*) contains a theological sentiment in which the ruling class often found consolation: cf. Nos. 185, *b*) and 188, *e*).

a) Quoted in A. R. Bayley, *The Great Civil War in Dorset* (1910), p. 55; *b*) *The History of the House of Stanley* (1799), pp. 213–17.

a) FORCE

[Lord Paulet gave] order to kill men, women and children without mercy; but to reserve such ministers as they could take that were well-wishers to Parliament for to be flayed alive, and such-like exquisite torments. . . . [He declared that] it was not fit for any yeoman to have allowed him from his labours any more than the poor moiety of £10 a year; and when the power should be totally on their side, they shall be compelled to live at that low allowance, notwithstanding their estates are gotten with a great deal of labour and industry.

b) FRAUD

As it is not . . . good that the common people should know their strength, so is it safest to keep them ignorant of what they may do, but rather give them daily occasion to admire the power and clemency of their Lord. . . . When the people are bent on mischief, it is folly rashly to oppose them without sufficient power and force, neither is it discretion to yield to them too much, for reason will never persuade a senseless multitude; but keeping your gravity and state, comply with them seemingly and rather defer the matter to another time, with assurance that you will forward their own desires, by which you may gain time, as if convinced by their reasons and not the fear of any danger from them; and by the next meeting you may have taken off some of their leading champions, and either by good words or fair promises softened them to your own will. . . . It is certain that the greater number of men are bad.

Part Seven

THE CIVIL WAR

The question in dispute between the King's party and us [was], as I apprehended, whether the King should govern as a God by his will and the nation be governed by force like beasts; or whether the people should be governed by laws made by themselves, and live under a government derived from their own consent.

Lieutenant-General Edmund Ludlow.

89. CAUSES OF CIVIL WARS

These generalisations, three written before and one after the Civil War, show what contemporaries thought were the causes of social and political unrest. Bacon (*b*) includes religious grievances among his causes, but his remedies are all economic and social. Hobbes, writing after the event (*d*), refers specifically to the Ship Money case (see No. 49). Note his reference to the example of successful bourgeois revolution in the Netherlands (cf. Nos. 67–8 and 101, *c*)).

a) James I, Preface to *A Counterblast to Tobacco* (1604); *b*) Bacon, *Essay* No. XV; *c*) Rushworth, I, pp. 604–5; *d*) Hobbes, *Leviathan* (Everyman), pp. 173–7.

a) JAMES I

WE are of all nations the people most loving and most reverently obedient to our prince, yet are we (as time hath often borne witness) too easy to be seduced to make rebellion upon very slight grounds. Our fortunate and oft-proved valour in wars abroad, our hearty and reverent obedience to our princes at home, hath bred us a long and a thrice-happy peace. Our peace hath bred wealth; and peace and wealth hath brought forth a general sluggishness, which makes us wallow in all sorts of idle delights and soft delicacies, the first seeds of the subversion of all great monarchies. Our clergy are become negligent and lazy, our nobility and gentry prodigal and sold to their private delights, our lawyers covetous, our common people prodigal and curious; and generally all sorts of people more careful for their private ends than for their mother the commonwealth.

b) BACON—OF SEDITIONS AND TROUBLES

The causes and motives of seditions are innovation in religion, taxes, alteration of laws and customs, breaking of privileges, general oppression, advancement of unworthy persons, strangers, dearths, disbanded soldiers, factions grown desperate; and whatsoever in offending people joineth and knitteth them in a common cause. . . .

The first remedy or prevention is to remove by all means possible that material cause of sedition whereof we spake; which is want and poverty in the estate. To which purpose serveth the opening and well balancing of trade; the cherishing of manufactures; the banishing of idleness; the repressing of waste and excess by sumptuary laws; the improvement and husbanding of the soil; the regulating of prices of things vendible; the moderating of taxes and tributes and the like. . . . The multiplying of nobility and other degrees of quality in an over-proportion to the common people doth speedily bring a state to necessity: and so doth likewise an overgrown clergy; for they bring nothing to the stock; and in like manner when more are bred scholars than preferments can take off. . . .

Above all things good policy is to be used that the treasure and moneys in a state be not gathered into few hands. For otherwise a state may have a great stock and yet starve. And money is like muck, not good except it be spread. This is done chiefly by suppressing, or at the least keeping a strait hand upon, the devouring trades of usury, ingrossing, great pasturages, and the like.

For removing discontentments, or at least the danger of them: there is in every state, as we know, two portions of subjects, the noblesse and the commonalty. When one of these is discontent, the danger is not great: for common people are of slow motion if they be not excited by the greater sort; and the greater sort are of small strength except the multitude be apt and ready to move of themselves. Then is the danger, when the greater sort do but wait for the troubling of the waters amongst the meaner, that then they may declare themselves. . . . It is a desperate case if those that hold with the proceedings of the state be full of discord and faction; and those that are against it be entire and united.

c) SPEECH BY JOHN PYM, 1628

The form of government is that which doth actuate and dispose every part and member of a state to the common good; and as those parts give strength and ornament to the whole, so they receive from it again strength and protection in their several stations and degrees.

If this mutual relation and intercourse be broken, the whole frame will quickly be dissolved and fall in pieces, and instead of this concord and interchange of support, whilst one part seeks to uphold the old form of government, and the other part to introduce a new, they will miserably consume and devour one another. Histories are full of the calamities of whole states and nations in such cases. It is true that time must needs bring some alterations, and every alteration is a step and degree towards a dissolution; those things only are eternal which are constant and uniform. Therefore it is observed by the best writers upon this subject, that those commonwealths have been most durable and perpetual which have often reformed and re-composed themselves according to their first institution and ordinance; for by this means they repair the breaches and counterwork the ordinary and natural effect of time. . . .

He desired their lordships to remember what profitable prerogatives the laws had appointed for the support of sovereignty—as wardships, treasures trove, felons' goods, fines, amercements and other issues of courts, wrecks, escheats, and many more too long to be enumerated; which for the most part are now by charters and grants of several princes dispersed into the hands of private persons; and that, besides the ancient demesnes of the crown of England, William the Conqueror did annex, for the better maintenance of his estate, great proportions of those lands which were confiscated from those English which persisted to withstand him; and of these very few remain at this day in the King's possession. And that since that time the revenue of the crown had been supplied by attainders . . . by the dissolution of the monasteries and chantries, near a third part of the whole land being come into the King's possession. He remembered further that constant and profitable grant of the subjects in the act of tonnage and poundage. And all these, he said, were so alienated, anticipated, overcharged with annuities and assignments, that no means were left for the pressing and important occasions of this time but the voluntary and free gift of the subjects in Parliament.

The hearts of the people, and their bounty in Parliament, is the only constant treasure and revenue of the crown, which cannot be exhausted, alienated, anticipated or otherwise charged and encumbered.

d) HOBBES, 1651

Of those things that weaken, or tend to the dissolution of, a commonwealth.

A fifth doctrine that tendeth to the dissolution of a commonwealth is "That every private man has an absolute property in his goods, such as excludeth the right of the sovereign." Every man has indeed a property that excludes the right of every other subject: and he has it only from the sovereign power, without the protection whereof every other man should have equal right to the same. But if the right of the sovereign also be excluded, he cannot perform the office they have put him into; which is to defend them both from foreign enemies and from the injuries of one another; and consequently there is no longer a commonweath. . . .

Often-times the example of different government in a neighbouring nation disposeth men to alteration of the form already settled. . . . I doubt not but many men have been contented to see the late troubles in England, out of an imitation of the Low Countries; supposing there needed no more to grow rich than to change, as they had done, the form of their government. . . .

There is sometimes in a commonwealth a disease which resembleth the pleurisy; and that is when the treasure of the commonwealth, flowing out of its due course, is gathered together in too much abundance in one or a few private men, by monopolies or by farms of the public revenues. . . . Another infirmity of a commonwealth is the immoderate greatness of a town, when it is able to furnish out of its own circuit the number and expense of a great army; as also the great number of corporations, which are as it were many lesser commonwealths in the bowels of a greater, like worms in the entrails of a natural man. To which may be added the liberty of disputing against absolute power by pretenders to political prudence; which though bred for the most part in the lees of the people, yet, animated by false doctrines, are perpetually meddling with the fundamental laws, to the molestation of the commonwealth.

90. HISTORICAL ANALYSES

Harrington's analysis of the causes of the Civil War was adopted by many of his contemporaries (see No. 92; cf. Nos. 1, *a*), 89, *b*)), and is regarded with great respect by modern historians. C. H. Williams (*The Tudor Despotism*, p. 159) says: "It has been estimated that out of the proceeds of the property confiscated by the state (at the dissolution of the monasteries) an amount equal to a yearly value of £90,000 was either given away for nothing or was sold—often at nominal prices—to a group of persons whose number did not reach much more than a thousand." But where Harrington speaks of "the people" (as the French revolutionaries spoke of "the third estate"), we should speak more precisely of the bourgeoisie (cf. notes to Nos. 77 and 92). With Harrington's first sentence compare No. 42, *b*). The second extract sadly confirms Harrington's analysis from a Royalist point of view, bitterly regretting the "good old days" of serfdom. (cf. No. 14, *d*).

a) Harrington, *Works* (1737), pp. 388–91, 69–70, 487; *b*) Sir Edward Walker, *Historical Discourses*, p. 50.

a) HARRINGTON, 1656–9

THE land in possession of the nobility and clergy of England, till Henry VII, cannot be esteemed to have overbalanced those held by the people less than four to one. Whereas in our days, the clergy being destroyed, the lands in possession of the people overbalance those held by the nobility at least nine in ten. . . . Henry VII, being conscious of the infirmity of his title, yet finding with what strength and vigour he was brought in by the nobility, conceived jealousies of the like power in case of a decay or change of affections. . . . Under the pretence of curbing riots he obtained the passing of such laws as did cut off . . . retainers, whereby the nobility wholly lost their officers. Then, whereas the dependence or the people upon their lords was of a strict tie or nature, he found a means to loosen this also by laws, which he obtained upon as fair a pretence, even that of population. . . . The nobility, who by the former laws had lost their officers, by this lost their soldiery. Yet remained to them their estates, till the same prince introducing the statutes for alienations, these also became loose. . . .

Henceforth the country lives and great tables of the nobility, which no longer nourished veins that would bleed for them, were fruitless and loathsome until they changed the air, and of princes became courtiers; where their revenues, never to have been exhausted by beef and mutton, were found narrow, whence followed racking of rents and at length sale of lands. . . .

The court was yet at Bridewell, nor reached London any further than Temple Bar. The latter growth of this City, and in that the declining of the balance to popularity, derives from the decay of the nobility and of the clergy. In the reign of the succeeding king were abbeys (than which nothing more dwarfs a people) demolished. . . .

The growth of the people of England, since the ruins mentioned of the nobility and the clergy, came in the reign of Queen Elizabeth to more than stood with the interest or indeed the nature or possibility of a well-founded or durable monarchy; as was prudently perceived, but withal temporised by her Council, who (if the truth of her government be rightly weighed) seem rather to have put her upon the exercise of principality in a commonwealth than of sovereign power in a monarchy. Certain it is that she courted not her nobility, nor gave her mind (as do monarchs seated upon the like foundation) to balance her great men or reflect upon their power now inconsiderable; but ruled wholly, with an art she had to high perfection, by humouring and blessing her people. For this mere shadow of a commonwealth is she yet famous, and shall ever be so; though had she introduced the full perfection of the orders requisite to popular government her fame had been greater. . . .

To this Queen succeeded King James, whom . . . neither his new peerage, which in abundance he created, nor the old availed him anything against that dread wherein, more freely than prudently, he discovered himself to stand of Parliaments, as now mere popular councils, and running to popularity of government like a bowl down a hill: not so much, I may say, of malice prepensed as of natural instinct, whereof the Petition of Right, well considered, is a sufficient testimony. . . . There remained nothing to the destruction of a monarchy, retaining but the name, more than a prince who by contending should make the people to feel those advantages which they could not see. And this happened in the next king [Charles I] who, too secure in that undoubted right whereby he was advanced to a throne which had no foundation, dared to put this to an unseasonable trial. . . .

A government founded upon the overbalance of property is legitimately founded, and so upon justice; but a government founded upon the underbalance of property must of necessity be founded upon force, or a standing army. . . . A monarchy divested of its nobility has no refuge under heaven but an army. Wherefore the dissolution of this government caused the [civil] war, not the war the dissolution of this government. . . . If the balance, or state of property in a nation, be the efficient cause of government, and, the balance not fixed, the government (as by the present narrative is evinced) must remain inconstant or floating: then the process in the formation of a government must be first by a fixation of the balance, and next by erecting such superstructures as to the nature thereof are necessary.

b) A ROYALIST

The gentry of this county [Cornwall] retain their old possessions, their old tenants, and expect from them their ancient reverence and obedience. And . . . if many of the nobility and gentry of this unhappy kingdom had not fallen from the lustre, virtue and honour of their ancestors, and by their luxury been necessitated to manumise their villeins, but had paid that awful reverence to the majesty and greatness of their sovereign as they ought, they might have expected the same proportionably from their inferiors and tenants; and instead of having them their companions, or rather masters (as now they are) they might have had them their servants, and then I believe this war, which (under pretence of religion and liberties) is to introduce heresy in doctrine, parity in conditions, and to destroy the king, nobility and gentry, in probability had not been.

91. CONTEMPORARY VIEWS OF THE CAUSES OF THE WAR

For the Grand Remonstrance (*a*), see No. 77. The letter (*d*) from Baillie (see No. 104) was written home just after a series of victories by the Royalist Montrose in Scotland had caused consternation there. For Walwyn (*f*), see Nos. 110, 121 and 125.

a) Gardiner, pp. 206–7; *b*) quoted in S. R. Brett, *John Pym* (1940), p. 230; *c*) Selden, *Table Talk*, pp. 196–7; *d*) Baillie, *Letters and Journals* (1775), II, p. 148, Public Letter of August 10th, 1645; *e*) Leveller Petition of November 23rd, 1647, in Wolfe, p. 237; *f*) Walwyn's *Just Defence* (1649), in H. and D., p. 384; *g*) *The Man in the Moon* (Royalist newspaper), July 4th–11th, 1649, p. 111.

a) FROM THE GRAND REMONSTRANCE

THE root of all this mischief we find to be a malignant and pernicious design of subverting the fundamental laws and principles of government upon which the religion and justice of this kingdom are firmly established. The actors and promoters hereof have been:—

(i) The Jesuited Papists, who hate the laws as the obstacles of that change . . . which they so much long for;

(ii) The bishops and the corrupt part of the clergy, who cherish formality and superstition as the natural effects and more probable supports of their own ecclesiastical tyranny and usurpation;

(iii) Such councillors and courtiers as for private ends have engaged themselves to further the interests of some foreign princes or states to the prejudice of his Majesty and the state at home.

b) PYM TO THE CITY FATHERS, 1642

We should never have stepped one step towards war if we might have had or hoped for such a peace as might have secured religion and liberty and the public good of the kingdom; but truly ill counsel did exclude us from such hope. . . . We shall pursue the maintenance of our liberties, liberties that may not only be the laws and statutes, but liberties that may be in practice and in execution. . . . For to have printed liberties, and not to have liberties in truth and reality, is but to mock the kingdom.

c) A CYNICAL PARLIAMENTARIAN

If men would say they took arms for anything but religion, they might be beaten out of it by reason; out of that they never can, for they will not believe you whatever you say.

The very *Arcanum* of pretending religion in all wars is that something may be found out in which all men may have interest. In this the groom has as much interest as the lord. Were it for land, one has one thousand acres, and the other but one; he would not venture so far as he that has a thousand. But religion is equal to both. Had all men land alike, . . . then all men would say they fought for land.

d) A SCOTTISH VIEW

The design of the misled court was, and is, by all means out of hell to fasten the yoke of tyranny on the necks both of our bodies and souls, for our times and the days of our posterity; and therefore, what we have done we were absolutely necessitated to it; and whatever troubles God has cast upon us for our present trial, we expect ere long a comfortable conclusion; albeit no thanks to them, be

[they] who they will, who either by their treachery, or cowardice, or untimeous divisions, or groundless jealousies, or neglect of the public, are the instruments of Scotland's woe. If yet they will not waken they will perish, not only without any wise man's compassion, but with a mark of infamy on their persons and families for ever.

e) THE LEVELLER VIEW

The ground of the late war between the King and you [Parliament], was a contention whether he or you should exercise the supreme power over us.

f) ANOTHER LEVELLER

As for Mr. Pym and Mr. Hampden, it's well known I honoured them much for what I saw was good in them, and never reproached them in my life; but was not satisfied, when they would make a war, that they would make it in the name of the King and Parliament. I could not understand it to be plain dealing, nor thousands more besides me.

g) A CYNICAL CAVALIER

[The goods and lands of Charles I were sold by Parliament after his execution in 1649.] This was the ground of their war, whatsoever they pretend to the contrary.

92. PARLIAMENTARY DEBATE ON CAUSES OF THE WAR

This debate took place in spring, 1659, in a Parliament summoned by Richard Cromwell: the proposed upper chamber ("the Other House") was under discussion, and suggestions that the establishment of the sovereignty of the representatives of the people had been the aim of the revolution led to a discussion of what the Civil War had in fact been about. No one suggested that it had been fought about religion (see Part IV). Neville and Baynes were followers of Harrington (see No. 90). Baynes speaks of "the people," but he is anxious that government should be "built upon property, else the poor must rule it." Clearly for him "the poor" are something different from "the people."

Burton, II, p. 390, III, pp. 133–4, 145–8, 186–8.

Mr. Scot: What was fought for, but to arrive at that capacity to make your own laws? . . .

Mr. Neville: The Commons, till Henry VII, never exercised a negative voice. All depended on the Lords. In that time it would have been hard to have found in this house so many gentlemen of estates. The gentry do not now depend upon the peerage. The balance is in the gentry. They have all the lands. Now Lords, old or new, must be supported by the people. There is the same reason why the Lords should not have a negative voice, as that the King should not have a negative: to keep up a sovereignty against nature. The people of England will not suffer a negative voice to be in those who have not a natural power over them. And for the militia, that power which was to be employed for the preserving of laws, that was employed against them. No power will acquiesce in the taking away their own power. When we are naturally free, why should we make ourselves slaves artificially? Let us not return to the government of the Long Parliament. It was an oligarchy, detested by all men that love a commonwealth: so that whosoever lays that upon us, it was not the government contended for. . . . It will be in vain to recognize any body, till you have provided for the liberty of the people. . . .

Lieutenant-general Ludlow: The great quarrel between the King and us was the militia. Either he or we were guilty. . . . When the interest of the nation was suitable to government by Kings (but that was when the constitution was another thing than now it is) the people might live peaceably and be happy under Kings. . . . [But now] if we take the people's liberties from them, they will snatch them back again. . . .

Captain Baynes: I hope the gentlemen in the Other House that have fought against the negative voice and for the militia, and got their estates by it, will not now turn contrary. . . . There are forty knights in this House, that represent more than the property of all the Other House. The House of Lords, heretofore, could draw to the field half the nation. They had great dependencies.

They had a foundation, a property, which was sufficient to support a third estate. The old Lords did stand in balance by their property.

We are not at the root and bottom of our business. The first thing is to see the materials. All government is built upon property, else the poor must rule it. All nations are so. Let us therefore consider things before persons. . . . The constitution of King, Lords and Commons can never be suitable to this nation as now constituted. When the Lords were not able to maintain themselves, some of them truckled under the King, some under the Parliament, as they could shift; and by late experience, what a screen and complete balance were the Lords between the King and the people! Do all that they could, the King, and themselves to boot, were most of them broken in pieces under the Commons.

The people were too hard for the King in property; and then in arms too hard for him. We must either lay the foundation in property, or else it will not stand. Property, generally, is now with the people; the government therefore must be there. If you make a single person, he must be a servant and not a lord. . . . If you can find a House of Lords to balance property, do it. Else let a senate be chosen by the election of the people, on the same account. There must be a balance. . . .

Major-General Lambert: For the transactions these 14 years, it is no matter whether the militia, negative voice or delinquency were the first occasion of the quarrel. . . . It was certainly a complicated quarrel, under all the united prerogatives and exorbitances of an old monarchy, and the defence of the people to reduce it to its just limits. The prerogative began too great and continued too great.

Therefore it is not amiss to look back into the parties concerned, on both sides. What party was the King's? What were the Parliament's dependencies? And what engagements had either side to bring such great bodies for their defence into the field? The King and Parliament were, as it were, the two great general heads of this difference. The universality of their quarrel engaged almost all the world on one side or the other; especially in England, Scotland and Ireland, scarce a family but was divided. All had their angry divisions, and something of interest too, bound up in this quarrel. . . .

For the King, it is plain that Papists, prelates and delinquents, all such as had places or titles, pluralists of honour or profit, and generally all debauched people, ran with that stream. For the Parliament's party, an honest, sober, grave people, that groaned under oppressions, thirsted after grace, the reformed party of the nation, that owned their country's service, that had no by-ends and expected no advantage from the King or from the court. And these were the arguments and interests that brought the parties into the field:

(i) The Papist had his toleration, and prerogative was that strength and source whence that was to proceed. . . . (ii) The Prelates, they had the advancement and the formalities, which all flowed from the same fountain. Preferment flowed readily on. (iii) Dependence upon places of honour or profit, in pensions or expectancies, engaged many, and led a great way; but when I spoke of honour I spoke of names, not things. (iv) Debauched people expected liberty, or rather license, to exercise their lusts and villanies without control. . . .

On the other side, there was only a sober, quiet, reformed people, generally thought—perhaps not universally so neither.

93. RELIGION OR CLASS INTERESTS?

From *A Remonstrance of Many Thousand Citizens* (July, 1646), an early Leveller pamphlet, probably by Overton (see Part IX). Its analysis of the causes and course of the war is from a more radical angle than the preceding extracts, but fits in with views we have already quoted. On the mixture of religion and economic interests, cf. No. 58 and Part VIII; on parsons as propagandists, cf. Nos. 52, 57, 113. Overton's view of who "the people" were contrasts with that of the Harringtonians (Nos. 90, 92); but even he suggests that

Parliament's first appeal was to "considerable substantial persons." This pamphlet heralds the advent of less "substantial" persons into politics, in opposition to the wealthier parliamentarians' desire to compromise with the royalists (cf. Nos. 105–6, Part IX). For "Norman bondage" as a symbol of feudalism, see No. 151.
Wolfe. pp. 117–29.

Time hath revealed hidden things unto us, things covered over thick and threefold with pretences of "the true reformed religion." . . . This nation, and that of Scotland, are joined together in a most bloody and consuming war by the waste and policy of a sort of lords in each nation, that were malcontents and vexed that the King had advanced others . . . to the managing of state affairs. . . .

Their work was to subvert the monarchical lords and clergy. . . . But this was a mighty work, and they were no wise able to effect it of themselves. "Therefore," say they, "the generality of the people must be engaged; and how must this be done? Why," say they, "we must associate with that part of the clergy that are now made underlings . . . and with the most zealous religious non-conformists; and by the help of these we will lay before the generality of the people all the Popish innovations in religion, all the oppressions of the bishops and High Commission, all the exorbitances of the Council-board and Star Chamber, all the injustice of the Chancery and courts of justice, all the illegal taxations . . . , whereby we shall be sure to get into our party the generality of the City of London, and all the considerable substantial people of both nations. . . ."

"But," say some, "this will never be effected without a war, for the King will have a strong party, and he will never submit to us."—"'Tis not expected otherwise", say they; "and great and vast sums of money must be raised, and soldiers and ammunition must be had, whereof we shall not need to fear any want; for what will not an oppressed, rich and religious people do to be delivered from all kinds of oppression, both spiritual and temporal, and to be restored to purity and freedom in religion, and to the just liberty of their persons and estates?

"All our care must be to hold all at our command and disposing; for if this people thus stirred up by us should make an end too soon with the King and his party, it is much to be doubted they would place the supreme power in their House of Commons, unto whom only of right it belongeth, they only being chosen by the people. . . . So . . . we must be careful the supreme power fall not into the people's hands, or the House of Commons'. . . . If any shall presume to oppose . . . us . . . we shall be easily able, by the help of the clergy, by our party in the House of Commons, and by their and our influence in all parts of both nations, easily to crush and suppress them. . . ."

The war might in the beginning have been prevented if ye had drawn a little more blood from the right vein. . . . Ye might have ended the war long ere this, if by sea or land ye had shewed yourselves resolved to make us a free people. But it is evident, a change of our bondage is the uttermost is intended us. . . .

Ye are extremely altered in demeanour towards us. In the beginning ye seemed to know what freedom was, made [no] distinction of honest men, whether rich or poor, all were welcome to you. . . . We cannot but expect to be delivered from the Norman bondage, . . . and from all unreasonable laws made ever since that unhappy conquest. . . . The work, ye must note, is ours and not your own, though ye are to be the partakers with us in the well or ill doing thereof; and therefore ye must expect to hear more frequently from us than ye have done, nor will it be your wisdom to take these admonitions and cautions in evil part. . . . We know we have store of friends in our neighbour countries.

94. THE PARLIAMENTARY ARMY AND NAVY

These extracts show the Parliamentary forces in formation. The first four illustrate the democratic principle on which Cromwell selected his officers and men. His troops were so much more successful than the rest of the Parliamentary armies that these principles ultimately became the basis of the New Model Army (see Nos. 105–6). Crawford, a Scot (*d*), stood for a more conservative point of view (see No. 103). Extract *e*) is a propaganda account of Parliamentary recruiting in the South-west. Extract *f*), a letter from the Earl of Warwick to John Pym (July 6th, 1642), illustrates pleasantly the sophistry of the Parliament's claim to fight on behalf of 'King and Parliament'. Cf. Nos. 80, *b*) and 91, *f*).

a) Abbott, I, p. 256; *b*) *ibid.*, p. 262; *c*) *ibid.*, IV, p. 471; *d*) *ibid.*, I, pp. 277-8; *e*) John Ashe, *A Perfect Relation* (1642), pp. 4-5; *f*) Rushworth IV, p. 752.

a) CROMWELL TO SUFFOLK COMMITTEE, AUGUST, 1643

You have no infantry at all considerable; hasten your horses;—a few hours may undo you, neglected. I beseech you be careful what captains of horse you choose, what men be mounted; a few honest men are better than numbers. . . . If you choose godly honest men to be captains of horse, honest men will follow them, and they will be careful to mount such. . . . I had rather have a plain russet-coated captain that knows what he fights for and loves what he knows, than that which you call a "gentleman" and is nothing else. I honour a gentleman that is so indeed.

b) TO THE SAME, SEPTEMBER 28TH, 1643

Gentlemen, it may be it provokes some spirits to see such plain men made captains of horse. It had been well that men of honour and birth had entered into these employments, but why do they not appear? Who would have hindered them? But seeing it was necessary the work must go on, better plain men than none.

c) CROMWELL TO HAMPDEN, 1642 OR 1643

"Your Troopers," said I, "are most of them old decayed serving-men and tapsters and such kind of fellows; and," said I, "their troopers are gentlemen's sons, younger sons, persons of quality. Do you think that the spirits of such base and mean fellows will be ever able to encounter gentlemen that have honour, courage and resolution in them? . . . You must get men of a spirit,—and take it not ill what I say, I know you will not—of a spirit that is like to go as far as a gentleman will go, or else I am sure you will be beaten still." . . . I told him I could do somewhat in it. . . . I raised such men as had the fear of God before them, and made some conscience of what they did; and from that day forward . . . they were never beaten.

d) CROMWELL TO MAJOR-GENERAL CRAWFORD, MARCH, 1644

The complaints you preferred to my Lord [Manchester] against your lieutenant colonel . . . have occasioned his stay here. . . . Surely you are not well advised thus to turn off one so faithful to the cause, and so able to serve you as this man is. Give me leave to tell you, I cannot be of your judgment. . . . Ay, but the man is an Anabaptist! Are you sure of that? Admit he be, shall that render him incapable to serve the public? . . .

Sir, the state in choosing men to serve them takes no notice of their opinions; if they be willing faithfully to serve them, that satisfies. I advised you formerly to bear with men of different minds from yourself: if you had done it when I advised you to it, I think you would not have had so many stumbling blocks in your way. It may be you judge otherwise, but I tell you my mind.

e) RECRUITMENT BY PARLIAMENT

Upon Friday morning they all marched together unto the place appointed for that day's meeting, in the town of Chewton [near Wells], and thither came unto us all the trained bands of that quarter of the shire, and especially Master Popham's regiment, complete in number, nay doubled twice over by means of volunteers, who came best armed and were most ready in the use of their arms.

At this place met some of your committees and some of your deputy lieutenants, to wit, Sir Edward Hungerford (who lent arms of his own unto 150 or 200 volunteers) [etc.] . . . and after we had been upon the place about one or two hours our company was increased to the number of about 40 thousand. . . . Many of these had no more weapons but their swords, yet all came to show their affections to the King and Parliament. . . . This great company was made up of all the gentry and yeomanry, and lastly youths that inhabited in the north-east part of the county; there came unto us every one of Master Smith's tenants, 40 yeoman well armed, and all the inhabitants in that quarter where [the royalist] Sir Ralph Hopton lived unto his very gates.

There came also out of those parts of Wiltshire near Sir Edward Hungerford's quarter about 2 or 3 hundred horsemen. . . . There came likewise 300 lusty stout men of very good rank and quality of the city of Bristol. . . . There came from Gloucestershire a company of foot well armed, consisting of 250 or 300 men . . . all volunteers.

f) THE FLEET IS WON OVER

I received his Majesty's letters for the discharging me of the command of the Fleet wherewith I was intrusted. . . . I called a Council of War, and acquainted them with his Majesty's letters, and likewise with the Ordinance of Parliament, sent from the Houses for me to continue my charge. I confess it was a great strait that I was in, between two commands that have so much power over me. But when I consider the great care which I have ever observed in the Parliaments of this Kingdom . . . and likewise that the trust of his fleet for the defence of his Majesty and the Kingdoms was committed to me by them; and knowing the integrity of my own heart to his Majesty and Parliament, I resolved not to desert that charge committed to my trust, . . . which having declared to my captains at the Council of War, all of them unanimously and cheerfully took the same resolution, excepting five, . . . all which five refused to come upon my summons, as having no authority over them, and got together round that night to make their defence against me. [But they were soon compelled to submit.]

95. THE ROYALIST ARMY

The Cavalier Army was very different in composition and behaviour from that of Parliament. These extracts help to explain why Parliament won in the end. The German Prince Rupert, Duke of Cumberland (Charles I's nephew), was known to Parliamentary wits as Prince Robber, Duke of Plunderland. Contemporaries said that he introduced the German word "plunder" into the English language. "Tush!" he is reported as saying; "we will have no law in England henceforward but the sword" (Lilly, *True History of King James I and King Charles I* (1651; ed. 1715), p. 9.

a) Warwick, *Memoirs*, p. 253; *b*) Aubrey, *Brief Lives* (1898), I, p. 157; *c*) Warburton, II, p. 191; *d*) Oglander, pp. 117–9.

a) AT THE BATTLE OF EDGEHILL, 1642

The King had given leave unto his own volunteer guard of noblemen and gentlemen, who, with their attendance, made two such troops as that they consisted of about 300 horse; . . . and I had the honour to be of the number, and to be one of the most inconsiderable persons of it; and when we valued the estates of the whole troop, we reckoned there was £100,000 per annum in that body staked that day in that engagement, against men of very disproportionable quality.

b) BAD RELATIONS BETWEEN OFFICERS AND MEN

Sir Robert Harley . . . has often said that generally the commanders of the King's army would never be acquainted with their soldiers, which was an extraordinary prejudice to the King's cause.

c) AN OFFICER REPORTS TO PRINCE RUPERT, MAY, 1643

Our men are not very governable, nor do I think they will be unless some of them be hanged, for they fall extremely to the old kind of plundering. . . . We have already driven a few sheep and some few cattle from a knight that is notoriously known to be ill-affected to the King's service. I am informed we shall find some more such to-morrow in our journey home; we shall do the like from them.

d) A ROYALIST'S COMPARISON

Truly all, or the greatest part, of the King's commanders were so debased by drinking, whoring and swearing that no man could expect God's blessing on their actions. . . . They imputed their failures to want of money, for they would idly spend it as fast as they had it, not caring how they burdened the country, thereby making of their friends their enemies.

The Lord Goring, having taken one Mr. Peard, a Parliament man, in Devonshire when he had the command of that county under his Majesty, 1645, . . . asked him, "And pray, what say they of me in the Parliament House?"

"Truly, sir," replied Mr. Peard, "they speak very well of you and are glad you came into this county, assuring themselves that you will prove one of the best friends they have."

"How, I?" answered Goring. "The Devil will sooner be their friend. But pray tell me what is their meaning by it?"

"Sir," answered Peard, "I pray excuse me, or I might have my throat presently cut by your army."

After Goring had long entreated him, with many oaths and protestations that no hurt should be done unto him, Peard said, "Truly, sir, the Parliament is confident that, through your looseness and debasement, which your army will imitate, and the great impositions that you will lay on the county, you will make them of our enemies become our friends." This proved true.

On the contrary, the Parliament took all course possible to civilize their soldiers, and therefore chose preaching commanders, no drunkards or swearers, kept their army in outward show very civil, duly paid them to avoid discontenting the country . . . [etc.].

96. PARLIAMENTARY FINANCE

These extracts show how Parliament paid for the war. Supported most strongly in London, the corporate towns and the rural clothing areas (see Part II), Parliament had far more wealth to draw on than the King (*a*)—from an Irish Catholic agent in Germany to Rome). But support came from ordinary people all over the country. Extract *c*) is an enemy's sneer, but shows the popularity of the Parliamentary cause (cf. *d*)—showing the growth *from below* of the famous Eastern Association). In Oxford, on the other hand, Charles I's headquarters, plate had to be forcibly requisitioned from some of the colleges. Extract *f*) shows how loans upon the public faith were gerrymandered to the advantage of the bourgeoisie (cf. No. 164, *b*)). When voluntary contributions proved insufficient, Parliament introduced a regular system of taxation, and also laid hands on the property of its opponents; *b*) shows how this fostered democratic control. Extract *g*), written after the event, shows how important was the City's support. It also makes an interesting anticipation of the labour theory of value (cf. No. 147, *a*)), and suggests how the moneyed men subsequently repented of the democratic revolution they had unleashed and helped to bring about the Restoration (cf. No. 188, *a*) and *d*).

a) *Historical Manuscripts Commission, Franciscan*, p. 232; *b*) Brilliana, Lady Harley, quoted in Notestein, *English Folk* (1938), p. 303; *c*) J. H[owell], *Some Sober Inspections made into the Carriage . . . of the late Long Parliament*, pp. 128–9; *d*) quoted in Kingston, *East Anglia and the Civil War* (1897), pp. 83–4; *e*) Warburton, II, p. 277; *f*) as *c*), p. 147; *g*) Hobbes, *English Works*, VI, pp. 299, 304, 320–1; *h*) Dugdale, pp. 112–4, 120, 127–8; *j*) Oglander, pp. 120–1.

a) A CATHOLIC ENVIES THE BOURGEOISIE'S WEALTH, 1642

Parliament . . . really rules, having in its possession the royal rents and the rents of the gentlemen who aid the King, the wealth of the City of London, the rents of the bishops, the hearts of the greater and better part of the cities of the realm, all the ships of the fleet, all the ports of the sea, immense contributions of money from all the counties. . . . What means has he [Charles I] to keep the machine going, while the Parliament holds all the money of the kingdom?

b) THE POOR CONTRIBUTE MOST

Those that have hearts have not means, and they that have means have not hearts.

c) VOLUNTARY CONTRIBUTIONS—A ROYALIST SNEER

Unusual voluntary collections were made both in town and country. The sempstress brought in her silver thimble, the chamber-maid her bodkin, the cook his silver spoon, the vintner his bowl into the common treasury of war. . . . And observed it was, that some sorts of females were freest in those contributions, as far as to part with their rings and ear-rings.

d) VOLUNTARY CONTRIBUTIONS IN SUFFOLK

Shimpling, the eighth day of March, Anno Domini 1643.

These whose names by us are here underwritten have given their consents to join in the Association according to the Book of Directions; and what arms they will find, as followeth:

John Wells, clerk [i.e. clergyman], will find a musket complete; but no pay.

Widow Copping will contribute 10*s*.

George Causon will contribute 10*s*. for the pay of Mr. Wells's musket.

Thomas Gardner will find a musket complete and 20*s*. of money.

William Gallant, Widow Hammond, Thomas Coe and John Smythe will find a musket complete and 20*s*. of money. . .

Richard Pawsey will find an old headpiece and a sword.

They that did join before the commissions was John Plampin, to find a musket and 20*s*. . . .

These are all that will find arms; the rest have consented to associate [26 names].

e) AN OFFICER REPORTS TO PRINCE RUPERT

Here is one Samuel Webb, a clothier, who both hath and doth assist the Parliament against the King. . . . He has sent a great quantity of cloth into Gloucester; and indeed there is scarcely one of all these clothiers but have both lent money and do maintain soldiers upon their own charges against his Majesty.

Painswick, 3 miles from Gloucester, the 7th Aug. 1643.

f) THE RICH PROFIT BY LOANS TO PARLIAMENT

When the lenders upon [the] public faith came to demand their moneys, they could not have them unless they doubled the first sum; . . . but if they *doubled* not both interest and principal, they should not be capable to have any lands allowed for their moneys. Divers to my knowledge have ruined themselves hereby, and though they clamoured and spoke high language at the Parliament's door, and were promised satisfaction, yet they could not get a penny to this day.

g) IMPORTANCE OF THE CITY OF LONDON

B.: What means had he [Charles I] to pay, what provision had he to arm, nay, means to levy, an army able to resist the army of the Parliament, maintained by the great purse of the City of London, and contributions of almost all the towns corporate in England? . . .

A.: Those that helped the King in that kind were only lords and gentlemen. . . .

B.: It seems not only by this but also by many examples in history, that there can hardly arise a long or dangerous rebellion that has not some such overgrown city with an army or two in its belly to foment it.

A.: Nay more; those great capital cities, when rebellion is upon pretence of grievances, must needs be of the rebel party: because the grievances are but taxes, to which citizens (that is, merchants), whose profession is their private gain, are naturally mortal enemies; their only glory being to grow excessively rich by the wisdom of buying and selling.

B.: But they are said to be of all callings the most beneficial to the commonwealth, by setting the poorer sort of people on work.

A.: That is to say, by making poor people sell their

labour to them at their own prices; so that poor people, for the most part, might get a better living by working in Bridewell, than by spinning, weaving and other such labour as they can do: saving that by working slightly [i.e. imperfectly] they may help themselves a little, to the disgrace of our manufacture. And as most commonly they [merchants] are the first encouragers of rebellion, presuming of their strength, so also are they, for the most part, the first to repent, deceived by them that command their strength.

h) METHODS OF FINANCE

[November 29th, 1642] there issued out an order from both Houses, that Committees should be named throughout all counties to take care for provisions of victual for the Army raised by the Parliament; as also for seizing on dragoon horses and draught-horses; and for borrowing of money or plate, to supply the army upon the *public faith*. Which committees had thereby power to send for and take such provisions, money, plate and horse as the owners did then neglect to bring in.

And having formerly ordered that the King and Queen's revenue coming into the Exchequer should be detained and employed for the public service; they seized on thirteen hundred quarters of corn which were then in the King's stores. Also, for explanation of their former ordinance touching the contribution of horse, money and plate . . . they ordered that the refusers should be distrained; and in default of distresses to be found, their persons to be imprisoned. . . .

They saw the people, by degrees, so patiently submit to many other burdens; they began to debate . . . how fit and necessary it would be for them to impose excise, upon wine, beer, tobacco, and such petty commodities . . . Whereas the first ordinance of excise was but only for maintenance of the army and payment of debts due by the Commonwealth, they passed another . . . upon such commodities as had not been formerly taxed; besides an alteration of the rates. Which commodities were strong-waters, medicinal drugs, haberdashers-ware, upholsterer's ware, salt, sallets, soap; all sorts of woollen cloth, papers, skins and glasses.

j) PERSONAL EXPERIENCE

Besides excise, customs, tonnage and poundage, all the King's lands, delinquents' lands under sequestration, all the King's goods, subjects that have been plundered, the Bishops' lands, the deans' and chapters' lands, all the Prince of Wales's estate and the tin and lead mines, the Parliament lays a tax on the kingdom of £90,000 for the army. Of which the Isle of Wight pays every month £305, and the parish of Brading pays every month £21 10*s*., and of this Sir John Oglander payeth £3 10*s*., and every week 18*s*.

97. ROYALIST FINANCE

Royalist finance was very different from that of Parliament. There were few voluntary contributions from any but great lords, bishops, Oxford and Cambridge colleges. Wealthy peers like the Earl of Glamorgan, later Earl and Marquis of Worcester (supposed to be the richest man in England) and the Marquis, later Duke, of Newcastle raised and financed whole armies. Here we have the Marquis of Worcester's bill, as he presented it after the Restoration. (For Newcastle, see No. 165, *b*)). Worcester made the most of his contribution, of course; but as a great Papist peer he had everything to lose by a victory of Parliament. That did not prevent him and his father driving a hard bargain, as *b*) shows. In 1646 Charles I sent Glamorgan to Ireland to arrange for a Papist army to be brought over to fight for the King in England; but the plot was exposed before it came to fruition. Charles gave Glamorgan a patent for a dukedom, but this promise was not honoured in 1660. For long after the Restoration the Marquis of Worcester (who had lived on £3 a week in the 'fifties) was in grave financial difficulties (see note to No. 194).

a) Warburton, III, pp. 523–30; *b*) *ibid*., pp. 140–1.

a) POST-RESTORATION CLAIMS BY THE MARQUIS OF WORCESTER

How came the then Marquis of Hertford, after his defeat in the West, with recruits to his Majesty at Oxford, but by my father's means and mine? The forces that I sent with him had cost me £8,000; and £2,000 my father lent him, ready money. How came Sir John Byron's regiment of horse to be first raised, but by £5,000 in gold, given him by my father? How came the Forest of Dean to be reduced; Goodrich strong castle to be taken; Monmouth itself, with its garrison, to be surprised; Chepstow, Newport and Cardiff to be taken and secured for his Majesty, but by my forces and my father's money? How came Raglan Castle to be first fortified and last rendered, but £50,000 disbursed therein by my father?

How came his Majesty's army to be considerable before Edgehill fight but by the men I brought? . . . At 14 days' warning I brought 4,000 foot and 800 horse to the siege of Gloucester, paying them £6,000 down upon the nail . . . besides my troop of Life Guard, consisting of six score noblemen and gentlemen, whose estates amounted to above three score thousand pounds a year, most of whom I furnished with horse and arms. . . .

I have spent, lent, . . . for my King and country, . . . £918,000.

b) CLAIMS IN 1642—A NOTE FOR THE KING

The effect of the message your Majesty desireth I should deliver to my father from your Majesty at Nottingham, the 9th of September, 1642.—That your Majesty, with many thanks, expressed yourself most sensible of the great expense and charge his lordship had been at for your service, far more than any man else. . . . If he and his friends could procure £10,000, your Majesty would suddenly, if it please God to restore you, see it repaid, and would presently, in token of thankfulness, send my father the Garter . . . and also . . . you would pass a patent of Marquis of what title my father should desire. . . . If this could possibly be performed, then the crown, which hitherto your Majesty confesseth to stay upon your head by his assistance, will be then confirmed by him.

98. EFFECTS OF WAR ON RELATIONS OF LANDLORD AND TENANT

To raise money, and to deprive Royalist landlords of their revenues, Parliament ordered tenants of Royalists to pay in their rents to the revolutionary committees set up by Parliament in the counties (*a*). Royalists who accepted the victory of Parliament were subsequently allowed to "compound" for their estates, i.e. to buy them back (*e*); cf. No. 166). Tenants took advantage of "these times of liberty and distraction" to refuse to pay rents due even to landlords who took the side of Parliament, to throw open enclosures, etc. (see also Nos. 99–100). Yet after Pride's Purge (see Part XI), Parliament had to take further action which a conservative Parliamentarian viewed with concern as stirring up tenants to disregard landlords' rights (*e*).

a) Firth and Rait, *Acts and Ordinances of the Interregnum*, I, pp. 106–8; *b*) *Memoirs of the Verney Family during the Civil War*, II, pp. 86, 90–1; *c*) *ibid.*, I, pp. 271–2; *d*) ed. W. Beaumont, *A Discourse of the War in Lancashire* (Chetham Soc., 1864), p. 131; *e*) Walker, Part II, p. 204.

a) PARLIAMENTARY ORDINANCE OF MARCH 27TH, 1643

[ESTATES of all supporters of the King to be seized by county sequestration committees.] And the said Sequestrators . . . are hereby authorised and required . . . to receive such rents, arrearages of rents . . . due or payable by their or any of their several and respective tenants or other person or persons: which said tenants and other persons are hereby required to pay the same to the said Sequestrators. . . . Yet so nevertheless that in respect of the hardness of the times and the great charges which otherwise lie upon the said tenants and others by occasion of this present war, every such tenant which shall pay to the said Sequestrators . . . shall upon their obedience and conformity to this Ordinance be considered out of the said rents, revenues and profits, and shall be discharged of his whole rent against his landlord or any other to whom the same is due, being . . . delinquents.

b) MRS. EURE TO RALPH VERNEY, 1642

I wish you all to take heed of women, for this very vermin have pulled down an enclosure, which some of them were put in prison for it by the Justices, that had their pipe to go before them, and their ale and cakes to make themselves merry when they had done their feats of activity. . . . I wish all were well ended, for things stand in so ill a condition here as we can make no money of our coal-pits. If rents fail and those fail too we shall be in a hard case. . . .

Times are so bad here as we have not made one penny of our coals, and we have not received one penny from Misterton, so my husband was forced to send for those rents as were gathered up to keep life and soul together, which was but £100. . . . I am in such a rage with the Parliament as nothing will pacify me, for they promised us all should be well if my Lord Strafford's head were off, and since then there is nothing better, but I think we shall be undone with taxes, and if we have no rents neither it will be a hard case.

c) LADY SUSSEX TO THE SAME, 1645

My estate is fallen so low, and the uncertainty of it and my life such, having neither lease nor inheritance, that any security from me cannot any way be considerable; . . . my plate being all gone, but a very little left; and some of my gems gone too; for this last year and a half I disbursed much more than my comings-in; my fifth and twentieth parts I paid, and £10 a week for an extraordinary; . . . contributions on both sides. . . . The whole kingdom being as it is, we cannot tell how long we may enjoy any thing; . . . and for my little rents that are due now I owe more than they come to. . . . I hope if I can get my rents in I may make it up. . . . Money is so hard a commodity to come by now that many suffer much.

d) A STEWARD TO HIS LORD, JUNE 17TH, 1646

The poorness of the people [of Hoole, Lancashire], neglect of calling upon them for their rents, together with these times of liberty and distraction, rendered them of that place incredibly forgetful, and many would deny to pay any rent.

e) INCITING TENANTS AGAINST LANDLORDS, 1649

"An Act for the relief of well-affected tenants against malignant landlords who have compounded for their estates, rack their tenants' rents, or turn them out of doors." This is a device . . . to stir up all the tenants of England (especially schismatics) to combine with them [Parliament] against their landlords, and deprive them of the legal use of their estates and the benefit of their compositions; for to what purpose shall gentlemen compound for their estates when they must let and set them at the discretion of domineering committees?

99. SOCIAL UNREST

In many places where lands had recently been enclosed the inhabitants seized the opportunity offered by the general confusion to re-establish their rights. There are many examples like those in *a*). Extract *b*) is a Royalist account of the destruction of manorial records, an exploit often repeated in the French and Russian Revolutions. The peasants felt that if the lord's evidence of his claims against them could be destroyed, his power to enforce his claims would also vanish. Extract *c*), written after the Restoration by a Royalist, shows women coming into politics—on the Parliamentary side (cf. No. 115).

a) *Lords' Journals*, IV, p. 262, V, p. 592; *b*) [Bruno Ryves] *Angliæ Ruina* (1647), pp. 31–4, 249; *c*) Butler, *Hudibras*, Part II, Canto 2, lines 775–80, 799–812.

a) FROM THE JOURNALS OF THE HOUSE OF LORDS

May 31st, 1641. The Earl of Hertford hath been in the quiet possession, some years since, of 160 acres of enclosed land, lying in Godney Moor in the county of Somerset; yet now of late, and sitting this present Parliament, some have disorderly and in a riotous manner broken down several parcels [i.e. parts] of the said enclosures, and put in their cattle into the said 160 acres; and give out threatening speeches that they will use violence to any man that shall offer to oppose such their doings. . . . [Ordered that they shall desist and be punished.]

February 7th, 1643. Divers of the inhabitants of the

towns of Sutton and Luton in the county of Lincoln have of late, in a riotous and tumultuous manner, entered upon the marsh called Sutton Marsh, and pulled down some of the dwelling houses and committed great waste and spoil in corn and other goods there, and have threatened the tenants to lay all the said marsh common unless they remove their dwellings before Shrove Tuesday next. . . . [Riots to be suppressed.]

b) DESTRUCTION OF FEUDAL RECORDS

On Monday the 15th of August, 1642, Sir Richard Minshall of Bourton in the county of Buckingham, knight, furnished with 10 horse and arms, began his journey into the north to wait upon the King, as in the duty of a servant and subject he was bound. . . . [His house was sacked.] They break open his library, and the place where he kept his evidences; they seize on all bills, bonds, deeds, evidences, writings and books which they find, whether Sir Richard's or his friends': some of these they take away with them, some they tear in pieces, some they bind in bundles and make them serve instead of fuel both to heat ovens and to roast meat for their supper; and would by no means suffer any of them to be redeemed, though large sums of money were offered for them. . . .

[At Peterborough Cathedral the looters] must needs swallow up the lands appertaining to that church; to which, that they might pretend the juster title, they broke open the charter-house, plundered away the great charter, all the evidences, leases and other writings belonging thereunto, manifesting their party's desire to have all estates of others to come and be at their arbitrary disposals.

c) WOMEN

Women, that were our first apostles,
Without whose aid we'd all been lost else;
Women, that left no stone unturned
In which the Cause might be concerned;

Brought in their children's spoons and whistles,
To purchase swords, carbines and pistols. . . .
What have they done, or what left undone,
That might advance the Cause at London?
Marched rank and file, with drum and ensign,
T' entrench the City for defence in;
Raised ramparts with their own soft hands,
To put the enemy to stands;
From ladies down to oyster-wenches
Laboured like pioneers in trenches,
Fell to their pickaxes and tools
And helped the men to dig like moles.
Have not the handmaids of the City
Chosen of their members a committee
For raising of a common purse
Out of their wages, to raise horse?

100. THE CLASS STRUGGLE

Class feeling ran high during and after the Civil War. Extracts *a*) and *c*) come from the notebook of Sir John Oglander, a Royalist who before the war was living well above his income, even allowing for dues in kind to the value of £300 a year which he received from tenants and "friends"; so naturally he disliked a situation in which "base men" got above themselves. He was twice imprisoned by Parliament. Extract *f*) is from a report by a Parliamentary journalist of what Henrietta Maria is alleged to have told her son when he left his exile in France to accept the crown of Scotland. It is not to be accepted literally, but is evidence of what contemporaries expected her to say.

a) Oglander, p. 104; *b*) Warburton, II, p. 122; *c*) Oglander, p. 109; *d*) *A Character of England*, in John Evelyn's *Miscellaneous Writings* (1825), p. 150; *e*) ed. Browning, *Memoirs of Sir John Reresby* (1936), pp. 21–2; *f*) Gardiner, *Charles II and Scotland in 1650*, pp. 19–20.

a) A ROYALIST IN THE ISLE OF WIGHT, 1642

I BELIEVE such times were never before seen in England, when the gentry were made slaves to the commonalty and in their power, not only to abuse but plunder any gentleman. No law and government, no assizes, no sessions, no justices that would be obeyed, no spiritual courts. If any notorious malefactor was sent to the gaol, the next soldiers that came released him by breaking up the gaol. . . . Our fears are that the worst is to come. . . .

b) PRINCE RUPERT'S DECLARATION AGAINST PARLIAMENT, 1643

Is it not their usual practice first to plunder a man's house of all plate and monies, and then imprison him as a delinquent, for no other fault but because he stood loyal to his prince? . . . Have they not now stuffed all the prisons in London with Earls, Lords, Bishops, judges and knights, masters of colleges, lawyers and gentlemen, of all conditions and counties? For what (God knows) they themselves know not; insomuch as now they are enforced to find new prisons for the knights, aldermen and substantial citizens of London, who are now thrust in thither only because they are suspected to love their King.

c) A SAD TIME FOR THE GENTRY

From Anno Domini 1641 till Anno Domini 1646, in our unnatural wars . . . most of the ancient gentry were either extinct or undone. The King's side were almost all gentlemen, and of the Parliament's few. As one said, "The King shot bullets of gold for lead." . . . There were in Yorkshire a hundred families extinct or undone, so that none of them could appear again as gentlemen. Death, plunder, sales and sequestrations sent them to another world or beggar's bush, and so all—or most—shires. I verily believe that in the quarrel of the Two Roses there were never half as many gentlemen slain, and so many base men, by the others' loss and slaughter, made gentlemen.

d) A VISITOR TO DEMOCRATIC ENGLAND

[At Rochester] how new a thing it appeared to me to see my confident host set him down cheek by jowl by me, belching and puffing tobacco in my face, you may easily imagine; till I afterwards found it to be the usual style of this country. . . . Arrived at the metropolis of civility, London, we put ourselves in coach with some persons of quality, who came to conduct us to our lodging; but neither was this passage without honour done to us—the kennel-dirt, squibs, roots and rams' horns being favours which were frequently cast at us by the children and apprentices without reproof. . . . Carmen . . . in this town domineer in the streets, overthrow the "hell-carts" (for so they name the coaches), cursing and reviling at the nobles. . . . I have greatly wondered at the remissness of the magistrate and the temper of the gentlemen; and that the citizens, who subsist only upon them, should permit so great a disorder, rather joining in the affronts than at all chastising the inhumanity. But these are the natural effects of parity, popular libertinism and insular manners.

e) SIR JOHN RERESBY IN 1658

The citizens and common people of London had then so far imbibed the custom and manners of a commonwealth that they could scarce endure the sight of a gentleman, so that the common salutation to a man well dressed was "French dog" or the like. Walking one day in the street with my valet de chambre, who did wear a feather in his hat, some workmen that were mending the street abused him and threw sand upon his clothes, at which he drew his sword, thinking to follow the custom of France in the like cases. This made the rabble fall upon him and me, that had drawn too in his defence, till we got shelter in a house, not without injury to our bravery and some blows to ourselves. There was little satisfaction in that town in those days, . . . so that the nobility and gentry lived most in the country.

f) THE QUEEN MOTHER'S ADVICE TO CHARLES II, 1650

She would . . . have him . . . remember that . . . he labour to make the noblemen and barons [of Scotland] unite to preserve their privileges against any attempt upon them by the people.

That he cause to be represented to them that otherwise than by a King they cannot hold what they have against the people.

That, if they should but think of a Commonwealth, the people there would be as free as they are in England.

That it is necessary that their Parliaments therefore be full of the nobility.

101. ADMINISTRATION BY PARLIAMENT

All these extracts are by Royalists, who naturally disliked the revolutionary administration set up by Parliament. Sir John Oglander (*a*) is particularly sour; his "poor Baxter" was a captain in the Parliamentary Army, and Mr. Maynard and Mr. Matthews at least were respectable citizens; but Sir John is horrified that anyone below the rank of gentleman should be concerned in local government. Extract *b*) is intended to make the reader's flesh creep. Again it is more important as evidence of what the ruling class feared than of what was actually happening, at least as early as 1643. The reference to "Christian liberty" shows the uses to which arguments drawn from religion might be put. Cleveland (1613–58), author of *c*), had a great reputation for wit which it is difficult for us to appreciate. But his "Character" is interesting because of its specific parallel with the revolutionary Netherlands (cf. Nos. 67, 89, *d*)). *Hogens-Mogens* ("high mightinesses") is the Dutch title for the ruling dignitaries of the Republic.

a) Oglander, pp. 105–6, 110, 129; *b*) [Ryves] *Angliæ Ruina*, pp. 26–7; *c*) J. Cleveland, *Works* (1687), pp. 72–6.

a) THE COMMITTEE FOR THE SAFETY OF THE ISLE OF WIGHT

O THE tyrannical misery that the gentlemen of England did endure from July, 1642, till April, 1643, and how much longer the Lord knoweth! They could call nothing their own, and lived in slavery and submission to the unruly, base multitude. *O tempora, O mores. . . .*

We had a thing here called a Committee, which overruled Deputy-Lieutenants and also Justices of the Peace; and of this we had brave men: Ringwood of Newport, the pedlar; Maynard, the apothecary; Matthews, the baker; Wavell and Legge, farmers; and poor Baxter of Hurst Castle. These ruled the whole island and did whatsoever they thought good in their own eyes. . . .

1649. John Baskett, Bowreman and Rolph bore the chiefest sway in our island, and, under them, poor Parson Ward's son of Yaverland, and Templar, a collar-maker in Newport, whom they made Marshall, bore all the sway under them.

b) SAD STATE OF AFFAIRS IN CHELMSFORD, 1643

It was lately certified from thence by a chief member of that town . . . that he finds the case there to be far worse than he expected; for while they [the supporters of Parliament] hoped that, the power being (traitorously) wrested out of the King's hand, they should have shared it amongst themselves, they find that either the power is fallen into their hands that are far beneath them, or else hath raised these men up far above them, for as he writes "The town is governed by a tinker, two cobblers, two tailors, two peddlars," etc.

And that the world may see . . . what principles they intend to rule by, I shall here set down certain preparatory prelusory propositions which they usually preach (for preach they do) to their own infatuated disciples: . . . and you shall have them in their own terms, viz.:—

"First, that Kings are the burdens and plagues of those peoples or nations over which they govern.

"Secondly, that the relation of master and servant hath no ground or warrant in the New Testament, but rather the contrary: for there we read 'In Christ Jesus there is neither bond nor free,' and 'We are all one in Christ.'

"Thirdly, that the honours and titles of Dukes, Marquises, Earls, Viscounts, Lords, Knights and gentlemen are but ethnical and heathenish distinctions amongst Christians.

"Fourthly, that one man should have £1,000 a year, another not £1, perhaps not so much, but must live by the sweat of his brows, and must labour before he eat, hath no ground, neither in nature nor in Scripture.

"Fifthly, that the common people, heretofore kept under blindness and ignorance, have a long time yielded themselves servants, nay slaves, to the nobility and gentry; but God hath now opened their eyes and discovered unto them their Christian liberty: and that therefore it is now fit that the nobility and gentry should serve their servants, or at least work for their own maintenance; and if they will not work they ought not to eat."

c) THE CHARACTER OF A COMMITTEE-MAN

A Committee-man is the relics of regal government, but, like the holy relics, he outbulks the substance whereof he is a remnant. There is a score of kings in a Committee, as in the relics of the cross there is the number of 20. . . . I have wondered often why the plundered countrymen should repair to him for succour. . . . The Star Chamber and the High Commission . . . are not extinct; they survive in him. . . . To speak the truth, he is the universal tribunal: for since these times all causes fall to his cognizance, as in a great infection all diseases turn oft to the plague. It concerns our masters the Parliament to look about them; if he proceedeth at this rate, the jack may come to swallow the pike, as the interest often eats out the principal. . . . There was a time when such cattle would hardly have been taken upon suspicion for men in office, unless the old proverb were renewed, that the beggars make a free company, and those their wardens. . . .

Take a state-martyr, one that for his good behaviour has paid the excise of his ears, [or] suffered captivity by the land-piracy of Ship Money; next a primitive freeholder, one that hates the King because he is a gentleman. . . . Add to these a mortified bankrupt, that helps out his false weights with some scruples of conscience. . . . These with a new blue-stockinged Justice, lately made of a good basket-hilted yeoman . . . together with two or three equivocal Sirs, whose religion, like their gentility, is the extract of their acres; . . . not forgetting the man of the law, whose corruption gives the hogan to the sincere junto. These are the simples of this precious compound; a kind of Dutch hotch-potch, the Hogan Mogan Committee-man.

102. ANXIETY OF THE ARISTOCRACY

As the class struggle sharpened, conservative elements on the Parliamentary side, especially big landowners, began to long for a peaceful compromise. In *a*) the shrewd Venetian Ambassador, unfriendly to Parliament, reports this fact home even before the outbreak of war. In *b*) Sergeant-Major R. Kirle gives his reasons for deserting Parliament. The unkind alleged that he changed sides because his family estates were under the control of the King's forces. He certainly changed back again as soon as Parliament was clearly winning. This is a propaganda pamphlet, but is evidence of what was expected to be believed. In *d*) Lord Willoughby writes despondently to the Earl of Denbigh. In fear of the democratic rank and file, peers like Willoughby were prepared to sell out to the King; but, thanks to the vigilance of Cromwell, Ludlow (*e*) and others they failed. The Self-denying Ordinance (No. 106, *a*)) put command of the Army into safe hands. The Earl of Essex, whom Willoughby attacked for excessive military zeal, then proclaimed that he would "devote his life to repressing the audacity of the common people."

a) *C.S.P. Ven.*, 1640-2, p. 284; *b*) Webb, *Memorials of the Civil War in Herefordshire* (1879), II, pp. 349-51; *c*) Warwick, *Memoirs*, pp. 200-1; *d*) Historical Manuscripts Commission, Fourth Report (1874), I, p. 268; *e*) Ludlow, I, pp. 105-6.

a) THE VENETIAN AMBASSADOR, JANUARY 31ST, 1642

THE majority of the upper House . . . sigh earnestly for a mutually satisfactory agreement [between King and both Houses], as they rightly foresee that if the lower House succeeds in beating down the royal authority, it will afterwards proceed to reduce the prerogatives of the nobility as well, and will take complete command of the government. . . . On the other hand the members of the lower House who are the chief architects of this machine encourage disturbance with all their might, in the assurance of raising their own estate upon the ruins of the sovereign's authority.

b) REASONS FOR CHANGING SIDES

About the time these distempers began here I returned from serving the Swede in Germany and the States in Holland. . . . So common were the grievances in that unhappy conjuction of time when I went abroad [late sixteen-thirties] that I retained the same impressions in me at my coming home [and took service under Parliament]. . . .

Master Sedgwick, chaplain to that regiment [the Earl of Stamford's] first opened my eyes . . . by the spirit . . . of fury and madness. He revealed the misery of this war, and in his inspired rage brake the shell (religion, safety of the King, liberty and property) and showed us the kernel (atheism, anarchy, arbitrary government and confusion). . . . What was meant else by encouraging violence and sharing in things plundered? . . . If they cannot prove any of quality to be a Papist, yet as he is a gentleman he shall want grace; and that is title enough to possess the estates of all that are more richer than themselves; and in truth had it not been [for this] persuasion, you might have made riots but not a war; for under the promise of malignants' estates are intended not only those that directly take part with the King, but all those too that shall not concur with you in all things.

c) FALSE POSITION OF HOUSE OF LORDS

This House of Commons, having thus fixed deeply their root [by executing the Earl of Strafford], it is no marvel they raise their top to that height, that ere long it shadowed the Lords' House; and by dripping upon them, in some few years caused them to be voted useless. And indeed that body of men (who resemble a king if not in unity, yet in paucity . . .), forgetting their own natural station, when they withdraw themselves from the cloth of state and dependence on the throne, where they are placed to support it and upon emergent occasions to screen the Commons from any scorching greatness of it, if they forget their duty to their prince and become popular themselves, it will not be long before they be themselves subjected to the commonalty: for it is not title, but useful power, that draws unto itself the reverence of greatness.

d) A PEER ANXIOUS FOR COMPROMISE, 1644

Here [London] we are all hasting to an early ruin, for I cannot see that anything else can satisfy, self-ends rules so much. For peace I cannot so much as ever expect it, nor see a thought by those that sit at the helm tending that way. Nobility and gentry are going down apace. If you that have the active part [in the army] do not preserve it, I am sure we that have the consultative part [will] down with it as fast as we can. We are reprehending my Lord General by a sharp letter for his disobedience in doing more for us against our wills than we would have had by our wills.

e) A REPUBLICAN'S VIEW

By this time [1644] it was clearly manifest that the nobility had no further quarrel with the King than till they could make their terms with him, having, for the most part, grounded their dissatisfactions upon some particular affront or the prevalency of a faction about him. But though it should be granted that their intentions in taking arms were to oblige the King to consent to redress the grievances of the nation; yet if a war of this nature must be determined by treaty, and the King left in the exercise of the royal authority after the utmost violation of the laws and the greatest calamities brought upon the people, it doth not appear to me what security can be given them for the future enjoyment of their rights and privileges; nor with what prudence wise men can engage with the Parliament, who being—by practice at least—liable to be dissolved at pleasure, are thereby rendered unable to protect themselves, or such as take up arms under their authority, if after infinite hardships and hazards of their lives and estates, they must fall under the power of a provoked enemy, who, being once re-established in his former authority, will never want means to revenge himself upon all those who, in defence of the rights and liberties of the nation, adventure to resist him in his illegal and arbitrary proceedings.

103. SCOTTISH ARMY *VERSUS* DEMOCRACY

The conservative Parliamentarians hoped to defeat the Cavaliers with the help of a Scottish army, and so avoid having to arm their own people. Holles (*a*) was a Presbyterian, who was expelled from Parliament in 1648 (see No. 139). He not unnaturally worked for the Restoration in 1660 and received a peerage. In extract *b*) the Levellers point out in 1646 what Holles subsequently admitted.

a) Denzil Holles, *Memoirs* (1699), pp. 9–11; *b*) Wolfe, pp. 123–4.

a) A PRESBYTERIAN LOOKS BACK

The House of Lords in the summer after the beginning of our troubles, . . . having resolved to deliver themselves and the kingdom from this Egyptian slavery, had prepared a message to the King, with overtures for an accommodation, and sent it down to the House of Commons on a Saturday, where the major part . . . after a long dispute and much opposition . . . agreed to some particulars, and, it growing late, adjourned the further debate till Monday morning; against which time these firebrands had set the City in a flame, as if there were a resolution to betray all to the King; and thereupon brought down a rabble of their party, some thousands, to the House of Commons' door, who gave out threatening speeches, and named among themselves (but so as they might be heard) some members of the House, whom they said they looked upon as enemies and would pull out of the House; which did so terrify many honest timorous men, and gave that boldness to the others, as contrary to all order they resumed the question that was settled on Saturday for going on with the business, and at last carried it by some voices to have it laid aside. . . .

This made some persons cast about how a stop might

be given to such violent proceedings, and to have other counsels admitted. . . . It was therefore proposed that our brethren of Scotland might be called in, who were known to be a wise people, lovers of order, firm to monarchy. . . . Their wisdom and moderation, as was presumed, might then have delivered us from that precipice of misery and confusion into which our charioteers were hurrying us amain.

b) A LEVELLER REMONSTRANCE TO THE COMMONS, 1646

Ye have never made that use of the people of this nation, in your war, as you might have done, but have chosen rather to hazard their [the Scots'] coming in than to arm your own native undoubted friends.

101. SCOTTISH ARMY IN ENGLISH POLITICS

These extracts are from letters written home by Baillie, Scottish representative in England. In all his theological and political negotiations with the English Parliamentarians, Baillie relied on the Scottish Army even more than on the Lord of Hosts. The Westminster Assembly was a body of divines convened by Parliament to draft a set of articles of belief more suitable to the new régime. Its deliberations were wholly ineffectual, all serious decisions being taken by the laymen in Parliament. But it helped to deceive some contemporaries and historians as to the importance of religious questions in the revolution (see also No. 108). Baillie, *Letters and Journals*, I, pp. 228, 432, II, pp. 33–4, 98, 204.

December 19th, 1640. God is making here a new world; no fear yet of raising [i.e. dissolving] the parliament so long as the lads about Newcastle lie still. . . .

February 18th, 1644. When we had agreed with Sir Henry Vane and the Solicitor [St. John] upon the draught [of an ordinance setting up a joint Anglo-Scottish Committee of Both Kingdoms], it was gotten through the House of Lords with little difficulty, where most was expected; . . . my Lord Northumberland joining effectually with all our desires, our army being now masters of his lands. . . .

July 5th, 1644. [After news of the victory at Marston Moor.] We dare not be too much exalted, only we bless God from our heart, who is beginning to shine on our army, and make it, after very long expectance and beating down of our pride, to be a fountain of joy and hope to those who love the welfare of religion. We hope things in the [Westminster] Assembly and parliament may go more after our mind. Our army oft signified to us, they conceived their want of success flowed most from God's anger at the parliament and assembly, for their neglect of establishing of religion. We oft told them the truth, that we had no hope of any progress here, till God gave them victories; and then, we doubted not, all would run both in parliament and assembly. . . .

April 25th, 1645. None need to talk of any fickleness or ingratitude of the English towards us, of any advancement of the Independent party; for no man here doubts but if once our army were in such a condition as easily, if we were diligent, might be, all these clouds would vanish, and we would regain this people's hearts, and do with all sectaries, and all things else, what we would. . . .

April 24th, 1646. Fie upon these enemies of Scotland, who mar the sending up of men hither, who by God's blessing might spare us a greater labour, and save much blood, which cannot but be shed if a war begin betwixt the nations. It is neither reason nor religion that stays some men's rage, but a strong army bridling them with fear.

105. CROMWELL DEMANDS AN ARMY THAT WILL FIGHT

At the beginning of the Civil War the peers and other great landlords who sided with Parliament were almost automatically given command of the troops raised in their localities, and the Earl of Essex was made Commander-in-Chief (*a*). But these were exactly the people who did not want to carry the war to a victorious conclusion (see Nos. 102–3). So all radicals demanded an army officered by men who really wanted to win the war. Oliver Cromwell led this agitation, in which social and military motives were combined.

a) Lilly, *King James I and Charles I*, p. 64; *b*) *C.S.P.D.*, 1644–5, p. 151; *c*) *Camden Miscellany*, VIII (1883), fifth item, p. 2; D. Holles, *Memoirs*, p. 18; *d*) Abbott, I, p. 323; *e*) *ibid.*, p. 314; *f*) *ibid.*, p. 128; *g*) *ibid.*, pp. 377–8.

a) SHORTAGE OF PEERS TO COMMAND THE PARLIAMENTARY ARMY

HAD Essex refused to be general, our cause in all likelihood had sunk in the beginning, we having never a nobleman at that time either willing or capable of that honour and preferment; indeed, scarce any of them were fit to be trusted.

b) AT A COUNCIL OF WAR, NOVEMBER 10TH, 1644

Earl of Manchester: If we beat the King 99 times, yet he is King still, and so will his posterity be after him; but if the King beat us once we shall be all hanged, and our posterity be made slaves.

Cromwell: My Lord, if this be so, why did we take up arms at first? This is against fighting ever hereafter. If so, let us make peace, be it never so base.

c) MANCHESTER TO HOUSE OF LORDS, DECEMBER, 1644

Lieutenant-General Cromwell's . . . expressions were sometimes against the nobility; that he hoped to live to see never a nobleman in England, and he loved such better than others because they did not love lords; and that it would not be well till [the Earl of Manchester] was but Mr. Montague.

d) ARCHBISHOP WILLIAMS TO CHARLES I

Cromwell . . . loves none that are more than his equals.

e) CROMWELL IN THE COMMONS, DECEMBER, 1644

It is now a time to speak, or for ever hold the tongue. The important occasion is now no less than to save a nation out of a bleeding, nay almost dying, condition, which the long continuance of this war hath already brought it into; so that without a more speedy, vigorous and effectual prosecution of the war . . . we shall make the kingdom weary of us and hate the name of a Parliament.

For what do the enemy say? Nay, what do many say

that were friends at the beginning of the Parliament? Even this, that the members of both Houses have got great places and commands, and the sword into their hands; and, what by interest in the Parliament, what by power in the army, will perpetually continue themselves in grandeur, and not permit the war speedily to end, lest their own power should determine with it. This I speak here to our own faces is but what others do utter abroad behind our backs. . . . I do conceive if the army be not put into another method, and the war more vigorously prosecuted, the people can bear the war no longer, and will enforce you to a dishonourable peace.

f) CROMWELL AND UNITY, 1641

Combination carries strength with it. It's dreadful to adversaries; especially when it's in order to the duty we owe to God, to the loyalty we owe to our King and sovereign, and to the affection due to our country and liberties.

g) BRISTOL HAS SURRENDERED, SEPTEMBER, 1645

Presbyterians, Independents, all had here the same spirit of faith and prayer; . . . they agree here, know no names of difference: pity it is it should be otherwise any-where. All that believe have the real unity. . . . As for being united in forms, commonly called uniformity, every Christian will for peace-sake study and do as far as con-science will permit; and from brethren in things of the mind we look for no compulsion but that of light and reason. In other things God hath put the sword into the Parliament's hand, for the terror of evil-doers and the praise of them that do well. If any plead exemption from it, he knows not the Gospel: if any would wring it out of your hands, or steal it from you under any pretence soever, I hope they shall do it without effect. That God may maintain it in your hands, and direct you in the use thereof, is the prayer of

Your humble servant,

OLIVER CROMWELL.

106. THE NEW MODEL ARMY

The army with which the Parliament began the war was locally raised, paid and controlled. Inefficiency resulted: it was difficult to get men to serve outside their own counties; and units were commanded by men who happened to be prominent locally, but were not necessarily distinguished for revolutionary determination or military ability. Thus both the more radical Parliamentarians, and those who desired an efficient army, called for the formation of a "New Model," paid by Parliament, under the effective command of one man, and able to go where he, and not some local committee, thought fit. This was achieved in 1645 by the Self-denying Ordinance. The removal at once of conservative officers and of local control by conservative lords-lieutenant and J.Ps. made easier the development of radical and sectarian ideas among the rank and file—as illustrated in *b*) and *c*). Hugh Peters (*b*) was subsequently executed as a regicide (see No. 110). Richard Baxter (*c*) joined the army after Naseby. As to William the Conqueror, see No. 151. Extract *d*) shows that the rank and file of the New Model Army were not all "spiritual-thriving."

a) Gardiner, pp. 287–8; *b*) "Mr. Peter's Message" (1646), in Woodhouse, *Puritanism and Liberty*, p. 387; *c*) Baxter, *Autobiography*, pp. 47–50, 61; Woodhouse, *op. cit.*, pp. 388–9; *d*) quoted in Webb, *Civil War in Herefordshire*, II, pp. 191–2.

a) THE SELF-DENYING ORDINANCE, APRIL 3RD, 1645

Be it ordained by the Lords and Commons assembled in Parliament, that all and every of the members of either House shall be . . . discharged at the end of forty days after the passing of this Ordinance, of and from all and every office or command military or civil, granted or conferred by both or either of the said Houses of this present Parliament. . . .

Provided that this Ordinance shall not extend to take away the power and authority of any Lieutenancy or Deputy-Lieutenancy in the several counties, cities or places, or of any Custos Rotulorum, or of any commission for Justices of Peace, or sewers, or any commission of Oyer and Terminer, or gaol-delivery.

Provided always . . . that those members of either House who had offices by grant from His Majesty before this

Parliament, and were by His Majesty displaced sitting this Parliament, and have since by authority of both Houses been restored, shall not by this Ordinance be discharged from their said offices or profits thereof, but shall enjoy the same.

b) A "SPIRITUAL-THRIVING" ARMY

I can say, your army is under a blessed conduct, their counsels godly and faithful. More love I have not seen, which I believe may spring from this root; that through grace we make godliness our interest, and not opinion, the which we wish were the spirit of the kingdom though we prescribe to none. . . . One thing there is most singular in this your army: that whereas soldiers usually spend and make forfeiture even of the civility they bring into other armies; here men grow religious, and more spiritual-thriving than in any place of the kingdom.

c) THE REVEREND RICHARD BAXTER

The army, being ready to march, was partly the envy and partly the scorn of the nobility and the lords-lieutenants and the officers which had been put out by the Self-denying vote; but their actions quickly vindicated them from contempt. . . .

When I came to the army, among Cromwell's soldiers I found a new face of things which I never dreamt of. I heard the plotting heads very hot upon that which intimated their intention to subvert both church and state. . . .

Abundance of common troopers and many of the officers I found to be honest, sober, orthodox men, and others tractable, ready to hear the truth, and of upright intentions. But a few proud, self-conceited, hot-headed sectaries had got into the highest places, and were Cromwell's chief favourites, and by their very heat and activity bore down the rest, or carried them along with them, and were the soul of the Army though much fewer in number than the rest. . . .

I perceived that they took the King for a tyrant and an

enemy, and really intended absolutely to master him or to ruin him; and that they thought, if they might fight against him, they might kill or conquer him; and if they might conquer, they were never more to trust him further than he was in their power. . . . They said, What were the lords of England but William the Conqueror's colonels, or the Barons but his majors, or the knights but his captains? They plainly showed me that they thought God's providence would cast the trust of religion and the kingdom upon them as conquerors. . . .

But their most frequent and vehement disputes were for liberty of conscience, as they called it; that is, that the civil magistrate had nothing to do to determine of anything in matters of religion by constraint or restraint, but every man might not only hold, but preach and do, in matters of religion, what he pleased; that the civil magistrate hath nothing to do but with civil things, to keep the peace, and protect the churches' liberties, etc. . . .

A great part of the mischief they did among the soldiers was by pamphlets which they abundantly dispersed; such as R. Overton's *Martin Mar-Priest*, and more of his, and some of J. Lilburne's, who was one of them; and divers against the King, and against the ministry, and for liberty of conscience, etc. . . .

The thing contrived [by the Agitators] was an heretical democracy.

d) SIR SAMUEL LUKE, 1645

I think these New Models knead all their dough with ale, for I never saw so many drunk in my life in so short a time. . . . I hear several officers have petitioned the General that they may have liberty to leave the Army, they being not able to live with the ungodly crew. They are grown so wild since they came near the enemy that our devout Christians cannot abide them.

107. NEUTRALS AND OTHERS

It would be wrong to suppose that all Englishmen were enthusiastic partisans in the Civil War. There is the story of the gentleman who got mixed up in a battle whilst fox-hunting. Many men took sides because of local rivalry or pure expediency (*a*). Extract *b*) shows a distinguished lawyer and antiquary, Sir Roger Twysden, genuinely unhappy at having to choose. (Perhaps his profession and his baronetcy pulled different ways.) He was in trouble successively with Charles I (for refusing Ship Money), with the Long Parliament (for refusing to lend them money), and with Charles II (about what he thought illegal taxation). But such men were exceptions. More important neutrals were the Clubmen (*d*). As the war progressed, the peasantry came to see that they paid for all (in taxation, plunder and free-quarter) and got nothing. They formed in some counties of the south-west (the clothing counties) a third party to impose peace. The threat from this popular movement, of which the Royalists tried to take advantage, helped to drive Parliament into establishing the New Model Army, a more democratic and disciplined force (see Nos. 105–6). But this Army itself produced even more radical demands (see Part X). Extract *c*) has been left in the original spelling.

a) *Oxinden Letters*, pp. 308–9; *b*) Sir R. Twysden, *Journal* (quoted in *Certain Considerations upon the Government of England* (Camden Soc., 1849, pp. xxii, lxxi–lxxii); *c*) Godwin, *The Civil War in Hants* (1882), p. 105; *d*) J. and W., p. 45.

a) A KENTISH GENTLEMAN IN DIFFICULTIES, JUNE 18TH, 1642

I AM much dissuaded and importuned by my best and dearest friends, on both sides, not to meddle with the [Parliamentary] militia. . . . All their arguments were too tedious to set down. I'll trouble you but with one or two. To sit still and take no parts, especially as a commander, is the wisest and safest way: next they allege the necessity why I should, and impossibility why I cannot, live upon the place, the latter because of my weak estate and multiplicity of [law-]suits, expenses and business to which I must give an assidual and necessary attendance. Then they urge the [King's] proclamation and invalidity of the [Parliament's] ordinance, and power of the King's punishment, which is death and confiscation if conqueror, the parliament having only power to fine and imprison.

b) A PERPLEXED LAWYER, *c*. 1642–3

Never did any man with more earnest expectation long for a Parliament than I did; seeing, to my understanding, the great necessity of one both for church and state; nor did any (so far as my calling led me) more than I oppose any illegal course [which] might retard the calling of one; as . . . [witness] the contest I had with one John Bristock, who, setting up a brew-house at Tunbridge, by a power, as he pretended, from court, prohibited men the brewing and selling beer of their own making, and thereupon uttered [i.e. sold] his own, not only at unreasonable rates, but (as was informed) issued out unwholesome drink; which being complained of, he was so proceeded against by that worthy patriot Mr. Dixon and myself, when others refused to meddle with it, as he made little further use of his patent; . . . never imagining a Parliament would have took upon them the redressing things amiss . . . by a way not traced out unto them by their ancestors; or the House of Commons would have assumed a power of commanding those who authorised their sitting in it, otherwise than by making laws that both were to obey. . . .

I did not love to have a King armed with book law against me for my life and estate. . . . Should his Majesty come in a conqueror (which I wished not) he could in so general a defection take away all men's estates. . . . Those which had somewhat must be only the losers by these wars.

c) THE WOMAN'S POINT OF VIEW

Most deare and loving husbane, my king love—

I remember unto you, hoping that you are in good helth, as I ame at the writting heareof. My little Willie have bene sicke this forknight. I pray you to come whome ife youe cane cum saffly. I doo marfull that I cannot heere from you ass well other nayberes do. I do desiere to heere from you as soone as youe cane. I pray youe to send me word when youe doo thenke you shall returne. You doe not consider I ame a lone woemane; I thought you woald never have leave me thuse long togeder, so I rest evere praying for your savese returne,

Your loving wife,
SUSAN RODWAY.

Ever praying for you tell deth I depart.

To my very loving husbane, Robert Rodway, a traine soudare [i.e. a soldier in one of the London trained bands] in the Red Reggiment, under the command of Captaine Warrin. Deliver this with spide, I pray youe.

d) DESIRES AND RESOLUTIONS OF THE COUNTIES OF DORSET AND WILTS, 1645

First, to maintain and defend the true reformed protestant religion and the inheritance of the crown.

Secondly, to join with and assist one another in the mutual defence of our liberties and properties against all plunderers and all other unlawful violence whatsoever.

Thirdly, we do hereby resolve and faithfully promise each to other, that if any person or persons whatsoever who shall concur with us and assist us in these our resolutions happen to suffer in his person or estate in the execution of the premises, that shall be accounted as the suffering of the generality and reparation shall be made to the party suffering according to his damages; and in case [of] loss of life, provision shall be made for his wife and children, and that at the county's charge.

Fourthly, we do hereby declare all such unworthy of our assistance as shall refuse to join with us in the prosecution of these our just intentions.

Part Eight

THE SECTS AND DEMOCRACY

. . . That liberty which the lower sort of citizens, under pretence of religion, do challenge to themselves. For what civil war was there ever in the Christian world which did not either grow from or was nourished by this root?

Thomas Hobbes.

108. RELIGION NOT THE ISSUE

Hardly less misleading than the view that the Civil War was fought about religion is the view that the distinction between the groupings which we call "Presbyterian" and "Independent" was merely religious. It was in fact also political (*c*) and social (see also No. 109). The Presbyterians were those conservative M.Ps. who favoured calling in a Scottish army rather than arming the people of England (No. 103). Baillie in *b*) makes it clear that many who were not Independents in religion opposed the imposition of a Presbyterian religious system on England. Extract *c*) was written by a Royalist.

a) Nalson, *Impartial Collection*, II, p. 665; *b*) Baillie, *Letters and Journals*, I, p. 437, II, pp. 107, 149–50, 161, 183; *c*) [Anon.] *A Memento* (*c*. 1660–5), p. 180.

a) SIR E. DERING IN THE COMMONS, NOVEMBER, 1641

MR. SPEAKER, there is a certain new-born, unseen, ignorant, dangerous, desperate way of Independency: are we, Sir, for this Independent way? Nay, Sir, are we for the elder brother of it, the Presbyterian form? I have not yet heard any one gentleman within these walls stand up and assert his thought here for either of these ways.

b) BAILLIE REPORTS HOME TO SCOTLAND

April 2nd, 1644. No man I know, in either of the Houses [of Parliament] of any note, is for them [the Independents]. . . .

May or June, 1645. The Erastian party in the Parliament is stronger than the Independent, and is like to work us much woe. Selden is their head. . . .

August, 1645. The most part of the House of Commons, especially the lawyers, whereof there are many, and divers of them very able men, are either half or whole Erastians, believing no church-government to be of divine right but all to be a human constitution, depending on the will of the magistrate. . . .

October 14th, 1645. Our greatest trouble for the time is from the Erastians in the House of Commons. They are at last content to erect presbyteries and synods in all the land, and have given out their orders for that end; yet they give to the ecclesiastic courts so little power that the [Westminster] Assembly, finding their petitions not granted, are in great doubt whether to set up anything till, by some powerful petition of many thousand hands, they obtain some more of their just desires. The only mean to obtain this, and all else we desire, is our recruited army about Newark. . . .

January 20th, 1646. The Independent party, albeit their number in the parliament be very small, yet being prime men, active and diligent, and making it their great work to retard all till they be first secured of a toleration of their separate congregations; and the body of the lawyers, who are another strong party in the House, believing all church government to be a part of the civil and parliamentary power, which nature and scripture has placed in them, and to be derived from them to the ministers only so far as they think expedient; a third party of worldly profane men, who are extremely affrighted to come under the yoke of ecclesiastic discipline; these three kinds making up two parts at least of the parliament, there is no hopes that ever they will settle the government according to our mind, if they were left to themselves.

c) A ROYALIST'S COMMENT

It makes me smile sometimes to hear how soberly men will talk of the *religion* of this or that faction. . . . He that would rightly understand them must read for Presbytery, *aristocracy*; and *democracy* for Independency.

109. PRESBYTERIANS AND INDEPENDENTS

Extract *a*) is by a Scottish Royalist. But it, like *c*)—by the author of No. 108, *c*)—gives a fair picture just because the authors are so sure that the principles of Independency have only to be stated to be abhorred. Extract *b*) shows that the division between Presbyterians and Independents in religion by no means always coincided with the division between the political parties to which we give those names. Haselrig was politically an Independent.

a) G. Wishart, *The Deeds of Montrose* (ed. Murdoch and Simpson, 1893), pp. 199–202; *b*) Clarendon, *History of the Rebellion* (ed. Macray, 1888), VI, p. 148; *c*) *A Memento*, p. 25.

a) A SCOTTISH EPISCOPALIAN, *c.* 1651

(*i*) *Presbyterians.* Into their meeting, which they call their presbytery, they co-opt such of the people as are most zealous for their way, chapmen, ploughmen, mechanics, sailors, tailors, colliers, cobblers, and the like. . . . These have the same right to vote as the ministers themselves. They are elected annually, and dignified with the title of lay or ruling elders. Among their ministers they pretend to maintain complete equality, a mere fiction upset in practice. Their real rulers are a small clique, advanced by the popular applause and the giddy conceit of the rabble, who lord it most tyrannically not only over their brethren but over peers of the realm and even the King himself. Ecclesiastical matters are all submitted to the presbytery, and not only so, but all matters, human or divine, under pretence of being scandals or stumbling-blocks. . . . Against such as resist or gainsay their decrees they thunder out anathemas and excommunications, by which, according to their teaching, body and soul are damned and delivered to the devil. By these means they exercise a wonderful terror not only over the poor ignorant mob but even over the nobility. They interdict all commerce and intercourse with the excommunicate, thus lightly tearing asunder and destroying the bonds that unite servants to masters, children to parents, wives to husbands, the people to their magistrate. . . . In their meetings they rail with the greatest bitterness against lords, princes and even kings. . . . By such arts they win favour and power with the people. . . .

(*ii*) *Independents.* They are called Independents, I suppose, because they acknowledge no dependence upon any superior. . . . They tolerate one another, and inflict no heavier punishment on those who differ in matters of religion than seclusion from the congregation. . . . The people elect their ministers. . . . They maintain that the people, meaning the lowest class only, excluding kings, princes and peers, have by divine right absolute power over the lives and fortunes of all. In this, as in most other respects, they agree with the Presbyterians, except that the power they [the latter] nominally ascribe to the people is in effect arrogated by the presbytery, to whose decrees the people are entirely subjected.

b) CLARENDON

Haselrig was as to the state perfectly repub[lican], and as to religion perfectly presbyterian.

c) A ROYALIST, *c.* 1660–5

The Presbyterians, having first asserted the people's cause against the prerogative, and attempting afterward to establish themselves, by using prerogative arguments against the people, found it a harder matter to erect an aristocracy upon a popular foundation than to subvert a monarchy upon a popular pretence; or to dispose the multitude (whom they themselves had declared to be the supreme power) to lay down their authority at the feet of their servants.

110. CONNECTION OF RELIGION AND POLITICS

Extract *a*), by the Leveller Walwyn, shows that the first step in a political campaign was to capture one's church congregation. The parish was the unit of local government, the basic political unit in the hierarchy leading up to Parliament. In *b*), from a hostile source, Hugh Peters, Oliver Cromwell's friend and a regicide, is shown using a religious text to preach revolutionary politics.

a) W. Walwyn, *A Whisper in the Ear of Mr. Thomas Edwards* (1646), p. 4; *b*) *Trial of the Regicides* (1713), pp. 183–4.

a) THE POLITICAL HIERARCHY

[HAVING reformed our church] our next endeavours were for the whole ward, wherein after much labour we so prevailed that the well-affected carried the choice of aldermen and common council men and all other officers in the ward. My next public business was with many others in a remonstrance to the Common Council, to move the Parliament to confirm certain infallible maxims of free government: wherein the power of Parliament was plainly distinguished from the King's office—so plainly that (had it taken effect) few men after due consideration thereof would through error of judgment have taken part against the Parliament, or befriended arbitrary power, as too many did for want of light.

b) A POLITICAL SERMON

Mr. Chace: My lord, I heard the prisoner at the bar preaching before Oliver Cromwell and Bradshaw, who was called Lord President of the High Court of Justice, and he took his text out of the Psalms in these words, "Bind your Kings with chains, and your nobles with fetters of iron"; that was part of the text. But says he in his sermon, "Beloved, it is the last psalm but one, and the next psalm hath six verses and twelve Hallelujahs, praise ye the Lord, praise God in his sanctuary, and so on. For what?" says he. "Look into my text, there is the reason of it—that Kings were bound in chains, etc.!"

111. RELIGION AND CLASSES

The Reformation had given ordinary people the opportunity to study the Scriptures for themselves; had cast down priests from their privileged monopoly position (cf. No. 55). It was the hitherto uneducated who found this most exciting: and they proceeded to draw lessons from the Bible which shocked their social superiors. Royalists never tired of jeering at the "mechanic" lay preachers on the Parliamentary side, nor of expressing horror at their heresies. *Eikon Basilike* (*b*), a devotional book, is one of the famous frauds of history. Published immediately after the execution of Charles I, it was attributed to the "Royal Martyr," and had so great a propaganda effect that Milton wrote *Eikonoklastes* to counter it. *Eikon Basilike* was probably written by John Gauden, who was rewarded with a bishopric at the Restoration. (For Baillie (*c*), cf. Nos. 108 and 114.)

a) Braithwaite, *The English Gentleman*, p. 120; *b*) *Eikon Basilike* (1876), p. 69; *c*) R. Baillie, *A Dissuasive from the Errors of the Time, Epistle Dedicatory* (2nd ed., 1646).

a) UNEDUCATED PREACHERS, 1630

WHENCE sprung all these schisms in the church, these many rents in Christ's seamless coat, but from those who of mechanics became divines, professing to teach before they were taught?

b) THE VULGAR CONTRASTED WITH THE GENTRY, 1649

That old leaven of innovations, masked under the name of reformation, . . . was never wont so far to infect the whole mass of the nobility and gentry of this kingdom, however it dispersed among the vulgar.

c) RELIGION AND THE BOURGEOISIE, 1646

The Parliament of England cannot have on earth so strong pillars and pregnant supporters of all their privileges as free protestant assemblies established by law and kept in their full freedom from the lowest to the highest, from the congregational eldership to the general synod of the nation. No such bars as these are imaginable either against tyranny or anarchy; they are the mightiest impediments both to the exorbitancy of monarchs, which has been and is our misery, and to the extravagancy of the common multitude, attempting to correct and subject all Parliaments to their own foolish desires,—which is like to be the matter of our next exercise and trouble.

112. SOCIAL ASPECTS OF ICONOCLASM, 1643

We hear a great deal about the "vandalism" of the Puritans. This account by a Royalist journalist shows that they were not always merely hostile to art for its own sake. There might be social and religious reasons for wishing to remove the insignia of worldly pomp and class distinction from the House of God. Cromwell's troops at Lincoln in September, 1644, were accused of shooting down "all scutcheons and arms of such lords and gentlemen as were benefactors or buried" in the Cathedral (*Mercurius Aulicus*). [Ryves] *Angliæ Ruina*, pp. 59–60.

In St. Mary's Church in Warwick, and the chapel (commonly called the Earl's chapel) adjoining to the choir of that church, are divers fair monuments of the Beauchamps, anciently Earls of that place. . . . Thomas Beauchamp (Earl of Warwick and Earl Marshal of England) . . . built the choir now standing, in the midst whereof is his monument; and adorned the windows with . . . pictures of himself, his wife and children, which were many; upon the surcoats of the men were their arms skilfully depicted, the women having the like, and mantles over which were the arms of their matches, their husbands being the prime nobility of those times. . . . Such is the barbarousness of the pretenders to reformation that upon Wednesday the 14th of this instant June [1643], the soldiers by the appointment and encouragement of one whom (in these degenerous times, wherein the dregs of the people are made commanders for the advancement of rebellion) men call Colonel Purefoy (a man of a mean desperate fortune, but by the means of the late Lord Brooke chosen burgess of Parliament for Warwick . . .) did beat down and deface those monuments of antiquity. . . . In which the world may observe that these men are the sworn enemies not only of pretended superstition, but of the ensigns of nobility and gentry; that if their Diana, I mean their parity, may take effect, posterity may forget and not read the distinction of noble from ignoble in these venerable monuments of ancient nobility: there being in these windows something indeed to instruct a herald, nothing to offend the weakest Christian.

113. FUNCTION OF PREACHERS

Before the revolution, parsons preached submission to the established order, except in the few parishes where a Puritan landlord was dominant, or where town corporations had installed Puritan lecturers (Nos. 57 and 58). It was therefore natural for Parliament to use ministers as propagandists and for Cavaliers or conservative Parliamentarians to fear the unsettling social consequences of such a step (*a*). All parties agreed that government must have the support of ministers

(No. 52). The report of Alderman Violet, a City goldsmith, is concerned with economic problems and the maintenance of social order (*b*). For this a first necessity is "godly ministers" in every parish, with "a competent subsistence," i.e. tithes. Hence the attack on tithes (Nos. 122, 154, 177, 186) was an attack on the existence of a state Church, and resisted as such by the partisans of "order." Walker (*a*) was a supporter of Parliament but a persistent enemy of Independents, sectaries and republicans. Overton (*c*) was one of the Leveller leaders.

a) Walker, Part II, pp. 156–7; *b*) *C.S.P.D.*, 1650, p. 180; *c*) R. Overton, *The Arraignment of Mr. Persecution* (1645), p. 25; *d*) Izaak Walton, *Life of Dr. Sanderson* (World's Classics), p. 380.

a) PARSONS AS PARTY PROPAGANDISTS

April 12th, 1649. It was referred to a Committee [of Parliament] to consider of a way how to raise pensions and allowances out of Deans' and Chapters' lands to maintain supernumerary itinerant ministers. . . . These wandering apostles are to preach anti-monarchical seditious doctrine to the people (suitable to that they call the present government) to raise the rascal multitude and schismatical rabble against all men of best quality in the kingdom, to draw them into associations and combinations with one another in every county and with the army, against all lords, gentry, ministers, lawyers, rich and peaceable men, and all that are lovers of the old laws and government, for the better rooting of them out.

b) REPORT OF ALDERMAN VIOLET TO THE COMMITTEE FOR THE MINT, MAY, 1650

[After describing the decay of trade.] I propose as remedies:—

First, to settle able and godly ministers in all churches throughout the nation, that will teach the people to fear God, to obey their superiors and to live peaceably with each other, with a competent subsistence for all such ministers.

c) THE BELLY HATH NO EARS

He that lives but a small time shall surely see a Presbyter as fat as ever was a Bishop; those are enemies to all knowledge. . . . All heads must be made even with the Presbyter's, none higher nor none lower, just as tall, and no taller, he that is too short must be stretched out, and he that is too long must be pared even, lest they should miss of their Prayers: "give us this day our daily tithes"; that the German proverb might be fulfilled. . . . "The covetousness of the Priests and the mercy of God endure for ever." I would exhort them to be otherwise minded, but that I know, venter non habet aures, the belly hath no ears.

d) ELECTED MINISTERS

The Bishops' power being now vacated, the common people were made so happy as every parish might choose their own minister, and tell him when he did and when he did not preach true doctrine; and by this and the like means several churches had several teachers, that prayed and preached for and against one another; and engaged their hearers to contend furiously for truths which they understood not.

114. INTERNATIONAL CONNECTIONS

Men still thought in terms of an international civil war (see Part V). In *a*) the conservative Scot, Baillie, is appealing to his friend, William Spang (in the Netherlands), to agitate there for support for the middle way in England and Scotland. The victory of the Cavaliers in England, Baillie argues, might lead to a reactionary coup in the Netherlands by supporters of the House of Orange-Nassau: and a triumph of "democratic anarchy" in England would spell disaster for the Dutch too. In *b*), written in Latin for a European audience, Milton reveals some of the high hopes the English revolution aroused. He is describing reactions to his defence of the execution of Charles I.

a) Baillie, *Letters and Journals*, II, pp. 26, 35; *b*) Milton, *Selected Prose* (World's Classics), p. 378.

a) FEARS, 1644

STRANGE that your divines of Holland will learn nothing from England! Do they sit still while we are a-dying! The calamity may shortly come over to them. . . . If the malignants [Cavaliers] prevail, all the force of this isle will be employed to put the Nassovian yoke on their neck, will they, nill they; and if the democratic anarchy vex our churches, ye are blind if ye see not that pest incumbent to you likewise. . . . No man doubts but, in spite of the devil, Britain and Holland must join hearts in hand for their common necessities.

b) HOPES, 1654

I seem to survey, as from a towering height, the far extended tracts of sea and land, and innumerable crowds of spectators, betraying in their looks the liveliest interest, and sensations the most congenial with my own. Here I behold the stout and manly prowess of the Germans disdaining servitude; there the generous and lively impetuosity of the French; on this side, the calm and stately valour of the Spaniard; on that, the composed and wary magnanimity of the Italian. Of all the lovers of liberty and virtue, the magnanimous and the wise, in whatever quarter they may be found, some secretly favour, others openly approve; some greet me with congratulations and applause; others, who had long been proof against conviction, at last yield themselves captive to the force of truth. Surrounded by congregated multitudes, I now imagine that, from the columns of Hercules [Straits of Gibraltar] to the Indian Ocean, I behold the nations of the earth recovering that liberty which they so long had lost.

115. SOCIAL ASPECTS OF RELIGIOUS SECTS

Thomas Edwards, a Presbyterian pamphleteer, led the attack on the sects in successive volumes of his *Gangræna* (*a*). The real implications of religious differences are made clear: the disgust at "mechanick" preachers; the horror at such democratic sentiments as that Christ died for all. The comparison of the sects with John of Leyden and the Anabaptists of Münster was a favourite theme amongst upholders of existing social privilege. It was a cry of "Communism" which enabled them to damn without argument. Note Edwards's reference to women preachers. As *b*) shows, the more democratic sects were the first to demand some equality of rights for women (cf. No. 99, *c*)).

a) Edwards, *Gangræna*, I. pp. 58, 64, 116, 119, III, pp. 261–2, 275; *b*) quoted in E. Rogers, *Life and Opinions of a Fifth-Monarchy Man* (John Rogers), 1847, p. 69.

a) DANGERS OF RELIGIOUS LIBERTY

THE Sectaries (though a contemptible number, and not to be named at the same time with the Presbyterians) have not waited upon the Parliament and [Westminster] Assembly for the Reformation, but preached against it and stirred up the people to embody themselves and to join in Church fellowship, gathering Churches, setting up Independent government, rebaptising and dipping many hundreds. . . .

They do on purpose (having got Churches void) keep many churches without ministers, seek out for none, stop (all they can) orthodox ministers from coming in, which they do for two reasons, i. that so they may pay no tithes: ii. that so they may have the liberty of the pulpits for all kind of sectaries and mechanic preachers, who come from London, the armies and other places to preach in and corrupt the people, and that the people, being as sheep without a shepherd, may be more easily now drawn away to error and schism. . . .

Among all the confusion and disorder in Church matters both of opinions and practices, and particularly of all sorts of mechanics taking upon them to preach and baptise, as smiths, tailors, shoemakers, pedlars, weavers, etc., there are also some women-preachers in our times, who keep constant lectures, preaching weekly to many men and women. . . . In her exercise she [i.e. Mrs. Attoway, a woman-preacher] delivered many dangerous and false doctrines: as, i. that it could not stand with the goodness of God to damn his own creatures eternally. . . . iv. that Christ died for all. . . .

Hence then we may clearly see from many of the principles and practices laid open in this book, that many of the sectaries of our times, anabaptists, libertines, Independents, are not only against government in the Church, all authoritative power of classes, synods, but against civil government too. Monarchy and aristocracy, both Kings and Lords have been cried down . . .; and for democracy, though in divers pamphlets they seem to contend for that, as in opposition to all kingly and lordly government, yet in pleading for it they have laid down such positions as are not consistent with any civil government at all, but what necessarily would bring any Commonwealth (the most popular) into a chaos and confusion. . . . In a word nothing pleases them, not the government nor any part of it; not the laws, their design is to have all pulled down, to have a total change made, that being abrasa tabula [i.e. the slate having been wiped clean] they might write in it what they pleased, and might come to have the new modelling of Church and Commonwealth. O how like are our sectaries to the old anabaptists of Munster and Germany! their very spirit having entered into our men. O how like is John Lilburne to John of Leyden, as if he had been spit out of his mouth, Mr. Dell to Thomas Muntzer. . . . I dare be bold to say, and can prove it, that the old anabaptists never delivered or held principles more destructive to human society to all kind of government, both political, ecclesiastical and economical, to all godliness and religion, than many of our sectaries. . . .

Certainly the House of Commons, so great and understanding a body, . . . cannot be so weak as to believe them, and to think if the sectaries get power into their hands, and overthrow the House of Peers, ministers, City, that they shall escape and not follow after: they have written, spoken, done as much against them as the House of Peers, ministers, City, and no question will again as they see their advantage, or are discontented, or upon some new light that they were not chosen by all the freemen of England but only by the prerogative men, the freeholders. No man knows where these sectaries will stop or stay, or to what principles they will keep, and is there any safety in adhering to such a party? . . . To conclude this corollary, I say, God keep me and all true Presbyterians from that liberty of conscience the sectaries would give us if we lay at their mercy, and liberty of conscience were theirs to give.

b) EQUAL RIGHTS FOR WOMEN

Let not men despise [women], or wrong them of their liberty of voting and speaking in common affairs. To women I say, I wish ye be not too forward, and yet not too backward, but hold fast your liberty; keep your ground, which Christ hath got and won for you, maintain your rights, defend your liberties even to the life. . . . Ye ought not by your silence to betray your liberty, trouble your consciences, lose your privileges and rights, or see the truth taken away or suffer before your eyes.

116. CROMWELL OPPOSES INTOLERANCE

Cf. Nos. 94, 105–6. After William the Silent, the leader in the revolt of the Netherlands, Cromwell was one of the earliest persons in a position of power who *on principle* practised toleration. But this toleration did not extend to Roman Catholics (*c*). There is neither hypocrisy nor inconsistency here. Catholicism was associated with all that the Parliamentarians were fighting against—absolutism, obscurantism, persecution: in Ireland it was the ally of Spain. So it could not be tolerated until the revolutionary order was secure (cf. No. 117, *b*) and note to No. 132).

a) Abbott, II, pp. 338–9; *b*) *ibid.*, p. 303; *c*) *ibid.*, p. 146; *d*) *ibid.*, III, p. 586.

a) FOR THE GOVERNOR OF EDINBURGH CASTLE, SEPTEMBER, 1650

You say that you have just cause to regret that men of civil employments should usurp the calling and employment of the ministry, to the scandal of the reformed kirks. Are you troubled that Christ is preached? Is preaching so inclusive in your function? Doth it scandalise the reformed kirks, and Scotland in particular? Is it against the Covenant? Away with the Covenant if it be so. . . . Your pretended fear lest error should step in is like the men that would keep all wine out of the country lest men should be drunk.

b) TO THE GENERAL ASSEMBLY OF THE KIRK OF SCOTLAND, AUGUST, 1650

I beseech you in the bowels of Christ, think it possible you may be mistaken.

c) TO THE GOVERNOR OF ROSS (IRELAND), OCTOBER, 1649

For that which you mention concerning liberty of conscience, I meddle not with any man's conscience. But if by liberty of conscience you mean a liberty to exercise the mass, I judge it best to use plain dealing and to let you know, where the Parliament of England have power that will not be allowed of.

d) SPEECH TO PARLIAMENT, JANUARY 22ND, 1655

Is there not yet upon the spirits of men a strange itch? Nothing will satisfy them unless they can put their finger upon their brethren's consciences, to pinch them there. To do this was no part of the contest we had with the common adversary. For religion was not the thing at the first contested for; but God brought it to that issue at last; and gave it unto us by way of redundancy; and at last it proved to be that which was most dear to us. And wherein consisted this more than in obtaining that liberty from the tyranny of the bishops to all species of Protestants to worship God according to their own light and consciences?

117. MILTON'S VIEWS ON LIBERTY

The royal censorship broke down with the abolition of the Star Chamber. *Areopagitica* (*b*) was written (in the form of an imaginary speech to Parliament) when the Presbyterian majority there proposed to introduce a censorship *before publication*. It is a magnificent defence of liberty, but it is not absolute. Like Cromwell and the Levellers, Milton did not propose to extend freedom to Papists, the enemies of freedom. Milton realised that, owing to lack of education and to propagandist education under the old régime, the mass of the population was incapable of the fullness of freedom which he advocated as the right of all men in *Areopagitica*. Hence his continual emphasis on the importance of education; hence too it is only a logical development of Milton's position that he acted as censor for the republican government in the 'fifties (cf. No. 141). Extract *c*) attacks those who had criticised Milton's advocacy of divorce.

a) J. Milton, *The Reason of Church Government* (Nonesuch Ed.), pp. 555, 561; *b*) *Areopagitica* (*ibid.*), pp. 696, 701–2, 707–8, 711–12, 716, 719–20, 722–3, 725; *c*) *ibid.*, p. 71; *d*) *ibid.*, p. 72.

a) 1641

I HAVE determined to lay up as the best treasure, and solace of a good old age (if God vouchsafe it me) the honest liberty of free speech from my youth. . . . Should the church be brought under heavy oppression, and God have given me ability the while to reason against that man that should be the author of so foul a deed . . . [should I not speak out] I foresee what stories I should hear within myself, all my life after, of discourage and reproach. "Timorous and ungrateful, the church of God is now again at the foot of her insulting enemies: and thou bewailest. What matters it for thee or thy bewailing? When time was, thou couldst not find a syllable of all that thou hadst read or studied to utter in her behalf. Yet ease and leisure was given thee for thy retired thoughts out of the sweat of other men. . . ." [I can only devote myself to poetry again when] the land had once enfranchised herself from this impertinent yoke of prelaty, under whose inquisitorious and tyrannical duncery no free and splendid wit can flourish.

b) 1644

It was from out the rind of one apple tasted that the knowledge of good and evil, as two twins cleaving together, leapt forth into the world. And perhaps this is that doom which Adam fell into, of knowing good and evil, that is to say of knowing good by evil. As therefore the state of man now is, what wisdom can there be to choose, what continence to forbear, without the knowledge of evil? He that can apprehend and consider vice with all her baits and seeming pleasures, and yet abstain, and yet distinguish, and yet prefer that which is truly better—he is the true wayfaring Christian. I cannot praise a fugitive and cloistered virtue, unexercised and unbreathed, that never sallies out and sees her adversary, but slinks out of the race where that immortal garland is to be run for, not without dust and heat. Assuredly we bring not innocence into the world, we bring impurity much rather: that which purifies us is trial, and trial is by what is contrary. . . . If every action which is good or evil in man at ripe years were to be under pittance and prescription and compulsion, what were virtue but a name, what praise could be then due to well-doing? . . . Many there be that complain of divine Providence for suffering Adam to transgress. Foolish tongues! When God gave him reason, he gave him freedom to choose; for reason is but choosing. . . .

To me it [censorship before publication] seems an undervaluing and vilifying of the whole nation. I cannot set so light by all the invention, the art, the wit, the grave and solid judgment which is in England as that it can be comprehended in any twenty capacities [of censors] how good soever. . . . Truth and understanding are not such wares as to be monopolized and traded in by tickets and statutes and standards. We must not think to make a staple commodity of all the knowledge in the land, to mark and license it like our broadcloth and our wool packs. . . . Nor is it to the common people less than a reproach; for if we be so jealous over them as that we dare not trust them with an English pamphlet, what do we but censure them for a giddy, vicious and ungrounded people; in such a sick and weak estate of faith and discretion as to be able to take nothing down but through the pipe of a licencer. . . .

If [a man] believe things only because his pastor says so, or the [Westminster] Assembly so determines, without knowing other reason, though his belief be true yet the very truth he holds becomes his heresy. . . .

Lords and Commons of England, consider what nation it is whereof ye are, and whereof ye are the governors; a nation not slow and dull, but of a quick, ingenious and piercing spirit, acute to invent, subtle and sinewy to discourse, not beneath the reach of any point the highest that human capacity can soar to. . . . Methinks I see in my mind a noble and puissant nation rousing herself like a strong man after sleep and shaking her invincible locks: methinks I see her as an eagle mewing her mighty youth and kindling her undazzled eyes at the full mid-day beam; purging and unscaling her long abused sight at the fountain itself of heavenly radiance; while the whole noise of timorous and flocking birds, with those also that love the twilight, flutter about amazed at what she means, and in their envious gabble would prognosticate a year of sects and schisms.

What should ye do then, should ye suppress all this flowery crop of knowledge and new light sprung up and yet springing daily in this city [London], should ye set an oligarchy of twenty ingrossers over it, to bring a famine upon our minds again, when we shall know nothing but what is measured to us by their bushel? Believe it, Lords and Commons, they who counsel ye to such a suppressing do as good as bid ye suppress yourselves; and I will soon show how. If it be desired to know the immediate cause of all this free writing and free speaking, there cannot be assigned a truer than your own mild and free and humane government; it is the liberty, Lords and Commons, which your own valorous and happy counsels have purchased us, liberty which is the nurse of all great wits: this is that which hath rarified and enlightened our spirits like the influence of heaven; this is that which hath enfranchised, enlarged and lifted up our apprehensions degrees above themselves. Ye cannot make us now less capable, less knowing, less eagerly pursuing of the truth, unless ye first make yourselves, that made us so, less the lovers, less the founders, of our true liberty. We can grow ignorant again, brutish, formal and slavish as ye found us; but then ye must first become that which ye cannot be, oppressive, arbitrary and tyrannous, as they were from whom ye have freed us. . . . Give me the liberty to know, to utter, and to argue freely according to conscience, above all liberties. . . .

Truth is strong next to the Almighty; she needs no policies, nor stratagems nor licencings to make her victorious; those are the shifts and the defences that error uses against her power. Give her but room, and do not bind her when she sleeps. . . . If it come to prohibiting, there is not ought more likely to be prohibited than truth itself; whose first appearance to our eyes bleared and dimmed with prejudice and custom is more unsightly and unplausible than many errors.

Yet if all cannot be of one mind, as who looks they should be? this doubtless is more wholesome, more prudent, and more Christian, that many be tolerated rather than all compelled. I mean not tolerated popery, and open superstition, which as it extirpates all religious and civil supremacies, so itself should be extirpate, provided first that all charitable and compassionate means be used to win and regain the weak and the misled: that also which is impious or evil absolutely either against faith or manners, no law can possibly permit, that intends not to unlaw itself: but those neighbouring differences, or rather indifferences, are what I speak of, whether in some point of doctrine, or of discipline, which though they may be many, yet need not interrupt the unity of spirit, if we could but find among us the bond of peace. . . .

And as for regulating the press, let no man think to have the honour of advising ye better than yourselves have done in that order published next before this, "that no book be printed, unless the printer's and the author's name, or at least the printer's, be registered." Those which otherwise come forth, if they be found mischievous and libellous, the fire and the executioner will be the timeliest and the most effectual remedy that man's prevention can use.

c) 1645

I did but prompt the age to quit their clogs
By the known rules of ancient liberty,
When straight a barbarous noise environs me
Of owls and cuckoos, asses, apes and dogs. . . .
[They] bawl for freedom in their senseless mood,
And still revolt when truth would make them free.
License they mean when they cry "Liberty,"
For who loves that must first be wise and good. . . .

d) 1646. ON THE NEW FORCERS OF CONSCIENCE UNDER THE LONG PARLIAMENT

Because you have thrown off your prelate lord,
And with stiff vows renounced his liturgy
To seize the widowed whore Plurality
From those whose sin ye envied, not abhorred,
Dare ye for this adjure the civil sword
To force our consciences that Christ set free. . . ?
New presbyter is but old priest writ large.

Part Nine

THE LEVELLERS

Further error No. 52—By natural birth all men are equally and alike born to like property, liberty and freedom.

The Rev. Thomas Edwards.

118. LEVELLERS AND DEMOCRACY

The Levellers drew their strength from classes below those represented in Parliament (*a*); cf. Nos. 42 and 93). The bourgeois revolutionaries might now repent of their rashness in stirring up the London populace against the reactionaries in Parliament and Charles I in 1640–1 (*b*); cf. No. 70). Extract *c*) is from a Cavalier satire on the Levellers, probably written in the sixteen-forties. It goes on to accuse the Levellers of opposing kings and priests, and of advocating community of women.

a) Edwards, *Gangræna*, III, p. 16 (i); *b*) Whitelock, *Memorials*, II, pp. 128–9; *c*) *The Rump* (1662), I, p. 262.

a) EXCLUDED FROM THE FRANCHISE, 1646

LET Lilburne, Overton, Larner and the rest of that rabble who talk so much of the House of Commons being their chosen ones . . . name any knight or burgess whom they chose or were capable to choose; for I believe they were of so mean estate that they had not so much free land per annum required by the statute; . . . and as for choosing burgesses in London where they lived, they were no livery men of any of those Companies who have voices in election.

b) DEMOCRACY TURNED AGAINST PARLIAMENT, 1647

This way of petitioning by multitude of hands to the Parliament, which was formerly promoted by some of both Houses as a means to carry on their designs at that time, began now to be made use of and returned upon them, to their great trouble and danger; wherein we may observe the justice of God in punishing sometimes undue and indirect means by the very same means afterwards brought about against the users of them.

c) THE LEVELLERS' RANT

'Tis we will pull down what e'er is above us,
And make them to fear us, that never did love us;
We'll level the proud, and make every degree
To our royalty bow the knee;
'Tis no less than treason
'Gainst freedom and reason
For our brethren to be higher than we.

119. SOVEREIGNTY OF PARLIAMENT—AND PEOPLE

The Levellers were more anxious than Parliament itself to assert the sovereignty of Parliament over the King (*a*): this sovereignty being derived from the people (*b*). If admitted, this would have justified the Leveller demand for parliamentary reform, to render Parliament truly representative of the people (cf. No. 132). With Lilburne's last remark, cf. Rainborough in No. 133.

a) Wolfe, p. 285; *b*) *ibid.*, p. 14.

a) LEVELLER PETITION OF SEPTEMBER 11TH, 1648

But to our exceeding grief we have observed that no sooner God vouchsafeth you victory, and blesseth you with success, and thereby enableth you to put us and the whole nation into an absolute condition of freedom and safety, but, according as you have been accustomed . . . ye betake yourselves to a treaty with him [the King], thereby putting him that is but one single person and a public officer of the commonwealth in competition with the whole body of the people, whom ye represent; not considering that it is impossible for you to erect any authority equal to yourselves.

b) LILBURNE IN DECEMBER, 1646

The only and sole legislative law-making power is originally inherent in the people, and derivately in their commissions chosen by themselves by common consent, and no other. In which the poorest that lives hath as true a right to give a vote as well as the richest and greatest.

120. DEMAND FOR LAW REFORM

With these Leveller criticisms, cf. Nos. 174–5. Extract *b*) is from R. Overton's *Certain Articles for the Good of the Commonwealth*, which were "presented to the consideration of his Excellency, Sir Thomas Fairfax, and to the officers and soldiers under his command" in July, 1647, when the Levellers hoped for great things from the Army (see Part X). In fact this reform was achieved in 1650 (No. 174, *d*)).

a) J. Lilburne, *Liberty vindicated against Slavery* (1646), Wolfe, p. 11; *b*) Wolfe, p. 192; *c*) *Several Proposals for Peace and Freedom by an Agreement of the People*, Wolfe, p. 316.

a) ONE LAW FOR RICH AND POOR ALIKE, 1646

WHAT is the reason of this their [imprisoned debtors'] great neglect? Because we are poor, poor I say, and not able to fee lawyers, attorneys, solicitors and gaolers; for if we had moneys to satiate these horse-leeches, then (though our causes were never so unjust, and debts never so great) we should no ways doubt the gaining of our liberties.

b) AGAINST MUMBO-JUMBO

That all the laws of the land (locked up from common capacities in the Latin or French tongues) may be translated into the English tongue. And that all records, orders, processes, writs and other proceedings whatsoever may be all entered and issued forth in the English tongue . . . that so the meanest English commoner that can but read written hand in his own tongue may fully understand his own proceedings in the law.

c) FOR EQUALITY BEFORE THE LAW, 1648

That in all laws made or to be made, every person may be bound alike; and that no degree of Lords, peers of Parliament (now or hereafter assembled) or others, no tenure, estate, charter or office soever shall confer any exemption from the ordinary course of justice whereunto others are subjected.

121. OPPOSITION TO ENCLOSURES

With these extracts, cf. No. 169. Extract *a*) is from the same source as No. 120, *b*). Extract *b*) is by a bitter enemy of the Levellers, but seems internally consistent. Walwyn came the nearest of all the Levellers to holding Communist views: he liked putting hypothetical cases in order to be able to express his opinions without danger. Cf. Winstanley's not dissimilar views in No. 153, *d*).

a) Wolfe, p. 194; *b*) *Walwyn's Wiles* (1649), H. and D., pp. 302–3.

a) CERTAIN ARTICLES FOR THE GOOD OF THE COMMONWEALTH, 1647

THAT all grounds which anciently lay in common for the poor, and are now impropriate, enclosed and fenced in, may forthwith (in whose hands soever they are) be cast out and laid open again to the free and common use and benefit of the poor.

b) COMMUNIST VIEWS ATTRIBUTED TO A LEVELLER

This Mr. Walwyn, to work upon the indigent and poorer sort of people, and to raise up their spirits in discontents and clamours, etc., did one time profess he could wish with all his heart that there was neither pale, hedge nor ditch in the whole nation, and that it was an unconscionable thing that one man should have £10,000 and another more deserving and useful to the commonwealth should not be worth 2*d*.—or to that purpose.

At another time discoursing of the inequality and disproportion of the estates and conditions of men in the world, [he] had words to this purpose, That it was a sad and miserable thing that it should so continue, and that it would never be well until all things were common; and it being replied "Will that be ever?" answered, "We must endeavour it." It being said, That this would destroy all government, answered that there would be less need of government, for then there would be no thieves, no covetous persons, no deceiving and abusing of one another, and so no need of government, etc.; but if in such a case they have a form and rule of government to determine cases, as may fall out, yet there will be no need of standing officers in a commonwealth, no need of judges, etc., but if any difference fall out, or any criminal fact be committed, take a cobbler from his seat, or a butcher from his shop, or any other tradesman that is an honest and just man, and let him hear the case and determine the same, and then betake himself to his work again.

122. AGAINST TITHES

For tithes see note to No. 113, also Nos. 154 and 186. They fell heavily on the poor (*b*), and were particularly resented when they went to maintain men who preached unpopular social and political doctrines, or to lay impropriators. The parties of the Left wished to disestablish the state Church and have ministers maintained by the voluntary contributions of their congregations; men of the Right had no doubt that very few would contribute if not compelled (*c*), *d*)). They also felt, as some M.Ps. put it, that tenants who wanted to be quit of tithes would soon want to be quit of rent. (Gardiner, *Great Civil War*, III, p. 124). The last sentence of *c*), by a Presbyterian, suggests that opponents of tithes were having the better of arguments drawn from the Bible. The author of *b*) was an Episcopalian. Extract *d*) comes, significantly, from a pamphlet advocating improved agricultural methods; the author is indignant at clerical opposition to enclosure (see No. 169), and warns ministers not to trust the common people whose interests they seek to defend.

a) Wolfe, pp. 193–4; *b*) [Anon.] *Good Works*, pp. 2–3; *c*) *Some Observations on the Late Dangerous Petition presented to the House of Commons*, p. 17; *d*) W. Blyth, *The English Improver Improved*, p. 77.

a) OVERTON, JULY, 1647

THAT the grievous oppressions by tithes and forced maintenance for the ministry be removed, and that the more easy and evangelical practice of contribution be granted and confirmed for the benefit of the subject and his freedom therein, for prevention of the lordliness in, and the commotions, oppressions and tyrannies that might happen by, the clergy.

b) PAID BY THE POOR, 1641

There is a great inequality of paying tithe in London, the rich men, for the most part, paying very little . . . so that the minister's maintenance ariseth, for the most part, from the meanest and poorest people, in which respect that little maintenance he hath falls short many years in a great part, especially in hard or sickly times . . .; the richest citizen in London hardly paying so much as a countryman that hath but £20 or £10 per annum in his occupation.

c) VOLUNTARY MAINTENANCE OF MINISTERS, 1648

That is, being interpreted, that excepting London and the adjacent counties all ministers should be expelled the realm of England; and how many, think you, would be left in the Dominion of Wales? . . . Within a while people would be so far from disputing of God that they would never think of him. . . . Tithes . . . were never urged by us as a precept of the gospels but as the law of England.

d) INGRATITUDE, 1652

The minister . . . might go barefoot, and his family a-begging, for what the common people would contribute to his subsistence.

123. A PEER AND THE LEVELLERS

Extracts from the journal of the Earl of Leicester, a great magnate who played an inglorious part during the revolution by trying to keep in with both sides. After quoting the Leveller newspaper, *The Moderate*, he adds his own revealing comments. His first remark, on what he regarded as the censorship and police duties of a *Christian* state, illuminates the connection between religion and politics once again. Ed. R. W. Blencowe, *Sidney Papers* (1825), pp. 78–9, 94–5.

The Moderate, July 31st–August 7th, 1649: Many honest people . . . argue it with much confidence, that *property is the original cause of any sin between party and party*, as to civil transactions; and that, since the tyrant is taken off, and the government altered *in homine*, so ought it really to redound to the good of the people *in specie*; which, though they cannot expect it in few years by reason of the multiplicity of the gentry in authority, command, etc., who drive on all designs for support of the old government, and consequently their own interest and the people's slavery; yet they doubt not but in time the people *will* herein discern their own blindness and folly.

The Earl of Leicester: It is a wonder that it hath been so long suffered, there being almost every week such passages like this almost in it—and such as would not be permitted in any Christian state, nor even amongst the heathen.

The Moderate: Wars have ever been clothed with the most specious of all pretences, viz. reformation of religion, the laws of the land, liberty of the subject, etc., though the effects thereof have proved most destructive to them; . . . taking away each man's birthright, and *settling upon a few a cursed property*, *the ground of all civil offences* and the greatest cause of most sins against the heavenly Deity.

The Earl of Leicester: His former wicked and desperate style, for which it is a wonder that he is not severely punished, but suffered still to write and to excite the people to overthrow all order and government.

124. REASON *VERSUS* PRECEDENT IN POLITICS

Before the revolution the Parliamentarians tried to find "precedents" from the feudal past for their attack on the monarchy. Much antiquarian research was devoted to the profitless task of proving that one side or the other was "right." Even after war started the leaders of the Parliamentary party still pretended that they were defending the old constitution, "King and Parliament," against the King's evil counsellors. This was partly due to intellectual timidity, to reluctance to break from traditional modes of thought; but it had its roots in the men of property's fear that the unfettered reason might draw conclusions hostile to their economic and political supremacy. Before the revolution it was rare for anyone to say, as Sir R. Phelips did once to Sir E. Coke, "If there be no precedent for this it is time to make one." But as the war continued new classes came into politics who had no vested interests to defend with the armoury of the past, and so there was a clean break from traditional arguments and antiquarianism, and the beginnings of a rational and scientific attitude to politics. No one could pretend there were precedents for the execution of Charles I. Overton's *Appeal* (*b*), significantly, is "from the degenerate representative body," the House of Commons, "to the body represented, the free people in general . . . and in especial" to Fairfax's army (cf. No. 77).

a) Wolfe, p. 114; *b*) *ibid.*, pp. 157–8.

a) A REMONSTRANCE OF MANY THOUSAND CITIZENS, JULY, 1646

WHATEVER our forefathers were, or whatever they did or suffered or were enforced to yield unto, we are the men of the present age and ought to be absolutely free from all kinds of exorbitancies, molestations or arbitrary power.

b) R. OVERTON—AN APPEAL, JULY 17TH, 1647

It is confessed that our English histories and records of the actions and transactions of our predecessors, both of ancient and late times (so far as I can understand) do not afford me any example or precedent for any appeal from Parliament to people: so that by such as prefer precedents and formalities, forms and figures, before the substance, life and spirit of all just precedents and laws, I may probably be censured and condemned for this present enterprise as an open and desperate enemy to Parliaments and magistracy, a subverter and destroyer of all national laws and government, and a reducer (to my power) of kingdoms and people into confusion. To such I shall return even the late words of our now degenerate Parliament, "that reason hath no precedent, for reason is the fountain of all just precedents."

125. LEVELLERS ON IRELAND

For Ireland, see No. 173. One oı two of the Levellers transcended religious differences sufficiently to realise that the English people had no interests in suppressing the national independence of Ireland. Extracts *a*) and *b*) were written by opponents of the Levellers; but they probably represent Walwyn's views not unfairly. Cf. No. 172, *d*).

a) Edwards, *Gangræna*, Part II, p. 27; *b*) *Walwyn's Wiles*, H. and D., p. 310; *c*) T. Prince, *The Silken Independents' Snare Broken* (1649), pp. 6–7.

a) DANGERS OF RELIGIOUS TOLERANCE, 1646

TOUCHING the rebellion in Ireland, Master Walwyn said the Irish did no more but what we would have done ourselves if it had been our case; and said "What had the English to do in their kingdom?" and that they were a better-natured people than we, and said "Why should not they enjoy the liberty of their consciences?"—Observe to what this pretended liberty of conscience brings men, namely to plead for treason, rebellion and all kinds of wickedness.

b) COMMON ENEMIES, 1649

. . . His constant endeavour to hinder the relief of Ireland by exhibiting arguments and reasons in justification of that bloody rebellion . . . arguing that the cause of the Irish natives in seeking their just freedoms, immunities and liberties was the very same with our cause here in endeavouring our own rescue and freedom from the power of oppressors.

c) FREEDOM BEGINS AT HOME

If England were settled as [the Levellers urged], the goodness of the government would invite the Irish with a desire unto it; there would then be some hopes (sending over faithful men, those who would make conscience of their ways, such as would keep their engagements) that the Irish would soon be reduced, as being willing to change their condition of bondage for freedom. . . .

All care ought to be taken, . . . when the Irish are overcome, that none of those employed do turn the gaining thereof to their own domination; a taste whereof, you know, is exercised in England. for what are we better for all the victories gained these eight years? Are not the people more burdened than ever? Wise and honest men will acknowledge it. . . .

And for keeping out of rebels, I am not only against any that shall invade the land from abroad; but I am against all that any ways invade our liberties within the nation.

Part Ten

ARMY DEMOCRACY

There is on earth a yet auguster thing,
Veiled though it be, than Parliament and King.

George Wither.

126. THE ARMY AS DEMOCRATIC CENTRE

Cf. No. 106, *c*). Walker, Part I, pp. 44, 59.

(1647) THE army . . . have sown the cockle of heresies and schism so abundantly in City and country (especially amongst the more beggarly sort) that these men, joining principles and interests with the army, weaken the hands of all opponents. . . . Their plausible way of prompting the people to petition against tithes, enclosures and copyhold fines uncertain was to encourage them to side with the army against all the nobility, gentry and clergy of the land (from whom the army did most fear an opposition) and to destroy monarchy itself: since it is impossible for any prince to be a King only of beggars, tinkers and cobblers.

127. SOLDIERS' DELEGATES

In February, 1647, the Presbyterian majority in Parliament decided to disband the Army (without providing for payment of the considerable arrears of pay) and to give those soldiers who wished the opportunity to volunteer for service in Ireland. The step was dictated by the conservatives' desire to "finish with the revolution," and by fear of the radical tendencies of the Army. The rank and file petitioned Parliament to reconsider its decision: inevitably the agitation took a *political* form (*a*). Delegates ("Agitators") were elected to represent the views of the rank and file: they prepared the *Solemn Engagement* signed by the soldiers at a general rendezvous (*c*).

a) J. and W., pp. 56–7; *b*) Rushworth, VI, p. 469; *c*) *ibid*., p. 510.

a) LETTER FROM SUFFOLK, APRIL 20TH, 1647

MOST houses where the soldiers quarter can testify their high discontented speeches against the parliament, and of their resolutions to go with the petition. I doubt not but you have heard how Ireton's regiment declared themselves at Ipswich last Thursday when the soldiers met; some of them made speeches crying out "All disband or none; all for Ireland or none." The soldiers conclude that they who have been so badly paid in England shall be wholly neglected if they shall go into Ireland. . . . As for the petition, they now speak of it openly, that they will send it up with two out of every troop, and they expect the parliament should clap them up [i.e. imprison them] who go up with it. And then they will presently set upon starving the City, where they doubt not but to find such a party as the parliament will be glad to let the soldiers out again. I hear they boast of apprentices and butchers by name [as their supporters]. . . .

The soldiers both in Norfolk and Suffolk sing one note; namely that they have fought all this time to bring the King to London, and to London they will bring the King. . . . Some of the soldiers do not stick to call the parliament-men tyrants. Lilburne's books are quoted by them as statute law.

b) VINDICATION OF THE OFFICERS, APRIL, 1647

The petition took its first rise from amongst the soldiers, and . . . we [the officers] engaged but in the second place to regulate the soldiers' proceedings and remove as near as we could all occasion of distaste.

c) THE SOLEMN ENGAGEMENT OF THE ARMY, JUNE 5TH, 1647

The soldiers of this army (finding themselves so stopped in their due and regular way of making known their just grievances and desires to and by their officers) were enforced to an unusual (but in that case necessary) way of correspondence and agreement amongst themselves, to choose out of the several troops and companies several men, and those out of their whole number to choose two or more for each regiment, to act in the name and behalf of the whole soldiery of the respective regiments, troops and companies.

128. ENCOURAGING THE OFFICERS

The rank and file having taken the lead, the Agitators employed a judicious combination of encouragements and threats to bring the officers into line. The officers, drawn largely from the lesser gentry, yeomanry and bourgeoisie, had common interests with the rank and file in desiring to keep the Army in being until arrears had been paid and an indemnity voted; but feared the extreme radicalism of some of the Agitators. So they wavered.

a) *Letter from the Agitators to the General and officers*, April 28th, 1647; *b*) *Clarke Papers* (ed. C. H. Firth, Camden Soc., 1891–1901), I, pp. 87–8.

a) AGITATORS TO THE OFFICERS, APRIL, 1647

THEREFORE, brave commanders, the Lord put a spirit of courage into your hearts, that you may stand fast; . . . if any of you shall not, he shall be marked with a brand of infamy for ever, as a traitor to his country and an enemy to his army. . . . Is it not better to die like men than to be enslaved and hanged like dogs?—which must and will be yours and our portion if not now looked unto. . . . We have been quiet and peaceable in obeying all orders and commands, yet now we have a just cause to tell you, if we be not relieved in these our grievances, we shall be forced to that which we pray God to divert.

b) LETTER FROM THE AGITATORS TO ALL REGIMENTS, MAY, 1647

The dividing and so the destroying designs are in hand. . . . No sooner came they [the officers] to speak on your behalfs, but they become the mark [to be shot at] instead of you. . . . Stand with your officers, and one with another; you need not fear. If you divide you destroy all. . . . [The officers] are yours while you are theirs.

129. THE OFFICERS FOLLOW

Those officers who did not fall in with the wishes of the men were driven out of the Army (*b*). The united Army accepted the Solemn Engagement of June 5th, which gave the Agitators a status in the governing organ of the Army and a say in its political deliberations. But already some of the officers were thinking of double-crossing the elected delegates (*d*) and *e*)). Extract (*c*) is from a version quoted by Lilburne.

a) *Clarke Papers*, I, p. 112; *b*) Wolfe, p. 246; *c*) *ibid.*, pp. 244–5; *d*) *Clarke Papers*, I, pp. 214–15; *e*) *Fairfax Correspondence*, III, p. 369.

a) END OF MAY, 1647

THE officers now own the soldiers and all that's done. . . . It is incredible the unity of officers and soldiers.

b) LILBURNE, DECEMBER 14TH, 1647

The whole army by agreement or joint consent cashiered all officers at Newmarket Heath [June 4th and 5th, 1647] that would not associate with them and engage to stand for common right and freedom, though against the Parliament, and so they hooted divers officers out of the field, unhorsed some and rent their clothes and beat them: and this in the face of the General, all which acts were death by martial law; but . . . officers at that time being only admitted by mutual consent they could have no power but what was entrusted to them by the soldiers.

c) THE SOLEMN ENGAGEMENT OF THE ARMY, JUNE 5TH, 1647

We do hereby declare, agree and promise to and with each other that we shall not willingly disband, nor divide, nor suffer ourselves to be disbanded or divided without satisfaction in relation to our grievances and desires, . . . and security that we as private men or other the free-born people of England shall not remain subject to the like oppression and injury as have been attempted, and this satisfaction and security to be such as shall be agreed unto by a Council to consist of those general officers of the army who have concurred with the army in the premises, with two commission officers and two soldiers to be chosen for each regiment, who have concurred and shall concur with us in the premises and in this Agreement.

d) A NEWS-LETTER, JULY 17TH, 1647

[The] Agitators, whom now in prudence we admit to debate; and it is not more than necessary they should be, considering the influence they have upon the soldiers; and the officer we hope hath such interest in them as, if any of more fierce disposition among them moderate not their reason, the officers can command it. . . . It is the singularest part of wisdom in the general and the officers so to carry themselves, considering the present temper of the army, so as to be unanimous in councils, including the new persons into their number. It keeps a good accord, and obtains ready obedience.

e) RUSHWORTH TO LORD FAIRFAX, JULY 20TH, 1647

Friday, July 16th, a general council of war called, consisting of about 100 officers besides Agitators. . . . The Agitators were higher in proposals than the officers, who were more expert in state affairs. I only mention this, that you may be assured the inferior, upon good reasons, submitted to the superior, so that it is not will but reason that guides the proceedings of the army.

130. DIRECT ACTION, JUNE 3RD, 1647

The Presbyterian majority in Parliament were plotting an agreement with Charles I at the Army's expense: already in April some in the Army had been discussing seizing the person of the King to hold as a pledge (No. 127, *a*)). This was now done, at the apparent initiative of the Agitators and on their sole authority; but Cromwell and the generals accepted the fact and used the situation to bring pressure on Parliament. This account was derived from an eye-witness.

Wood, *Fasti Oxonienses* (ed. Bliss, 1813–20), II, pp. 138–40.

June 3rd, 1647. About midnight came that party of horse, which in good order drew up before the house or palace at Holdenby, and at all avenues placed guards. This done, the officer that commanded the party alighted and demanded entrance. . . . He answered, his name was Joyce, a cornet in Col. Edw. Whalley's regiment, and his business was to speak with the King. "From whom?" said they. "From myself," said Joyce; at which they laughed, and thereupon Joyce said 'twas no laughing matter. . . . During this short treaty . . . the soldiers on each side had conference together, and so soon as they understood that they were fellow soldiers of one and the same army, they . . . opened the gates and doors, shook one another by the hand and bade them welcome. . . .

Cornet Joyce, being come unto the door, he in rude manner knocked. Those within asked who it was that, in such an uncivil manner and unseasonable time, came to disquiet the King's rest. The cornet answered, "My name is Joyce, an officer of the army, and sorry I am that I should disquiet the King, but I cannot help it, for speak with him I must, and that presently." This strange confidence of his, and the posture he was in, having a cocked pistol in his hand, amazed the four grooms of the bedchamber. . . .

The King then said, ". . . Give me a sight of your instructions." "That," said Cornet Joyce, "you shall see presently"; and forthwith drawing up the greatest and best part of the party into the inner court, as near as he could unto the King, said, "These, sir, are my instructions."

131. ARMY'S DECLARATION, JUNE 14TH, 1647

These famous words, accepted by the Army Council, form the Army's justification for its intervention in politics in 1647. H. and D., p. 55.

WE were not a mere mercenary army, hired to serve any arbitrary power of a state; but called forth and conjured by the several declarations of Parliament, to the defence of our own and the people's just rights and liberties. And so we took up arms in judgment and conscience to those ends, and have so continued them, and are resolved . . . to assert and vindicate the just power and rights of this kingdom in Parliament, for those common ends premised, against all arbitrary power, violence and oppression, and against all particular parties or interests whatsoever.

132. THE AGREEMENT OF THE PEOPLE

This is the first Agreement of the People. It was presented by the Agitators to the General Council of the Army at Putney in October, 1647 (No. 133). In Leveller theory the Agreement acted both as the guarantee of fundamental human rights and as a sort of entrance certificate into the state to which everyone had to subscribe before admission. It would serve to keep out Royalists. The revised Agreement of May 1st, 1649, excluded Catholics from all state offices, on political grounds. The Agreement is a social contract; those outside it are in effect in a state of war. Even within the state created by subscription to the Agreement, there is no explicit demand for manhood suffrage. The Agreement may be compared with the six points of the People's Charter, 1838. Gardiner, pp. 333–5.
Gardiner, pp. 333—5.

An Agreement of the People for a firm and present peace upon grounds of common right.

Having by our late labours and hazards made it appear to the world at how high a rate we value our just freedom, and God having so far owned our cause as to deliver the enemies thereof into our hands, we do now hold ourselves bound in mutual duty to each other to take the best care we can for the future to avoid both the danger of returning into a slavish condition and the chargeable remedy of another war; for, as it cannot be imagined that so many of our countrymen would have opposed us in this quarrel if they had understood their own good, so may we safely promise to ourselves that, when our common rights and liberties shall be cleared, their endeavours will be disappointed that seek to make themselves our masters. Since, therefore, our former oppressions and scarce-yet-ended troubles have been occasioned, either by want of frequent national meetings in Council, or by rendering those meetings ineffectual, we are fully agreed and resolved to provide that hereafter our representatives be neither left to an uncertainty for the time nor made useless to the ends for which they are intended. In order whereunto we declare:—

I

That the people of England, being at this day very unequally distributed by counties, cities, and boroughs for the election of their deputies in Parliament, ought to be more indifferently proportioned according to the number of the inhabitants; the circumstances whereof for number, place, and manner are to be set down before the end of this present Parliament.

II

That, to prevent the many inconveniences apparently arising from the long continuance of the same persons in authority, this present Parliament be dissolved upon the last day of September which shall be in the year of our Lord 1648.

III

That the people do, of course, choose themselves a Parliament once in two years . . . [to sit for not more than six months].

IV

That the power of this, and all future Representatives of this nation, is inferior only to theirs who choose them, and doth extend, without the consent or concurrence of any other person or persons, to the enacting, altering and repealing of laws, to the erecting and abolishing of offices and courts, to the appointing, removing, and calling to account magistrates and officers of all degrees, to the making of war and peace, to the treating with foreign states, and, generally, to whatsoever is not expressly or implicitly reserved by the represented to themselves:

Which are as followeth:

i. That matters of religion and the ways of God's worship are not at all entrusted by us to any human power, because therein we cannot remit or exceed a tittle of what our consciences dictate to be the mind of God without wilful sin: nevertheless the public way of instructing the nation (so it be not compulsive) is referred to their discretion.

ii. That the matter of impresting and constraining any of us to serve in the wars is against our freedom; and therefore we do not allow it in our Representatives; the rather, because money (the sinews of war), being always at their disposal, they can never want numbers of men apt enough to engage in any just cause.

iii. That after the dissolution of this present Parliament, no person be at any time questioned for anything said or done in reference to the late public differences, otherwise than in execution of the judgments of the present Representatives or House of Commons.

iv. That in all laws made or to be made every person may be bound alike, and that no tenure, estate, charter, degree, birth, or place do confer any exemption from the ordinary course of legal proceedings whereunto others are subjected.

v. That as the laws ought to be equal, so they must be good, and not evidently destructive to the safety and well-being of the people.

These things we declare to be our native rights, and therefore are agreed and resolved to maintain them with our utmost possibilities against all opposition whatsoever; being compelled thereunto not only by the examples of our ancestors, whose blood was often spent in vain for the recovery of their freedoms, suffering themselves through fraudulent accommodations to be still deluded of the fruit of their victories, but also by our own woeful experience, who, having long expected and dearly earned the establishment of these certain rules of government, are yet made to depend for the settlement of our peace and freedom upon him [Charles I] that intended our bondage and brought a cruel war upon us.

133. THE PUTNEY DEBATES

By a fortunate chance, the verbatim record of the debates in the General Council of the Army at Putney in October, 1647, have come down to us. They give a brilliant picture of a spontaneous discussion on the foundations of the state between Cromwell and Ireton on the one side, Colonel Rainborough and the Agitator Sexby (see No. 184) on the other. The latter were reinforced by two civilian Levellers from London, Wildman and Petty. The arguments used are familiar. Almost up to the present day they have been employed on both sides of the debate as to whether or not a vote should be dependent on a "stake" in the country. Ireton's speeches may be compared with the views expressed against the Reform Bills in 1832 and 1867. Those speakers had few new ideas above those with which Ireton provided them. On the other side this is not so true. Democratic ideas have since obtained a tremendous impetus from, among others, Bentham and Marx. The Levellers could only base their claims on a self-evident natural right. Ireton was able to show that a theory of absolute natural right might involve Communism and not merely democracy. The Levellers consequently found themselves on the horns of a dilemma. They denied, truthfully, they were Communists. But they could find no other basis for democratic theory than natural right—and that Ireton showed to involve Communism. In the Agreement of May 1st, 1649, in addition to Royalists, servants and those receiving alms are excluded from the franchise: since voting was by show of hands, the last two classes could hardly have flouted the views of their masters. But in effect the Levellers too were modifying natural right with a kind of property qualification. Woodhouse, *Puritanism and Liberty*, pp. 1–78, 122.

First day, October 28th, 1647

Sexby (*Agitator*): The cause of our misery [is] upon two things. We sought to satisfy all men, and it was well. . . . We have laboured to please a King, and I think, except we go about to cut all our throats, we shall not please him;

and we have gone to support . . . the Parliament, which consists of a company of rotten members. . . .

Commissary-General Ireton: I shall declare it again that I do not seek, or would not seek, nor will join with them that do seek, the destruction either of Parliament or King. Neither will I consent with those, or concur with them, who will not attempt all the ways that are possible to preserve both, and to make good use, and the best use that can be, of both for the kingdom. . . .

Lieutenant-General Cromwell: Truly this paper [the Agreement] does contain in it very great alterations of the very government of the kingdom, alterations from that government that it hath been under, I believe I may almost say, since it was a nation. . . . And what the consequences of such an alteration as this would be, if there were nothing else to be considered, wise men and godly men ought to consider. . . . I think we are not only to consider what the consequences are if there were nothing else but this paper, but we are to consider the probability of the ways and means to accomplish [the thing proposed]: that is to say, whether, according to reason and judgment, the spirits and temper of the people of this nation are prepared to receive and to go on along with it. . . . [He also urged that they must first take into consideration the obligations and engagements that lie upon the army by reason of their public declarations.]

Colonel Rainborough: I hear [it] said [that] it's a huge alteration, it's a bringing in of new laws, and that this kingdom hath been under this government ever since it was a kingdom. If writings be true there have been many scufflings between the honest men of England and those that have tyrannised over them; and if it be [true what I have] read, there is none of those just and equitable laws that the people of England are born to but are entrenchment[s on the once enjoyed privileges of their rulers] altogether. But [even] if they were those which the people have been always under, if the people find that they are [not] suitable to freemen as they are, I know no reason [that] should deter me, either in what I must answer before God or the world, from endeavouring by all means to gain anything that might be of more advantage to them than the government under which they live....

Mr. Wildman: The other [thing I would mention] is a principle much spreading, and much to my trouble, . . .: that when persons once be engaged, though the engagement appear to be unjust, yet the person must sit down and suffer under it; and that therefore, in case a Parliament, as a true Parliament, doth anything unjustly, if we be engaged to submit to the laws that they shall make, though they make an unjust law . . . yet we must swear obedience. . . . This principle is . . . contrary to what the Army first declared: that they stood upon such principles of right and freedom, and the laws of Nature and Nations, whereby men were to preserve themselves though the persons to whom authority belonged should fail in it. . . .

Commissary-General Ireton: If you will resort only to the law of Nature, by the law of Nature you have no more right to this land, or anything else, than I have. I have as much right to take hold of anything that is for my sustenance, [to] take hold of anything that I have a desire to for my satisfaction, as you. But here comes the foundation of all right that I understand to be betwixt men, as to the enjoying of one thing or not enjoying of it: we are under a contract, we are under an agreement, and that agreement is what a man has for matter of land that he hath received by a traduction from his ancestors, which according to the law does fall upon him to be his right. . . . This I take to be [the foundation of all right] for matter of land. For matter of goods, that which does fence me from that [right] which another man may claim by the Law of Nature of taking my goods, that which makes it mine really and civilly, is the law. . . .

[Debate adjourned with the appointment of a Committee to confer with the Agitators with regard to the Agreement and the Army's declarations and engagements; and with a decision to hold a prayer-meeting before the resumption of the debate on the morrow.]

Second day, October 29th, 1647

[The Agreement read in full; then the first Article by itself.]

Commissary-General Ireton [asked]: Whether those men whose hands are to it, or those that brought it, do know so much of the matter as [to know] whether they mean that all that had a former right of election [are to be electors], or [that] those that had no right before are to come in. . . .

Mr. Petty: We judge that all inhabitants that have not lost their birthright should have an equal voice in elections.

Colonel Rainborough: I desired that those that had engaged in it [might be included]. For really I think that the poorest he that is in England has a life to live, as the greatest he; and therefore truly, sir, I think it's clear, that every man that is to live under a government ought first by his own consent to put himself under that government, and I do think that the poorest man in England is not at all bound in a strict sense to that government that he hath not had a voice to put himself under. . . .

Commissary-General Ireton: I think that no person has a right to an interest or share in the disposing of the affairs of the kingdom, and in determining or choosing those that shall determine what laws we shall be ruled by here—no person hath a right to this, that hath not a permanent fixed interest in this kingdom. . . . But that by a man's being born here he shall have a share in that power that shall dispose of the lands here, and of all things here, I do not think it a sufficient ground. . . . Those that choose the representatives for the making of laws by which this state and kingdom are to be governed are the persons who, taken together, do comprehend the local interest of this kingdom; that is, the persons in whom all land lies, and those in corporations in whom all trading lies. . . .

Colonel Rainborough: I do not find anything in the Law of God, that a lord shall choose twenty burgesses, and a gentleman but two, or a poor man shall choose none. . . . I . . . am still of the same opinion, that every man born in England cannot, ought not, neither by the Law of God nor the Law of Nature, to be exempted from the choice of those who are to make laws for him to live under, and for him, for aught I know, to lose his life under. . . .

Commissary-General Ireton: Now I wish we may all consider of what right you will challenge that all the people should have right to elections. Is it by the right of nature? If you will hold forth that as your ground, then I think you must deny all property too, and this is my reason. For thus: by that same right of nature (whatever it be) that you pretend, by which you can say, one man hath an equal right with another to the choosing of him that shall govern him—by the same right of nature, he hath the same [equal] right in any goods he sees—meat, drink, clothes—to take and use them for his sustenance. . . .

Colonel Rainborough: That there's a property, the Law of God says it; else why [has] God made that law, THOU SHALT NOT STEAL? . . .

Colonel [Nathaniel] Rich: I confess [there is weight in] that objection that the Commissary-General [Ireton] last insisted upon; for you have five to one in this kingdom that have no permanent interest. . . . If the master and servant shall be equal electors, then clearly those that have no interest in the kingdom will make it their interest to choose those that have no interest. It may happen, that the majority may by a law, not in a confusion, destroy property; there may be a law enacted, that there shall be an equality of goods and estate. . . . If we strain too far to avoid monarchy in kings [let us take heed] that we do not call for emperors to deliver us from more than one tyrant.

Mr. Wildman: I conceive that's the undeniable maxim of government: that all government is in the free consent of the people. If [so], then upon that account there is no person that is under a just government, or has justly his own, unless he by his own free consent be put under that government. . . .

Commissary-General Ireton: I do acknowledge that which you take to be so general a maxim, that . . . the original of power of making laws . . . does lie in the people [but by the people is meant those] that are possessed of the permanent interest in the land. . . .

Sexby (Agitator): We have engaged in this kingdom and ventured our lives, and it was all for this: to recover our birthrights and privileges as Englishmen; and by the arguments urged there is none. There are many thousands of us soldiers that have ventured our lives; we have had little property in the kingdom as to our estates, yet we have had a birthright. But it seems now, except a man has a fixed estate in this kingdom, he has no right in this kingdom. I wonder we were so much deceived. If we had not a right to the kingdom, we were mere mercenary soldiers. . . . I do think the poor and meaner of this kingdom—I speak as in relation [to the condition of soldiers], in which we are—have been the means of the preservation of the kingdom. . . .

Colonel Rainborough: I would fain know what the soldier has fought for all this while? He has fought to enslave himself, to give power to men of riches, men of estates, to make him a perpetual slave. We do find in all presses that go forth none must be pressed that are freehold men. When these gentlemen fall out among themselves they shall press the poor scrubs to come and kill [one another for] them.

Commissary-General Ireton: I confess I see so much right in the business that I am not easily satisfied with flourishes. . . . I [will] tell you what the soldier of the kingdom has fought for. First, the danger that we stood in was that one man's will must be a law. The people of the kingdom must have this right at least, that they should not be concluded [but] by the Representative of those that had the interest of the kingdom. So[m]e men fought in this because they were immediately concerned and engaged in it. Other men who had no other interest in the kingdom but this, that they should have the benefit of those laws made by the Representative, yet [fought] that they should have the benefit of this Representative. . . . The liberty of all those that have the permanent interest, . . . *that* is provided for. And liberty cannot be provided for in a general sense if property be preserved. For if property be preserved, [so] that I am not to meddle with such a man's estate, his meat, his drink, his apparel or other goods, then the right of nature destroys liberty. By the right of nature I am to have sustenance rather than perish; yet property destroys it for a man to have [this] by the right of nature, suppose there be no human constitution. . . .

Sexby (Agitator): I confess, many of us fought for those ends which, we since saw, were not those which caused us to go through difficulties and straits, to venture all in the ship with you. It had been good in you to have advertised us of it, and I believe you would have [had] fewer under your command to have commanded. . . .

Commissary-General Ireton: No man . . . will stand to that interest more than I do, of having Parliaments successive and not perpetual, and the distribution of elections [more equal]. But, notwithstanding, my opinion stands good, that it ought to be a distribution amongst the fixed and settled people of this nation. . . .

Mr. Petty: The rich would very unwillingly be concluded by the poor. And there is as much reason that the rich should conclude the poor as the poor the rich—and indeed no reason. There should be an equal share in both. . . .

Third day, November 1st, 1647

Commissary-General Ireton: Any man that makes a bargain, and does find afterwards 'tis for the worse, yet is bound to stand to it.

Mr. Wildman: They were cozened, as we are like to be.

134. ANXIETIES OF RANK AND FILE

After the deadlock at Putney, the tension between officers and rank and file increased, till finally (November, 1647) the generals broke decisively with the Agitators at a general rendezvous at Ware (*d*). The Army Council was dissolved. All these extracts are from Leveller pamphlets. The reference in *a*) to "new Agents" rises from the fact that some of the troopers' representatives had been "recalled" (because suspected of desiring to compromise with the officers) and replaced by others more radical. The title of *d*) refers to events in March, 1649, when eight troopers petitioned the Council of Officers for a restoration of democratic liberties, and five of them (the "beagles") were cashiered under degrading circumstances; the "foxes" are Cromwell and Ireton.

a) *A Letter from the Agents*, p. 3; *b*) *A Call to all the Soldiers*, pp. 3–4, 7; *c*) *A Letter sent from the Several Agitators of the Army*, pp. 6 7; *d*) probably by R. Overton, *The Hunting of the Foxes by Five Small Beagles*, Wolfe, pp. 363, 370.

a) LETTER FROM NEW AGENTS OF FIVE CAVALRY REGIMENTS, OCTOBER 28TH, 1647

LET it be remembered, that if you had not joined together at first and chosen your agents to act for you, when your officers thought it not safe for them to appear, you had been now in no capacity to plead for your own or the people's freedoms.

b) A CALL TO ALL THE SOLDIERS, OCTOBER 29TH, 1647

Your agitators (we hear) are esteemed but as a burden to the chief officers. . . . They a long time staggered before they engaged with you; and certainly had never engaged but that they saw no other way nor means to shelter and preserve themselves. . . . YE CAN CREATE NEW OFFICERS: necessity hath no law.

c) LETTER FROM AGITATORS TO THEIR REGIMENTS, NOVEMBER 11TH, 1647.

We hope it will be no discouragement to you though your officers, yea the greatest officers, should oppose you. It's well known, that the great officers which now opposed did as much oppose secretly when we refused to disband. . . . Those resolutions to stand for freedom and justice began amongst the soldiers only. . . . You have been fed with paper too long; we desire that there may be a general rendezvous, and no parting each from other till we be fully assured we shall not return to burden the country by free-quarter, and till our arrears be actually secured, and the foundations of our freedom, peace and security in the Agreement [of the People] established.

d) OVERTON LOOKS BACK, 1649

These things the soldiery beholding and observing endeavoured to restore their agents to a competent power and ability, to make good the faith of the army to the people, but then they found the hottest opposition from Cromwell and Ireton with his faction of officers, as whoever calls but to mind the business of Ware, when Col. Eyer was imprisoned, and Mr. Arnold a private soldier was shot to death for promoting and assisting the work of the soldiery in reference to the Solemn Engagement of the Army, may know.

And then it may be remembered how insolent and furious Cromwell deported himself against the honest observers of the faith of the army, it being then made death to observe the Engagement or but speak for the Agitators. O let that day never be forgotten! Let not the blood of that innocent person be here had out of remembrance, till justice be had for the same; neither let our Engagement or the perfidious perjured subverters thereof be forgotten; for here the Engagement was utterly cast aside, and the Agitators laid by. . . .

You shall scarce speak to Cromwell about anything but he will lay his hand on his breast, elevate his eyes and call God to record; he will weep, howl and repent even while he doth smite you under the fifth rib. . . . Thus it is evident to the whole world that the now present interest of the officers is directly contrary to the interest of the soldiery.

135. ARMY DEMOCRACY SABOTAGED

Both of these are Leveller accounts; they give a fair enough story of the way in which the Army Council was dissolved after the deadlock at Putney (Nos. 133 and 134). At the rendezvous at Ware in November, 1647, the rank and file were forced to sign the "short declaration" referred to in the last sentence of *b*).

a) R. Overton, *The Hunting of the Foxes by Five Small Beagles*, Wolfe, pp. 359–60; *b*) *The People's Friend.*

a) THE GENERALS DISLIKE THE ARMY COUNCIL

THE private soldiery (to interpose betwixt the people and their destroyers) drew themselves into that solemn Engagement of June 5th, 1647; in the attempting and transaction of which they found no small opposition (as may well be remembered) amongst the officers. . . . It was somewhat of a scorn to them [the generals] that a private soldier (though the representor of a regiment) should sit cheek by jowl with them, and have with an officer an equal vote in that Council. This was a thing savoured too much of the people's authority and power. . . . Hence followed secret murmurings and whisperings amongst the prerogative officers against the session and power of the Agitators, and at length palpable endeavours broke forth to suppress them.

b) THE ARMY COUNCIL DISSOLVED, NOVEMBER, 1647

Their [the officers'] spirits could not bear any co-partners with them in power, and therefore they first discouraged the Agitators as meddling with matters which did not concern them, then they questioned their power, by whom indeed themselves were settled in the power they had; and then they introduced all officers into the Councils; . . . and at last they quite dissolved the Council, and some few (if not one alone) drew up a short declaration contrary to their first Engagement.

Part Eleven

THE END OF THE OLD ORDER

To maintain religion, the King's person and authority, both Houses of Parliament, the laws and liberties of the people, i.e. so far as they could . . . be kept together, was the CAUSE: but when that was impossible, then their work was to maintain what they could of it, viz. the liberties of the people and their representatives: and this was the GOOD OLD CAUSE.

John Rogers: Mr. Prynne's Good Old Cause, 1659.

It is not a disgrace but an endearment of the Good Old Cause, that it destroys King, Queen, Prince, Lords and Kingdom in their political capacity.

H. S[*tubbe*]*:* The Commonwealth of Israel, 1659.

136. "THE ANARCHY," 1648

A Royalist ballad *a*) describes an imaginary mass meeting held to settle the future religion and government of England. Extract *b*) illustrates even more subversive demands that were actually made in 1649 (cf. No. 172, *d*)).

a) Firth in *Trans. Royal Historical Soc.*, 3rd Series, VI, pp. 61-3; *b*) [Anon] *Tyranipocrit Discovered*, in Orwell and Reynolds, *British Pamphleteers* (1948), I, p. 107.

a) FICTITIOUS DEMANDS, 1648

[*A Member of Parliament addresses the meeting:*]

Now that, thanks to the powers below,
We have e'en done out our do,
The mitre is down,
And so is the crown
And with them the coronet too;
Come clowns, and come boys,
Come hobber de hoys
Come females of each degree,
Stretch your throats, bring in your votes,
And make good the anarchy.

And "thus it shall go," says Alice;
"Nay, thus it shall go," says Amy;
"Nay, thus it shall go," says Taffy, "I trow";
"Nay, thus it shall go," says Jamy.

["Ah, good people," says the speaker, "the truth is a difficult thing to discover; you must decide what the truth is and which of your sects has it." Again the answer is discordant.]

"Sure, I have the truth," says Numph,
"Nay, I have the truth," says Clem,
"Nay, I have the truth," says Reverend Ruth,
"Nay, I have the truth," says Em.

["Well," says the speaker, "let truth be where it will, these divisions in religion reduce our power; take one religion and stick to it, here are forty to choose from."]

"Then we'll be of this," says Meg;
"Nay, we'll be of that," says Tib;
"Come we'll be of all," says pitiful Paul;
"Nay, we'll be of none," says Gib.

["After all," replies the speaker, "religion does not really matter, the question of government is really the important one."]

"Then let's have King Charles," says George,
"Nay, let's have his son," says Hugh,
"Nay, let us have none," says jabbering Joan,
"Nay, let's all be kings," says Prue.

[Despairing of arriving at any agreement, since even when the populace is victorious it can do nothing but debate, the speaker appeals to the Royalists:]

"Come royalists then do you play the men
And cavaliers give the word,
Now let us see at what you would be,
And whether you can accord."

"A health to King Charles," says Tom,
"Up with it," says Ralph like a man,
"God bless him," says Doll, "and raise him," says Moll,
"And send him his own," says Nan.

b) REAL DEMANDS, 1649

If the rulers of this world cannot make all the poor rich, yet they can [make] the richest poorer; for their sin is not so much in that some men are too poor, as it is in that some are too rich. The magistrates' duty is equally to divide and share such goods as God hath given them a power to dispose of: and when they have done that, then they have done their duty. O impious world, thou art not so much to be blamed because there are abuses, as because thou maintainest them. Do thou take away the superfluous riches from the rich, and divide them amongst the poor. . . . Once in a year, or oftener, thou must examine every man's estate to see if they have not made their goods uneven; and if they have, then thou must make it even again.

137. THE LOWER ORDERS IN POWER

The *coup d'état* of 1648-9 (Nos. 139-40) bought new men to power. A revolutionary dictatorship was established. Extract *c*) shows that some of the gentry opposing the new régime thought that liberty and property were the same thing; *a*), *b*) and *d*) that the government was able to rally lower-class support. With *a*), whose optimism proved premature, cf. Part XII and No. 200, *b*). Extract *b*) is by a Royalist who subsequently became Cromwell's physician.

a) [Anon.], *Anglia Liberata* (1651), pp. 67-8; *b*) [Bate], *A Short Narrative of the Late Troubles in England*, p. 131; *c*) Bayley, *The Great Civil War in Dorset*, p. 352; *d*) Dunlop, *Ireland under the Commonwealth* (1913), I, pp. 52-3.

a) A REAL REVOLUTION

ENGLAND hath received many a sudden change, but never such a change as now. Heretofore the poor people toiled themselves, in shifting one tyrant out of the saddle to set up another; but now they have driven out not only the tyrant, but tyranny itself; and cashiered not only a single king, but all kings for ever. It is an easy matter for particulars to supplant one another in government, because the interest stands deposited in a single hand; but when the whole frame of government is altered from what it was, and the interest of state lies diffused in the hands of the people, it is almost impossible to alter it again without such a tract of time as may produce new dispositions and opportunities for the effecting a new alteration. Besides, it is very rarely observed . . . that ever kingly government was suddenly restored in any country, after it had been once cashiered by the people.

b) "SORDID MEN" GOVERN LONDON, 1649

The Common Council of the City of London (that was wont to consist of the most wealthy and grave citizens) they ["the Oligarchians," i.e. the members of the Long Parliament after Pride's Purge] thrust out of their places, . . . substituting in their places the most sordid men and of the vilest condition, many of them being but youths; but more of a desperate fortune.

c) DECLARATION OF THE COUNTY OF DORSET, JUNE, 1648

We demand . . .:—

(iv) That our liberties (purchases of our ancestors' blood) may be redeemed from all former infringements and preserved henceforth inviolable; and that our ancient liberties may not lie at the mercy of those that have none, nor [be] enlarged and repealed by the votes and revotes of those that have taken too much liberty to destroy the subjects'. . . .

(vii) That we may no longer subjugate our necks to the boundless lusts and unlimited power of beggarly and broken committees, consisting generally of the tail of the gentry, men of ruinous fortunes and despicable estates, whose insatiable desires prompt them to continual projects of pilling and stripping us; and that we be not awed by their emissaries . . . generally the most shirking and cunning beggars that can be picked out of a county.

(viii) That, instead, we may be governed in military affairs and civil by men of visible estates and of unquestioned repute, . . . well-beloved by us.

d) COMMISSIONERS AT BELFAST TO COUNCIL OF STATE, SEPTEMBER, 1651

The Isle of Man, . . . (if our intelligence be true) will be gained [for the Parliament] without much difficulty; the inhabitants being (as we are informed) weary of their landlords and desirous to be under your government.

138. IGNORANCE NECESSARY TO GOVERNMENT

These extracts, written in 1649 by men who had been driven from power by the republicans, show what the Presbyterians thought was the way to treat the lower orders. (For Holles, see notes to Nos. 78 and 103.)

a) Walker, Part I, pp. 140–1; *b*) D. Holles, *Memoirs*, p. 1.

a) PEARLS BEFORE SWINE

THE engaged party [i.e. the Army and its supporters] have laid the axe to the very root of monarchy and

Parliament; they have cast all the mysteries and secrets of government, both by Kings and Parliaments, before the vulgar (like pearls before swine) and have taught both the soldiery and people to look so far into them as to ravel back all governments to the first principles of nature. . . . They have made the people thereby so curious and so arrogant, that they will never find humility enough to submit to a civil rule. . . . There can be no form of government without its proper mysteries, which are no longer mysteries than while they are concealed. Ignorance, and admiration arising from ignorance, are the parents of civil devotion and obedience.

b) THE WORST HAS HAPPENED

The wisest of men saw it to be a great evil that servants should ride on horses and princes walk as servants on the earth: an evil now both seen and felt in our unhappy kingdom. The meanest of men, the basest and vilest of the nation, have got the power into their hands; trampled upon the crown; baffled and misused the Parliament; violated the laws; destroyed or suppressed the nobility and gentry of the kingdom.

139. PRIDE'S PURGE

The Second Civil War had been brought about by an agreement between Charles I and the Scots. After that the Army decided that no settlement was possible while Charles lived. But as long as in the Parliament a Presbyterian majority, from fear of the Left, was ready to come to an agreement with Charles on any terms, the trial and execution of the King was impossible. Accordingly, on December 6th, 1648, about 140 members were excluded from the House of Commons, leaving a "rump" of about fifty to sixty to carry on the business. Ludlow was an Army grandee and Member of Parliament, but a convinced republican, suspected at this time of association with the Levellers.

Ludlow, I, pp. 208–10.

Some of our Commissioners who had been with the King pleaded in the House for a concurrence with him, as if they had been employed by him. . . . The corrupt party in the House, having bargained for their own and the nation's liberty, resolved to break through all hazards and inconveniences to make good their contract, and after twenty-four hours debate, resolved by the plurality of votes, "That the King's concessions were ground for a future settlement." . . . The day following some of the principal officers of the army came to London, with expectation that things would be brought to this issue; and consulting with some members of Parliament and others, it was concluded after a full and free debate, that the measures taken by the Parliament were contrary to the trust reposed in them, and tending to contract the guilt of the blood that had been shed upon themselves and the nation: that it was therefore the duty of the army to endeavour to put a stop to such proceedings; having engaged in the war, not simply as mercenaries, but out of judgment and conscience, being convinced that the cause in which they were engaged was just, and that the good of the people was involved in it . . . We agreed that the army should be drawn up the next morning, and guards placed in Westminster Hall, the Court of Requests and the Lobby; that none might be permitted to pass into the House but such as had continued faithful to the public interest. . . . Col. Pride commanded the guard that attended at the Parliament-doors, having a list of those members who were to be excluded, preventing them from entering into the House, and securing some of the most suspected under a guard.

140. THE END OF CHARLES I

The second extract shows the duplicity of Charles I, who in all his negotiations with Parliament tried to play off one section of his enemies against another so as to retain his power. This finally decided even Oliver Cromwell that there could be no settled government with Charles on the throne, and he was handed over to a High Court of Justice to be tried. Extract *e*) shows how far the logic of revolution had driven the revolutionaries from their original claim that they were fighting merely against the evil counsellors of the King, not against his person. Now Charles is arraigned as a traitor to the commonwealth of England. Extract *f*) contains a summing up by the republican Scot in February, 1659. These words formed part of the charge against him after the Restoration, when he was hanged, disembowelled and quartered.

a) Warburton, III, p. 149; *b*) *Letters of Charles I*, p. 176; *c*) Gardiner, pp. 373–4; *d*) In *Letters of Charles I*, p. 255; *e*) Gardiner, pp. 377–80; *f*) Burton, III, pp. 109–10.

a) PRINCE RUPERT TO THE DUKE OF RICHMOND, JULY, 1645

HIS Majesty hath now no way left to preserve his posterity, kingdom and nobility, but by a treaty. I believe it a more prudent way to retain something than to lose all.

b) CHARLES I TO LORD DIGBY, MARCH, 1646

I am endeavouring to get to London . . . being not without hope that I shall be able so to draw either the Presbyterians or Independents to side with me, for extirpating the one or the other, that I shall be really King again.

c) THE CHARGE AGAINST THE KING, JANUARY 20TH, 1649

. . . All which wicked designs, wars, and evil practices of him, the said Charles Stuart, have been, and are carried on for the advancement and upholding of a personal interest of will, power, and pretended prerogative to himself and his family, against the public interest, common right, liberty, justice, and peace of the people of this nation, by and from whom he was entrusted as aforesaid [i.e. with a limited power to govern by and according to the laws of the land and not otherwise].

d) THE LORD PRESIDENT OF THE HIGH COURT OF JUSTICE, JOHN BRADSHAW

How far you have preserved the privileges of the people, your actions have spoke it; but truly, Sir, men's intentions ought to be known by their actions; you have written your meaning in bloody characters throughout the whole kingdom.

e) SENTENCE ON CHARLES I, JANUARY 27TH, 1649

The said Charles Stuart, being admitted King of England and therein trusted with a limited power to govern by and according to the law of the land, and not otherwise; and by his trust, oath and office being obliged to use the power committed to him for the good and benefit of the people, and for the preservation of their rights and liberties; yet nevertheless, out of a wicked design to erect and uphold in himself an unlimited and tyrannical power to rule according to his will, and to overthrow the rights and liberties of the people, and to take away and make void the foundations thereof, and of all redress and remedy of misgovernment, which by the fundamental constitutions of this kingdom were reserved on the people's behalf in the right and power of frequent and successive Parliaments, or national meetings in council; he, the said Charles Stuart, for accomplishment of such his designs, and for the protecting of himself and his adherents in his and their wicked practices, to the same end hath traitorously and maliciously levied war against the present Parliament and people therein represented. . . . Whereupon the proceedings and judgment of this Court were prayed against him as a tyrant, traitor and murderer, and public enemy to the commonwealth. . . .

This Court is in judgment and conscience satisfied that he, the said Charles Stuart, is guilty of levying war against the said Parliament and people. . . . For all which treasons and crimes this Court doth adjudge that he, the said Charles Stuart, as a tyrant, traitor, murderer and public enemy to the good people of this nation, shall be put to death by the severing of his head from his body.

f) A REGICIDE JUSTIFIES HIMSELF TEN YEARS LATER

It is impossible that any man should delight in a man of so much blood as the King was. . . . He was seven or eight times sent to with propositions, and would not yield. . . . So long as he was above ground, in view, there were daily revoltings among the army, and risings in all places; creating us all mischief, more than a thousand kings could do us good. It was impossible to continue him alive.

141. MILTON DEFENDS REGICIDE

Throughout Europe news of the execution of Charles was received with horror. England, like Russia after 1917, was ostracised. English representatives abroad were insulted and assassinated. John Milton took up the pen to defend the execution of a King. He showed that society has a right to call its rulers to account; and he based his argument on a version of the social contract which was to be preserved in the work of John Locke. Government was established by men to defend and preserve them against the danger of each man being his own judge. But the authority of the government came from the people and to them could be returned. J. Milton, *Tenure of Kings and Magistrates* (*Selected Prose*, World's Classics), pp. 326, 331–4, 336.

If men within themselves would be governed by reason, and not generally give up their understanding to a double tyranny, of custom from without, and blind affections within, they would discern better what it is to favour and uphold the tyrant of a nation. But being slaves within doors, no wonder that they strive so much to have the public state conformably governed to the inward vicious rule by which they govern themselves. For indeed none can love freedom heartily, but good men; the rest love not freedom but license; which never hath more scope or more indulgence than under tyrants. . . .

No man who knows aught can be so stupid to deny that all men naturally were born free, being the image and resemblance of God himself, and were by privilege above all the creatures born to command and not to obey: and that they lived so, till from the root of Adam's transgression, falling among themselves to do wrong and violence, and foreseeing that such courses must needs tend to the destruction of them all, they agreed by common league to bind each other from mutual injury, and jointly to defend themselves against any that gave disturbance or opposition to such agreement. Hence came cities, towns and commonwealths. And because no faith in all was found sufficiently binding, they saw it needful to ordain some authority that might restrain by force and punishment what was violated against peace and common right. This authority and power of self-defence and preservation being originally and naturally in every one of them, and unitedly in them all, for ease, for order, and lest each man should be his own partial judge, they communicated and derived either to one, whom for the eminence of his wisdom and integrity they chose above the rest, or to more than one whom they thought of equal deserving: the first was called a King; the other magistrates. Not to be their Lords and Masters . . . but to be their Deputies and Commissioners, to execute by virtue of their entrusted power that justice which else every man by the bond of nature and of covenant must have executed for himself, and for one another. . . . These for a while governed well . . . till the temptation of such a power left absolute in their hands perverted them at length to injustice and partiality. Then did they, who now by trial had found the danger and inconveniences of committing arbitrary power to any, invent laws either framed or consented to by all, that should combine and limit the authority of [those] whom they chose to govern them: that so man, of whose failing they had proof, might no more rule over them, but law and reason abstracted as much as might be from personal errors and frailties. . . . When this would not serve, but that the law was either not executed, or misapplied, they were constrained from that time, the only remedy left them, to put conditions and take oaths from all Kings and magistrates at their first instalment to do impartial justice by law: who upon those terms and no other received allegiance from the people, that is to say, bond or covenant to obey them in execution of those laws which they the people had themselves made or assented to. And this oft-times with express warning, that if the King or magistrate proved unfaithful to his trust, the people would be disengaged. They added also counsellors and Parliaments, nor to be only at his beck, but with him or without him, at set times, or at all times, when any danger threatened, to have care of the public safety . . . What can be more just, . . . if a subject for certain crimes be to forfeit by law . . . all his inheritance to the King, than that a King, for crimes proportional, should forfeit all his title and inheritance to the people? Unless the people must be thought created all for him, he not for them, and they all in one body inferior to him single; which were a kind of treason against the dignity of mankind to affirm. . . .

It follows, that to say Kings are accountable to none but God is the overturning of all law and government. For if they may refuse to give account, then all covenants made with them at coronation, all oaths, are in vain, and mere mockeries, all laws which they swear to keep, made to no purpose; for if the King fear not God, as how many of them do not? we hold then our lives and estates by the tenure of his mere grace and mercy, as from a God, not a mortal magistrate. . . .

It follows lastly, that since the King or magistrate holds his authority of the people, both originally and naturally for their good in the first place, and not his own, then may the people, as oft as they shall judge it for the best, either choose him or reject him, retain him or depose him though no tyrant, merely by the liberty and right of freeborn men to be governed as seems to them best.

142. ESTABLISHMENT OF THE REPUBLIC

Although the sovereignty of the representatives of the people was declared nearly a month before the execution of Charles I (*a*), it was over two months before the monarchy and the House of Lords were formally abolished (*b*), *c*)), another two months before England was proclaimed a republic (*d*). The republicans were afraid of committing themselves until their late Leveller allies had been rendered powerless (see Part XIII). The republican régime remained to do great deeds, as Haselrig proudly proclaimed ten years later (*e*).

a) *Commons Journals*, VI, p. 111; *b*) Gardiner, pp. 385–6; *c*) *ibid.*, p. 387; *d*) *ibid.*, p. 388; *e*) Burton, III, p. 97.

a) RESOLUTION OF THE COMMONS, JANUARY 4TH, 1649

THE people are, under God, the original of all just power . . . The Commons of England in Parliament assembled, being chosen by and representing the people, have the supreme power in this nation; . . . whatsoever is enacted or declared for law by the Commons in Parliament assembled hath the force of law, and all the people of this nation are concluded thereby, although consent and concurrence of King or House of Peers be not had thereunto.

b) ACT ABOLISHING THE MONARCHY, MARCH 17TH, 1649

Whereas it is and hath been found by experience that the office of a King . . . is unnecessary, burdensome and dangerous to the liberty, safety and public interest of the people . . .; be it therefore enacted and ordained . . . that the office of a King in this nation shall not henceforth reside in or be exercised by any one single person.

c) ACT ABOLISHING THE HOUSE OF LORDS, MARCH 19TH, 1649

The Commons of England assembled in Parliament, finding by too long experience that the House of Lords is useless and dangerous to the people of England to be continued, have thought fit to ordain and enact . . . that from henceforth the House of Lords in Parliament shall be and is hereby wholly abolished and taken away.

d) ACT DECLARING ENGLAND A REPUBLIC, MAY 19TH, 1649

The people of England and of all the territories thereunto belonging are and shall be . . . a Commonwealth and Free State, and shall from henceforth be governed as a Commonwealth and Free State by the supreme authority of this nation, the representatives of the people in Parliament, and by such as they shall appoint and constitute as officers and ministers under them for the good of the people, and that without any King or House of Lords.

e) SIR ARTHUR HASELRIG LOOKS BACK, FEBRUARY 7TH, 1659

We continued four years before we were put an end to. In which time, I appeal to all if the nation, that had been blasted and torn, began not exceedingly to flourish. At the end of the four years, scarce a sight to be seen that we had had a war. Trade flourished; the City of London grew rich; we were the most potent by sea that ever was known in England. Our navy and armies were never better.

143. DISTRUST OF PROPERTIED REPUBLICANS

After May, 1649, the social basis of the republican régime was very narrow. Royalists and Presbyterians opposed it on the Right, Levellers on the Left. Extract *a*) shows mistrust of the men of property as early as 1647; *b*) and *c*) illustrate the same anxieties two years later. The Independent Grandees *could* not be consistent democratic revolutionaries (see No. 133); after the break with the Left, they were ultimately forced back into agreement with the defeated Royalists and Presbyterians, whose hold over local government had in many parts of England never been broken (*d*). Musgrave, the author of this extract, had his own private quarrel with the republican Sir Arthur Haselrig, but there is no reason to doubt the substantial accuracy of his picture of conditions in Cumberland and Westmorland.

a) [Anon.] *A general charge of impeachment of high treason in the name of Justice-Equity against the communalty*, quoted in D. W. Petegorsky, *Left-Wing Democracy in the English Civil War* (1940), p. 101; *b*) Lilburne, *Legal Fundamental Liberties*, Wolfe, p. 423; *c*) [Anon.] *Certain Queries*, quoted in Woodhouse, *Puritanism and Liberty*, p. 246; *d*) J. Musgrave, *A true and exact relation of the great and heavy grievances the well-affected of the northern bordering counties lie under, by Sir A. Haselrig's misgovernment and placing in authority there for Justices of the Peace, Commissioners for Militia, Ministry and Sequestrations, malignants and men disaffected to the present government* (1650), pp. 36, 47.

a) DISTRUST OF THE GENTRY, 1647

CONSIDER how impossible it is for those that oppress you to ease and free you from your oppressions. For who are the oppressors but the nobility and gentry; and who are oppressed—is it not the yeoman, the farmer, the tradesman and the labourer? Then consider, have you not chosen oppressors to relieve you from oppression? . . . It is naturally inbred in the major part of the nobility and gentry to oppress the persons of such that are not as rich and honourable as themselves, to judge the poor but fools and them wise. . . . It is they that oppress you, insomuch that your slavery is their liberty, your poverty is their prosperity.

b) LEVELLER ANXIETY, 1649

Although they have beheaded the King, yet I am confidently persuaded their enmity is such at the people's liberties that they would sooner run the hazard of letting the Prince in to reign in his father's stead than further a really just Agreement [of the People], or endure the sight of a new Parliament rightly constituted.

c) A DILEMMA, 1649

How can the Kingdom be the Saints' when the ungodly are electors and elected to govern?

d) NO SOCIAL REVOLUTION IN THE NORTH, 1650

There is not a Committee-man in Cumberland, nor Justice of the Peace in . . . Cumberland or Westmorland, saving one or two at the most, but many ways have discovered his malignancy and disaffection to the present proceedings of this Parliament. . . . Here the whole gentry are malignants, delinquents, papists, popish or base temporizers. Here not 10 of the gentry in both these counties, nay, I dare say, not so many, have proved cordial to the state.

144. THE NEED FOR TERROR

This Parliamentarian reporter at The Hague was tolerably well informed about Charles II's design to invade England via Scotland, which led to his defeat at Worcester in 1651. He draws the moral that continued watchfulness and firmness against opponents are needed. In the course of the next ten years, however, "respect to cousin and county" proved stronger than democratic vigilance. Gardiner, *Charles II and Scotland in 1650*, pp. 119–21.

THOUGH you may perhaps think it something improbable [that] you should be invaded by sea, and that it will be impossible to provide a navy, either so secretly as you should not know it, or so great as you should not be able to deal with it, they [the cavaliers in exile in Holland] are of another mind, and think to bring it about by a trick of address that you shall not prevent. They say they have made their party everywhere ready to join with them; . . . a few shall land at first, and his [the King's] party flock to them by multitudes, and this would draw your forces to one place; and so soon as these distractions are among you, then the hungry Scots like a swarm of locusts to come in upon you, man and mother's son, to make happy and fertile England as miserable by a war as their own country is without it. . . . This is the evil that threatens you; I need not prescribe you a process for cure. . . . But . . . take heed of being cheated by a beaten, fawning spaniel. They are here most afraid of your High Court of Justice, which they doubt may much discourage their party, and they wish you would not renew the power of it when what they have shall expire. . . . And indeed the Court is of almost as much use to you as an army, and will prevent the rising of as many enemies as the other will destroy; only you must be sure to execute justice there with all severity. A few of the first stirrers taken away by the power thereof, without respect to cousin or county, will keep all the rest quiet: but whoever that Court condemns let them be as already dead. If the Parliament give pardons in these cases they will much weaken their own security.

Part Twelve

THE DIGGERS

Everyone talks of freedom, but there are but few that act for freedom, and the actors for freedom are oppressed by the talkers and verbal professors of freedom. . . . If we be suffered to speak, we shall batter to pieces all the old laws, and prove the maintainers of them hypocrites and traitors to this commonwealth of England.

Gerrard Winstanley.

145. THE DIGGERS' FIRST APPEARANCE

These extracts speak for themselves. Extract *c*) was signed by Gerrard Winstanley "for myself and in the behalf of my fellow commoners." For the theory of the Norman Yoke (*c*), see No. 151.

a) *Clarke Papers*, II, pp. 209–10; *b*) *ibid.*, pp. 210–11; *c*) *ibid.*, pp. 218–19.

a) THE COUNCIL OF STATE TO FAIRFAX, APRIL 16TH, 1649

RELATION hath been made to this Council of a disorderly and tumultuous sort of people assembling themselves together . . . at a place called St. George's Hill; and although the pretence of their being there by them avowed may seem very ridiculous, yet that conflux of people may be a beginning whence things of a greater and more dangerous consequence may grow, to the disturbance of the peace and quiet of the Commonwealth. We therefore recommend it to your Lordship's care that some force of horse may be sent to Cobham in Surrey and thereabouts with order to disperse those people so met, and to prevent the like for the future, that a malignant and disaffected [i.e. Royalist] party may not under colour of such ridiculous people have any opportunity to rendez-vous themselves in order to a greater mischief.

b) INFORMATION OF HENRY SANDERS, WALTON-UPON-THAMES, APRIL 16TH, 1649

One Everard, once of the army but was cashiered, who termeth himself a prophet, one Stewer and Colten, and two more, all living at Cobham, came to St. George's Hill in Surrey, and began to dig on that side the Hill next to Camp Close, and sowed the ground with parsnips and carrots and beans. On Monday following they were there again, being increased in their number. . . . On Friday last they came again, between 20 and 30, and wrought all day at digging. They did then intend to have two or three ploughs at work, but that they had not furnished themselves with seed corn, which they did on Saturday at Kingston. They invite all to come in and help them, and promise them meat, drink and clothes. They do threaten to pull down and level all park pales, and lay open; and intend to plant there very shortly. They give out they will be four or five thousand within ten days. . . . It is feared they have some design in hand.

c) DIGGERS TO FAIRFAX AND HIS COUNCIL OF WAR, DECEMBER, 1649

Now, Sir, the end of our digging and ploughing upon the common land is this, that we and all the impoverished poor in the land may get a comfortable livelihood by our righteous labours thereupon; which we conceive we have a true right unto (I speak in the name of all the poor commoners) by virtue of the conquest over the King; for while he was in power he was the successor of William the Conqueror, and held the land as a conqueror from us, and all lords of manors held title to the common lands from him. But seeing the common people of England by joint consent of person and purse have cast out Charles our Norman oppressor, we have by this victory recovered ourselves from under his Norman yoke, and the land now is to return into the joint hands of those who have conquered—that is, the commoners—and the land is to be held no longer from the use of them [the commoners] by the hand of any [who] will uphold the Norman and kingly power still. . . . [Otherwise] we that are impoverished by sticking to the Parliament and you shall lose the benefit of all our taxes, free quarter and blood, and remain slaves still to the kingly power in the hands of lords of manors.

146. ORIGINS OF PROPERTY

Note that Winstanley uses the words "God" and "Reason" interchangeably. The Declaration (*b*) was signed by forty-five Diggers "for and in behalf of all the poor oppressed people of England and the whole world." With Winstanley's views on the origin of landed property compare those of Thomas Spence, quoted in Max Morris's *From Cobbett to the Chartists*, pp. 38–9.

a) Winstanley, *The True Levellers' Standard Advanced* (1649), Hamilton, pp. 37–8; *b*) Winstanley, *A Declaration from the Poor Oppressed People of England* (1649), Hamilton, p. 44.

a) In the beginning of time the great creator, Reason, made the earth to be a common treasury, to preserve beasts, birds, fishes and man, the lord that was to govern this creation. . . . But not one word was spoken in the beginning that one branch of mankind should rule over another. . . . But . . . selfish imaginations . . . did set up one man to teach and rule over another. And thereby . . . man was brought into bondage, and became a greater slave to such of his own kind than the beasts of the field were to him.

And hereupon the earth . . . was hedged in to enclosures by the teachers and rulers, and the others were made . . . slaves. And that earth, that is within this Creation made a common storehouse for all, is bought and sold and kept in the hands of a few, whereby the great Creator is mightily dishonoured, as if he were a respecter of persons, delighting in the comfortable livelihood of some and rejoicing in the miserable poverty and straits of others. From the beginning it was not so. . . .

Wherefore is it that there is such wars and rumours of wars in the nations of the earth? And wherefore are men so mad to destroy one another? but only to uphold civil property of honour, dominion and riches one over another. . . . But when once the earth becomes a common treasury again, as it must . . . then this enmity of all lands will cease, and none shall dare to seek dominion over others, neither shall any dare to kill another, nor desire more of the earth than another.

b) We whose names are subscribed do in the name of all the poor oppressed people in England declare unto you that call yourselves lords of manors and lords of the land that . . . the power of enclosing land and owning property was brought into the Creation by your ancestors by the sword; which first did murder their fellow creatures, men, and after plunder or steal away their land, and left this land successively to you, their children. And therefore, though you did not kill or thieve, yet you hold that cursed thing in your hand by the power of the sword; and so you justify the wicked deeds of your fathers, and that sin of your fathers shall be visited upon the head of you and your children to the third and fourth generation, and longer too, till your bloody and thieving power be rooted out of the land.

147. ECONOMIC THEORIES

Extract *a*) contains an anticipation of the labour theory of value (cf. No. 96, *g*)).

a) Winstanley, *The Law of Freedom in a Platform* (1652), Hamilton, p. 118; *b*) Winstanley, *Fire in the Bush* (1650), p. ix; *c*) Winstanley, *The Law of Freedom*, Hamilton, p. 157.

a) No man can be rich but he must be rich either by his own labours or by the labours of other men helping him. If a man have no help from his neighbour he shall never gather an estate of hundreds and thousands a year. If other men help him to work, then are those riches his neighbour's as well as his; for they be the fruit of other men's labours as well as his own. . . . Rich men receive all they have from the labourer's hand, and what they give, they give away other men's labours, not their own.

b) Be not like the rats and mice, that draw the treasures of the earth into your holes to look upon, whilst your fellow members, to whom it belongs as well as to you by the law of creation, do starve for want.

c) This is the bondage the poor complain of, that they are kept poor by their brethren in a land where there is so much plenty for everyone.

148. ADVANTAGES OF COMMON OWNERSHIP

Note Winstanley's hostility in *b*) to the wage-labour system, to which the dispossessed peasantry were being subjected; and the connection in his mind between this feature of capitalism and his anticipation of Marx's view that under capitalism the workers have no country.

a) Winstanley, *The True Levellers' Standard Advanced*, Hamilton, p. 42; *b*) Winstanley, *An Appeal to All Englishmen* (1650), Hamilton, p. 103.

a) TRULY, you counsellors and powers of the earth, know this, that wheresoever there is a people thus united by common community of livelihood into oneness, it will become the strongest land in the world; for then they will be as one man to defend their inheritance; and salvation (which is liberty and peace) is the walls and bulwarks of that land or city.

Whereas on the other side, pleading for property and single interest divides the people of a land and the whole world into parties, and is the cause of all wars and bloodshed and contention everywhere.

b) This Commonwealth's freedom will unite the hearts of Englishmen together in love, so that if a foreign enemy come in we shall all with joint consent rise up to defend our inheritance, and shall be true to one another. Whereas now the poor see, if they fight and should conquer the enemy, yet either they or their children are like to be slaves still, for the gentry will have all. . . . For, say they, "We can as well live under a foreign enemy working for day wages as under our own brethren, with whom we ought to have equal freedom by the law of righteousness."

149. FREEDOM

"Freedom" was a word which had been used by all parties during the Civil War; but its meaning had never been very clearly defined. Winstanley's definition includes economic as well as political liberty.

a) Winstanley, *A Letter to the Lord Fairfax and His Council of War* (1649), Hamilton, p. 58; b) Winstanley, *The Law of Freedom*, Hamilton, pp. 122–3; c) Winstanley, *A Watchword to the City of London and the Army* (1649), Hamilton, p. 67.

a) If the common people have no more freedom in England but only to live among their elder brothers [landlords] and work for them for hire, what freedom then have they in England more than we can have in Turkey or France?

b) True freedom lies where a man receives his nourishment and preservation, and that is in the use of the earth. . . . A man had better to have no body than to have no food for it. . . . True freedom lies in the free enjoyment of the earth.

c) All men have stood for freedom . . .; and now the common enemy is gone you are all like men in a mist, seeking for freedom and know not where nor what it is. . . . Freedom is the man that will turn the world upside down, therefore no wonder he hath enemies.

150. THE DIGGERS AND THE POOR

The Diggers' attempt at communal farming on St. George's Hill was disrupted by the lord of the manor and the local freeholders. With c), cf. No. 158. The Diggers claimed to be the "True Levellers."

a) Winstanley, *A Watchword to the City of London and the Army*, Hamilton, pp. 69, 78; b) Winstanley, *Fire in the Bush*, Hamilton, pp. 33–4; c) Winstanley, *A New Year's Gift for the Parliament and Army* (1650), Hamilton, p. 97.

a) The poorest man hath as true a title and just right to the land as the richest man. . . . I see the poor must first be picked out and honoured in this work, for they begin to receive the word of righteousness; but the rich generally are enemies to true freedom.

b) If you would find true majesty indeed, go among the poor despised ones of the earth; for there Christ dwells, and there you shall see light and love shine in majesty indeed, rising up to unite the Creation indeed into the unity of spirit and bond of peace.

c) Jesus Christ, who is that powerful spirit of love, is the head Leveller.

151. THE END OF FEUDALISM

Extract *a*) comes from a pamphlet by John Hare, *St. Edward's Ghost, or Anti-Normanism*, written in 1642, first published in 1647. Its thesis is that all the wrongs of the people of England date from the Norman Conquest, 1066, when an alien ruling class subjected the mass of the population. This is almost as unscientific as some of the revolutionaries' appeals to the Scriptures. But men have to think with the ideas of the past; the theory of the Norman Yoke has a long history, going back at least to the thirteenth century; and through it the oppressed peasantry had arrived at its own crude class analysis of politics. Hare's conclusions are revolutionary enough: he advocated expropriation of the aristocracy, complete equality before the law, and a thoroughgoing reform of the legal system. The theory was taken up by the Levellers, and survived in the working class until Chartism, but Winstanley pushed it to its most logical conclusion (*b*) and *d*)). Some nineteenth-century liberal historians adopted the theory of "free Anglo-Saxons," but with them it was reduced to racialism: liberty was thought of as something essentially Germanic. The important core of truth in the theory is that it records a memory of a more equal society common to *all* peoples. Its weakness (apart from its "racialism") is that it looks backward. With the Levellers and the Diggers, revolutionary-democratic thought began to free itself from the tyranny of the past and to see that a free and equal state of society was something to be justified by human reason rather than by appeal to dubious precedents (*b*) and *c*) and Nos. 124, 133).

a) J. Hare, *St. Edward's Ghost, Harleian Miscellany*, VIII, pp. 95–99; *b*) Winstanley, *A Letter to the Lord Fairfax*, Hamilton, pp. 56–7; *c*) Winstanley, *The Law of Freedom*, Hamilton, pp. 182, 185; *d*) Winstanley, *An Appeal to the House of Commons* (1649), Hamilton, pp. 62–5.

a) HARE

Is it then suitable to the dignity, or tolerable to the spirit of this our nation . . . not only to remain but contentedly to rest under the disgraceful title of a conquered nation, and in captivity and vassalage to a foreign power? . . . If we contemplate the heraldry and titles of our nobility, there is scarce any other matter than inventories of foreign villages, that speak them not to be of English blood; but tell us . . . that their progenitors conquered this land by the sword. . . .

We are by this pretended conquest cast into such a predicament and condition, as makes us incapable of acquiring new honour ever after, so long as we remain therein; the evidence of this we may descry in our own laws, wherein we find that such as are in the nature of villeins are incapable of enjoying freehold lands, but though they purchase never so much it belongs all to their lords. . . .

It is but the carcass of an enemy that we have to remove out of our territories, even the carcass and bones of the Norman Duke's injurious and detested perpetrations. . . . Let us either confess and profess ourselves for ever mere vassals and slaves, or else attempt to uncaptive ourselves. —The end and scope of this whole discourse . . . is effectually, yet orderly and legally, to endeavour these following particulars:—

. . . (iii) That all the Norman nobility and progeny amongst us repudiate their names and titles brought over from Normandy, assuming others consistible with the honour of this nation, and disclaim all right to their possessions here, as heirs and successors to any pretended conquerors.

(iv) That all laws and usages introduced from Normandy be . . . abolished.

b) WINSTANLEY

We desire that your lawyers may consider these questions:—

. . . (viii) Whether all laws that are not grounded upon equity and reason, not giving a universal freedom to all but respecting persons, ought not to be cut off with the King's head? We affirm they ought.

c) The Kings' old laws cannot govern a free commonwealth. . . . They are called the Kings' laws because they are made by the Kings. If any say they were made by the commoners, it is answered, they were not made by the commoners as the commoners of a free commonwealth are to make laws. For in the days of the Kings none were to choose nor be chosen Parliament-men, or law-makers, but lords of manors and free-holders. . . . All inferior people were neither to choose nor to be chosen. . . .

The laws of Kings have always been made against such actions as the common people were most inclinable to, on purpose to ensnare them into their sessions and courts; that the lawyers and clergy, who were the Kings' supporters, might get money thereby and live in fulness by other men's labours.

d) Seeing we have with joint consent of purse and person conquered [William the Conqueror's] successor Charles, and the power now is in your hand, the nation's representative, O let the first thing you do be this, to set the land free! Let the gentry have their enclosures free from all Norman enslaving entanglements whatsoever, and let the common people have their commons and waste lands set free to them, from all Norman enslaving lords of manors. . . .

If you do not set us free from the Norman yoke, now after you have taken our taxes and free-quarter from us, whereby we have dearly bought our freedom, and you thereupon promised freedom and you have power now to give it, . . . you give a just occasion to the common people of England never to trust the fair words of a Parliament any more, as you were always very slow in trusting the King when he swore by the word of a King, because you found that subtlety and self lay under, and no reality. . . .

. . . Let it not be said in the ears of posterity that the gentry of England assembled in Parliament proved covenant-breakers . . . to God and the common people, after their own turn was served. . . . Surely if you found out the Court of Wards to be a burden and freed lords of manors and gentry from paying fines to the King; and freed their children from the slavery of falling ward, let the common people be set free too from paying homage to lords of manors.

152. THE REVOLUTION NOT YET COMPLETED

Winstanley regards Parliament as representing exclusively the gentry: the "poor common people" are outside (*a*).

a) Winstanley, *A New Year's Gift for the Parliament and Army*, Hamilton, pp. 80–3; *b*) Winstanley, *A Watchword to the City of London and the Army*, Hamilton, p. 74; *c*) Winstanley, *The Law of Freedom*, Hamilton, p. 171.

a) KINGLY power is like a great spread tree; if you lop the head or top bough, and let the other branches and root stand, it will grow again and recover fresher strength. . . .

While this kingly power reigned in one man called Charles, all sorts of people complained of oppression. . . . Thereupon you that were the gentry, when you were assembled in Parliament, you called upon the poor common people to come and help you. . . . That top bough is lopped off the tree of Tyranny, and the kingly power in that one particular is cast out. But alas, oppression is a great tree still, and keeps off the sun of freedom from the poor commons still.

b) Therefore, England, beware: . . . William the Conqueror's army begins to gather its head again, and the old Norman prerogative law is the place of their rendez-vous. For though their chief captain, Charles, be gone, yet his colonels, which are lords of manors, his councillors and divines, which are our lawyers and priests, his inferior officers and soldiers, which are the freeholders and landlords, . . . [are still there].

c) Therefore, you Army of England's Commonwealth, look to it. The enemy could not beat you in the field, but they may be too hard for you by policy in counsel, if you do not stick close to see common freedom established. For if so be that kingly authority be set up in your laws again, King Charles hath conquered you and your posterity by policy, and won the field of you, though you seemingly have cut off his head.

153. THE LAW NOT YET REFORMED

a) Winstanley, *A New Year's Gift for the Parliament and the Army*, Hamilton, p. 86; *b*) Winstanley, *Fire in the Bush*, Hamilton, p. 32; *c*) Winstanley, *The Law of Freedom*, Hamilton, p. 112; *d*) *ibid.*, pp. 118–19; with this, cf. No. 120, *b*).

a) ENGLAND is a prison; the variety of subtleties in the laws preserved by the sword are bolts, bars and doors of the prison; the lawyers are the jailors, and poor men are the prisoners.

b) The law is the fox, poor men are the geese; he pulls off their feathers and feeds upon them.

c) The main work of reformation lies in this, to reform the clergy, lawyers and law; for all the complaints of the land are wrapped up within them three, not in the person of a King.

d) IN THE FREE COMMONWEALTH

Shall we have no lawyers?

There is no need of them, for there is to be no buying and selling; neither any need to expound laws; for the bare letter of the law shall be both judge and lawyer, trying every man's actions. And seeing we shall have successive Parliaments every year, there will be rules made for every action a man can do.

154. PRIESTS

With these extracts compare the *Last Will and Testament* of the Owenite Henry Hetherington (Max Morris, *From Cobbett to the Chartists*, pp. 237–9), and Marx's view that religion is "the opium of the people."

a) Winstanley, *The Law of Freedom*, Hamilton, p. 143; *b*) Winstanley, *An Appeal to all Englishmen*, Hamilton, p. 101; *c*) Winstanley, *The Law of Freedom*, Hamilton, p. 167; *d*) *ibid.*, pp. 125–6.

a) WHAT is the reason that most people are so ignorant of their freedoms and so few fit to be chosen commonwealth's officers?

Because the old kingly clergy . . . are continually distilling their blind principles into the people, and do thereby nurse up ignorance in them. For they observe the bent of the people's minds, and make sermons to please the sickly minds of ignorant people, to preserve their own riches and esteem among a charmed, befooled and besotted people.

b) [Priests] lay claim to heaven after they are dead, and yet they require their heaven in this world too, and grumble mightily against the people that will not give them a large temporal maintenance. And yet they tell the poor people that they must be content with their poverty, and they shall have their heaven hereafter. But why may not *we* have our heaven here (that is, a comfortable livelihood in the earth) and heaven hereafter too, as well as you?

c) While men are gazing up to heaven, imagining after a happiness or fearing a hell after they are dead, their eyes are put out, that they see not what is their birthrights, and what is to be done by them here on earth while they are living. . . . And indeed the subtle clergy do know that if they can but charm the people . . . to look after riches, heaven and glory when they are dead, that then they shall easily be the inheritors of the earth and have the deceived people to be their servants. This . . . was not the doctrine of Christ.

d) [The ministers say] "The doctrine of faith must not be tried by reason." No, for if it be their mystery of iniquity will be discovered, and they would lose their tithes.

155. SCIENCE *VERSUS* RELIGION

Winstanley, who hated Oxford and Cambridge as centres of reaction and mystification, shows himself in tune with those tendencies in the science of his day that look back to Bacon and forward to the Royal Society. Winstanley, *The Law of Freedom*, Hamilton, p. 163.

To know the secrets of nature is to know the works of God. . . . And indeed if you would know spiritual things, it is to know how the spirit or power of wisdom and life, causing motion or growth, dwells within and governs both the several bodies of the stars and planets in the heavens above; and the several bodies of the earth below, as grass, plants, fishes, beasts, birds and mankind. For to reach God beyond the Creation, or to know what he will be to a man after the man is dead, if any otherwise than to scatter him into his essences of fire, water, earth and air of which he is compounded, is a knowledge beyond the line or capacity of man to attain to while he lives in his compounded body.

156. WINSTANLEY'S OBJECTIVES

The aim of Communism, says Winstanley, is to establish a society in which *all* will be happier because freer, even those who see their economic interest in exploiting others. Winstanley, *A Watchword to the City of London and the Army*, p. 12; partly in Hamilton, p. 75.

Take notice of this, you lords of manors and Norman gentry, though you should kill my body or starve me in prison, yet know that the more you strive, the more troubles your hearts shall be filled with; and do the worst you can to hinder public freedom, you shall come off losers in the latter end. . . . Alas! you poor blind earth moles, you strive to take away my livelihood, and the liberty of this poor weak frame my body of flesh, which is my house I dwell in for a time; but I strive to cast down your kingdom of darkness, and to open hell gates, and to break the devil's bonds asunder wherewith you are tied, that you my enemies may live in peace; and that is all the harm I would have you to have.

157. THE DIGGERS' SONG, 1649

This song may be either by Winstanley or by Robert Coster, another Digger poet. *Clarke Papers*, II, pp. 221–5.

You noble Diggers all, stand up now, stand up now,
You noble Diggers all, stand up now,
  The waste land to maintain, seeing Cavaliers by name
  Your digging do disdain and persons all defame.
Stand up now, stand up now.

Your houses they pull down, stand up now, stand up now,
Your houses they pull down, stand up now;
  Your houses they pull down to fright poor men in town
  But the gentry must come down, and the poor shall wear the crown.
Stand up now, Diggers all!

With spades and hoes and ploughs, stand up now, stand up now,
With spades and hoes and ploughs stand up now,
  Your freedom to uphold, seeing cavaliers are bold
  To kill you if they could, and right from you to hold.
Stand up now, Diggers all! . . .

The gentry are all round, stand up now, stand up now,
The gentry are all round, stand up now;
  The gentry are all round, on each side they are found,
  Their wisdom's so profound to cheat us of the ground.
Stand up now, stand up now.

The lawyers they conjoin, stand up now, stand up now.
The lawyers they conjoin, stand up now;
  To arrest you they advise, such fury they devise,
  The devil in them lies and hath blinded both their eyes.
Stand up now, stand up now.

The clergy they come in, stand up now, stand up now,
The clergy they come in, stand up now;
  The clergy they come in and say it is a sin
  That we should now begin our freedom for to win.
Stand up now, Diggers all! . . .

'Gainst lawyers and 'gainst priests stand up now, stand up now,
'Gainst lawyers and 'gainst priests stand up now;
  For tyrants are they both, even flat against their oath,
  To grant us they are loath free meat and drink and cloth.
Stand up now, Diggers all! . . .

To conquer them by love, come in now, come in now,
To conquer them by love, come in now;
  To conquer them by love, as it does you behove,
  For He is King above, no power is like to love.
Glory *here*, Diggers all.

Part Thirteen

THE DEFEAT OF THE LEVELLERS

You have no other way to deal with these men but to break them in pieces. . . . If you do not break them they will break you.

Oliver Cromwell.

158. THE LEVELLERS REPUDIATE THE DIGGERS

The Levellers and Diggers did not unite against their common enemies. Here we see Lilburne savagely attacking the Diggers. (Contrast Winstanley's views in No. 156.) During the 'fifties the Leveller leaders either made money and were absorbed into the bourgeoisie, or relapsed into a mystical quietism. Lilburne died a Quaker in 1657 (but see No. 160). There is no evidence for the oft-repeated statement that Winstanley also turned Quaker: it is due to incorrect dating of one of his early pamphlets. The whole development of his thought seems to have been away from religion. J. Lilburne, *Apologetical Narrative* (1652), pp. 68–9.

THIS conceit of levelling of property and magistracy is so ridiculous and foolish an opinion, as no man of brains, reason or ingenuity can be imagined such a sot as to maintain such a principle, because it would, if practised, destroy not only all industry in the world, but raze the very foundation of government. . . . For as for industry and valour by which the societies of mankind are maintained and preserved, who will take pains for that which when he hath gotten is not his own, but must equally be shared in by every lazy, simple, dronish sot? Or who will fight for that wherein he hath no other interest but such as must be subject to the will and pleasure of another, yea of every coward and base low-spirited fellow?

159. THE LEVELLER REVOLT OF 1649

In March, 1649, when discontent among the rank and file of the Army was again rising, Lilburne published *The Second Part of England's New Chains*, appealing for a restoration of the General Council of the Army with elected Agitators, and for a new Parliament on the basis of the Agreement of the People. Parliament declared this seditious and tending to mutiny; Lilburne, Walwyn, Overton and Prince were arrested, and hauled before the Council. In *a*) Lilburne is addressing its President, Bradshaw, and trying to hold the new government to the letter of its published declaration. Cromwell's answer is a forcible statement of the class realities of the situation; he seems to regard "the blood and treasure" spent in the Civil War as a kind of investment.

In April, Robert Lockyer, one of the defenders of the Agreement of the People at Ware (No. 134), was executed for leading a mutiny. Londoners turned his funeral (*b*) into a mass demonstration. Sea-green colours were first worn as distinguishing Leveller colours at Rainborough's funeral (November, 1648) after his assassination by Royalists. Note that the "higher sort" found it risky to associate publicly with the democracy of the lower classes. In May began a more serious revolt near Banbury led by Corporal William Thompson (*c*). The Agreement referred to in his manifesto is the version of the Agreement of the People (No. 132) produced on May 1st, 1649, by Lilburne and his friends in the Tower. This revolt was also crushed, Thompson escaping. At the same time a revolt broke out among regiments near Salisbury. But the danger was short-lived. In *d*) Fairfax reports his victory over the remaining mutineers at Burford. Thompson was discovered and killed on May 17th. The Levellers were finally defeated.

a) H. and D., pp. 195–204; *b*) *The Moderate*, April 24th–May 1st, 1649, p. 483; *c*) *England's Standard Advanced in Oxfordshire, or a Declaration from Mr. Will Thompson and the oppressed people of this nation now under his conduct*; *d*) *For the Honourable William Lenthall, Esq., Speaker of the honourable House of Commons* (1649).

a) LILBURNE BEFORE THE COUNCIL OF STATE, APRIL, 1649

"THE laws and liberties of England are my inheritance and birthright. . . . In your late Declaration . . . [of] the grounds . . . of your doing justice upon the late King, and why you have abolished kingly government and the House of Lords, you declare in effect the same; and promise to maintain the laws of England, in reference to the peoples' liberties and freedoms. . . . I cannot but look upon this irregular, unjust and illegal hostile action of yours as one of the . . . issues of your new-created tyranny, to amuse and debase my spirit, and the spirits of the people of this free nation, to fit me and them for bondage and slavery: this being the very practice of the Earl of Strafford before you. . . . I had rather die than basely betray my liberties into their martial fingers, who, after fighting for our freedoms, would now destroy them. . . ."

After we were all come out . . . I laid my ear to their door and heard Lieutenant-General Cromwell (I am sure of it) very loud, thumping his fist upon the Council table till it rang again . . . speak in these very words, or to this effect: "I tell you, Sir, you have no other way to deal with these men, but to break them in pieces"; and thumping upon the Council table again, he said: "Sir, . . . if you do not break them they will break you; yea, and bring all the guilt of the blood and treasure shed and spent in this kingdom upon your heads and shoulders; and frustrate and make void all that work, that with so many years industry, toil and pains you have done, and so render you to all rational men in the world as the most contemptiblest generation of silly low-spirited men in the earth, to be broken and routed by such a despicable contemptible generation of men as they are. And therefore, Sir, I tell you again, you are necessitated to break them."

b) FUNERAL OF ROBERT LOCKYER

April 29th. Mr. Lockyer, that was shot Friday last at [St.] Paul's, was this day brought . . . through the heart of the City. . . . The manner of his funeral was most remarkable, considering the person to be in no higher quality than a private trooper. . . . The body . . . was accompanied with many thousand citizens, who seemed by countenance much dejected and more discontented for the death of the said party. About 1,000 went before the corpse, by five and six on file together; the corpse then came with six trumpets dolefully sounding a soldiers' knell. . . . The trooper's horse advanced in the rear of this regiment, clothed all over in mourning, and led by a footman (a funeral honour equal to a chief commander). The corpse was adorned with bundles of rosemary on each side; one half of each was stained in blood, and the sword of the deceased with them. Some thousands succeeded these in rank and file, and the women brought up the rear. . . . Most of this great number that thus attended the corpse had sea-green and black ribbons in their hats, or pinned to their black ribbons on their breasts. By that time the corpse came to the new churchyard, some thousands of the higher sort (that said they would not endanger themselves, to be publicly seen marching through the City) were there ready to attend it with the same colours of sea-green and black. Some people derided them with the name of Levellers. . . . Others [said] that King Charles had not had half so many mourners to attend his corpse when interred, as this trooper.

c) THOMPSON'S DECLARATION, MAY 6TH, 1649

Whereas it is notorious to the whole world, that neither the faith of the Parliament, nor yet the faith of the Army . . . hath been at all observed, or made good, but both absolutely declined and broken, and the people only served with bare words, and fair promising papers, and left utterly destitute of all help or delivery: And that this hath principally been by the prevalency and treachery of some eminent persons . . . is most evident. The solemn Engagement of the Army at New-Market and Triplo-Heaths, by them destroyed, the Council of Agitators dissolved, the blood of war shed in time of peace, petitioners for common freedom suppressed by force of arms . . . the lawful trial by twelve sworn men of the neighbourhood subverted and denied, bloody and tyrannical courts (called an High Court of Justice, and the Council of State) erected, the power of the sword advanced and set in the seat of the magistrates, the civil law stopped and subverted, and the military introduced . . . whereby all the lives, liberties, and estates are all subdued to the wills of those men, no law, no justice, no right or freedom, no care of grievances, no removal of unjust barbarous taxes . . . while utter beggary and famine . . . hath broke in upon us, and already seized upon several parts of the nation.

Wherefore, through an unavoidable necessity, no other means left under heaven, we are enforced to betake ourselves to the law of Nature, to defend and preserve ourselves and native rights; and therefore are resolved as one man . . . to endeavour the redemption of the magistracy of England, from under the force of the sword, to vindicate the Petition of Right, to set the unjustly imprisoned free, to relieve the poor, and settle the Commonwealth upon the ground of common right, freedom and safety . . . to have justice for the blood of Mr. Arnold, shot at Ware, and for the blood of Mr. Robert Lockyer and divers others, who of late by martial law, were murdered at London. . . .

We declare . . . we will endeavour the absolute settlement of this distracted nation, upon that form and method, by way of an Agreement of the People, . . . promising and resolving to the utmost hazard of our lives and abilities to pursue the speedy and full accomplishments thereof, and to our power to protect and defend all such as shall assent or adhere thereunto; and particularly, for the protection of Lieut. Col. John Lilburne, Mr. William Walwyn, Mr. Thomas Prince, Mr. Richard Overton, Capt. Bray, and Mr. William Sawyer, from their barbarous and illegal imprisonments . . . resolving to stop the payment of all taxes and assessments whatsoever, or of excise, tithes, and the tax of £90,000 per mensem, etc. And having once obtained a new Representative, according to the said Agreement, upon such terms and limitations therein expressed, we shall then freely lay down our arms, and return to our several habitations and callings.

d) FAIRFAX TO THE SPEAKER

Sir, I thought it my duty, having received another pledge and token of the mercy and goodness of God to this poor nation, to give you a speedy account thereof. . . . [At] Burford . . . and in the adjacent villages, we took (I think) almost the whole party [of the mutineers]. . . . Sir, I hope this is none of the last mercies, I pray God you and we may make good use of it, it will be your glory and your honour to settle this poor nation upon foundations of justice and righteousness, and I hope this mercy will the more encourage you to do so; for the poor people, however deluded by some cunning and turbulent spirits, yet they may see you will improve your power for their good, and then your enemies shall be found liars, which I am confident you will; so I cease you further trouble, and remain

Your most humble servant

THO. FAIRFAX.

Burford, 14th May, midnight, 1649.

160. QUAKER SOCIAL DOCTRINES

The early Quakers were no pacifists. They were strong in the Army; in the late 'fifties many of the propertied classes feared that they might lead an armed revolt. The word "Quaker," like "Anabaptist," was just a loose term of abuse, like "Red" to-day; there were some pacifist Quakers, and in the disillusionment after the Restoration these began to preponderate and to organise the sect. But their early connection with the Levellers, and the similarity of their views, is made clear by these extracts. The Quakers denied the gloomy and oligarchical doctrine of Calvinism, that only a minority ("the elect") can be saved, and advanced the egalitarian views (*a*) which a major found dangerous to the supremacy of the ruling class (tacitly identified with the elect, poverty being God's punishment for wickedness). Thurloe (*a*) and *b*)) was Cromwell's Secretary of State, the most powerful man (under Oliver) in the Government; Henry Cromwell (*b*) was Oliver's second son, Commander-in-Chief in Ireland. He had been sent there to reduce the influence of men of the Left.

a) *Thurloe State Papers*, VI, p. 162; *b*) *ibid.*, IV, p. 508; *c*) Firth, *Scotland and the Protectorate*, pp. 362–3.

a) MAJOR RICHARDSON TO THURLOE, APRIL 2ND, 1657

HIS tenets are dangerous, maintaining perfection in this life.

b) HENRY CROMWELL TO THURLOE, FEBRUARY 6TH, 1655

I think their principles and practices are not very consistent with civil government, much less with the discipline of an army. Some think them to have no design, but I am not of that opinion.

c) COLONEL DANIEL TO GENERAL MONCK, JULY 16TH, 1657

My Captain-Lieutenant . . . is much confirmed in his principles of quaking, making all the soldiers his equals (according to the Levellers' strain) that I dare say in short time his principles in the army shall be the root of disobedience. My Lord, the whole world is governed by superiority and distance in relations, and when that's taken away, unavoidably anarchy is ushered in. . . . I am afraid lest by the spreading of these humours the public suffer, for they are a very uncertain generation to execute commands, and liberty with equality is so pleasing to ignorance that proselites will be daily brought in, and any rational person that speaks or acts against it shall be censured as proud or a disturber of liberty; and when I think of the levelling design that had like to have torn the army to pieces, it makes me more bold to give my opinion that these things be curbed in time. . . . Where all are equals I expect little obedience in government.

161. THE QUAKER MENACE TO SOCIETY

James Nayler was a Quaker who in October, 1656, rode into Bristol on horseback, whilst women flung their cloaks in his path and sang, "Holy, Holy, Holy!" He was charged with blasphemy, since he had "assumed the gestures, words, names and attributes of our Saviour." His case was the subject of lengthy debates in Parliament. The tone of these extracts and the savageness of the sentence show that it was social anxiety rather than religious bigotry that animated the M.Ps. Burton, I, pp. 24–5, 55, 60, 68–9, 73, 128, 158.

Major-General Skippon: It has always been my opinion that the growth of these things is more dangerous than the most intestine or foreign enemies. I have often been troubled in my thoughts to think of this toleration. . . . Their [the Quakers'] great growth and increase is too notorious, both in England and Ireland; their principles strike both at ministry and magistracy. Many opinions are in this nation (all contrary to the government) which would join in one to destroy you if it should please God to deliver the sword into their hands. . . .

Mr. Drake: Did he [Nayler] not suffer himself to be honoured as our Saviour in his riding through all the towns? What would you do if one should ride triumphantly through the country as a ruler of the nations? Were not he to be proceeded against as a traitor? . . .

Mr. Downing: Observe how careful they are not to give honour to any authority. You saw how he behaved himself at the bar. Not a cap to you, though you be gods in one sense; yet he will take cap, knee, kisses and all reverence. . . .

Colonel Sydenham: It is against the civil peace; for, by this rule [Nayler's], we must lay aside all civil submission to any supreme power, and throw down the sceptre at Christ's feet wherever we find him reigning, though in this impostor. . . . These Quakers or Familists affirm that Christ dwells personally in every believer. . . .

Colonel Gorges: I would demand this question of these gentlemen [Nayler's defenders]: Is there such a thing as blasphemy? Consider what he said at the bar. He said the voice, the spirit that spoke in him were the words of Christ. If he be infallible, then let us worship him. If fallible, what is that less than blasphemy to own such a spirit in him? His practice is idolatrous: his excuse is, Christ is within him. . . .

Mr. Church: The Quakers are not only numerous but dangerous, and the sooner we put a stop, the more glory we shall do to God, and safety to this commonwealth. . . . Whatever they pretend, they cannot be a people of God. Christ's spirit is a meek spirit, but they are full of bitterness in reviling the ministers and magistrates. . . .

Resolved, that James Nayler be set on the pillory . . . during the space of two hours on Thursday next, and be whipped by the hangman through the streets of Westminster to the Old Exchange, London; and there likewise to be set upon the pillory; . . . and that at the Old Exchange his tongue shall be bored through with a hot iron, and that he be there also stigmatised in the forehead with the letter B [Blasphemer]; and that he be afterwards sent to Bristol . . . and there also publicly whipped; . . . and that from thence he be committed to prison in Bridewell, London, and there restrained from the society of all people and kept to hard labour until he be released by the Parliament.

162. GEORGE FOX'S VIEWS

Fox was one of those responsible for the final emergence of the Quakers after the Restoration as a pacifist sect; yet in 1657 he had spoken with approval of a crusade to spread Protestantism all over Europe, and these extracts show that he too shared many of the social views of the Levellers and Winstanley. With *a*) compare No. 154, with *b*) Nos. 38, *d*), 120, 174, 175, *d*), and with *c*) Lilburne's behaviour before the Star Chamber in 1637 (No. 35).

a) G. Fox, *Journal* (Everyman), p. 23; *b*) *ibid.*, p. 37; *c*) *ibid.*, pp. 126–7; *d*) G. Fox, *Journal* (1902), I, p. 312.

a) [1649] The black earthly spirit of the priests wounded my life; and when I heard the bell toll to call people together to the steeplehouse, it struck at my life; for it was just like a market-bell, to gather people together that the priest might set forth his ware to sale. Oh! the vast sums of money that are gotten by the trade they make of selling the Scriptures and by their preaching, from the highest bishop to the lowest priest.

b) [1650] In this time of my imprisonment I was exceedingly exercised about the proceedings of the judges and magistrates in their courts of judicature. I was moved to write to the judges concerning their putting men to death for [stealing] cattle, and money and small matters; and to show them how contrary it was to the law of God in old time.

c) [1656] [Captain Bradden said] "When Major Ceely and I came by you, as you were walking in the Castle Green, he put off his hat to you, and said 'How do you do, Mr. Fox? Your servant, sir.' Then you said to him, 'Major Ceely, take heed of hypocrisy and of a rotten heart; for when came I to be thy master and thou my servant? Do servants cast their masters into prison?' "

d) [1656] Persecution was blind in all ages, and madness and folly led it; yet persecution got always a form or pretence of godliness.

Part Fourteen

ECONOMIC PROBLEMS OF THE REVOLUTION

> I love old England very well, but as things are carried here the gentry cannot joy much to be in it.
>
> *Sir Ralph Verney* 1655.

163. WARDS AND FEUDAL TENURES

For the Court of Wards and feudal tenures, see No. 31. Their abolition (*a*) was confirmed by Act of Parliament in 1656. When the Parliament of 1660 decided to recall Charles II, their next business was the further confirmation of this abolition; such was the importance attached to it. Charles II was given £100,000 a year in compensation for his loss of revenue, instead of the £200,000 offered in 1610; and the £100,000 was to be raised not by a land tax but by the Excise, i.e. it would be paid not by the gentry who benefited from the abolition of feudal tenures, but by the lower classes who did not. With the views of Lord Keeper Guilford (*b*), cf. No. 31; note his reference to "the country," where he means "the landed class."

a) Gardiner, p. 290; *b*) R. North, *Lives of the Norths* (1826), II, pp. 82–3.

a) ORDER OF THE TWO HOUSES OF PARLIAMENT, 1646

THAT the Court of Wards and Liveries, and all wardships . . . be from this day taken away; and that all tenures by homage, and all fines, licences, seizures, pardons for alienation, and all other charges incident thereunto, be likewise taken away; and that all tenures by knight service, either of his Majesty or others, . . . be turned into free and common socage.

b) A CONSERVATIVE VIEW

What can the people, that are always designing to diminish the just powers of the crown, expect but that the crown should always design to repair itself by a provision of force? . . . These considerations made his lordship [Lord Keeper Guilford] ever set himself against the republicans and resist their intended encroachments upon the crown. He thought the taking away of the [feudal] tenures a desperate wound to the liberties of the people of England, and must by easy consequence procure the establishment of an army. For when the legal dependence of the monarchy and the country upon each other is dissolved, what must succeed but force?

164. CONFISCATION AND SALE OF LANDS

Early in the Civil War, Parliament seized the lands of the King, Church and leading Royalists (Nos. 96, 98). They were thenceforward under continuous pressure to sell these lands to meet their current expenses, though this was resisted in the name of the sanctity of property. Before the establishment of the republic, only bishops' lands had been sold, for the reasons succinctly given in *b*). In 1649 crown and dean and chapter lands were sold; in 1651 those of leading Royalists. In addition, many Royalists were forced to sell estates privately to meet their debts, fines and taxation (see note to No. 165). The social consequences of the transfer of the property of the Church are suggested in *c*), translated from a memorandum drawn up for Cardinal Mazarin in July, 1654. The purchasers of the lands were those of the bourgeoisie and gentry who had confidence in the stability of the new régime. Many "new men" joined the landed class by purchase of confiscated estates. As J.Ps. and through Parliament, they henceforth had a say in government; and Parliament's dominance of the state was now secure. So these purchasers became conservative, having no desire to see a subversion of the social order that guaranteed their property. This helps to account for the move to the right under the Protectorate of Oliver Cromwell (see Nos. 177, 181–7). Much corruption was alleged against Members of Parliament and their officials, as in *d*).

a) Winstanley, *A New Year's Gift for the Parliament and Army*, Hamilton, p. 94; *b*) Baillie, *Letters and Journals*, II, p. 244; *c*) Guizot, *History of Cromwell and the English Commonwealth*, II, p. 435; *d*) J. Musgrave, *A true and exact relation . . .*, p. 41

a) LAND HUNGER, 1650

Do not all strive to enjoy the land? The gentry strive for land, the clergy strive for land, the common people strive for land; and buying and selling is an art, whereby people endeavour to cheat one another of the land.

b) BISHOPS' LANDS, 1646

The £200,000 was all told on Friday last. . . . We have had . . . much ado to get the great sum. . . . It was my dear friend Dr. Burgess's singular invention, that all who contribute to this sum would have as much of his old debt, with all the annual rents [i.e. with interest], counted to him, and for all make a good pennyworth [bargain] of the bishops' lands; so the bargain being exceeding advantageous, the strife was, who should come in with his money soonest. By this means we got the bishops' lands on our back, without any grudge, and in a way that no skill will get them back again.

c) VIEWS OF A FRENCH DIPLOMAT, 1654

[Cromwell] considers that—as in England and everywhere else where heresy has ruined the church—if the neighbour of an ecclesiastical property sees that he can appropriate it with impunity, . . . he will easily allow himself to give way to that temptation; in a short time this will produce a whole host of imitators. In fact it is certain that the properties of the church, which the Holy Ghost has maintained by the charity of the faithful to be the support of the faith in the mouth and in the hands of those who are worthy ministers, have become quite the opposite by the sacrilegious practice of those who possess them in the greatest abundance. That is the cause for which the church has most to fear ruin at the hands of its enemies. For it must fall when its goods are taken away, as has happened everywhere where the church has fallen; and what is worse, its ruin is so much the easier to bring about for those who plot it, in that the church's own children will become her enemies for the purpose of stripping her of her property.

d) PURCHASERS, 1650

By sitting there [in Parliament] they become great, purchasers of lands and manors. . . . If I had been a solicitor or agent for cavaliers at Goldsmiths' Hall, to the Committee of Sequestrations or to the Parliament, I might have got wealth, and had the countenance of the great ones, and found ready despatch of business. I know one poor solicitor that way hath gained £2,000 or £3,000 at the least. But I, agitating for a poor plundered people, could never gain the favour as [= of] the reading of a petition.

165. LOSSES OF ROYALIST LANDLORDS

The Cavaliers suffered severely in the Civil War. First they had to subscribe to the royal cause. Then their lands were sequestrated by the revolutionary Parliamentary committees in the counties (Nos. 96, 98). As long as his estates remained in the hands of these committees, the landlord received no rent. He could only recover his lands (but not arrears of rent) by paying a composition fine to the Committee at Goldsmith's Hall, calculated at anything from one-tenth to one-half of the capital value of his estate, according to the degree of his delinquency. After this he had to pay his one-fifth and one-twentieth to the Committee at Haberdashers' Hall to finance the Parliamentary cause. (The halls of the City companies were the centres of the financial organisation created by Parliament.) In 1655 the Cavalier landowner had to pay a special Decimation Tax of one-tenth of his rent. Nor was he exempt from normal taxation, which was heavy. Many Royalists were not allowed to compound, and some did not choose to: their lands were sold outright. Of the rest, almost all would be forced to sell or mortgage some land in order to pay composition fines and taxes; lands thus privately sold were not restored after 1660. The effect of the land transactions of the revolution was thus to transfer a great number of estates to those who in the sixteen-fifties had ready money. For effects of diminished revenue on the estate management of Cavaliers and for the behaviour of purchasers, see No. 166. With the Duke of Newcastle's balance sheet (*b*) compare that of the Marquis of Worcester (No. 97). Extract *a*) is by Lilly, the astrologer; *c*) is by Thomas Jordan.

a) Lilly, *True History of King James I and King Charles I*, pp. 6–7, 68; *b*) Newcastle, pp. 77–9; *c*) F. W. Fairholt, *Lord Mayors' Pageants* (Percy Soc., 1843), pp. 215, 221.

a) THE KING LETS DOWN THE GENTRY

[CHARLES I] loved not greatly the ancient nobility or gentry of this nation, but did rather prefer creatures of his own or father's making. How much he loved any of the nobility or gentry but for his own ends, he made it plainly appear at Oxford, where he procured sundry of the English nobles and many gentlemen, members of the House of Commons, to recede from the Parliament at Westminster and convene at Oxford, where himself was; and after that this mock Parliament, to satisfy his desire, had convened and assembled, done what they could, and thereby engaged their persons and estates for him: yet, because they would not in all things comply with his tyrannical humour, in a letter of his unto the Queen he complains of them unto her and said "He was so troubled with a *mongrel Parliament* he could do nothing," etc. . . .

The English noblemen he cared not much for, but only to serve his own turns by them; yet such as had the unhappiness to adventure their lives and fortunes for him, he lived to see them and their families ruined only for his sake. Pity it is many of them had not served a more fortunate master, and one more grateful.

b) THE DUKE OF NEWCASTLE'S BALANCE-SHEET

The loss of my Lord's estate . . . is as followeth:—

The annual rent of my Lord's lands, viz. £22,393 10*s*. 1*d*., being lost for the space of 18 years . . . amounts to £403,083. But being accounted with the ordinary use [i.e. interest] at 6 in the hundred, . . . it amounts to £733,579. . . .

Concerning the loss of his parks and woods . . . 'tis as follows:

1. Clipston Park and woods, cut down to the value of £20,000.
2. Kirkby Woods, for which my Lord was formerly proferred £10,000.
3. Woods cut down in Derbyshire, £8,000.
4. Red Lodge Wood, Rome Wood, and others near Welbeck, £4,000.
5. Woods cut down in Staffordshire, £1,000.
6. Woods cut down in Yorkshire, £1,000.
7. Woods cut down in Northumberland, £1,500. The total, £45,000.

The lands which my Lord hath lost in present possession are £2,015 per annum, which at 20 years' purchase come to £40,300; and those which he hath lost in reversion are £3,214 per annum, which at 16 years' purchase amount to the value of £51,424.

The lands which my Lord since his return has sold for

the payment of some of his debts occasioned by the wars . . . come to the value of £56,000, to which out of his yearly revenue he has added £10,000 more, which is in all £66,000.

Lastly, the composition of his brother's estate was £5,000, and the loss of it for 8 years comes to £16,000.

All which, if summed up together, amounts to £941,303.

c) AT THE LORD MAYOR'S PAGEANT, DECEMBER, 1659

Filcher, a cheat: Your roaring cavalier
Who, when he had the chink,
Would bravely domineer
In dicing, drabs and drink:
Go ask him now for money
And he hath none at all,
But cries, "'Tis in my counting-house
In Haberdashers' Hall. . . ."

Moll Medlar: I was bred a gentlewoman,
But our family did fall
When the gentry's coin grew common
And the soldiers shared it all. . . .

166. CONSEQUENCES FOR TENANTS

Cavaliers who had compounded (*a*) and new purchasers (*b*) both had to squeeze money out of their tenants, and so resorted to rack-renting and extortion. The land transfers of the revolutionary period thus expedited the transition to fully capitalist tenurial relations (*c*). The regicide John Cook (*a*) assumes that landlords are likely to be Cavaliers and tenants Roundheads (cf. Nos. 168, 174–5). Cook read the charge against Charles I (140, *c*)), and was executed at the Restoration.

a) J. Cook, *The Poor Man's Case* (1648), pp. 71–2; *b*) *Thurloe State Papers*, I, p. 633; *c*) *The Agreement between the Commissioners of Parliament and his Excellency Sir Thomas Fairfax*, p. 4.

a) THE POOR MAN'S CASE

Ah, what a sad thing is it to think that poor men should pay their [cavaliers'] compositions! Now poor tenants and others are arrested by scores for old debts and rents upon extremities, when they could keep no cattle in the grounds for fear of plundering. "But," says the old miser, "*I* must pay many thousand pounds to the Parliament, and must get it up again!" I profess it melts my very heart to think upon it. How happy a thing had it been if old usurers and griping landlords, which have been delinquents, had been ordered upon their compositions to have released and discharged all poor men which were not able to pay them, at least to have provided that they should not presently cast such poor wretches in prison—specially if a poor man have been well-affected to the Parliament and stands any ways engaged to a compounder. "Oh," says he, "I'll be sure to be revenged on that Roundhead," just like the devil, that because he cannot hurt the divine majesty he vents his malice against God's people, because the Parliament is out of his reach.

b) INTERCEPTED ROYALIST LETTER, 1653

[Tenants of former Church and Crown lands] do perfectly hate those who bought them, as possibly men can do; for these men are the greatest tyrants everywhere as men can be; for they wrest the poor tenants of all former immunities and freedoms they formerly enjoyed.

c) PETITION OF SURREY FARMERS TO FAIRFAX, 1647

Your petitioners, all rack-rented, have for nigh 6 years past born the charge of free-quartering soldiers, without any deduction of rent of the landlord's part; till now of late, since the army's advance from London, this charge doubles, and, with some of us, trebles our rent; so decaying our estates that little subsistence is (for ourselves, for our families, and for those many labourers employed by us) left us for the present; and for afterwards, likely none at all, unless your Excellency relieve us. For your petitioners, though racked in their rents already, and unable to pay our rents and to continue to bear this charge of quartering without allowance, are still charged as owners, and the landlords as yet go free, and most of them refuse absolutely to bear any part of this charge, upon tender of their rents, unless they shall be enforced thereunto by ordinance of Parliament; and many of them have threatened, and some of them have already commenced suits in law to recover their full rents; and others of them have sealed leases of ejectment, for the outing of such of their tenants as desired deduction of rent for this charge. . . .

[The petitioners asked Fairfax to represent their case to Parliament: which he did.]

167. CONSEQUENCES FOR TAXATION

Taxation was unfairly assessed before the Revolution (No. 48). This Declaration urges a new assessment—a demand not fully met until the land tax of William III. *A Perfect Account of the Daily Intelligence*, February 18th–25th, 1653.

Declaration of Commissioners for assessment in Yorkshire, February, 1653.

TYRANNY and kingship were not things personal, but . . . there was a deputation and concatenation of tyrants throughout the whole nation, whereby the burdens of war and peace were unequally supported, the manors of courtiers, demesne lands, forests, parks, warrens, tithes, Bishops' lands, with the whole endowment both of church and court, either exempt from all public contributions, or assessed in that disproportion as is not now suitable for England free. And though perhaps some of ourselves may have succeeded into the benefit of the old unequal distribution yet . . . we willingly do, and desire all men of estate to, aspire no higher than a fellow-commonership in the nation. . . . It was the wisdom of our forefathers to hide the wealth of the nation, and hinder a true estimate of men's estates. [But now that the rapaciousness of Kings is ended and we are all of one family, there should be a new survey and re-assessment of real estate.]

168. LAND NATIONALISATION PROPOSED

Chamberlen advocated keeping all confiscated Church, Crown and Royalists' lands in the hands of the state and using them as a public stock to provide employment for the poor. (Cf. the views of Thomas Spence in *From Cobbett to the Chartists*, p. 38.) If the lands are sold, Chamberlen argued, they will go to the rich, who have not subscribed to the Parliamentary cause; prices will fall in a glutted market. "Were it not better to lend them to the poor to be improved?"—the poor to choose whether they will work the land in common (cf. Part XII) or lease in parcels. Chamberlen thought that workhouses—the great remedy against unemployment for the next 200 years—created vagabondage and begging by destroying men's self-respect. Most contemporaries held that the poor were poor because they were wicked: Chamberlen saw that their "vices" were the result, not the cause, of their poverty. The rich had their way, and the land fund was sold, no provision being made in the way of credits for purchase by the poor (as was done in the French Revolution). Peter Chamberlen, *The Poor Man's Advocate* (1649), "Epistle," and pp. 9, 12, 14, 20.

KEEP your lands and keep your credit. Sell your lands and sell your credit. . . . Keep whole the public stock. Provide for the poor and they will provide for you. Destroy the poor and they will destroy you. And if you provide not for the poor, they will provide for themselves. . . .

Employment and competencies do civilise all men, and makes them tractable and obedient to superiors' commands. . . . None more intractable than idle beggars. . . .

It is reported that the poor should not be poor, were the rich but so honest as to let the poor have their own. . . . Nine men will not work to maintain one of their own rank idle, but they will be diligent task-masters (for that little which they shall need to work) to each other, and every single man will have nine overseers. . . . He that can and will not labour shall not eat. . . .

The poor (excepting some officers) are the army. . . .

[If confiscated lands are sold] How shall the money be disposed of? To grease the fat Sow? . . . Shall the rich still be paid, and the poor taxed? . . . The poor is a creditor as well as the rich. . . . The honest rich . . . will not offer to justify all that have been dabbling in contracts with this Parliament.

169. DIVERSE VIEWS ON ENCLOSURE

Enclosure had been proceeding for centuries (see Nos. 19–23); the land transfers of the Revolution only accelerated it. But in the sixteenth century orthodox opinion was opposed to enclosure. The pamphlets of Halhead (*a*) and the Rev. John Moore, a Leicestershire minister (*b*) and *c*)) are almost the last protests that get into print. The views of the Rev. Joseph Lee (*d*) are typical for the next century and a half: enclosure is socially necessary and therefore desirable; land is a commodity like everything else in bourgeois society; men can do what they like with their own: "the advancement of private persons will be the advantage of the public." Naturally, Lee related the agitation against enclosure to the Leveller movement. Extract *f*) is from a near-Digger pamphlet.

a) H. Halhead, *Inclosure Thrown Open*, p. 11; *b*) J. Moore, *The Crying Sin of England of not caring for the Poor*, pp. 7–14; *c*) J. Moore, *A Scripture Word against Enclosure*, p. 3; *d*) J. Lee, *A Vindication of Regulated Enclosure*, pp. 20–9, 9; *e*) Traditional; *f*) [Anon.] *More Light Shining in Buckinghamshire*, pp. 10–11.

a) ABSENTEE LANDLORDS, 1650

THE depopulating encloser . . . lives either in London, or in some city or town corporate, and gets heaps of money. . . . The richer sort are gone away, the poorer sort are cruelly handled. For there is some bailiff set over them; . . . they do so rack them and strain them that at length they break their hearts.

b) ENCLOSURE AND UNEMPLOYMENT, 1653

[The enclosers] care not how many beggars they make, so themselves may be gentlemen; nor how many poor they make, so themselves may be rich. . . . But they will plead, it's beside their intention to make beggars. Answer, It may be it is not the end of the workman, but sure I am, it's the end of the work of such enclosure. . . .

[An enclosing landlord said] "The poor increase like fleas and lice, and these vermin will eat us up unless we enclose." . . . They usually upon such enclosure treble the price of their land.

c) A PARSON ATTACKS THE PROFIT MOTIVE, 1656

So long as [tenants are] serviceable, drudge them, rack their rents, buy them to get by them and then sell them. . . . When lesser gain comes in by them they sell them or buy them upon that account as may serve their turns (Judas-like) to fill the bag.

d) A PARSON DEFENDS THE PROFIT MOTIVE, 1656

All things are not of an evil report in the Scripture sense which the multitude decry as evil; the best things nowadays are worst spoken of by the multitude; the very name of reformation is as much exploded by the vulgar as enclosure; those sacred ordinances of magistracy and ministry . . . are now become offensive to the levelling multitude. . . . A hedge in the field is as necessary in its kind as government in the church or commonwealth. . . . The ruder sort of people [are those most offended at enclosures.] . . .

It is a very strange principle and unheard-of paradox, that nothing can be done to God's glory which tends to man's profit. Do not tradesmen in following their vocations aim at their own advantage, do none of them glorify God thereby? . . . May not everyone lawfully put his commodity to the best advantage, provided he do it without prejudice to others? Do not all tradesmen cast to lay out their money upon such wares as will be most advantageous to themselves? Have not landholders as much reason, and may they not with as good conscience put their land to the best advantage? . . . Everyone by the light of nature and reason will do that which makes for his greatest advantage.

e) "ONE LAW FOR RICH AND POOR ALIKE"

The law locks up the man or woman
Who steals the goose from off the common,
But leaves the greater villain loose
Who steals the common from the goose.

f) PROPERTY IS THEFT, 1649

Mark this, you great Curmudgeons, you hang a man for stealing for his wants, when you yourselves have stolen from your fellow brethren all lands, creatures, etc.

170. NO LEGISLATION FOR THE POOR

The last attempt to prevent the hardship caused by enclosure was made by Major-General Whalley in 1656. His Bill (*a*) did not condemn enclosure altogether. It merely proposed to prevent depopulation and improve wastes. Nevertheless, it was defeated on the second reading. Similar failure had met an attempt to prevent extortionate fines on inheritance or alienation of copyholders (*b*). The Master of the Rolls (*a*) was Lenthall, late Speaker of the Long Parliament.

a) Burton, I, pp. 175–6; *b*) *Commons Journals*, VII, p. 433.

a) DEBATE IN PARLIAMENT, DECEMBER, 1656

Major-General Whalley brought in a Bill concerning the dividing of Commons, etc. Read the first time.

The Master of the Rolls was for rejecting of it, for he never liked any Bill that touched upon property.

It can never be made a good Bill what in itself had a tendency to any inconvenience; this the putting of the power of determining property in three persons. Time was when I durst hardly have trusted the justice of peace with determining of a cow grass. You have good justices now: who can tell what may be hereafter?

Major-General Whalley: I shall rather be loser than gainer by this Bill, for I have no commons; all mine are enclosed. It is for the general good, to prevent depopulation and discourage[ment] to the plough, which is the very support of the commonwealth. . . .

Mr. Fowell: This is the most mischievous Bill that ever was offered to this House. It will wholly depopulate many, and destroy property.

Resolved, that this Bill be not read the second time.

Resolved, that this Bill be rejected.

b) PROPERTY RIGHTS MAINTAINED, OCTOBER, 1656

A bill for ascertaining of arbitrary fines upon descent or alienation of copyholds of inheritance was this day read the second time. This bill being brought in with a clause that ascertains the fine to be one year's value, exceptions was taken against the same, as being contrary to the orders of the house, that any bill should be brought in to charge any of the people in their inheritance. . . .

The bill, upon the question, was rejected.

171. FOR FREE TRADE

Industrial monopolies came to an end in 1641, but not the privileged position of the City trading companies, whose financial support was so valuable to Parliament. The Left wing, the smaller merchants and industrialists, demanded freedom for all traders, especially exporters. The author of *a*), referring to the greater prosperity of the Netherlands, and almost quoting Bacon (No. 89, *b*)), wants to liberate trade, "especially that of cloth and other woollen manufactures." Extract *b*), coming from an outport at a time of acute crisis, when the Presbyterians of the City companies were out of favour in government circles, is a more direct attack. This theme was a familiar one with the Levellers. But although the companies found it difficult to enforce their privileges against interlopers under the republic, they were gradually reasserted during the Protectorate of Oliver Cromwell as part of the general move to the Right.

a) J. and W., p. 237; *b*) *ibid.*, p. 236.

a) FOR THE ENLARGEMENT OF TRADE, APRIL, 1645

THE strength of a kingdom consists in the riches of many subjects, not of a few, in so much that were this trade [cloth export] enlarged, it would tend to the multiplying of able and wealthy merchants; it would disperse it to a greater latitude . . . and prevent the increase of poor men and beggars up and down the land; for it is one of the main reasons why there are fewer beggars seen in commonwealths than in kingdoms, because of community and freedom of trading, by which means the wealth of the land is more equally distributed amongst the natives.

. . . Trade . . . is like dung, which being close kept in a heap or two stinks, but being spread abroad it doth fertilize the earth and make it fructify. . . . There are two main things that conduce to make a trade flourish, plenty of merchandise and multitude of merchants.

b) PETITION FROM THE GARRISON OF PORTSMOUTH, 1649

There is by sad experience found (especially to the poor) a daily decay of trade (the main pillar of this commonwealth's subsistence) occasioned by the continuation of monopolizing charters and associated companies, who have power to interrupt and deter all other natives from the exercise of free trade and commerce. . . .

For remedy whereof we humbly desire that you will declare that all free denizens of this nation, and friends to the weal public, may enjoy their rights by employment and improvement of their estates and stocks [i.e. capital] without the aforesaid restrictions in free traffic and commerce both foreign and domestic; and that all such monopolizing and encroaching charters may be abolished.

172. TRADE AND IMPERIAL EXPANSION

The Navigation Act, passed by the Rump in 1651 (*a*), was the first of a series of Acts designed to foster English shipping by limiting the circumstances under which foreign shipping might bring foreign produce to English shores. It was initially directed against the Dutch, England's chief commercial rival (see No. 68). The Act helped to bring about the Anglo-Dutch War of 1652–4 (*b*), which ended in victory for England. Adam Smith in *The Wealth of Nations* remarked that although the Act was not favourable to foreign commerce, its regulations were as wise as if they had been dictated by the most deliberate wisdom, because they tended to "diminution of the naval power of Holland, the only naval power which could endanger the security of England" (Everyman Ed., I, p. 408). The Act's direct effect on trade is impossible to estimate. But it is probable that it assisted by helping to develop the naval power of England and by giving English merchants a monopoly of trade with English colonies. The Navigation Code was not finally repealed till 1849. The Dutch War was followed by a naval campaign to win bases in the West Indies and open up Spanish America to English trade (*c*). Marvell, Milton's friend, remained true to the cause after the Restoration (see No. 198). Extract *d*) is from a left-wing pamphlet published in Holland in 1649. Cf. Nos. 125 and 136, *b*).

a) Gardiner, pp. 468–9; *b*) J. and W., p. 235; *c*) A. Marvell, *Poems* (1927), pp. 115–18; *d*) [Anon.] *Tyranipocrit Discovered*, in Orwell and Reynolds, *British Pamphleteers* (1948), I, pp. 90–1.

a) THE NAVIGATION ACT, OCTOBER 9TH, 1651

FOR the increase of the shipping and the encouragement of the navigation of this nation, which . . . is so great a means of the welfare and safety of this Commonwealth: be it enacted . . . that . . . no goods or commodities whatsoever of the growth, production or manufacture of Asia, Africa or America . . . shall be imported . . . into this Commonwealth of England, or into Ireland, or any other lands . . . to this Commonwealth belonging . . . in any other ship or ships . . . but only in such as do truly . . . belong only to the people of this Commonwealth, or the plantations thereof . . .; and whereof the master and mariners are also for the most part of them of the people of this Commonwealth. . . .

And it is further enacted . . . that no goods or commodities of the growth, production, or manufacture of Europe . . . shall . . . be imported . . . into . . . England, or into Ireland, or any other lands . . . to this Commonwealth belonging . . . in any ship or ships . . . but such as do . . . belong only to the people of this Commonwealth . . . except only such foreign ships . . . as do . . . belong to the people of that country or place, of which the said goods are the growth, production or manufacture; or to such ports where the said goods can only be, or most usually are, first shipped for transportation.

b) A LETTER FROM AMSTERDAM, MARCH, 1652

The talk holds high still here [Holland], and preparations [for war] go on, but yet they are not half so high as they are in Zeeland. . . . They find . . . that the Parliament's Act of Navigation sits a little too hard upon their shoulders, and if they can rant down that, then they have their ends; for how slight soever they pretended to make of it at its first coming forth, yet upon cooling consideration it touches to the quick. But what is that to England? Who are to mind their own honours and advantages, and not another state's, in framing and maintaining acts for the benefit of their own nation.

c) ON BLAKE'S VICTORY OVER THE SPANIARDS, 1657

Peace, against you, was the sole strength of Spain.
By that alone those islands she secures;
Peace made them hers, but war will make them yours . . .
Two dreadful navies there at anchor fight;
And neither has or power or will to fly:
There one must conquer, or there both must die.
Far different motives yet engag'd them thus:
Necessity did them, but choice did us. . . .
Ages to come your conquering arms will bless.
There they destroy what had destroy'd their peace;
And in one war, the present age may boast,
The certain seeds of many wars are lost.

d) RELIGION AND EMPIRE

Our merchants, they travel by sea and land to make Christian proselites . . . ; but consider their practices, and the profit that we have by their double-dealing: first in robbing of the poor Indians of that which God and nature hath given them, and then in bringing of it home to us, that we thereby may the better set forth and show the pride of our hearts, in decking of our proud carcasses and feeding of our greedy guts with superfluous, unnecessary curiosities. And although their dealing concerning the Indians' goods be bad, yet they deal worser with their persons; for they either kill them, which is bad, or make them their slaves, which is worse. I know not what to say concerning such impious proceedings with them poor innocent people.

173. CROMWELL IN IRELAND

We can only glance at Irish affairs (see Nos. 61 and 71). The revolution in England gave the occasion in 1641 for a national rising in Ireland against English overlordship, which took the form of a war of Roman Catholic landlords and peasants against Protestants (mostly landlords). Parliament could only turn serious attention to Ireland after the consolidation of the new régime in England: then Oliver Cromwell went over to establish colonial order in Ireland. Extracts *a*)–*c*) show how he did it. Extract *d*) gives the gist of the Cromwellian land settlement, which aimed at the wholesale expropriation of native landowners and their replacement by Protestant Englishmen. The land fund so created was used to pay the wages of the English Army. But the surveying of Ireland took so long that most of the rank and file had to sell their claims to land (at a discount) to officers and other speculators. So the project of colonising Ireland with English freeholders broke down: some of the Irish were allowed to remain in the English area, not from motives of humanity, but to provide cheap labour for absentee English landlords. The name of Cromwell has been hated in Ireland ever since, and it is a tragic foretaste of subsequent English history that the victories of democracy at home should have led to imperialist exploitation abroad. Some of the Levellers, alone of all English parties, refused to be blinded by religious passion, and saw the connection between their cause and that of the Irish patriots (No. 125).

a) Abbott, II, pp. 126–7; *b*) *ibid.*, p. 143; *c*) *ibid.*, pp. 197–8, 205; *d*) Gardiner, pp. 394–8.

a) CROMWELL TO THE SPEAKER, SEPTEMBER 17TH, 1649

THE Governor [of Drogheda], Sir Arthur Aston, and divers considerable officers being there, our men getting up to them were ordered by me to put them all to the sword. And indeed, being in the heat of action, I forbade them to spare any that were in arms in the town, and, I think, that night they put to the sword about 2,000 men, divers of the officers and soldiers being fled over the bridge into the other part of the town. . . . These, being summoned to yield to mercy, refused, whereupon I ordered the steeple of St. Peter's church to be fired, where one of them was heard to say in the midst of the flames: "God damn me, God confound me; I burn, I burn."

The next day, the other two towers were summoned, in one of which was about 6 or 7 score; but they refused to yield themselves, and we knowing that hunger must compel them set only good guards to secure them from running away until their stomachs were come down. From one of the said towers, notwithstanding their condition, they killed and wounded some of our men. When they submitted, their officers were knocked on the head, and every tenth man of the soldiers killed, and the rest shipped for the Barbadoes [to forced labour] . . .

I am persuaded that this is a righteous judgment of God upon these barbarous wretches, who have imbrued their hands in so much innocent blood; and that it will tend to prevent the effusion of blood for the future, which are the satisfactory grounds to such actions, which otherwise cannot but work remorse and regret.

b) CROMWELL TO THE SPEAKER, OCTOBER 14TH, 1649

This town [Wexford] is now so in your power, that [of] the former inhabitants I believe scarce one in twenty can challenge any property in their houses. Most of them are run away, and many of them killed in this service. And it were to be wished that an honest people would come and plant [i.e. settle] here, where are very good houses and other accommodation fitted to their hands, and may by your favour be made of encouragement to them, as also a seat of good trade, both inward and outward, and of marvellous great advantage in the point of the herring and other fishing. The town is pleasantly seated and strong. . . .

Thus it hath pleased God to give into your hands this other mercy, for which, as for all, we pray God may have all the glory. Indeed your instruments are poor and weak, and can do nothing but through believing, and that is the gift of God also.

c) CROMWELL'S DECLARATION, MARCH 21ST, 1650

Remember, ye hypocrites, Ireland was once united to England. Englishmen had good inheritances which many of them purchased with their money—they or their ancestors, from many of you and your ancestors. They had good leases from Irishmen for long time to come; great stocks thereupon; houses and plantations erected at their cost and charge. They lived peaceably and honestly amongst you. You had generally equal benefit of the protection of England with them, and equal justice from the laws, saving what was necessary for the state (out of reasons of state) to put upon some few people apt to rebel upon the instigation of such as you. You broke this union! You, unprovoked, put the English to the most unheard-of . . . massacre (without respect of sex or age) that ever the sun beheld. And at a time when Ireland was in perfect peace, and when, through the example of the English industry, through commerce and traffic, that which was in the natives' hands was better to them than if all Ireland had been in their possession and not an Englishman in it. . . .

We come (by the assistance of God) to hold forth and maintain the lustre and glory of English liberty in a nation where we have an undoubted right to do it; wherein the people of Ireland (if they listen not to such seducers as you [priests] are) may equally participate in all benefits, to use liberty and fortune equally with Englishmen, if they keep out of arms.

d) ACT FOR SETTLEMENT OF IRELAND, AUGUST 12TH, 1652

To the end . . . that the people of that nation [Ireland] may know that it is not the intention of the Parliament to extirpate that whole nation, but that mercy and pardon . . . may be extended to all husbandmen, ploughmen, labourers, artificers and others of the inferior sort . . ., they submitting themselves to the Parliament of the Commonwealth of England and living peaceably and obediently under their government, . . . be it enacted: . . .

I. That all and every person and persons, who at any time before the 10th day of November 1642, . . . have contrived, advised, counselled, promoted or acted the rebellion, murders or massacres done or committed in

Ireland . . . or have . . . aided, assisted, promoted, acted, prosecuted or abetted the said rebellion . . . be excepted from pardon of life and estate. . . .

V. That all . . . persons in Ireland that are in arms or otherwise in hostility against the Parliament . . . and shall not within eight and twenty days after publication hereof . . . lay down arms and submit to the power and authority of the said Parliament and Commonwealth, as the same is now established, be excepted from pardon for life and estate.

VI. That all other . . . persons . . . who have borne command in the war of Ireland against the Parliament of England . . . be banished during the pleasure of the Parliament . . . and their estates forfeited [two-thirds confiscated outright, the equivalent of one-third allowed to their wives and children where Parliament shall assign —i.e. in Connaught]. . . .

VIII. That all . . . persons of the Popish religion who have resided in Ireland at any time from the first day of October, 1641, to the first of March, 1650, and have not manifested their constant good affection to the interest of the Commonwealth of England . . . shall forfeit one third part of their estates in Ireland to the said Commonwealth, to be disposed of for the use, benefit and advantage of the said Commonwealth; and [shall keep] the other two third parts [or an equivalent elsewhere].

Part Fifteen

GROWING CONSERVATISM

Rich men are none of the greatest enemies to monarchy.
Chamberlen, The Poor Man's Advocate, 1649.

The King's blood was not our burden, it was those oppressing Norman laws whereof he enslaved us that we groaned under.
Gerrard Winstanley.

174. OPPOSITION TO LAW REFORM

Compare Nos. 120 and 153, and with *c*) compare Ireton's remarks in No. 133.

a) Whitelock, *Memorials*, II, pp. 553–4; *b*) Ludlow, I, p. 246; *c*) [Anon.] *England's Complete Law-judge and Lawyer*, pp. viii, 20; *d*) Firth and Rait, *Acts and Ordinances of the Interregnum*, II, pp. 455–6.

a) PETITION FROM NORFOLK TO FAIRFAX, MARCH, 1649

THAT all courts in the country be put down [i.e. abolished], and all causes under £10 value to be judged by two or three neighbours to be chosen by the parties; and perjury and subornation of it to be death. All suits in equity to be tried by juries, [but] not by common law.

Witnesses to be examined before the judge, except between two nobles, knights, etc., who are able to stand a long suit in chancery. No cause to hang above two terms; lawyers to be reduced to a smaller number, and their fees to be less and certain; and but one counsel in small causes.

That who will may purchase lands to be freehold in socage for a reasonable fine; and that the base oath of fealty and homage may make no more perjured souls in the kingdom.

b) A RICH MAN'S LAW, 1650

[Cromwell told me] that it was his intention to contribute the utmost of his endeavours to make a thorough reformation of the clergy and law: "but," said he, "the sons of Zeruiah are yet too strong for us; and we cannot mention the reformation of the law but they presently cry out, we design to destroy property: whereas the law as it is now constituted serves only to maintain the lawyers and to encourage the rich to oppress the poor."

c) LAW AND PROPERTY, 1656

There must be a jealousy lest the laws be altered, and the principles of property and privileges lost by degrees.

. . . The liberty of man is precious, and so are goods; for property is little if liberty be encroached on, and liberty little if property be taken away.

d) ACT FOR TURNING THE LAW INTO ENGLISH, NOVEMBER, 1650

The Parliament have thought fit to declare and enact . . . that all the report-books of the resolutions of judges, and other books of the law of England, shall be translated into the English tongue. . . .

From and after the first return of Easter Term which shall be in the year 1651 . . . all proceedings whatsoever in any courts of justice within this Commonwealth, and which concerns the law and administration of justice, shall be in the English tongue only . . .; and . . . shall be written in an ordinary, usual and legible hand and character.

175. MORE RADICAL REFORM NEEDED

Extract *a*) is from S. Chidley's *A Cry against a Crying Sin*. The complaint in *c*) had been true for centuries: what was new and revolutionary was that the complaint could now get into print—though there was no reform at this period.

a) *Harleian Miscellany*, VIII, p. 461; *b*) *ibid.*, II, pp. 555–7; *c*) *The Copyholder's Plea*, quoted in Margaret James, *Social Problems and Policy in the Puritan Revolution*, p. 95; *d*) Abbott, IV, p. 274.

a) TO THE COMMISSIONERS OF NEWGATE, 1652

RIGHT HONOURABLE, I am sorry to see you go on still in your wonted course of arraigning men for their lives merely for theft. I have observed that the persons who are arraigned before your honours are poor labourers and such creatures, who stole things of a small value, peradventure for mere necessity; yet you arraign them for their lives, when the Law of God requireth their preservation in such a way that they may make satisfaction, and not, if disabled [by mutilation as a legal punishment], to force them into a necessity of stealing again; but they are great sinners indeed who rob men of their precious lives. And the worst of men are such as despise and destroy thieves that steal merely to satisfy their hunger. . . . For life is above liberty and estate: the jewel of one man's life all your estates cannot balance.

b) PROPOSALS FOR LAW REFORM, 1653

The Law's Discovery: or a brief detection of sundry notorious errors and abuses contained in our English laws, whereby thousands are annually stripped of their estates, and some of their lives. . . . The author was a gentleman born to a fair estate, by degree a barrister, who, partly through sickness and partly for conscience, deserted the profession of our laws as epidemically evil. He spent divers of his last years in supervising the defects thereof. . . .

XVII. That insolvent debtors be freed from imprisonment, or else detained some short time at the creditor's charge till their cause be determined. . . .

XX. Whereas poor men can seldom put in bail, for want whereof they suffer unheard many months' imprisonment till their day of hearing comes, and are thereby often ruined; therefore for prevention, that the plaintiff by his own oath, or of some credible person allowed by the judge, declare the truth of the cause; wherein if he failed the prisoner, giving authority for his appearance, to be dismissed without bail; or (which is better) that the judge be authorised to determine of law, fact and equity, to avoid the formality and charge of pleading. . . .

XXVIII. That the uncertain fines of copyholders may be reduced to a certainty, either of an easy yearly rent, or moderate fine; also that the like might be done in servile tenures and heriots. This would prevent many Chancery suits and oppression by lords. . . .

XXX. That trial by combat may be suppressed as a reasonless law, and unwarrantable by God's Word.

c) CLASS AND LAW, 1653

The chancellor or judges (before whom the reasonableness [of manorial custom] dependeth to be determined) are themselves lords of such copyholders, and biassed with their own interest and concernment.

d) CROMWELL. SPEECH OF SEPTEMBER 17TH, 1656

There is one general grievance in the nation. It is the law. . . . The great grievance lies in the execution and administration. . . . The truth of it is, there are wicked abominable laws, that will be in your power to alter. To hang a man for sixpence, threepence, I know not what; to hang for a trifle, and pardon murder, is in the ministration of the law, through the ill-framing of it. . . . And to see men lose their lives for petty matters! This is a thing that God will reckon for.

176. POPULAR ANXIETY

This extract speaks for itself. It is from pp. 1–2 of the pamphlet.

The humble remonstrance of many thousands in and about the City of London, on behalf of all the free commoners of England, to his Excellency the Lord General Cromwell (and the officers) 21st April, 1653 [the day after the dissolution of the Rump], pp. 1–2.

God gave your enemies into your hands, and gave you large possessions, houses that you built not. . . . Was all this that you only might live in peace, ease and rest, and say you have wives, have farms, parks, manors and kingly houses to fee; and forget the vows you then made? Surely no. Are the people free? . . . Is not justice as necessary now as when the Parliament began?

177. RADICALISM'S LAST CHANCE

After the forcible dissolution of the Rump in April, 1653, power remained in the hands of Cromwell and the generals. To give a show of legality to their dictatorship and to broaden their basis of support, they called an assembly of delegates nominated by Independent congregations and sifted by the officers. This was the Little or "Barebones" Parliament, so called after one of its members, Praise Barbon, nicknamed Praise-God Barebones. From our knowledge of the political role of the Independent congregations, we can see how natural it was to summon a congress of delegates from them to advise the government; nor shall we imagine that they would concern themselves merely with theological matters. The legend is, however, widely spread that the Barebones Parliament was an assembly of religious maniacs. These extracts from its proceedings should show how very business-like it was in its approach to reform of the law, of the Church, of taxation, and to land sales, etc. It also agreed to legislation uniting England and Scotland for the first time. There were two parties: a conservative-military majority, composed of those who later supported the Protectorate; and a democratic minority, the last appearance in high politics of the reforming spirit which had motivated the Levellers and the Left-wing sectaries. The latter proved unexpectedly strong: it was their vote for the abolition of tithes which led to the dissolution of the Little Parliament (see No. 178). *Commons Journals*, VII, pp. 282–363.

July 6th, 1653. Resolved, That the title of Parliament shall be given to this Assembly. . . .

July 19th. Resolved, That the consideration of the property of incumbents in tithes be referred to a committee. . . .

July 20th. Resolved, That there be [committees] for the business of the law; . . . for inspecting the treasurers and regulating of officers and salaries; . . . for the business of trade and corporations; and for receiving propositions for the advantage of the commonwealth; . . . for the poor, and regulating commissions of the peace throughout the nation; . . . to consider of public debts; and to receive accusations of bribery, public frauds and breach of public trust; . . . for prisons and prisoners . . .; for advancement of learning.

Ordered, That it be referred to the committee for the law to prepare an Act for redress of delays and mischiefs arising on writs of error, writs of false judgment and arrests of judgment. . . .

July 23rd. Ordered, That it be referred to a committee to consider how relief may be given unto tenants against the oppression of delinquent, malignant or popish landlords, or lords of manors; and to prepare an Act for that purpose. . . .

August 8th. A bill touching marriages and the registering thereof [i.e. civil marriage] and also of births and burials . . . was . . . committed to a grand committee. . . .

August 10th. Ordered . . . That there be a High Court of Justice erected for the trial of offenders against the Commonwealth. . . .

August 17th. A bill entitled "A further additional Act for the sale of several lands and estates forfeited to the Commonwealth for treason" . . . was . . . read the first and second time.

August 20th. Resolved, . . . That an Act shall be brought in for exposing to sale two parts (in three parts to be divided) of all the lands and real estates of recusants [Roman Catholics] now vested in the Commonwealth by virtue of several Acts of Parliament made in the several reigns of Queen Elizabeth and of the late King James. . . .

August 22nd. Resolved, . . . That a bill be brought in touching idiots, lunatics and infants. . . .

September 9th. A bill entitled "An additional Act for the more speedy administration of justice in the Court of Admiralty" was . . . read the first and second time. . . .

September 12th. Resolved, That a bill be brought in for sale of some castles and houses belonging to the late King, formerly exempted from sale. . . .

Ordered, That the same committee do prepare a bill for the sale of remainders of Deans' and Chapters' land. . . .

September 21st. Resolved, That a bill be brought in for

sale of the estates of such persons as have been delinquents since the 30th of January 1649 [date of the execution of Charles I]. . . .

October 5th. The House this day resumed the debate upon the Act for relief of creditors and poor prisoners. . . .

October 14th. Mr. Anlaby reports from the Grand Committee touching the equality of taxes. . . . Resolved, . . . That the next assessment throughout the nation shall be by a fixed sum on each respective county; . . . that the fixed sums upon each respective county shall be levied by pound rate upon the estates real and personal; . . . that a committee be appointed to consider how these votes may be made practicable with the greatest equality. . . .

October 22nd. A bill entitled, "An Act for the de-afforestation, sale and improvement of the forests and the honours, manors, lands, tenements and hereditaments within the usual limits . . . of the same, heretofore belonging to the late King, Queen and Prince", was . . . read the first time. . . .

October 25th. The House was this day in a grand committee upon debate of the bill for uniting and incorporating Scotland into one free state and commonwealth with England. . . .

October 29th. A bill for regulating the great exorbitances of fees in the law and elsewhere . . . was read the first and second time. . . .

November 1st. Ordered, That it be referred to the committee of the law to bring in a bill for taking away holidays [i.e. holy days] and the observation of those days which are not juridical.

November 3rd. A bill for taking away the High Court of Chancery, and appointing Commissioners and judges to hear and determine as well causes now depending as also future matters of equity, and putting in order other matters of law which were within the jurisdiction of that court, and regulating divers abuses in the courts of common law . . . was . . . read the first and second time. . . .

November 7th. Resolved, That a bill be brought in

whereby tenants in tail may be enabled to pass away their estates. . . .

November 17th. Resolved, . . . That the power of patrons to present to benefices shall from henceforth be taken away. . . .

December 10th. The House proceeded in the debate of the report from the committee for tithes. . . .

December 12th. It being moved in the House this day, That the sitting of this Parliament any longer, as now constituted, will not be for the good of the Commonwealth; and that therefore it was requisite to deliver up unto the Lord General Cromwell the powers which they received from him, and that motion being seconded by several other members, the House rose.

178. FAILURE OF THE BAREBONES PARLIAMENT

The Barebones Parliament was welcomed by one contemporary "because there are not so many lords of manors in it" as usual: but there proved to be too many. These extracts are from *An Exact Relation of the Proceedings and Transactions of the Late Parliament* (1654), by L.D. He emphasises the respectability even of the Left-wing minority to which he adhered: they were solid bourgeoisie and freeholders, if not privileged (and debt-ridden) aristocrats, "as formerly it hath been."

a) *Somers Tracts*, X, pp. 90, 98–9; *b*) *ibid.*, p. 95.

a) WHY IT WAS DISSOLVED

THERE were four great votes that passed in the time of the sitting of the House, which some interests were much displeased at, and they passed not without great debate:—

First, a vote for abolishing and taking away the Court of Chancery;

Secondly, a vote for a new body or model of the law;

Thirdly, a vote to take away the power of patrons to make presentations;

Fourthly, that innocent negative vote of not agreeing with the report of the committee for tithes . . . upon which followed presently the dissolution of the House. . . .

The afore-mentioned [fourth] vote passing as it did,

those gentlemen that missed of their expectations and were crossed of having their wills, greatly fearing, as it seemeth, it would go ill with those corrupt interests of the lawyers and clergy, which they endeavoured to support, they took the pet, and were exceeding wroth, divers of them: and that afternoon and the next day . . . they took counsel with and among themselves, holding cabals and there consulting the overthrow and dissolution of the House. . . . Rising early and coming betimes to put in practice their design . . . those gentlemen, without hearing their fellows, or admitting the debate, or putting the question, rose up out of their places to be gone, and others in simplicity followed.

b) A DEFENCE OF ITS MEMBERS

"Oh the Parliament-men [they say], many of them are such as would destroy all property!"—As if they had none themselves, when as, though all of them had not very bulky estates, yet they had free estates, and were not of broken fortunes, or such as owed great sums of money, £10,000 and more (and those to whom they were so in debt knew not how to get a penny of it) and stood in need of privilege and protection, as formerly it hath been.

179. THE LORD PROTECTOR

The dissolution of the Barebones Parliament left the generals supreme. They made Cromwell Lord Protector. Clarendon cannot contain his amazement and horror at the continued powerlessness of the old landed aristocracy. Clarendon, *History of the Rebellion* (ed. Macray, 1888), V, pp. 287–8.

In this manner, and with so little pains, this extraordinary man, . . . without the assistance and against the desire of all noble persons or men of quality, or of three men who in the beginning of the troubles were possessed of £300 land by the year, mounted himself into the throne of three kingdoms, without the name of king but with a greater power and authority than had been ever exercised or claimed by any king.

180. CROMWELL'S THEORY OF REVOLUTION

The sense of co-operating with God's purposes played an important part in the political theory of the Puritan. It made him feel that his cause was righteous and would prevail, and that his motives in fighting for it were not merely selfish. Justice and history were on his side. This view, which Milton held and Cromwell here justifies, was not without its nobility; it disposed of the vulgar view (still held) that great revolutions can be brought about by the "agitation" of a group of conspirators. But Cromwell's version conveniently veiled the class issues at stake. Its dangers are apparent. God's wishes cannot be verified; and the theory may degenerate into justification by success. Cromwell comes near to so justifying his dictatorship in this speech of January 22nd, 1655. He continually had to defend himself against the charge of "making necessities in order to plead them": not altogether successfully. Milton was a supporter of Cromwell in the 'forties and early 'fifties, but in *Paradise Lost* (1665) he speaks bitterly of "necessity, the tyrant's plea." Abbott, III, pp. 590–2.

SUPPOSING this cause, or this business, must be carried on, either it is of God, or of man. If it be of man, I would I had never touched it with a finger; if I had not had a hope fixed in me that this cause and this business is of God, I would many years ago have run from it. If it be of God, He will bear it up. If it be of man, it will tumble, as everything that hath been of man, since the world began, hath done. And what are all our histories and other traditions of actions in former times but God manifesting Himself that He hath shaken and tumbled down and trampled upon everything that He hath not planted? . . . Let men take heed and be twice advised, how they call His revolutions, the things of God and His working of things from one period to another, how, I say, they call them necessities of men's creations. . . .

They say in other countries "There are five or six cunning men in England that have skill; they do all these things." Oh what blasphemy is this! . . . Therefore whatsoever you may judge men for, and say "this man is cunning and politic and subtle," take heed, again I say, how you judge of His revolutions as the product of men's inventions.

181. SOCIAL BASIS OF PROTECTORATE

By the time of the Protectorate the social basis of the government had become so narrow that the Army, to maintain itself, had to seek to broaden the basis of its support. Extracts *a*) and *b*) illustrate two types of property-holders whom Cromwell tried to attract; Royalists were still excluded, but the Instrument of Government on which the Protectorate was originally founded (*b*), by redistributing Parliamentary seats and franchise, was designed to bring the electoral system into something like correspondence with property distribution in the country. Many of the Army leaders were of "mean" extraction (*c*). But they were now themselves property-holders on a sufficient scale to desire a property-qualification. As the Protectorate moved to the Right, the Humble Petition and Advice (1657) restored the old franchise, which survived till 1832.

a) Quoted by M. Ashley, *Financial and Commercial Policy under the Cromwellian Protectorate* (1934), p. 16; *b*) Gardiner, pp. 410–11; *c*) Burton, I, p. 331.

a) THE FRENCH AMBASSADOR, JUNE, 1654

IT is agreed that the merchants have very great influence in England.

b) INSTRUMENT OF GOVERNMENT, DECEMBER, 1653

XIV. All and every person and persons, who have aided, advised, assisted or abetted in any war against the Parliament, since the first day of January, 1641, . . . shall be disabled and incapable to be elected, or to give any vote in the election of any members to serve in the next Parliament, or in the three succeeding triennial Parliaments.

XV. All such who have advised, assisted, or abetted the rebellion of Ireland, shall be disabled and incapable for ever to be elected, or give any vote in the election of any member to serve in Parliament; as also all such who do or shall profess the Roman Catholic religion. . . .

XVIII. All and every person and persons seized or possessed to his own use of any estate, real or personal, to the value of £200, and not within the aforesaid exceptions, shall be capable to elect members to serve in Parliament for counties.

c) GOSSIP ABOUT CROMWELL'S OFFICERS, JANUARY, 1657

That night I was with Mr. Moore and Mr. Paine at the Bull's Head, and with Mr. Booth and Col. Browne at the Half-Moon. They observed that Captain Philip Jones, who has now £7,000 per annum, was born but to £8 or £10 a year, Sir John Barkstead was a thimble-maker, Kelsey sold leather-points, Major-General Bridge was a common dragooner in Yorkshire, not long since a sneaking, etc.; and they reckoned up the mean extraction of many more Major-Generals.

182. REPUBLICANS ON THE PROTECTORATE

The establishment of the Protectorate broke Cromwell's last links with the Left. These extracts point out that Cromwell was compelled to become increasingly reliant on the "corrupt interests" of the nation. Many ex-Royalists became prominent members of his government.

a) Ludlow, I, pp. 376–7; *b*) Mrs. Hutchinson, *Life of Colonel Hutchinson*, II, pp. 202–4.

a) EDMUND LUDLOW

THE most weighty arguments which were then used to persuade me to continue in my employments were, that supposing Cromwell to be a tyrant, to have no just call to his present employment, and a wicked man, as most of them were so ingenuous to acknowledge him to be; yet they declared themselves to be of opinion, that a good man might act under him. . . . To this I answered, that though in an evil government already established, an honest man may take an employment, and bless God for such an opportunity of doing good, yet our case seemed to me to be very different, the dispute lying now between tyranny and liberty; and that I durst not in any measure contribute to the support of tyranny against the liberty of my country. Another argument much pressed was that by declining my station I should neglect an occasion of doing some good, and lay a necessity upon those in power to employ others, who might do mischief. To this

I replied, that it was not lawful to do the least evil for the attaining the greatest good; and that I apprehended it to be an evil thing to fortify Cromwell in his usurpation; that I hoped I should do more good by my open protestation against his injustice, and declining to act under him, than by the contrary means: for should all men who continued well affected to the interest of the Commonwealth refuse to act in the present state of affairs, there could be no way thought of, in my opinion, more probable to reduce the usurper to his right senses; who not daring to trust such as had acted against him, must of necessity by this means be left destitute of instruments to carry on his unjust designs. A third argument was that I should wait to see how he would use his power, which if he improved to evil ends, I should then find many others to join with, who would be as ready to oppose him as my self. To this also I answered, that I was fully convinced of the injustice of his undertaking; that he had betrayed his masters, under colour that they would not reform the law and the clergy; and that having called an assembly, in order, as he pretended, to accomplish that work, he had now broken them also for endeavouring to do it; that as soon as he had made the corrupt interests of the nation sensible of their danger, he had contracted an alliance with them, and was become their Protector; that it could not be reasonably expected that he should do anything towards their reformation, because every step he should take towards the lessening of their credit would tend to the weakening of his own authority; and that he was no less necessitated to be a vassal to them than he designed the rest of the nation to be slaves to him.

b) LUCY HUTCHINSON

He weeded, in a few months' time, above a hundred and fifty godly officers out of the army, with whom many of the religious soldiers went off, and in their room abundance of the king's dissolute soldiers were entertained; and the army was almost changed from that godly religious army, whose valour God had crowned with triumph, into the dissolute army they had beaten, bearing yet a better name. . . . His court was full of sin and vanity, and the more abominable, because they had not yet quite cast away the name of God, but profaned it by taking it in vain upon them. . . . Almost all the ministers everywhere fell in and worshipped this beast, and courted and made addresses to him. So did the City of London, and many of the degenerate lords of the land, with the poor-spirited gentry. The cavaliers, in policy, who saw that while Cromwell reduced all the exercise of tyrannical power under another name, there was a door opened for the restoring of their party, fell much in with Cromwell, and heightened all his disorders. . . . At last he took upon himself to make lords and knights, and wanted not many fools, both of the army and gentry, to accept of, and strut in, his mock titles.

183. THE REPUBLICAN ALTERNATIVE

This pamphlet, by one of the leading republicans, was published just before the elections to Oliver's second Parliament; it resulted in the imprisonment of its author. It pleads for an alliance of the republicans with the Army based on the suffrage of the "whole body of adherents to the cause." An opening is even left for Cromwell to return to the fold. Notable is the realisation that without army support there could be no republican solution; and the proposal of a self-perpetuating executive. Sir Henry Vane, *A Healing Question Propounded and Resolved* (1656), pp. 2–5, 7, 9, 11–13, 17, 20.

In the management of this war, it pleased God . . . so to bless the counsel and forces of the persons . . . engaged in this cause, as . . . to make them absolute . . . conquerors over their common enemy. And by this means they had added unto the natural right which was in them before . . . the right of conquest for the strengthening of their just claim to be governed by . . . successive representatives of their own election. . . . This they once thought they had been in possession of when it was ratified, as it were, in the blood of the last King. But of late a great interruption having happened unto them in their former expectations, and instead thereof, something rising up that seems rather accommodated to the private and selfish interest of a particular part (in comparison) than truly adequate to the common good . . . of the whole body engaged in this cause: hence it is that this compacted body is now falling asunder into many dissenting parts . . . and if these breaches be not timely healed, and the offences (before they take too deep root) removed, they will certainly work more to the advantage of the common enemy than any of their own unwearied endeavours and dangerous contrivances in foreign parts put all together. . . .

That which is first to be opened is the nature and goodness of the cause; which had it not carried in it its own evidence, would scarce have found so many of the people of God adherers to it . . . without which the military force alone would have been little available to subdue the common enemy, and restore to this whole body their just natural rights in civil things, and true freedom in matters of conscience. . . . For the first of these, . . . natural right, . . . it lies in this:—

They are to have and enjoy the freedom . . . to set up meet persons in the place of supreme judicature and authority amongst them . . . and through the orderly exercise of such measure of wisdom . . . as the Lord . . . shall please to give unto them, to shape . . . all subordinate . . . administrations of rule and government. . . .

The second branch which remains briefly to be handled, is . . . matters of religion. . . .

This freedom . . . consists . . . in the magistrate's forbearing to put forth the power of rule and coercion in things that God has exempted out of his commission. . . .

The . . . last reserve therefore which they [i.e. the supporters of the cause] have had . . . has been their military capacity. . . . By this mutual and happy transition which may be made between the party of honest men in the three nations virtually in arms, and those actually so now in power at the head of the army, how suddenly would the union of the whole body be consolidated, and made so firm as it will not need to fear all the designs and attempts of the common enemy. . . .

It is not then the standing and being of the present army and military forces in the three nations that is liable to exception of offence from any dissenting judgments at this time amongst the honest well affected party. . . . That wherein the offence lies, and which causes such great thoughts of heart amongst the honest party . . . is in short this:—

That when the right and privilege is . . . restored by conquest unto the whole body (that forfeited not their interest therein) of freely disposing themselves in such a constitution of righteous government, as may best answer the ends held forth in this cause; that nevertheless, either through delay they should be withheld . . . or through design they should come at last to be utterly denied the exercise of this their right, upon pretence that they are not in capacity as yet to use it; which indeed has some truth in it, if those that are now in power, and have the command of the arms, do not prepare all things requisite thereunto. . . .

And if this [unity] which is so essential to the well being and right constitution of government, were once obtained, the dispute about the form would not prove so difficult. . . . For if, as the foundation of all, the sovereignty be acknowledged to reside originally in the whole body of adherents to this cause . . . and then if in consequence hereof, a supreme judicature be set up . . . from the free choice and consent of the whole body . . . what could be propounded afterwards as to the form of the administration that would much stick? . . .

[Makes various suggestions regarding the administration: such as, a Council of State elected for life and filling up its own vacancies; the execution of the laws to be entrusted to a single person who would yet be subject to the regulative power.]

The very persons now in power are they unto whose lot it would fall to set about [the] preparatory work. . . .

The most natural way for which would seem to be by a general council or convention of faithful, honest, and discerning men, chosen for that purpose by the free consent of the whole body of adherents to this cause in the several parts of the nations . . . by order from the present ruling power, but considered as General of the army.

184. VIEWS OF A FORMER AGITATOR

Some Levellers, despairing of the Army as a means to power, turned to the exiled Charles II and offered support for a restoration in return for a guarantee of their programme. One such was Sexby, now Lieut.-Colonel (see No. 133). He and Colonel Titus (a Presbyterian turned Royalist) drafted *Killing no Murder*, which advocates the assassination of Cromwell: it was published under the name of William Allen. Not long after, Sexby was captured in England while preparing to assassinate Oliver himself. He died in the Tower. *Killing no Murder* (1657), Preface.

To his Highness, Oliver Cromwell.

May it please your Highness:

How I have spent some hours of the leisure your Highness has been pleased to give me, this following paper will give your Highness an account. How you will please to interpret it I cannot tell, but I can with confidence say, my intention in it is to procure your Highness that justice nobody yet does you, and to let the people see, the longer they defer it, the greater injury they do both themselves and you. To your Highness justly belongs the honour of dying for the people, and it cannot choose but be unspeakable consolation to you in the last moments of your life to consider with how much benefit to the world you are like to leave it. 'Tis then only (my Lord) the titles you now usurp, will be truly yours; you will then be indeed the deliverer of your country, and free it from a bondage little inferior to that from which Moses delivered his. You will then be that true reformer which you would be thought. Religion shall be then restored, liberty asserted and Parliaments have those privileges they have fought for. We shall then hope that other laws will have place besides those of the sword, and that justice shall be otherwise defined than the will and pleasure of the strongest; and we shall then hope men will keep oaths again, and not have the necessity of being false and perfidious to preserve themselves, and be like their rulers. All this we hope from your Highness's happy expiration, who are the true father of your country; for while you live we can call nothing ours, and it is from your death that we hope for our inheritances. Let this consideration arm and fortify your Highness's mind against the fears of death and the terrors of your evil conscience, that the good you will do by your death will something balance the evils of your life. And if in the black catalogue of high malefactors few can be found that have lived more to the affliction and disturbance of mankind than your Highness has done, yet your greatest enemies will not deny but there are likewise as few that have expired more to the universal benefit of mankind than your Highness is like to do. To hasten this great good is the chief end of my writing this paper; and if it have the effects I hope it will, your Highness will quickly be out of the reach of men's malice, and your enemies will only be able to wound you in your memory, which strokes you will not feel. That your Highness may be speedily in this security is the universal wishes of your grateful country. This is the desires and prayers of the good and of the bad, and it may be is the only thing wherein all sects and factions do agree in their devotions, and is our only common prayer. But amongst all that put in their requests and supplications for your Highness's speedy deliverance from all earthly troubles, none is more assiduous, nor more fervent than he, that with the rest of the nation has the Honour to be

May it please your Highness:

Your Highness's present slave and vassal

W. A.

185. CROMWELL ATTACKS THE LEFT

Gloves off now. No more pretence. If the commonwealth must suffer—better from rich men than poor men (*b*). With regard to the charge of Leveller correspondence with Cavaliers, see No. 184.

a) Abbott, III, pp. 435–6; *b*) *ibid.*, pp. 584–5.

a) SPEECH TO PARLIAMENT, SEPTEMBER 4TH, 1654

WHAT was the face that was upon our affairs as to the interest of the nation? to the authority of the nation? to the magistracy? to the ranks and orders of men, whereby England hath been known for hundreds of years? A nobleman, a gentleman, a yeoman? (That is a good interest of the nation, and a great one.) The magistracy of the nation, was it not almost trampled underfoot, under despite and contempt, by men of Levelling principles? . . . Did not that Levelling principle tend to the reducing of all to an equality? . . . What was the design, but to make the tenant as liberal a fortune as the landlord? Which, I think, if obtained, would not have lasted long! The men of that principle, after they had served their own turns, would have cried up interest and property then fast enough!

b) SPEECH TO PARLIAMENT, JANUARY 22ND, 1655

A company of men [i.e. the Levellers and republicans] . . . have been and yet are endeavouring to put us into blood and into confusion; more desperate and dangerous confusion than England ever yet saw. And I must say, as when Gideon commanded his son to fall upon Zeba and Zalmunna and slay them, they thought it more noble to die by the hand of a man than of a stripling . . . so is it some satisfaction, if a Commonwealth must perish, that it perish by men, and not by the hands of persons differing little from beasts; that if it must needs suffer, it should rather suffer from rich men than from poor men. . . .

The correspondence held with the interest of the Cavaliers [was] by that party of men called Levellers, and who call themselves Commonwealth's-men; whose declarations were framed to that purpose, and ready to be published at the time of their common rising.

186. A CONSERVATIVE CHURCH SETTLEMENT

A conservative political settlement meant a conservative Church settlement. Even Richard Baxter could approve (*b*), for Cromwell himself had now turned against the "mechanic" preachers. For Fox, on the other hand, Cromwell's achievement seemed very different.

a) Abbott, III, p. 440; *b*) Baxter, *Autobiography*, pp. 70–1; *c*) Fox, *Journal* (Everyman), pp. 192–3.

a) OLIVER TO PARLIAMENT, SEPTEMBER 4TH, 1654

THIS government . . . hath endeavoured to put a stop to that heady way . . . of every man making himself a minister and a preacher. It hath endeavoured to settle a way for the approbation of men of piety and ability for the discharge of that work. And I think I may say it hath committed that work to the trust of persons, both of the Presbyterian and Independent judgments, men of as known ability, piety and integrity, as I believe any this nation hath. . . . [The government] hath taken care, we hope, for the expulsion of all those who may be judged any way unfit for this work; who are scandalous, and who are the common scorn and contempt of that administration.

b) BAXTER ON THE TRIERS

One of the chief works he did was the purging of the ministry. . . . A society of ministers, with some others, were chosen by Cromwell to sit at Whitehall, under the name of Triers, who were mostly Independents, but some sober Presbyterians with them, and had power to try all that came for institution or induction, and without their approbation none were admitted. . . . The truth is, . . . to give them their due, they did abundance of good to the Church. They saved many a congregation from ignorant, ungodly, drunken teachers. . . . So that, though they were many of them somewhat partial for the Independents, separatists, Fifth Monarchy men and Anabaptists, and against the Prelatists and Arminians, yet so great was the benefit above the hurt which they brought to the Church that many thousands of souls blessed God for the faithful ministers whom they let in, and grieved when the Prelatists afterward cast them out again.

c) THE LOST LEADER

And though O.C. at Dunbar fight had promised to the Lord that if He gave him the victory over his enemies he would take away tithes, etc., or else let him be rolled into his grave with infamy; but when the Lord had given him victory and he came to be chief, he confirmed the former laws that if people did not set forth their tithes they should pay treble, and this to be executed by two justices of peace in the country, upon the oath of two witnesses.

But when the King came in, they took him up and hanged him; and buried him under Tyburn, where he was rolled into his grave with infamy. And when I saw him hanging there, I saw his word justly come upon him.

187. THE CROWN OFFERED TO OLIVER

The offer of the crown to Oliver was the outcome of an agreement with the Presbyterians, which widened the social basis of the régime to the Right and freed the government from dependence on a still too radical Army. But it made the political issue clear: radical elements in the Army and outside could deceive themselves no longer. Their outcry was used by the Army Grandees, who, amidst the compliments being exchanged between Cromwell and the Presbyterians, found themselves left out in the cold, to compel him to refuse the crown. The Humble Petition and Advice, here introduced by the prominent London merchant and alderman, Sir Christopher Packe, was accepted without the title of king. A Second Chamber was re-established, with Packe (and many of the Grandees) as members. But for Cromwell's death on September 3rd, 1658, the monarchy might well have been re-established in the family of Cromwell. Burton, I, p. 378.

SIR CHRISTOPHER PACKE presented a paper to the House, declaring it was somewhat come to his hand tending to the settlement of the nation, and of liberty and of property; and prayed it might be received and read: and it being much controverted, whether the same should be read without further opening thereof,

And the question being put,

The House was divided.

The Noes went forth.

Noes. 54. Colonel Sydenham and Mr. Robinson, Tellers.

Yeas. 144. Sir Charles Wolseley and Colonel Fitzjames, Tellers.

So it passed in the affirmative, and it was

Resolved, that this paper, offered by Sir Christopher Packe, be now read.

The said paper was read accordingly, and was intituled "The humble Address and Remonstrance of the Knights, Citizens and Burgesses, now assembled in the Parliament of this Commonwealth."

Resolved, that a candle be brought in.

Resolved, that the debate upon this paper be resumed to-morrow morning.

Part Sixteen

THE RESTORATION AND AFTER

If Aristotle . . . were to come again to the world he could not find words to explain the manner of this government. It has a monarchical appearance, and there is a King, but it is very far from being a monarchy.

The French Ambassador to Louis XIV.

188. PROPERTY AND THE RESTORATION

Oliver was succeeded by his son Richard in 1658; but the latter was soon overthrown by the Army Grandees. Military rule became a naked reality. The problem of raising money to pay the armed forces became acute. Men's minds reverted to the methods of 1649–53—confiscation and sale of lands. This produced general anxiety among men of property. Those Parliamentarians who had got all they wanted from the revolution began to wish for a deal with the Cavaliers and a restoration of the monarchy: only so could they get rid of the expensive and dangerously radical Army. Sir George Booth's revolt was led by such men (*a*). A few months later Charles offered himself as a Parliamentary king, and was accepted. His Declaration (*b*) shows what were thought to be the important issues in April, 1660:—(i) a general pardon, which meant that no one was to be called in question for the violent acts of the revolution (except the regicides; see No. 191); (ii) religious toleration—a promise which Parliament subsequently made the King dishonour because of its fear of the Left wing; (iii) reference of property questions to Parliament; (iv) pay for the Army. In face of the swing to the Right among the wealthier Parliamentarians, the only hope of the Left lay in arming the lower classes (*c*), *d*), *e*)). Newcome (*d*) was a Presbyterian minister who was ejected from his living in the general purge of 1662. One would therefore expect him to look back favourably to the period before the Restoration. But no; he put security for his property before the prevalence of his religious views.

a) Ed. J. A. Atkinson, *Tracts relating to the Civil War in Cheshire, 1641–59*, p. 186; *b*) Gardiner, pp. 465–7; *c*) Pepys, I, p. 106; *d*) ed. R. Parkinson, *Autobiography of Henry Newcome* (Chetham Soc., 1852), pp. 118–19; *e*) Baxter, *The Holy Commonwealth*, pp. 92–4, 226–31.

a) BOOTH'S DECLARATION, AUGUST, 1659

AND what will be the issue of all this? A mean and schismatical party must depress the nobility and understanding commons, the land must waste itself, and foreigners or others [i.e. the common people] must take the advantage of all. I dare say, I profess for myself and the greatest part with me, [we] have no aspect but this singly, [to see] that we be not possessed as waste ground is, only by the title of occupancy; or that the next that gets into the saddle ride us.

b) THE DECLARATION OF BREDA

Nor do we desire more to enjoy what is ours than that all our subjects may enjoy what by law is theirs. . . .

We do grant a free and general pardon . . . to all our subjects . . . who, within 40 days after the publishing hereof, shall . . . by any public act declare . . . that they return to the loyalty and obedience of good subjects; excepting only such persons as shall hereafter be excepted by Parliament. . . . Let all our subjects, how faulty soever, rely upon the word of a King, solemnly given by this present declaration, that no crime whatsoever, committed against Us or Our royal father before the publication of this, shall ever rise in judgment, or be brought in question, against any of them to the least endamagement of them, either in their lives, liberties or estates, or (as far forth as lies in our power) so much as to the prejudice of their reputations by any reproach or term of distinction from the rest of our best subjects; we desiring and ordaining that henceforth all notes of discord, separation and difference of parties be utterly abolished among all our subjects, whom we invite and conjure to a perfect union among themselves, under our protection, for the resettlement of our just rights and theirs in a free Parliament, by which, upon the word of a King, we will be advised. . . .

We do declare a liberty to tender consciences, and that no man shall be disquieted or called in question for differences of opinion in matter of religion which do not disturb the peace of the kingdom; and that we shall be ready to consent to such an Act of Parliament as, upon mature deliberation, shall be offered to us for the full granting that indulgence.

And because in the continued distractions of so many years and so many and great revolutions many grants and purchases of estates have been made to and by many officers, soldiers and others, who are now possessed of the same, and who may be liable to actions at law upon several titles, we are likewise willing that all such differences, and all things relating to such grants, sales and purchases, shall be determined in Parliament. . . .

We will be ready to consent to any Act or Acts of Parliament to the purposes aforesaid, and for the full satisfaction of all arrears due to the officers and soldiers of the army under the command of General Monck; and that they shall be received into our service upon as good pay and condition as they now enjoy. . . .

At our Court at Breda, this 4–14 day of April, 1660, in the twelfth year of our reign.

c) PEPYS. THE ALTERNATIVES

April 18th, 1660. It is now clear that either the fanatics must now be undone, or the gentry and citizens throughout England, and clergy, must fall, in spite of their militia and army, which is not at all possible I think.

d) THE REV. HENRY NEWCOME, AFTER 1662

And though soon after the settlement of the nation we saw ourselves the despised and cheated party, . . . yet in all this I have suffered since I look upon it as less than my trouble was from my fears then [1659–60]. They [the pre-restoration governments] did me no hurt; took nothing from me. These [the post-restoration government] have taken all; and yet I feel it not, comparatively, to what I felt from my fears then; and I would not change conditions . . . to have it as it was then, as bad as it is.

(i) Their malice and rage was so desperate and giddy and lawless. Affliction by law is known, and one may know how to frame to it, and more than is law cannot be inflicted. Then we lay at the mercy and impulse of a giddy, hot-headed, bloody multitude.

(ii) A Munsterian [i.e. Communist] anarchy we escaped, far sadder than particular persecution.

(iii) And methinks the trouble that befalls me, though it be more sharp, yet is more kindly, and is better taken, since coming from a lawful sovereign, than less that was inflicted by many usurpers.

e) THE REVEREND RICHARD BAXTER, 1659

All this stir of the Republicans is but to make the seed of the serpent to be the sovereign rulers of the earth. Were not this multitude restrained they would presently have the blood of the godly. . . . That the major vote of the people should ordinarily be just and good is next to an impossibility. . . .

He knoweth not what prudence and piety are, or knoweth not England or mankind, that knoweth not that the major part of the vulgar are scarcely prudent and pious men. . . . The rabble hate both magistrates and ministers. . . . Many a time have I heard them say, "It will never be a good world, while knights and gentlemen make us laws, that are chosen for fear and do but oppress us, and do not know the people's sores. It will never be well with us till we have Parliaments of countrymen like ourselves, that know our wants."

189. MILTON ON THE RESTORATION

Barely two months before the Restoration, when most others as closely associated as he with the execution of the King had fled or were in hiding, Milton raised his voice once more at the hateful prospect of a return to monarchy, and defended a free commonwealth. At the Restoration, Milton only narrowly escaped execution for his repeated defence of regicide. J. Milton, *Ready and Easy Way to establish a Free Commonwealth, Selected Prose* (World's Classics), pp. 452–3; 470–6.

If we return to kingship and soon repent, as undoubtedly we shall . . . we may be forced perhaps to fight over again all that we have fought, and spend over again all that we have spent, but are never like to attain thus far as we are now advanced to the recovery of our freedom, never to have it in possession as we now have it . . . making vain and viler than dirt the blood of so many thousand faithful and valiant Englishmen, who left us in this liberty, bought with their lives . . .

What government comes nearer to [the] precept of

Christ than a free commonwealth; wherein they who are the greatest are perpetual servants and drudges to the public at their own costs and charges, neglect their own affairs, yet are not elevated above their brethren; live soberly in their families, walk the streets as other men, may be spoken to freely, familiarly, friendly, without adoration? . . .

More just it is, doubtless, if it come to force, that a less number compel a greater to retain, which can be no wrong to them, their liberty, than that a greater number, for the pleasure of their baseness, compel a less most injuriously to be their fellow-slaves. They who seek nothing but their own just liberty, have always right to win it and to keep it, whenever they have power, be the voices never so numerous that oppose it. . . .

But if the people be so affected as to prostitute religion and liberty to the vain and groundless apprehension that nothing but kingship can restore trade . . . our condition is not sound but rotten, both in religion and all civil prudence. . . .

What I have spoken is the language of that which is not called amiss, "the Good Old Cause." . . . Thus much I should perhaps have said though I were sure I should have spoken only to trees and stones; and had none to cry to but with the Prophet, "O Earth, Earth, Earth!" to tell the very soil itself what her perverse inhabitants are deaf to. Nay, though what I have spoke should happen (which Thou suffer not, who didst create mankind free; nor Thou next, who didst redeem us from being servants of men!) to be the last words of our expiring liberty. But I trust I shall have spoken persuasion to abundance of sensible and ingenuous men; to some perhaps whom God may raise of these stones to become children of reviving liberty.

190. DEMOCRACY NEEDS A MATERIAL BASIS

Milton was very depressed at the prospect of the overthrow of the republic (No. 189). Wall here puts his finger on the economic reasons for the failure of democracy. Men could not be free so long as their minds were dulled by poverty. Real freedom for the masses must wait until an expansion of productivity had made a decent standard of living possible for all. In fact, the radical movement at the end of the eighteenth century, after the Industrial Revolution, picked up the cause of democracy where the bourgeois revolutionaries had been compelled to leave it in 1660.
Masson, *Life of Milton*, V, pp. 602–3; quoted in Jack Lindsay, *John Bunyan*, p. 200, with valuable comments.

Moses Wall to Milton, May, 1659

You complain of the non-progressency of the nation, and of its retrograde motion of late, in liberty and spiritual truths. It is much to be bewailed; but yet let us pity human frailty. When those who had made deep protestations of their zeal for our liberty both spiritual and civil, and made the fairest offers to be asserters thereof, and whom we thereupon trusted; when these, being instated in power, shall betray the good thing committed to them . . . and by that force which we gave them to win us liberty hold us fast in chains; what can poor people do? . . .

Besides, whilst people are not free but straightened in accommodations for life, their spirits will be dejected and servile. . . . There should be an improving of our native commodities, as our manufactures, our fishery, our fens, forests and commons and our trade at sea, etc., which would give the body of the nation a comfortable subsistence

191. THE END OF THE REVOLUTIONARIES

Deprived of much of the satisfaction they had expected from a restoration (see No. 194), the Royalists wreaked an exemplary revenge on those regicides they were able to capture.

a) *Trial of the Regicides*, pp. 55–6; *b*) *The Speeches and Prayers of M. G. Harrison* . . . [and others], 1660, pp. 6–7; *c*) Traditional.

a) MAJOR-GENERAL HARRISON'S SPEECH AT HIS TRIAL, OCTOBER 11TH, 1660

MY lords, the matter that hath been offered to you [the execution of Charles I] . . . was not a thing done in a corner. I believe the sound of it hath been in most nations. I believe the hearts of some have felt the terrors of that presence of God that was with His servants in those days (however it seemeth good to Him to suffer this turn to come on us) and are witnesses that the things were not done in a corner . . . I humbly conceive that what was done was done in the name of the Parliament of England, that what was done was done by their power and authority; and I do humbly conceive that it is my duty to offer unto you in the beginning that this court, or any court below the high court of Parliament, hath no jurisdiction of their actions.

b) HARRISON ON THE WAY TO THE SCAFFOLD

As he went to the place of execution . . . he called several times . . . , "I go to suffer upon the account of the most glorious cause that ever was in the world." As he was going to suffer one in derision called to him . . . : "Where is your Good Old Cause?" He with a cheerful smile clapped his hand on his heart and said: "Here it is, and I am going to seal it with my blood."

c) THE GENERAL VERDICT

Many men love the treason though they hate the traitor.

192. THE REVOLUTIONARIES LOOK TO POSTERITY

In defeat the best of the revolutionaries did not lose confidence in their cause; but they came to see that their aspirations could only be turned into realities by the efforts of later generations. Extract *a*) is from a tract written by Sir John Eliot in prison. "Socrates" stands for Eliot himself, "Athenians" for Englishmen.

a) Sir John Eliot, *Apology for Socrates*, p. 30; *b*) Harrington, *Works*, p. 385; *c*) Milton, *The Likeliest Means to remove Hirelings out of the Church*, *Prose Works* (Bohn), III, p. 41; *d*) Burton, IV, pp. 72, 105; *e*) Lilburne, *England's New Chains Discovered*, H. and D., p. 166; *f*) Winstanley, *A Watchword to the City of London and the Army*, Hamilton, p. 66.

a) SIR JOHN ELIOT, 1631

I WILL not tell you . . . what he suffered in his fortune, what he suffered in his person, in his liberty, in his life: to be made poor and naked; to be imprisoned and restrained; nay, not to be at all; not to have the proper use of anything, not to have knowledge of society; not to have being and existence; his faculties confiscate[d]; his friends debarred his presence; himself deprived [of] the world—I will not tell you of all this suffered by your Socrates; all this suffered for your service, for you most excellent Athenians, for your children, your posterity, to preserve your rights and liberties; that as they were the inheritance of your fathers, from you likewise they may again devolve to them.

b) HARRINGTON, 1659

If this age fails me, the next will do me justice.

c) MILTON, 1659

If I be not heard nor believed, the event will bear me witness to have spoken truth; and I in the meanwhile have borne my witness, not out of season, to the church and to my country.

d) SIR HENRY VANE, 1659

God is almighty. Will you not trust him with the consequences? He that has unsettled a monarchy of so many descents, in peaceable times, and brought you to the top of your liberties, though he drive you back for a while into the wilderness, he will bring you back. He is a wiser workman than to reject his own work. . . . When a man is asleep, he finds no hunger till he wake. I doubt the people of England will be hungry when they awake.

e) LILBURNE, 1649

Posterity, we doubt not, shall reap the benefit of our endeavours, whatever shall become of us.

f) WINSTANLEY, 1649

When these clay bodies are in grave, and children stand in place,
This shows we stood for truth and peace and freedom in our days;
And true-born sons we shall appear of England that's our mother,
No priests' nor lawyers' wiles to embrace, their slavery we'll discover.

193. MILTON STILL HAS CONFIDENCE IN HIS CAUSE

Many of the Puritans, after the Restoration had blasted their hopes, decided that God's Kingdom was not of this world, that they must abstain from politics (see note to No. 160). But not Milton. *Samson Agonistes* was published seven years after the Restoration, when the hopes of the revolutionaries were beginning to revive. Samson is a symbol not only for the poet himself, "now blind, disheartened, shamed, dishonoured, quelled"; he is also a symbol of the revolutionary cause, "in bonds under Philistian yoke." In his first speech he echoes the Army Declaration of June, 1647 (No. 131). Samson has been defeated by treachery and by his own excessive self-confidence; great is his humiliation, great the triumph of the Philistines; but the moral is not passivity. God still has glorious work for Samson to do for his country: he shall end the tyranny of the Philistines. Milton certainly intends us to see an allusion to Restoration England. He still has hopes for the Good Old Cause, although "servile minds" had given Samson up to "their masters," "whence to this day they serve." For although Samson lost his life in destroying the lords, "the vulgar only 'scaped who stood without." Milton (Nonesuch Ed.), pp. 495, 445–6, 446.

Samson: My nation was subjected to your Lords.
It was the force of conquest: force with force
Is well ejected when the conquered can. . . .
I was no private, but a person raised
With strength sufficient and command from Heaven
To free my country. If their servile minds
Me their deliverer sent would not receive,
But to their masters gave me up for nought,
Th' unworthier they; whence to this day they serve.
I was to do my part from Heaven assigned,
And had performed it if my known offence
Had not disabled me, not all your force. . . .
My heels are fettered, but my fist is free. . . .

[Samson was led off to perform feats of strength at a festival of his enemies.]

Messenger: [Samson] At last with head erect thus cried aloud:
"Hitherto, Lords, what your commands imposed
I have performed, as reason was, obeying,
Not without wonder or delight beheld.
Now of my own accord such other trial
I mean to show you of my strength, yet greater,
As with amaze shall strike all who behold."
This uttered, straining all his nerves he bowed,
As with the force of winds and waters pent
When mountains tremble, those two massy pillars
With horrible convulsion to and fro,
He tugged, he shook, till down they came and drew
The whole roof after them, with burst of thunder,
Upon the heads of all who sate beneath—
Lords, ladies, captains, councillors or priests,
Their choice nobility and flower, not only
Of this but each Philistian city round

Met from all parts to solemnise this feast.
Samson with these immixed, inevitably
Pulled down the same destruction on himself:
The vulgar only 'scaped who stood without. . . .

Chorus: All is best, though we oft doubt
What th' unsearchable dispose
Of highest wisdom brings about;
And ever best found in the close.
Oft he seems to hide his face
But unexpectedly returns
And to his faithful champion hath in place
Born witness gloriously; whence Gaza mourns,
And all that band them to resist
His uncontrollable intent.
His servants he, with new acquist
Of true experience from this great event
With peace and consolation hath dismissed
And calm of mind, all passion spent.

194. THE ROYALISTS SACRIFICED

To make the Restoration possible, Charles II had had to confirm the Parliamentarians' Civil War gains. This meant sacrificing those Royalists at whose expense these gains had been made. The fact that only regicides were excepted out of the Act of Indemnity reduced the recompense expected from punishment of the King's former enemies. In theory, all the estates of the King, the bishops, deans and chapters, and those Royalists whose lands had been confiscated and sold were returned to their original owners after 1660. The much greater mass of lands which had been privately sold by Royalists forced to find ready money to pay their composition fines or taxation (see Nos. 164–5) was not restored. And there is reason to believe that not all the owners of estates nominally restored in fact got them back. The old owners had to take legal action against them; and law and juries in the seventeenth century always favoured the man in possession if he had money.

a) Burnet, *History of My Own Time* (ed. Airy), I, pp. 287–9; *b*) quoted in Feiling, *History of the Tory Party, 1640–1714*, p. 101.

a) BURNET

THE act of indemnity passed with very few exceptions; at which the cavaliers were highly dissatisfied, and made great complaints of it. In the disposal of offices and places, as it was not possible to gratify all, so there was little regard had to men's merits or services. . . . When the cavaliers saw they had not that share in places that they expected, they complained of it so high that the earl of Clarendon, to excuse the King's passing them by, was apt to beat down the value they set on their services. This laid the foundation of an implacable hatred in many of them, that was completed by the extent and comprehensiveness of the act of indemnity, which cut off their hopes of being reimbursed out of the fines, if not the confiscations, of those who had during the course of the war been on the parliament side. . . . The angry men that were thus disappointed of all their hopes made a jest of the title of it, AN ACT OF OBLIVION AND INDEMNITY, and said the king had passed an act of oblivion for his friends and of indemnity for his enemies.

b) ROGER L'ESTRANGE

[The restoration land settlement] made the enemies to the constitution masters, in effect, of the booty of three nations.

195. SOCIAL CONSEQUENCES OF THE REVOLUTION

The old and the new ruling class are fusing. Many of the feudal powers of landlords survive the revolution (*a*). But feudal England has gone; wickedness of all kinds has been introduced by the revolution; the clock cannot now be set back (*b*). Money has triumphed (*c*). Even a bishop accepts the new standards (*d*). With *a*) cf. No. 6, *a*).

a) [Anon.] *A Discourse for a King and Parliament* (1660), pp. 1-2; *b*) Colonel Roger Whitley, quoted in J. W. Hyde, *The Post in Grant and Farm* (1894), p. 344; *c*) Skinner, *Life of Monck* (1724), p. 384; *d*) Thomas Sprat, *History of the Royal Society* (1667), p. 408.

a) ENGLAND RULED BY THE GENTRY, 1660

THIS island . . . is . . . governed by the influence of a sort of people that live plentifully and at ease upon their rents, extracted from the toil of their tenants and servants, . . . each of whom within the bounds of his own estate acts the prince; he is purely absolute; his servants and labourers are in the nature of his vassals; his tenants indeed are free, but in the nature of subjects, whom he orders in his courts, draws supplies from by his fines, and awes by his power and oaths of fealty to infinite submissions. . . .

Into this rank do our commanders, citizens and burghers aspire to be enrolled; so that no sooner, by arms, office or trade, do they acquire a competent stock, but forthwith for land it is disposed; and then disowning the title of soldiers, citizens or burghers, they take to themselves the degree and name of gentlemen; . . . for England within itself has been so often shuffled from high to low that scarce any artificer but may find his name in the Heralds' book, though not his pedigree, which ingenuity and goodwill may easily supply. . . . For by gentry, I intend not only such as are so in blood, but so in quality; such as live easefully and like princes, upon the labours of [their] dependants.

Now that this sort of people have by influence and in effect the command of this nation, at this instant appears evident in this, that they sit at the helm in the supreme council; they command in chief at sea and land; they impose taxes, and levy it by commissioners of the same quality. Out of this rank select we sheriffs, Justices of Peace, and all that execute the authority of a judge; by the influence of which powers, they so order all elections to Parliament or otherwise that the whole counties follow their respective factions, and the commonalty in the votes are managed by them as the horse by his rider.

b) THE DEPUTY POSTMASTER-GENERAL, *c.* 1670

In times past (before the wicked Rebellion), a nobleman or great officer of state or court would have half a score or a dozen gentlemen to attend him, but now all is shrunk into a *valet de chambre*, a page, and 5 or 6 footmen; and this is part of our cursed Reformation.

c) MONCK SETS A GOOD EXAMPLE

He very well knew . . . how unable the nobility are to support their own esteem and order, or to assist the crown, whilst they make themselves contemptible and weak by the number and weight of their debts and the continual decay of their estates. And if the wealth of the nation come to centre most among the lower and trading part of the people, at one time or other it will certainly be in their power, and probably in their desires, to invade the government. These and the like considerations had moved the Duke of Albermarle to become as great an example to the nobility of honourable good husbandry as he had been before of loyalty and allegiance.

d) THE NEW ARISTOCRACY

Traffic and commerce have given mankind a higher degree than any title of nobility.

196. POLITICAL CONSEQUENCES OF THE REVOLUTION

The restoration of the monarchy was not a restoration of the old order: Charles II was ultimately responsible to the House of Commons. He "did not want to go on his travels again," and never carried opposition to the wishes of the ruling class too far. James II took the fiction of his sovereignty seriously, and had to be deposed (No. 199). In *b*) the old Cromwellian, Pepys, records the remarks of the son of a Royalist officer: they are a striking confirmation of *a*). Now that the absolute monarchy had been abolished, the two sections of the ruling class, whatever their individual differences, were united in opposition to a standing army and to taxation that was expended on court extravagance rather than on a foreign policy conducted in the interests of English trade.

a) Aubrey, *Brief Lives*, I, p. 291; *b*) Pepys, VII, p. 17

a) HARRINGTON

I WELL remember he [Harrington] several times (at the breaking up [of the Commonwealth]) said, "Well, the King will come in. Let him come in, and call a Parliament of the greatest cavaliers in England, so they be men of estates, and let them sit but 7 years, and they will all turn commonwealth's men."

b) SEVEN YEARS LATER

July 12th, 1667. Sir H. Cholmly, as a true English gentleman, do decry the King's expenses of his privy purse . . . and the guards, which for his part, says he, "I would have all disbanded, for the King is not the better by them, and would be as safe without them; for we have had no rebellions to make him fear anything." But, contrarily, he is now raising of a land army, which this Parliament and kingdom will never bear; . . . but the design is, and the Duke of York [afterwards James II], he says, is hot for it, to have a land army, and so to make the government like that of France; but our princes have not brains, or at least care and forecast enough to do that.

It is strange how he and everybody do nowadays reflect upon Oliver, and commend him, what brave things he did, and made all the neighbour princes fear him; while here a prince, come in with all the love and prayers and good liking of his people, who have given greater signs of loyalty and willingness to serve him with their estates than ever was done by any people, hath lost all so soon that it is a miracle what way a man could devise to lose so much in so little time.

197. ALTERNATIVE PATHS FOR THE REVOLUTIONARIES

Some of the revolutionaries accepted the compromise of 1660 and concentrated on getting on in the world; others continued the struggle for democracy. Sir William Petty (*a*) is an example of the former. He started life as a cabin boy, and became successively seaman, doctor, Professor of

Anatomy at Oxford, physician to the Cromwellian Army in Ireland, contractor for the Survey of Ireland, economist and statistician. He made a good thing of his survey of confiscated lands in Ireland, was knighted at the Restoration, and became the founder of the great Shelburne and Landsdowne family. Miss Petty, the reader will be glad to hear, subsequently became Countess of Kerry. Richard Rumbold (*b*) took the other path. A Leveller in the 'forties, promoted from the ranks in the 'fifties, he became an underground conspirator after the Restoration. In 1683 he was involved in the Rye House Plot and fled to Holland. Thence he sailed with Argyle to make an unsuccessful rising in Scotland in 1685, was captured and executed. The famous words in *b*) are from his last speech.

a) Ed. Lansdowne, *Petty Papers*, II, p. 255; *b*) *State Trials*, XI (1811), p. 881.

a) PATERNAL ASPIRATIONS, 1679

My pretty little Pussling and my daughter Anne,
That shall be a countess, if her papa can.
If her papa cannot, then I make no doubt
But my little Pussling will be content without.
If my little Pussling prove an ugly carron
Then it will be well enough
If she get but a baron.
But if her fortune should be so
As to get but a knight,
Then I trow her cake is dough
And hopes are all beshite.

b) REFLECTIONS ON THE SCAFFOLD, 1685

I am sure there was no man born marked of God above another; for none comes into the world with a saddle on his back, neither any booted and spurred to ride him.

198. REPUBLICANISM SURVIVES

Harrington's prophecy (No. 196, *a*)) was being fulfilled. Charles II was increasingly at odds with his Parliament. Andrew Marvell, in this dialogue between Ralegh (see No. 46) and Britannia, hopes that the end of monarchy is coming, and quotes the Venetian republic as an example.

Marvell, *Poems* (1927), p. 188.

Britannia and Ralegh, c. 1675

Ralegh: Once more, great Queen, thy darling try to save;
Rescue him again from scandal and the grave;
Present to his thought his long-scorn'd Parliament
(The basis of his throne and government);
In his deaf ear sound his dead father's name;
Perhaps that spell may his erring soul reclaim. . . .
Britannia: Ralegh, no more; too long in vain I've tried
The Stuart from the tyrant to divide. . . .
Tyrants like leprous kings for public weal
Must be immur'd, lest their contagion steal
Over the whole. . . .
And shall this stinking Scottish brood evade
Eternal laws by God for mankind made?
No!
To the serene Venetian state I'll go,
From her sage mouth fam'd principles to know,
With her the prudence of the ancients read
To teach my people in their steps to tread.

199. 1688—AND AFTER

The ex-Cavaliers hated making the revolution of 1688; but by this date their mode of life was too bound up with bourgeois society for them to support a monarchy of the pre-1640 type (*a*). There was the further complication of James II's Catholicism. This strengthened his position in that the greatest reactionary power of the day, Louis XIV's France, might lend him assistance; but it alienated many owners of confiscated monastic lands. Accepting the necessity of deposing James II, the Tories wished to rush through the transfer of the throne to William and Mary as quickly as possible, so as to forestall any revival of democratic republicanism. Ludlow returned from his twenty-nine years' exile, hoping that the day of the Good Old Cause had dawned at last; but he was very soon bundled out of the country (*b*). Those days had passed.

a) Ed. Browning, *Memoirs of Sir John Reresby*, pp. 532–3; *b*) Ludlow, II, p. 511.

a) CRUEL NECESSITY

LORD WILLOUGHBY said it [1688] was the first time that any Bertie was ever engaged against the Crown . . . but there was a necessity either to part with our religion and properties, or do it.

b) LETTER OF JOHN HEYLER, NOVEMBER 7TH. 1689

This day Sir Ed. Seymour, with a noble company of gentlemen, waited on King William to desire him to issue out a proclamation with a reward to apprehend Colonel Ludlow, lately arrived from Switzerland. Sir Edward told the King that the House [of Commons] admired [i.e. wondered] why so deadly an enemy both to the monarchy and to the King of England should have the impudence to appear here, when he was attainted by Act of Parliament, and when he was one of those detestable regicides that murdered his grandfather; and that the opinion of the House was that he was sent for over by the [republican] faction to head them, that when opportunity should serve he might use his endeavours to the subversion of church and state. The King answered that the Address was both reasonable and just, and that he should make no difficulty to issue out a Proclamation immediately.

200. THE VERDICT OF THE WORKING-CLASS MOVEMENT

These extracts show nineteenth-century Radicals and Socialists looking back to the seventeenth-century revolution. Both are one-sided, yet each brings out an important point.

Cobbett's *Grammar* (*a*), written in 1817, was "intended . . . more especially for the use of soldiers, sailors, apprentices and plough-boys." He wanted to make the knowledge and culture of the ruling class accessible to the working class, so that each working man might "be able to assert with effect the rights and liberties of his country." He used political examples to hammer home grammatical points. (For Prynne, see No. 35, *a*).) Extract *b*) was written by Bronterre O'Brien in 1837. His analysis of the seventeenth-century revolution conflicts with the then fashionable Whig interpretation of history and looks forward to Marx.

with the then fashionable Whig interpretation of history and looks forward to Marx.

a) Cobbett, *A Grammar of the English Language* (1906), pp. 11–12; *b*) Bronterre O'Brien, *London Mercury*, May 7th, 1837 (in *From Cobbett to the Chartists*, p. 161).

a) FROM WILLIAM COBBETT

WHEN you come to read the history of those laws of England by which the freedom of the people has been secured . . .; when you come to read the history of the struggles of our forefathers by which these sacred laws have, from time to time, been defended against despotic ambition; . . . by which their violators have never failed, in the end, to be made to feel the just vengeance of the People; when you come to read the history of these struggles in the cause of freedom, you will find that tyranny has no enemy so formidable as the pen. And, while you will see with exultation the long-imprisoned, the heavily fined, the banished WILLIAM PRYNNE, returning to liberty, borne by the people from Southampton to London, over a road strewed with flowers; then accusing, bringing to trial and to the block, the tyrants from whose hands he and his country had unjustly and cruelly suffered; . . . your heart and the heart of every young man in the kingdom will bound with joy at the spectacle.

b) FROM BRONTERRE O'BRIEN

Political revolutions seldom go beyond the surface of society. They seldom amount to more than a mere transfer of power from one set of political chiefs to another. At best they only substitute one aristocratic form of government for another, and hence all political revolutions of which history makes mention have left the world pretty much as they found it—not wiser—not happier—not improved in any one essential particular. . . . Even the establishment of our "commonwealth" after the death of Charles I was a mere political revolution. It gave parliamentary privilege a temporary triumph over royal prerogative. It enabled a few thousand landowners to disenthral themselves from the burdens of feudal services, and to throw upon the people at large the expenses of maintaining the government. . . . For the millions it did nothing.

ACKNOWLEDGEMENTS

OUR thanks are due to the publishers who have kindly given us permission to quote from the following works:—

Letters of Charles I, ed. Sir Charles Petrie (Cassell & Co.). *Memoirs of the Verney Family during the Civil War*, ed. Lady Verney; *England during the Interregnum*, ed. M. James and M. Weinstock; *Tudor Economic Documents*, ed. R. H. Tawney and E. Power (Longmans Green & Co.). *Statutes and Constitutional Documents, 1558-1625*, ed. G. W. Prothero; *Constitutional Documents of the Puritan Revolution*, ed. S. R. Gardiner; *The Wiltshire Woollen Industry in the 16th and 17th Centuries*, by G. D. Ramsay; Bishop Burnet's *History of My Own Time*, ed. O. Airy, and *Supplement* ed. H. C. Foxcroft; *Memoirs of Edmund Ludlow*, ed. C. H. Firth; *History of the Tory Party 1640-1714*, by K. Feiling; Aubrey's *Brief Lives*, ed. A. Clark (the Clarendon Press, Oxford). *Strafford* by Lady Burghclere (A. P. Watt and Son and Messrs. Macmillan). *Charles II and Scotland in 1650*, ed. S. R. Gardiner (the Scottish History Society). *The Commonwealth of England*, by Sir T. Smith, ed. Alston; *Tudor Constitutional Documents*, ed. J. R. Tanner; *Constitutional Documents of the Reign of James I*, ed. J. R. Tanner; *Economic Writings of Sir W. Petty*, ed. C. H. Hull; *Ferrar Papers*, ed. B. Blackstone (Cambridge University Press). *Ireland under the Commonwealth*, by R. Dunlop (Manchester University Press). *Poems of Raleigh and Others*, ed. J. Hannah; *Diary of Samuel Pepys*, ed. H. B. Wheatley; *English Economic History, Select Documents*, ed. A. E. Bland, P. A. Brown and R. H. Tawney (G. Bell & Sons). *Puritanism and Liberty*, ed. A. S. P. Woodhouse (J. M. Dent & Sons). *Left Wing Democracy in the English Civil War*, by D. W. Petegorsky (Victor Gollancz). *Society in the Elizabethan Age*, by H. Hall (George Allen & Unwin). *John Pym*, by S. R. Brett (John Murray). *English Political Thought 1603-60*, by J. W. Allen; *A Royalist's Notebook*, ed. F. Bamford; *The Oxinden Letters*, ed. D. Gardiner; *The Petty Papers*, ed. Lansdowne (Constable & Co.). *The Selected Writings of Gerrard Winstanley*, ed. L. D. Hamilton (Cresset Press). *Wiltshire Quarter Session Records of the 17th Century*, ed. B. H. Cunnington (Wiltshire Gazette). *English Folk*, by W. Notestein (Jonathan Cape). *Memoirs of the Earl of Monmouth* (Alexander Moring, King's Classics). *The Memoirs of Sir John Reresby*, ed. A. Browning (Jackson, Son & Co.). *The Clarke Papers*, ed. C. H. Firth; *Diary of the Rev. Ralph Josselin*, ed. E. Hockliffe; Sir Thomas Wilson's *State of England* (1600), ed. F. J. Fisher; *Memorials of the Holles Family*, by G. Holles, ed. A. C. Wood (Camden series and Miscellany, Royal Historical Society). *Transactions of the Royal Historical Society*, 3rd series, vi, C. H. Firth (Royal Historical Society). *Selected Works, A. Crowley*, ed. J. M. Cowper; *Social Policy during the Puritan Revolution*, by M.

James; *Poems* of George Wither, ed. H. Morley (Routledge & Kegan Paul). *The Tudor Despotism*, by C. H. Williams; *Leveller Manifestoes of the Puritan Revolution*, ed. D. Wolfe (Thomas Nelson & Sons, London and New York). *A Short Narrative of the late Troubles in England*, by G. Bate, ed. A. Almack (F. R. Robinson & Co.). *Journal*, New Series, Vol. XVIII (the Derbyshire Archaeological and Natural History Society). *Financial and Commercial Policy under the Cromwellian Protectorate*, by M. Ashley (Oxford Historical Series, Oxford University Press). *Alderman Cockayne's Project and the Cloth Trade*, by A. Friis (Einar Munksgaard, Copenhagen and Oxford University Press). *Writings and Speeches of Oliver Cromwell*, ed. W. C. Abbott; *James I: Works*, ed. C. H. McIlwain (Harvard University Press). *Journal of Sir Simonds D'Ewes*, ed. Notestein; *The English Yeoman*, by M. Campbell; *Commons Debates, 1621*, ed. Notestein, Relf and Simpon (Yale University Press). *The Leveller Tracts*, ed. W. Haller and G. Davies (Columbia University Press). *Life of Sir John Digby*, ed. G. Bernard (Camden Miscellany, Vol. XII, Royal Historical Society.)

INDEX OF

PERSONS, AUTHORS, AND SEVENTEENTH-CENTURY COLLECTIONS

Authors are included only if they flourished in the 17th century

SUBJECT INDEX